VOL.2: **THE SUMMER WITH YOU**

MY **SUMMER** OF **YOU**

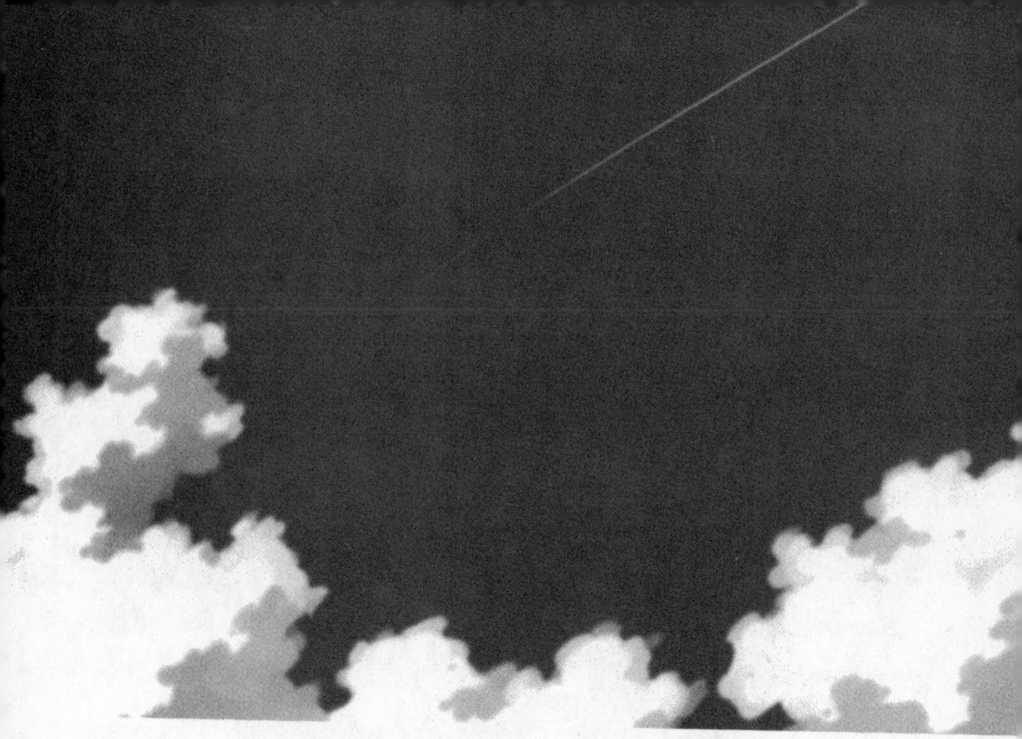

MY **SUMMER** OF **YOU**

VOL.2: **THE SUMMER WITH YOU**

CONTENTS

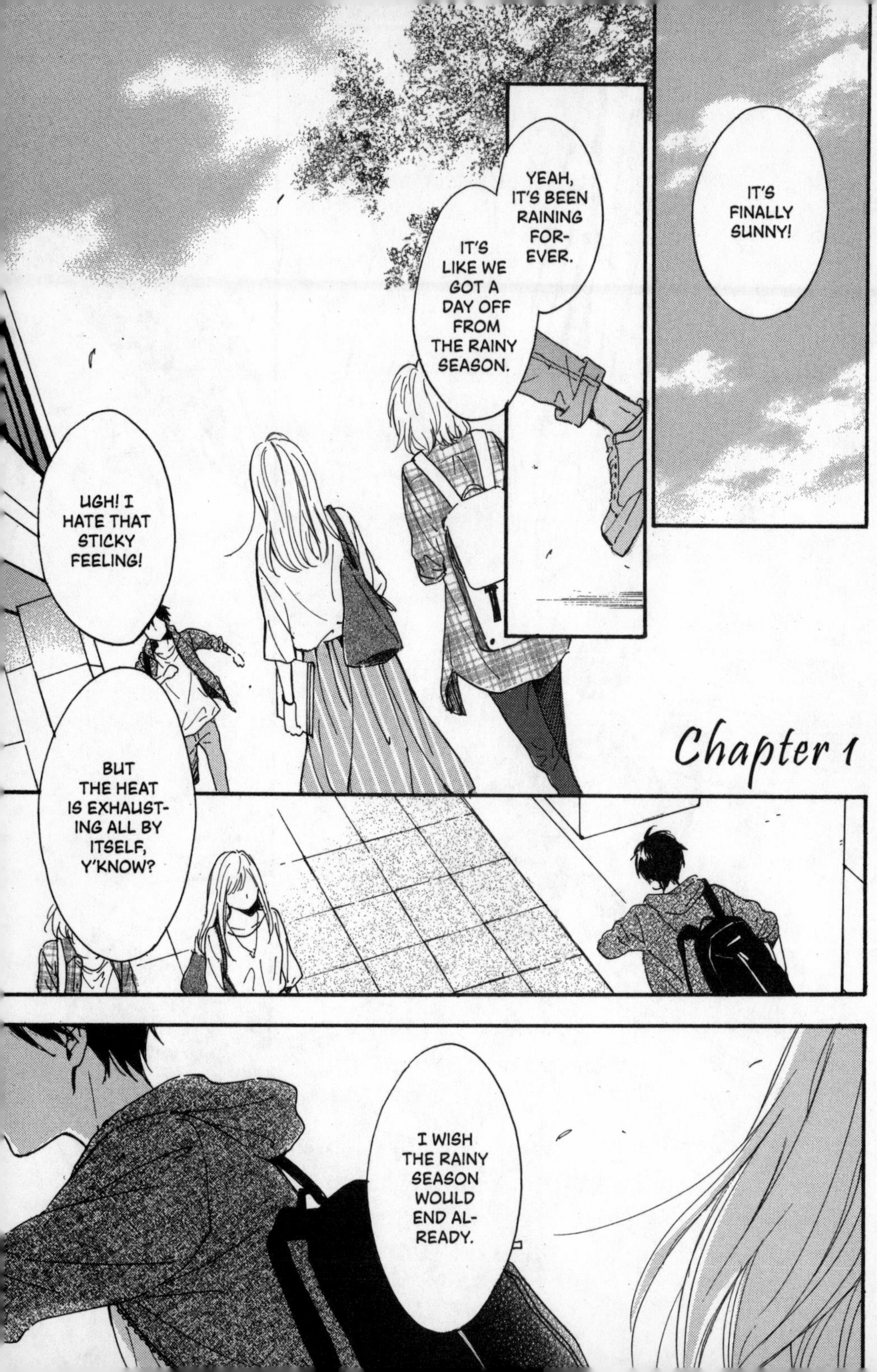
IT'S FINALLY SUNNY!
YEAH, IT'S BEEN RAINING FOR-EVER.
IT'S LIKE WE GOT A DAY OFF FROM THE RAINY SEASON.
Chapter 1
UGH! I HATE THAT STICKY FEELING!
BUT THE HEAT IS EXHAUSTING ALL BY ITSELF, Y'KNOW?
I WISH THE RAINY SEASON WOULD END AL-READY.

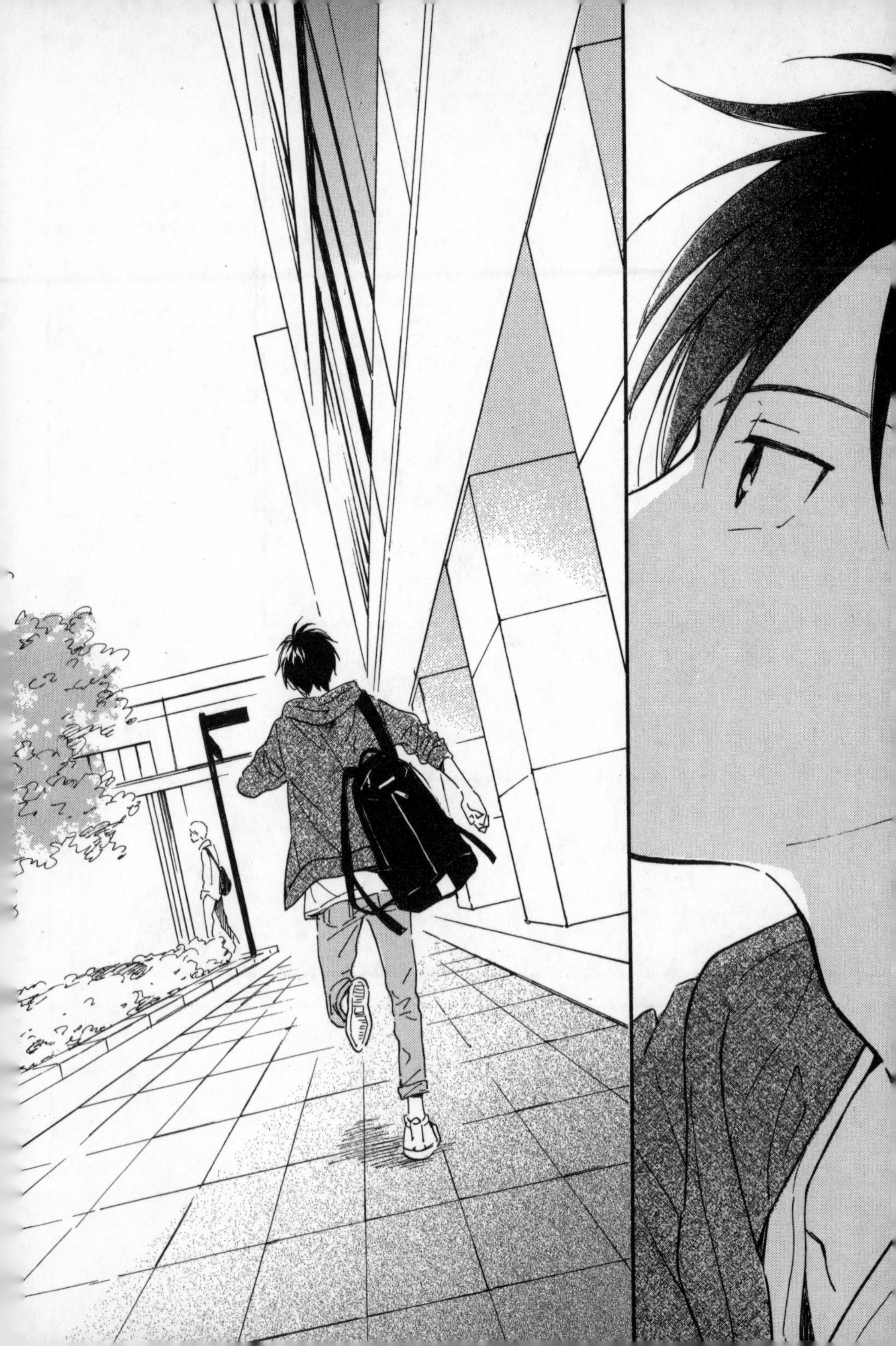

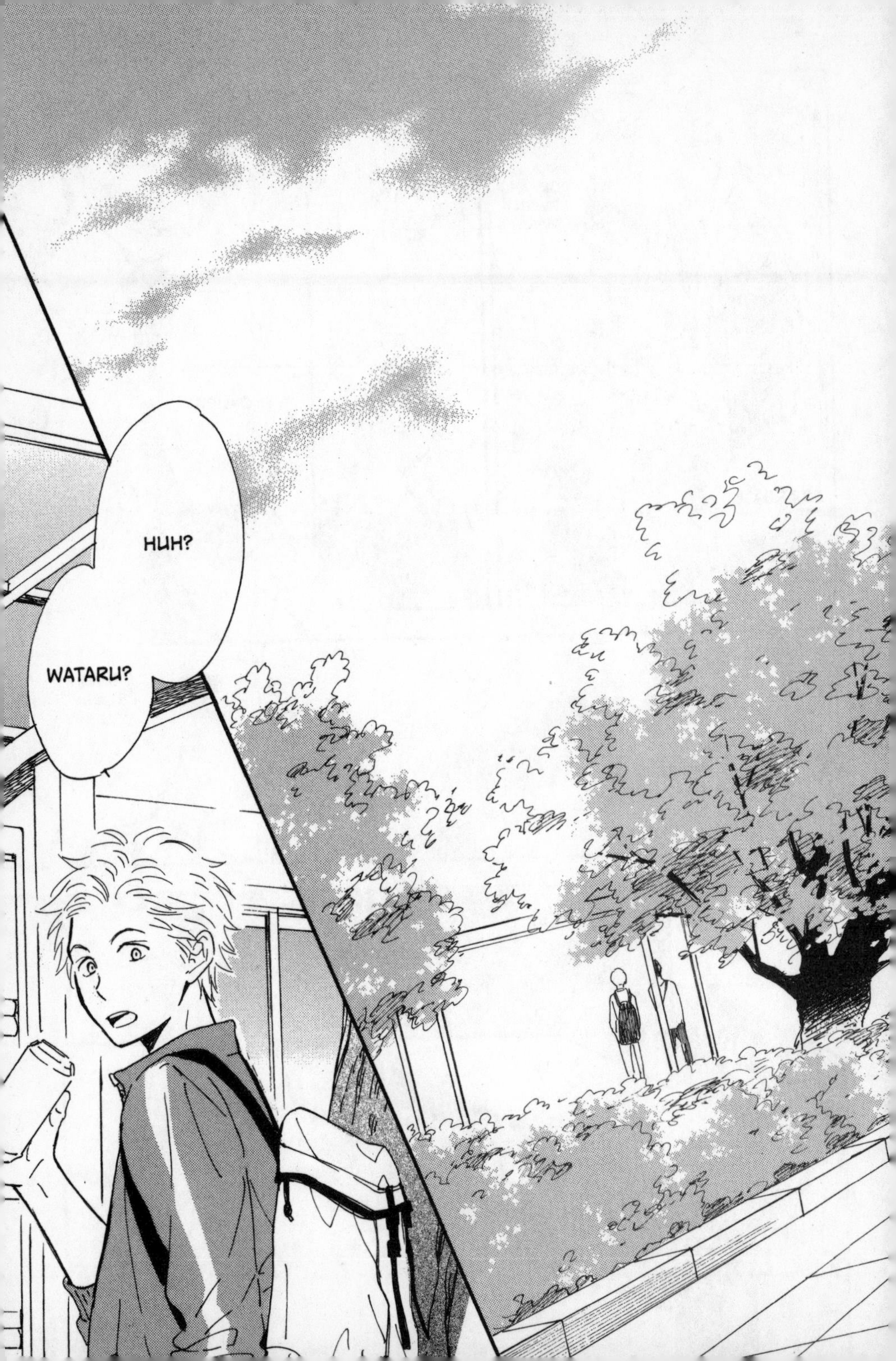
HUH?
WATARU?

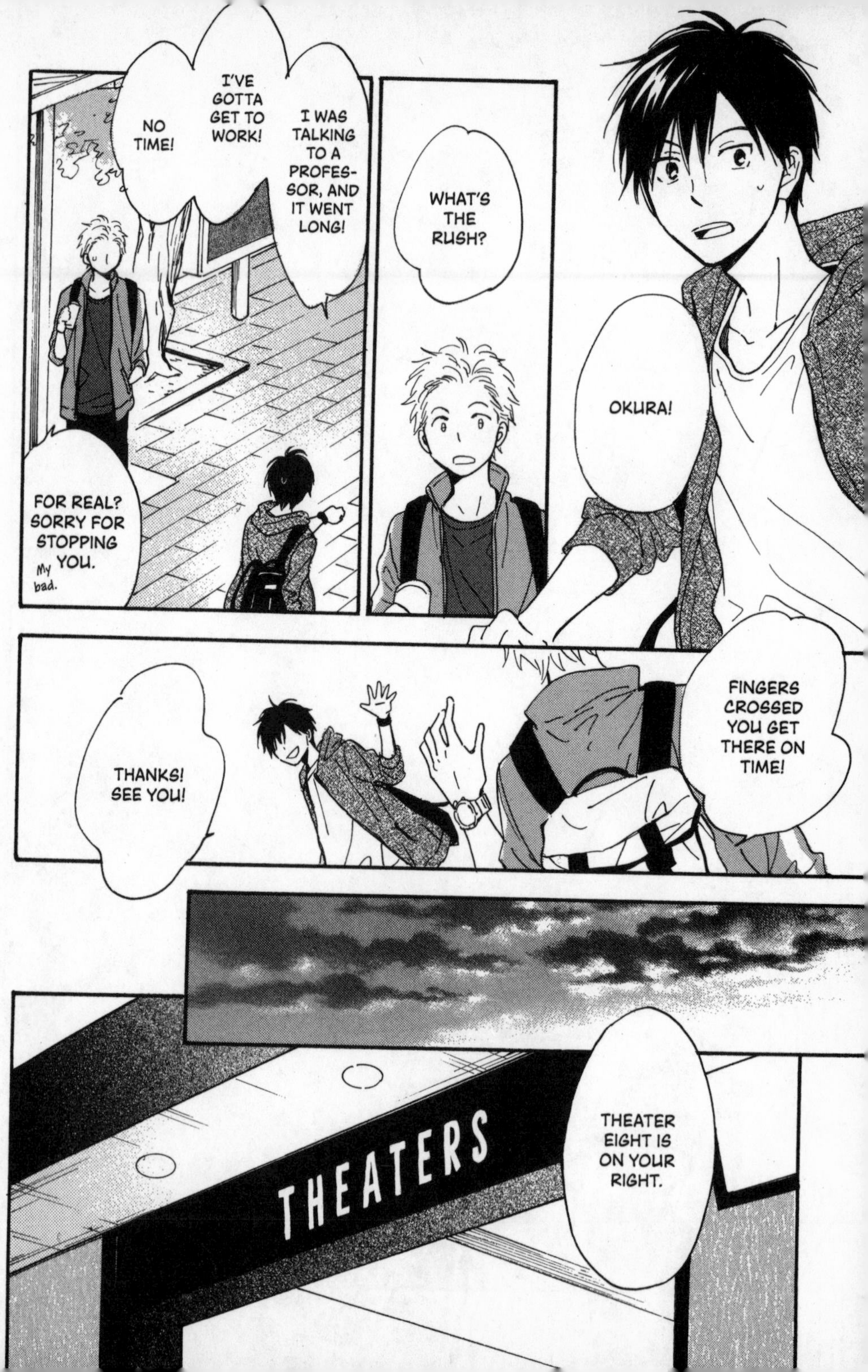
OKURA!
WHAT'S THE RUSH?
I WAS TALKING TO A PROFESSOR, AND IT WENT LONG!
I'VE GOTTA GET TO WORK!
NO TIME!
FOR REAL? SORRY FOR STOPPING YOU.
My bad.
FINGERS CROSSED YOU GET THERE ON TIME!
THANKS! SEE YOU!
THEATER EIGHT IS ON YOUR RIGHT.
THEATERS

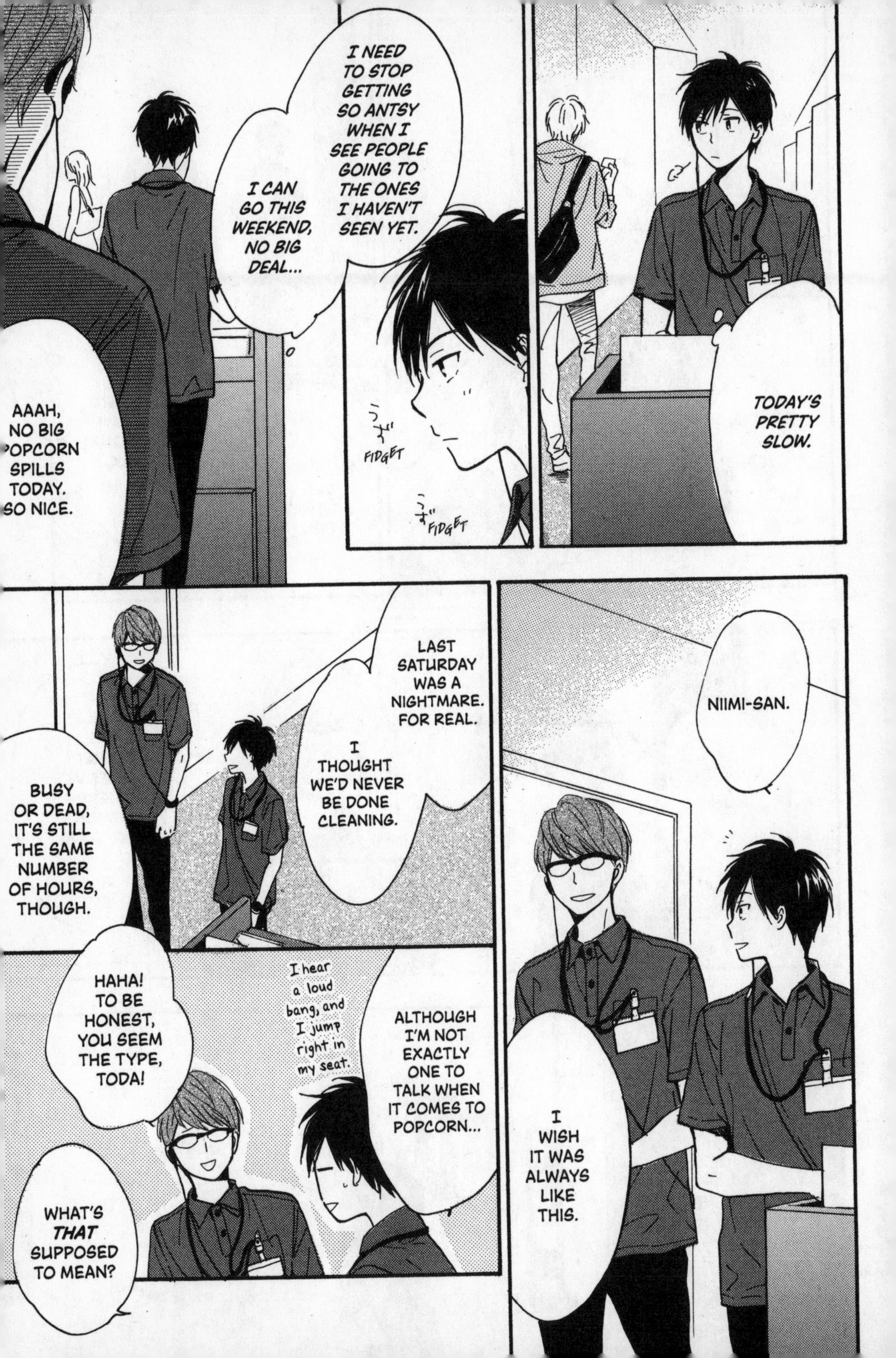
TODAY'S PRETTY SLOW.
I NEED TO STOP GETTING SO ANTSY WHEN I SEE PEOPLE GOING TO THE ONES I HAVEN'T SEEN YET.
I CAN GO THIS WEEKEND, NO BIG DEAL...
うず FIDGET
うず FIDGET
AAAH, NO BIG POPCORN SPILLS TODAY. SO NICE.
NIIMI-SAN.
I WISH IT WAS ALWAYS LIKE THIS.
LAST SATURDAY WAS A NIGHTMARE. FOR REAL.
I THOUGHT WE'D NEVER BE DONE CLEANING.
BUSY OR DEAD, IT'S STILL THE SAME NUMBER OF HOURS, THOUGH.
ALTHOUGH I'M NOT EXACTLY ONE TO TALK WHEN IT COMES TO POPCORN...
I hear a loud bang, and I jump right in my seat.
HAHA! TO BE HONEST, YOU SEEM THE TYPE, TODA!
WHAT'S *THAT* SUPPOSED TO MEAN?

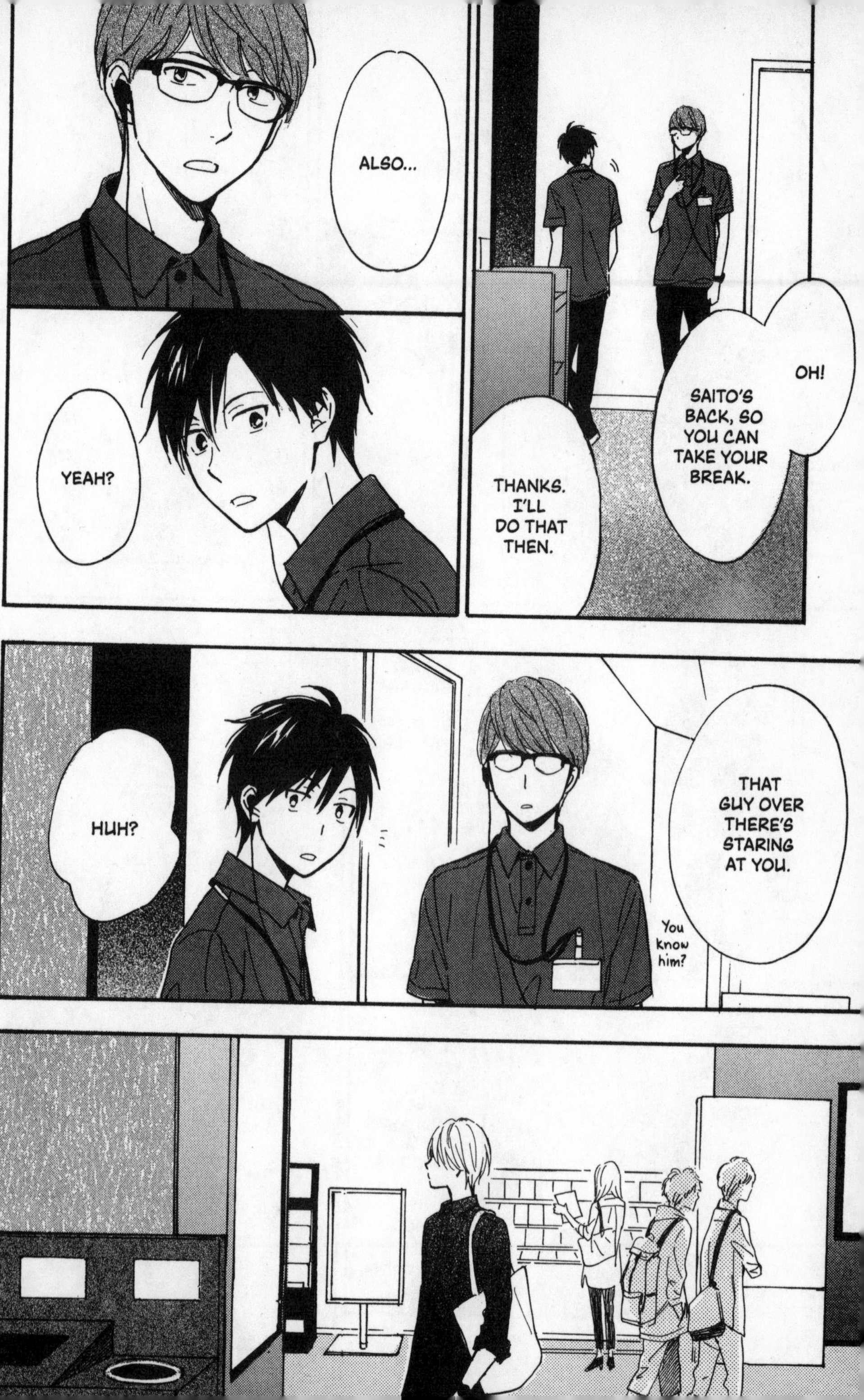
OH!
SAITO'S BACK, SO YOU CAN TAKE YOUR BREAK.
THANKS. I'LL DO THAT THEN.
ALSO...
YEAH?
THAT GUY OVER THERE'S STARING AT YOU.
You know him?
HUH?

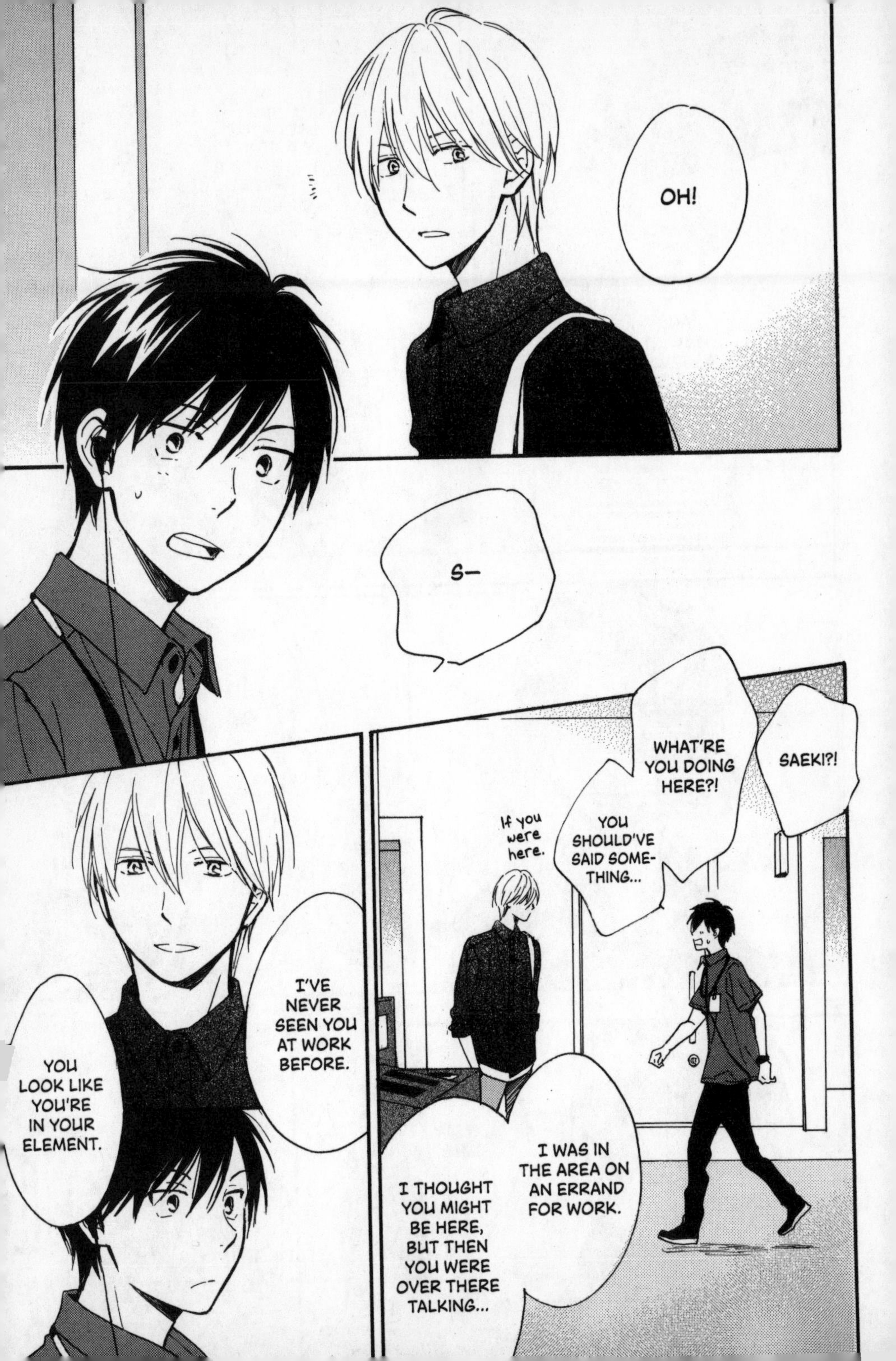
OH!
S—
SAEKI?!
WHAT'RE YOU DOING HERE?!
YOU SHOULD'VE SAID SOME-THING...
If you were here.
I WAS IN THE AREA ON AN ERRAND FOR WORK.
I THOUGHT YOU MIGHT BE HERE, BUT THEN YOU WERE OVER THERE TALKING...
I'VE NEVER SEEN YOU AT WORK BEFORE.
YOU LOOK LIKE YOU'RE IN YOUR ELEMENT.

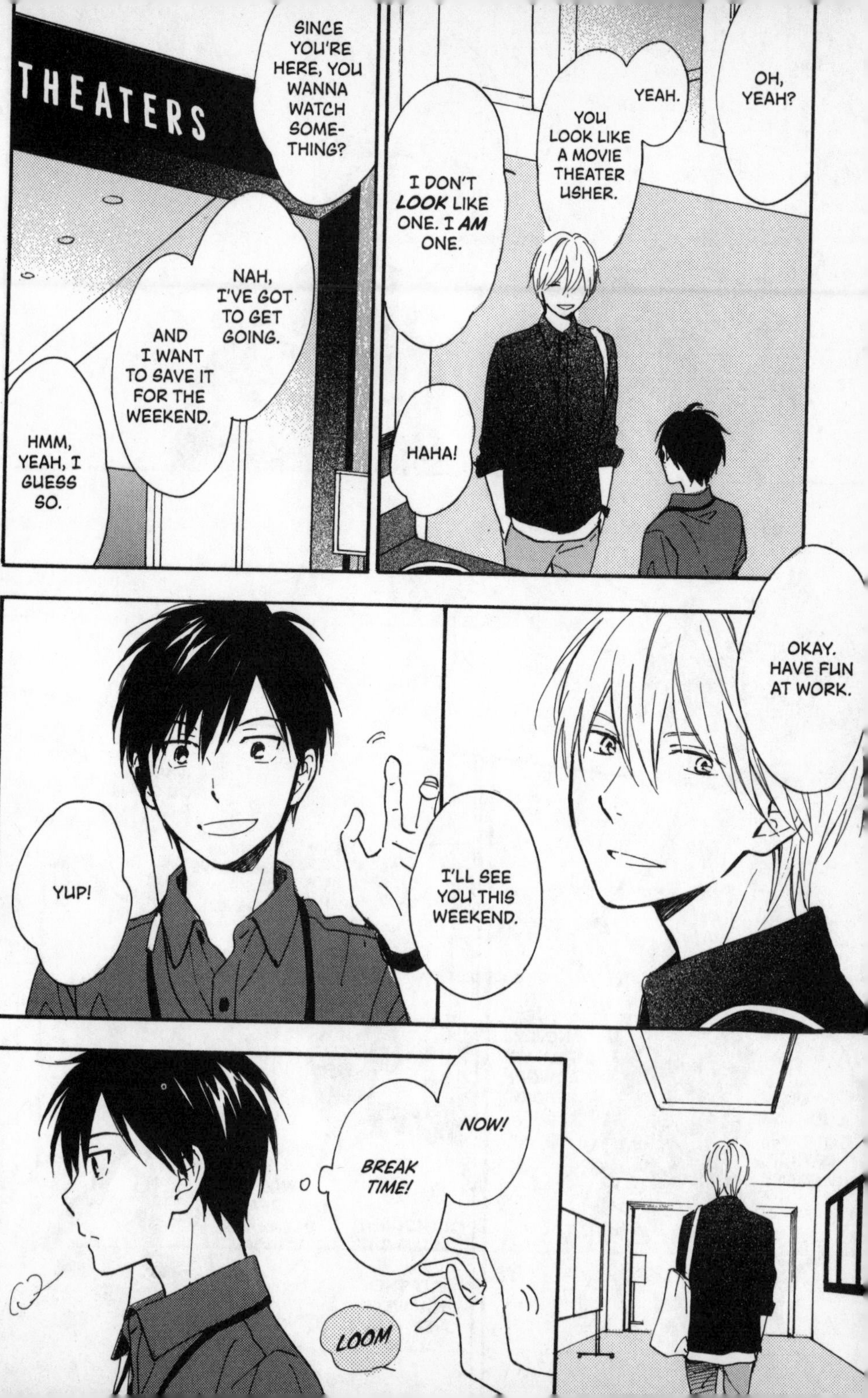
OH, YEAH?
YEAH.
YOU LOOK LIKE A MOVIE THEATER USHER.
I DON'T *LOOK* LIKE ONE. I *AM* ONE.
HAHA!
THEATERS
SINCE YOU'RE HERE, YOU WANNA WATCH SOMETHING?
NAH, I'VE GOT TO GET GOING.
AND I WANT TO SAVE IT FOR THE WEEKEND.
HMM, YEAH, I GUESS SO.
OKAY. HAVE FUN AT WORK.
I'LL SEE YOU THIS WEEKEND.
YUP!
NOW!
BREAK TIME!
LOOM

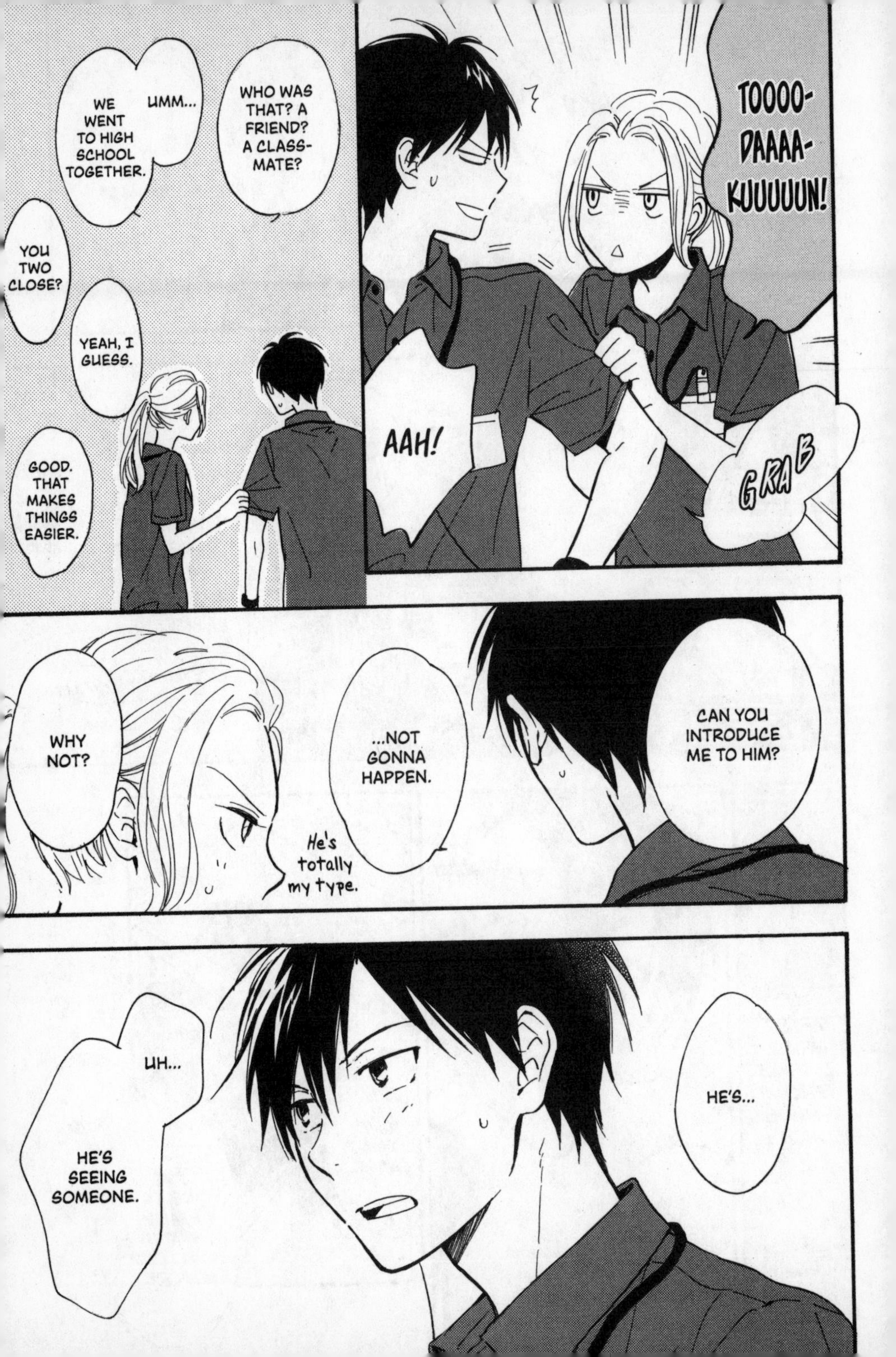
TOOOO-DAAAA-KUUUUUN!
AAH!
GRAB
WHO WAS THAT? A FRIEND? A CLASS-MATE?
UMM...
WE WENT TO HIGH SCHOOL TOGETHER.
YOU TWO CLOSE?
YEAH, I GUESS.
GOOD. THAT MAKES THINGS EASIER.
CAN YOU INTRODUCE ME TO HIM?
...NOT GONNA HAPPEN.
He's totally my type.
WHY NOT?
HE'S...
UH...
HE'S SEEING SOMEONE.

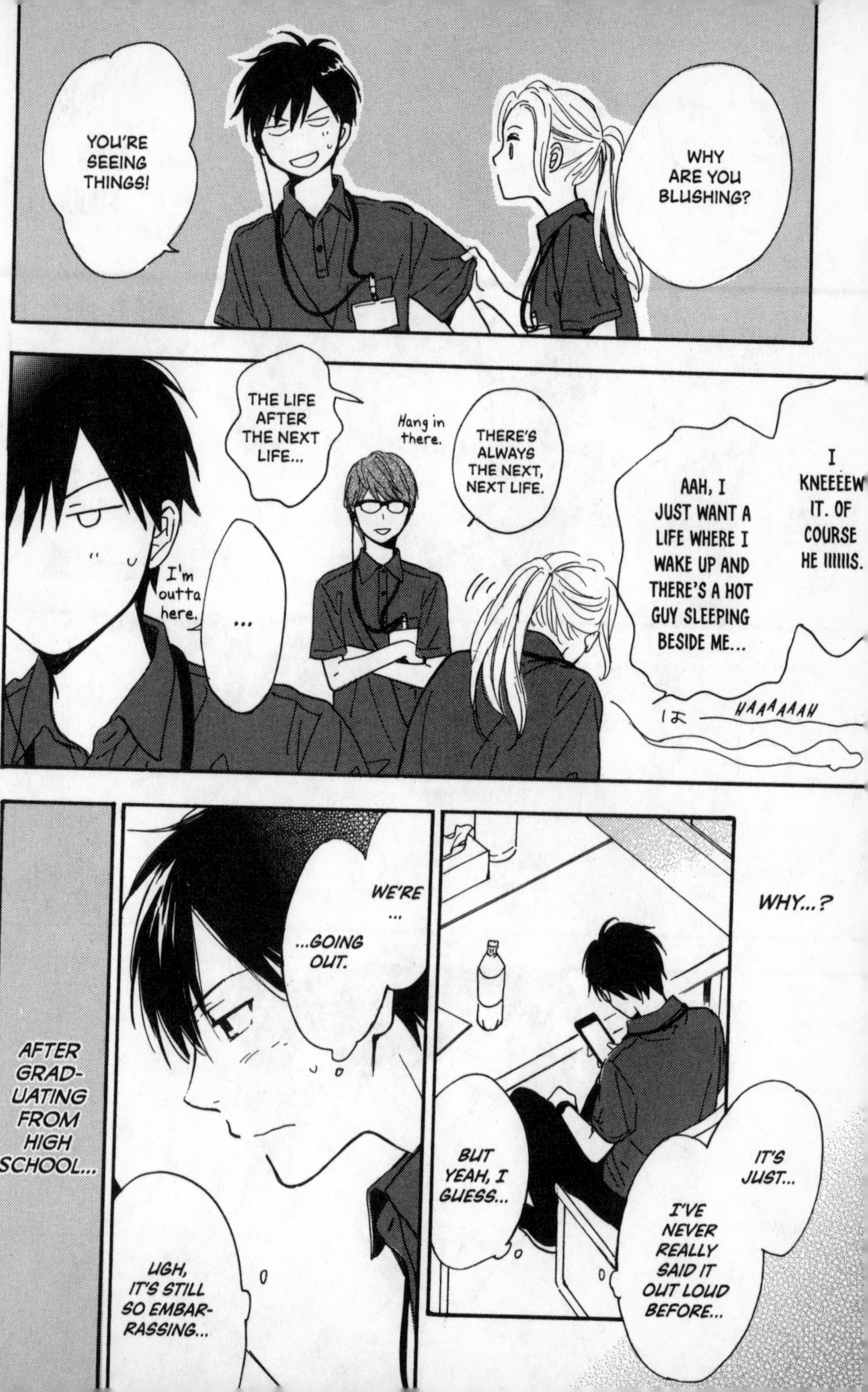
WHY ARE YOU BLUSHING?
YOU'RE SEEING THINGS!
I KNEEEEW IT. OF COURSE HE IIIIIIS.
AAH, I JUST WANT A LIFE WHERE I WAKE UP AND THERE'S A HOT GUY SLEEPING BESIDE ME...
は HAAAAAAH
THERE'S ALWAYS THE NEXT, NEXT LIFE.
Hang in there.
THE LIFE AFTER THE NEXT LIFE...
...
I'm outta here.
WHY...?
IT'S JUST...
I'VE NEVER REALLY SAID IT OUT LOUD BEFORE...
BUT YEAH, I GUESS...
WE'RE...
...GOING OUT.
UGH, IT'S STILL SO EMBARRASSING...
AFTER GRADUATING FROM HIGH SCHOOL...

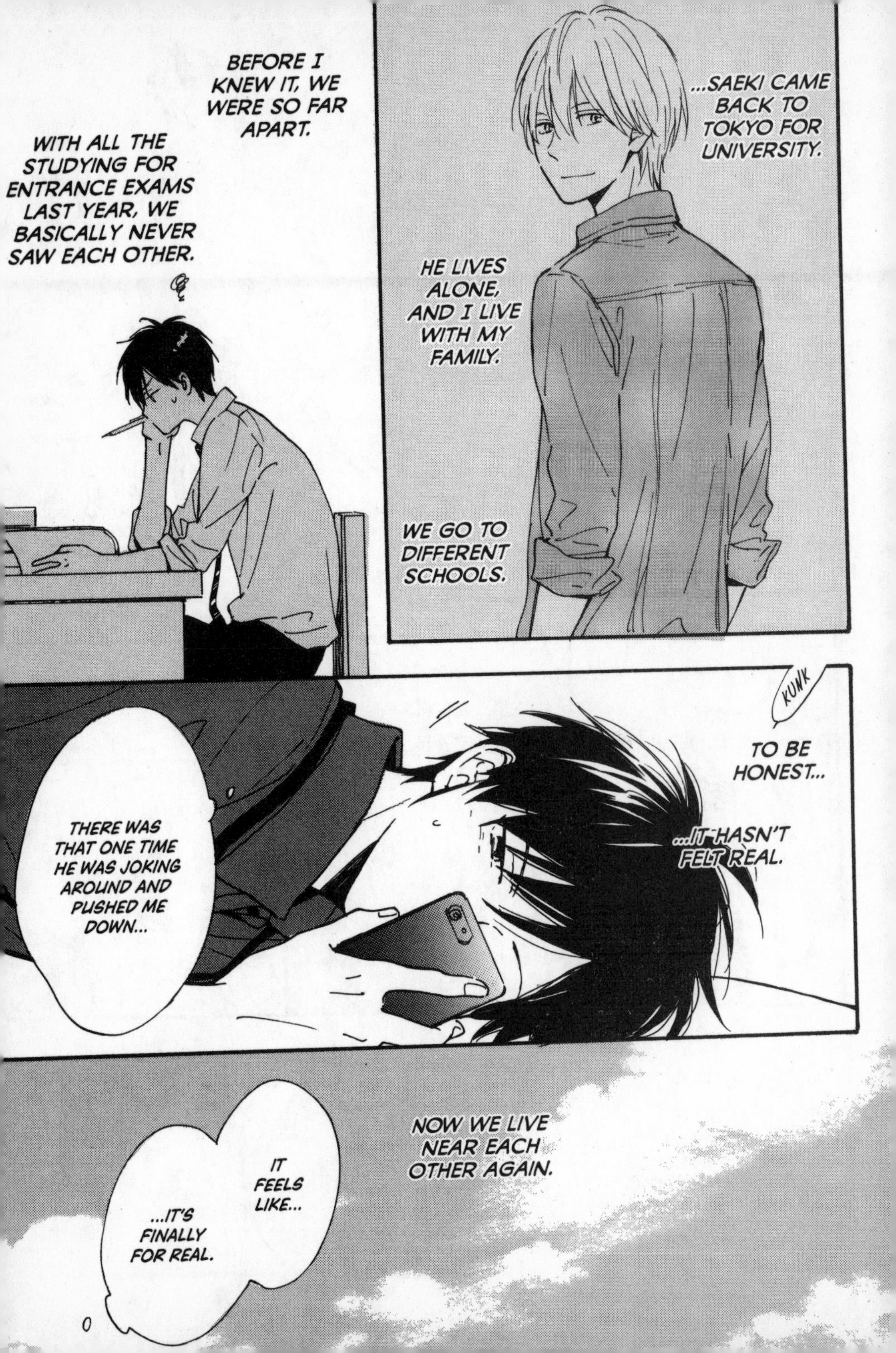
...SAEKI CAME BACK TO TOKYO FOR UNIVERSITY.
HE LIVES ALONE, AND I LIVE WITH MY FAMILY.
WE GO TO DIFFERENT SCHOOLS.
BEFORE I KNEW IT, WE WERE SO FAR APART.
WITH ALL THE STUDYING FOR ENTRANCE EXAMS LAST YEAR, WE BASICALLY NEVER SAW EACH OTHER.
KUNK
TO BE HONEST...
...IT HASN'T FELT REAL.
THERE WAS THAT ONE TIME HE WAS JOKING AROUND AND PUSHED ME DOWN...
NOW WE LIVE NEAR EACH OTHER AGAIN.
IT FEELS LIKE...
...IT'S FINALLY FOR REAL.

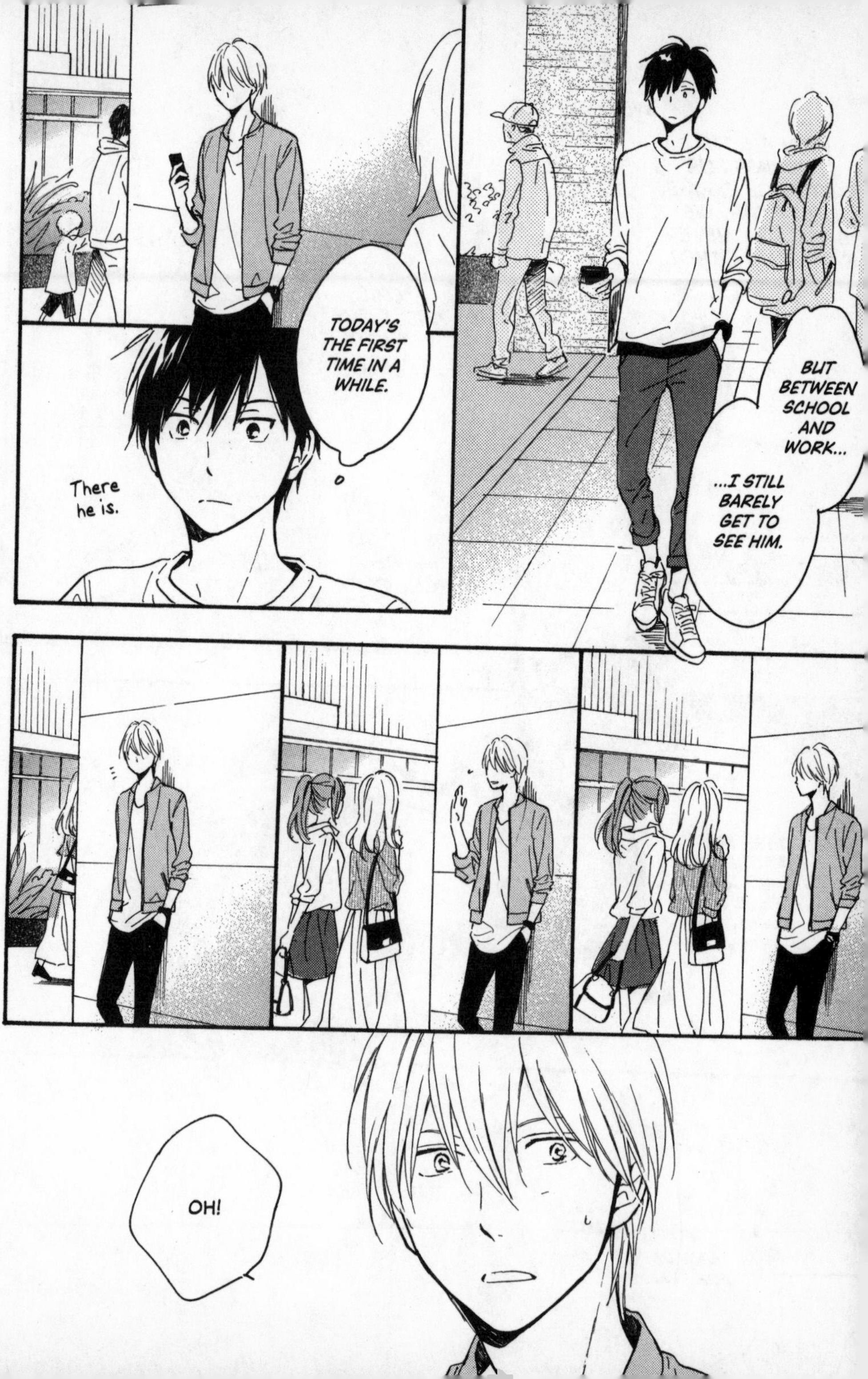
BUT BETWEEN SCHOOL AND WORK...
...I STILL BARELY GET TO SEE HIM.
TODAY'S THE FIRST TIME IN A WHILE.
There he is.
OH!

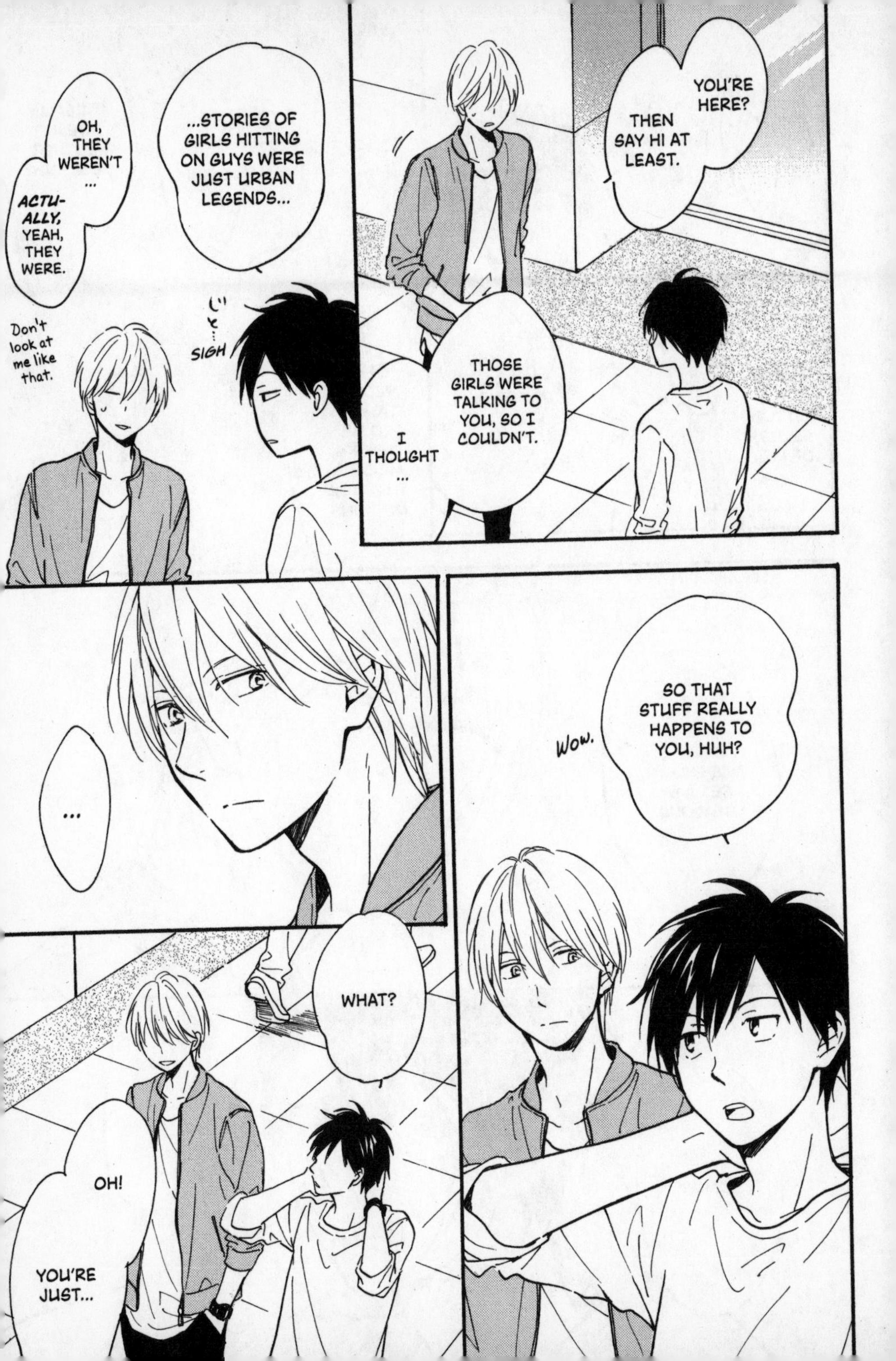
YOU'RE HERE?
THEN SAY HI AT LEAST.
THOSE GIRLS WERE TALKING TO YOU, SO I COULDN'T.
I THOUGHT ...
...STORIES OF GIRLS HITTING ON GUYS WERE JUST URBAN LEGENDS...
OH, THEY WEREN'T ... ACTU-ALLY, YEAH, THEY WERE.
じと…
SIGH
Don't look at me like that.
SO THAT STUFF REALLY HAPPENS TO YOU, HUH?
Wow.
...
WHAT?
OH!
YOU'RE JUST...

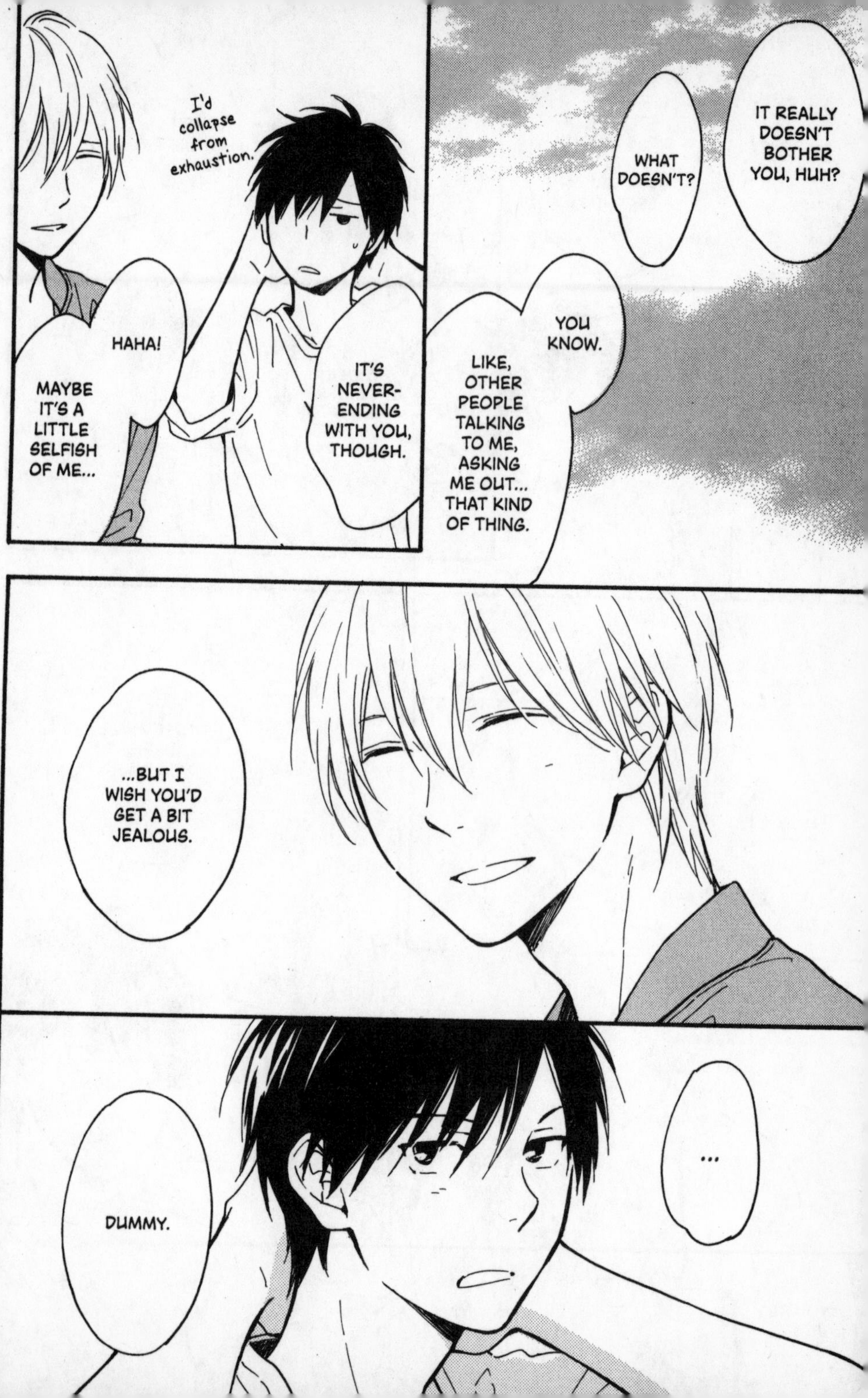
IT REALLY DOESN'T BOTHER YOU, HUH?
WHAT DOESN'T?
YOU KNOW.
LIKE, OTHER PEOPLE TALKING TO ME, ASKING ME OUT... THAT KIND OF THING.
IT'S NEVER-ENDING WITH YOU, THOUGH.
I'd collapse from exhaustion.
HAHA!
MAYBE IT'S A LITTLE SELFISH OF ME...
...BUT I WISH YOU'D GET A BIT JEALOUS.
...
DUMMY.

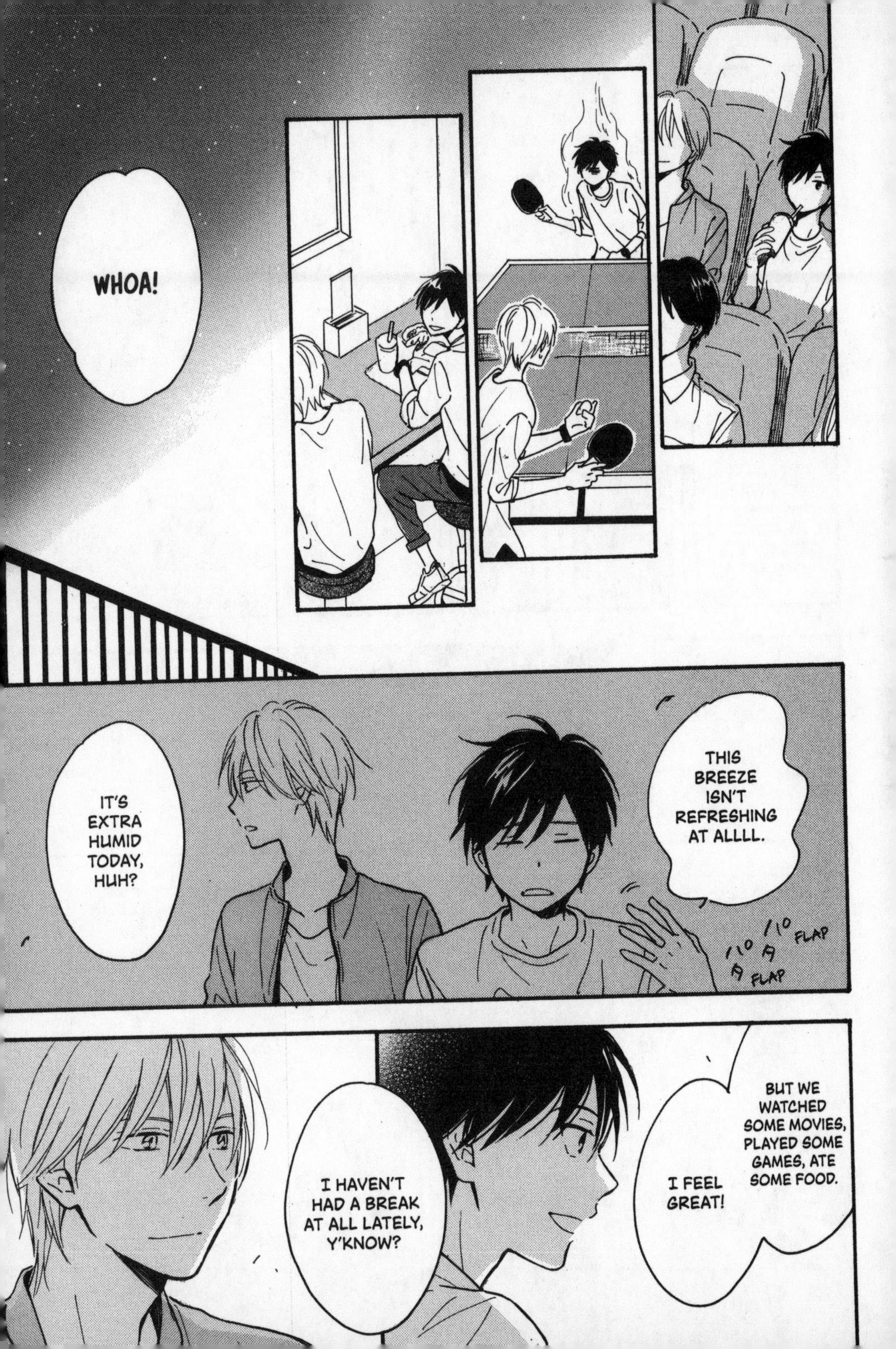
WHOA!
THIS BREEZE ISN'T REFRESHING AT ALLLL.
FLAP FLAP
IT'S EXTRA HUMID TODAY, HUH?
BUT WE WATCHED SOME MOVIES, PLAYED SOME GAMES, ATE SOME FOOD.
I FEEL GREAT!
I HAVEN'T HAD A BREAK AT ALL LATELY, Y'KNOW?

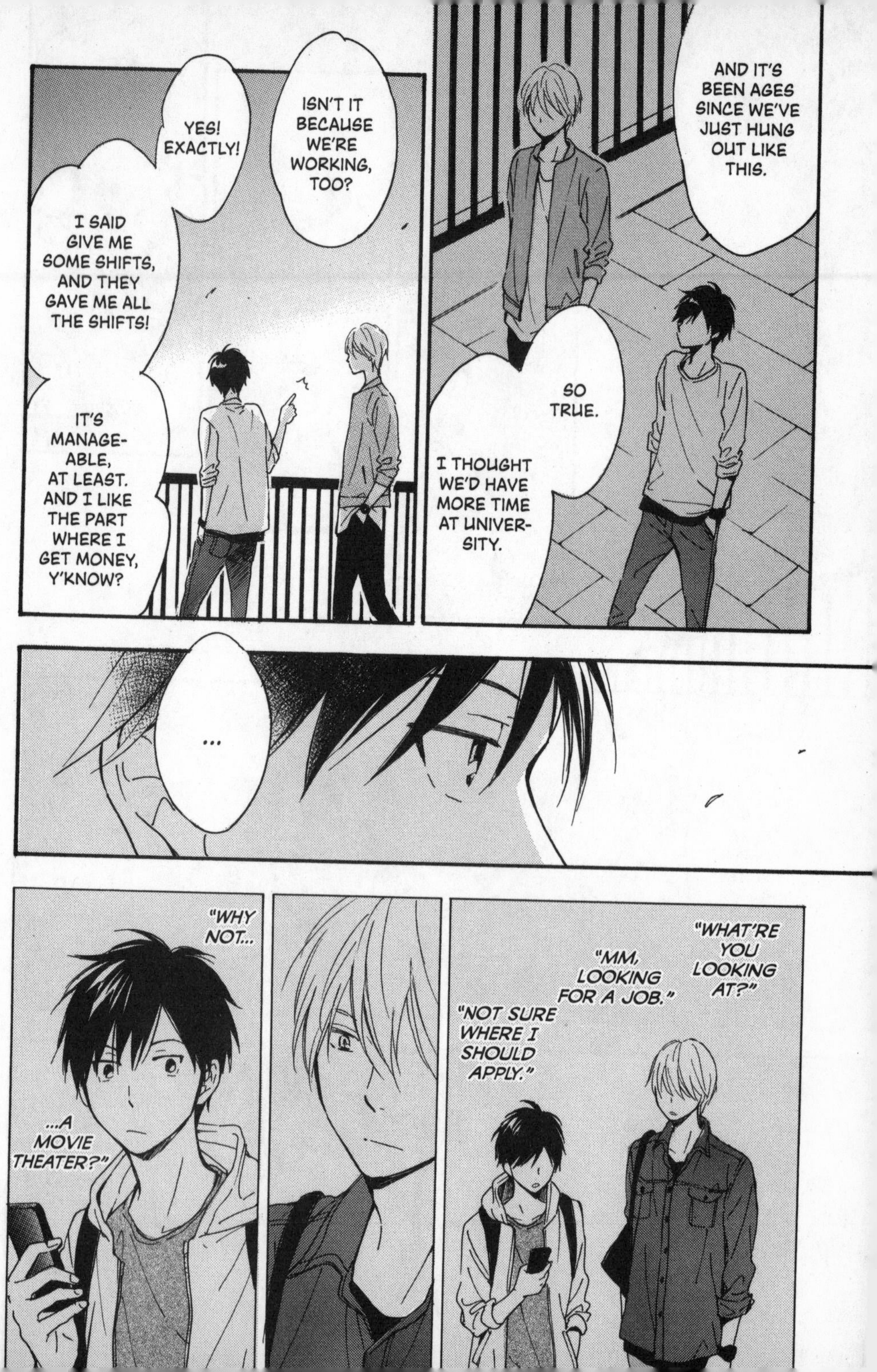
AND IT'S BEEN AGES SINCE WE'VE JUST HUNG OUT LIKE THIS.
SO TRUE.
I THOUGHT WE'D HAVE MORE TIME AT UNIVERSITY.
ISN'T IT BECAUSE WE'RE WORKING, TOO?
YES! EXACTLY!
I SAID GIVE ME SOME SHIFTS, AND THEY GAVE ME ALL THE SHIFTS!
IT'S MANAGEABLE, AT LEAST. AND I LIKE THE PART WHERE I GET MONEY, Y'KNOW?
...
"WHAT'RE YOU LOOKING AT?"
"MM, LOOKING FOR A JOB."
"NOT SURE WHERE I SHOULD APPLY."
"WHY NOT...
...A MOVIE THEATER?"

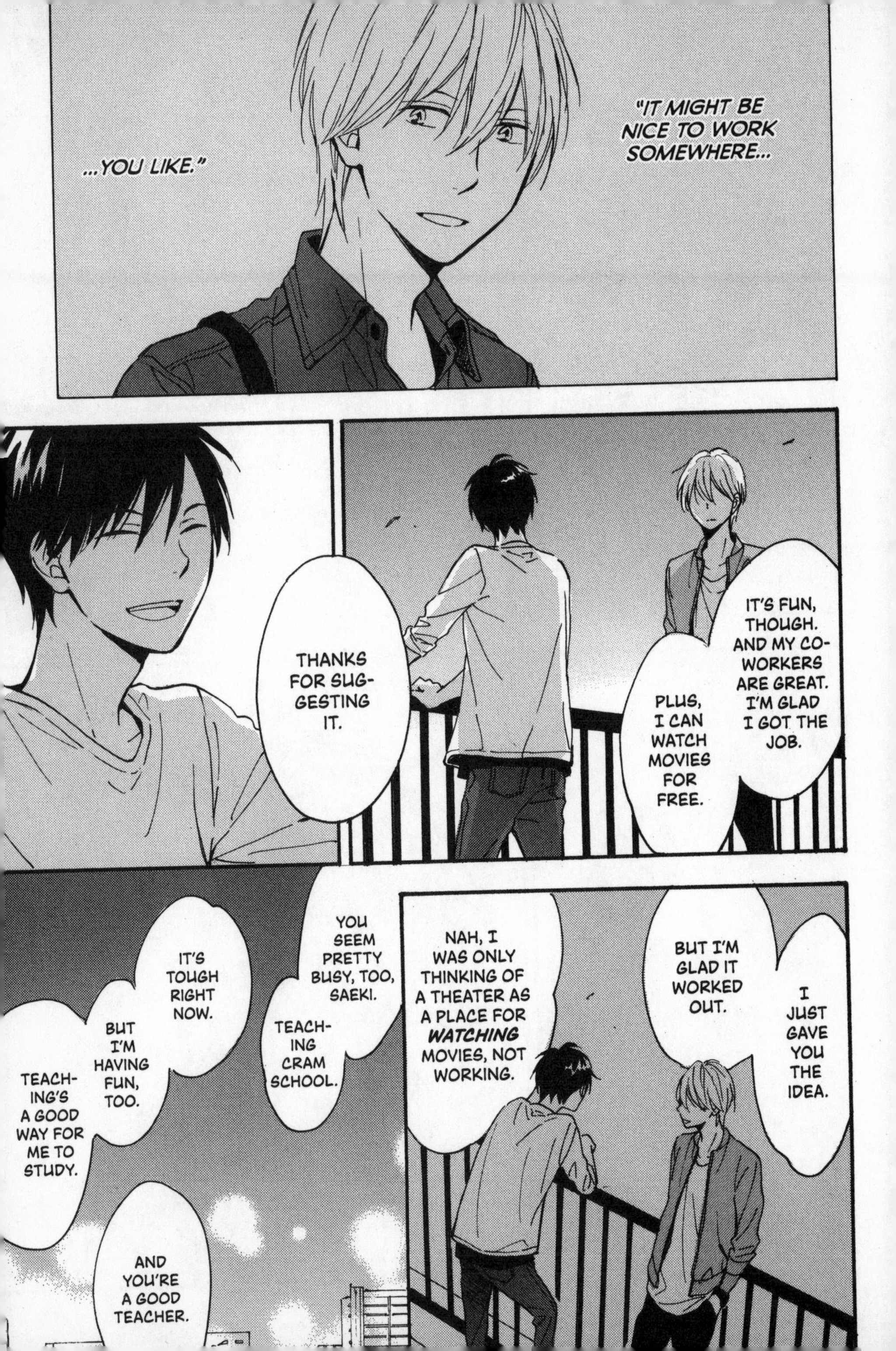
"IT MIGHT BE NICE TO WORK SOMEWHERE...
...YOU LIKE."
IT'S FUN, THOUGH. AND MY CO-WORKERS ARE GREAT. I'M GLAD I GOT THE JOB.
PLUS, I CAN WATCH MOVIES FOR FREE.
THANKS FOR SUG-GESTING IT.
NAH, I WAS ONLY THINKING OF A THEATER AS A PLACE FOR *WATCHING* MOVIES, NOT WORKING.
I JUST GAVE YOU THE IDEA.
BUT I'M GLAD IT WORKED OUT.
YOU SEEM PRETTY BUSY, TOO, SAEKI.
TEACH-ING CRAM SCHOOL.
IT'S TOUGH RIGHT NOW.
BUT I'M HAVING FUN, TOO.
TEACH-ING'S A GOOD WAY FOR ME TO STUDY.
AND YOU'RE A GOOD TEACHER.

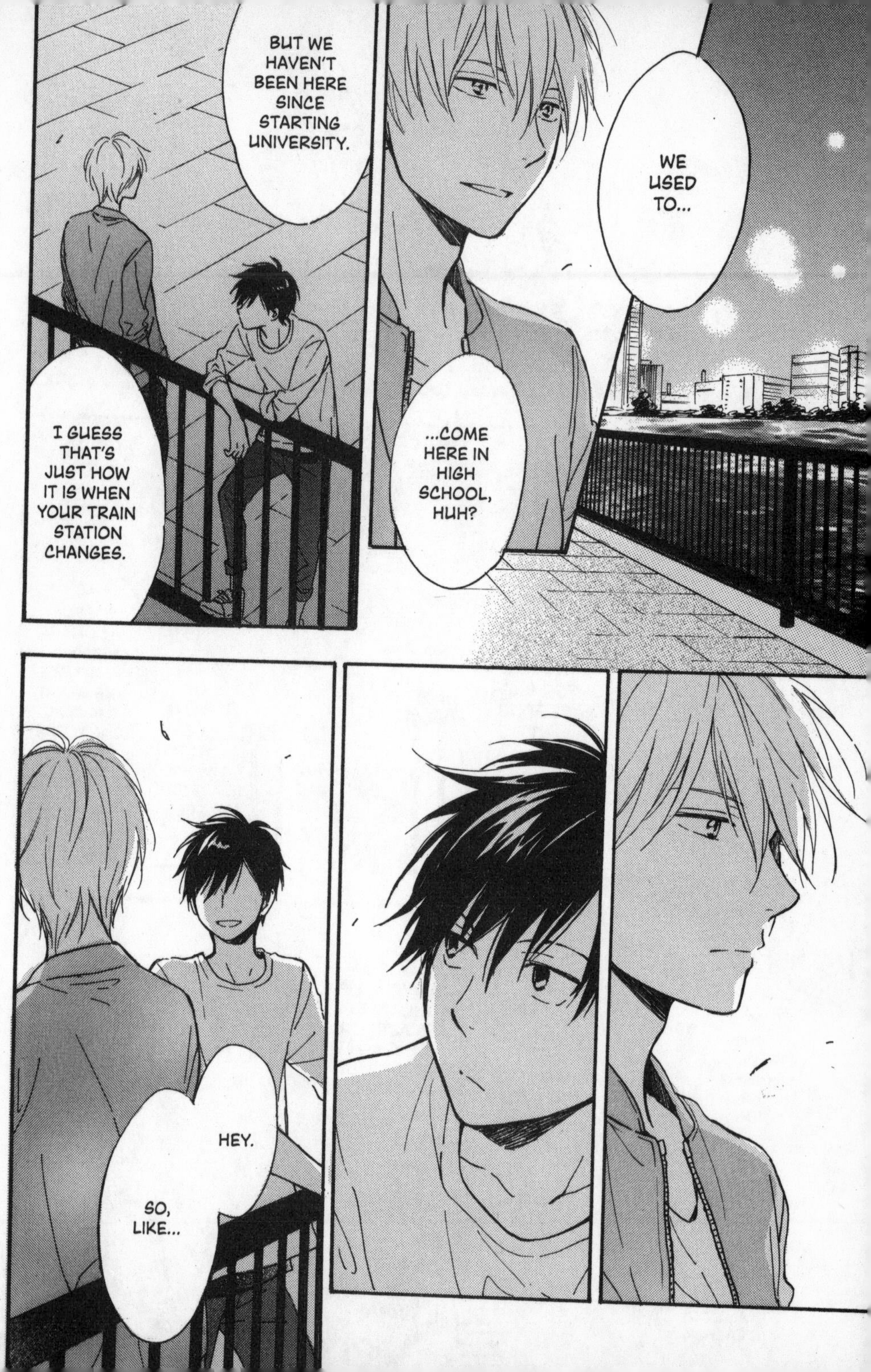
WE USED TO...
...COME HERE IN HIGH SCHOOL, HUH?
BUT WE HAVEN'T BEEN HERE SINCE STARTING UNIVERSITY.
I GUESS THAT'S JUST HOW IT IS WHEN YOUR TRAIN STATION CHANGES.
HEY.
SO, LIKE...

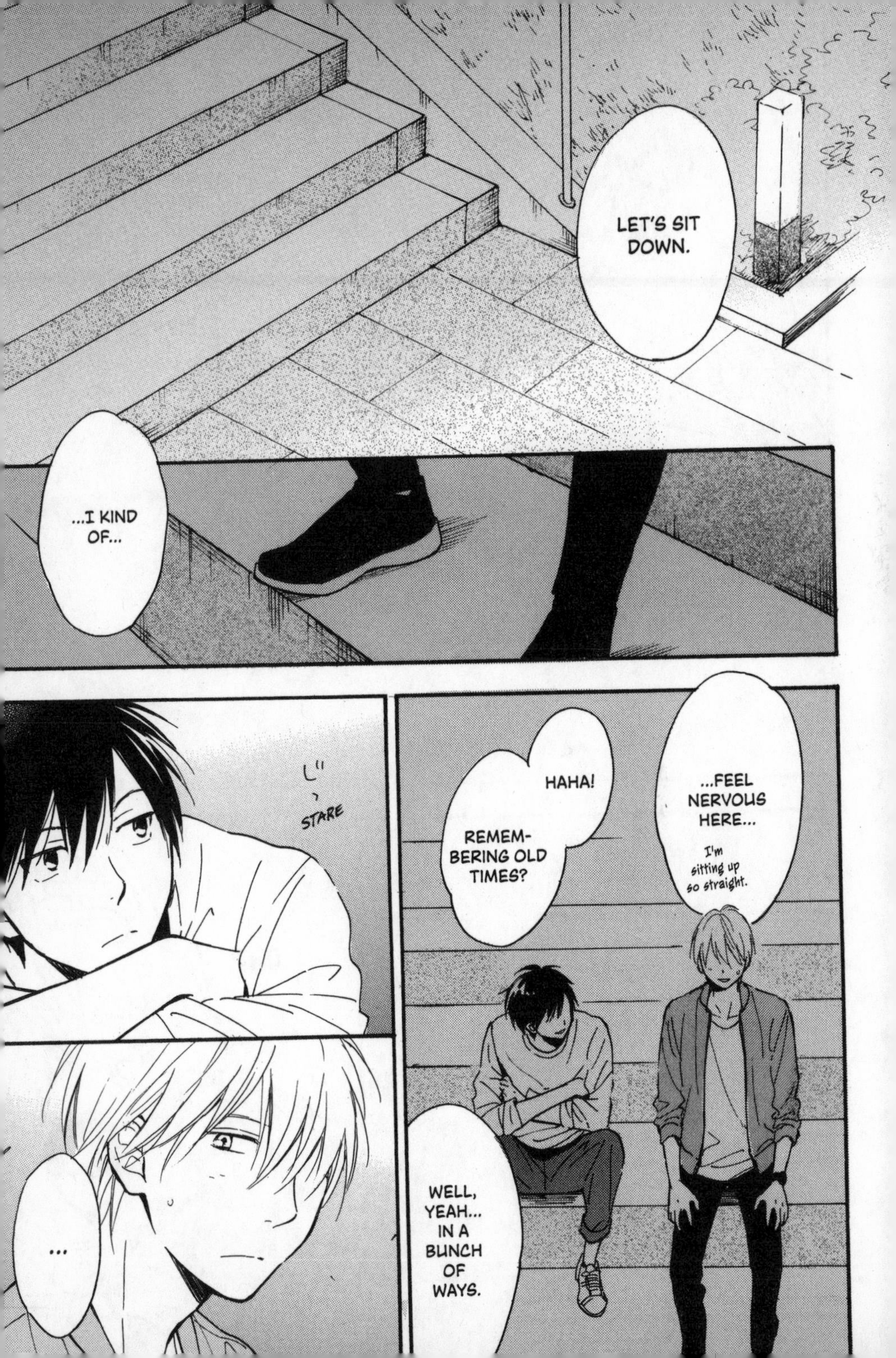
LET'S SIT DOWN.
...I KIND OF...
...FEEL NERVOUS HERE...
I'm sitting up so straight.
HAHA!
REMEM-BERING OLD TIMES?
WELL, YEAH... IN A BUNCH OF WAYS.
じっ
STARE
...

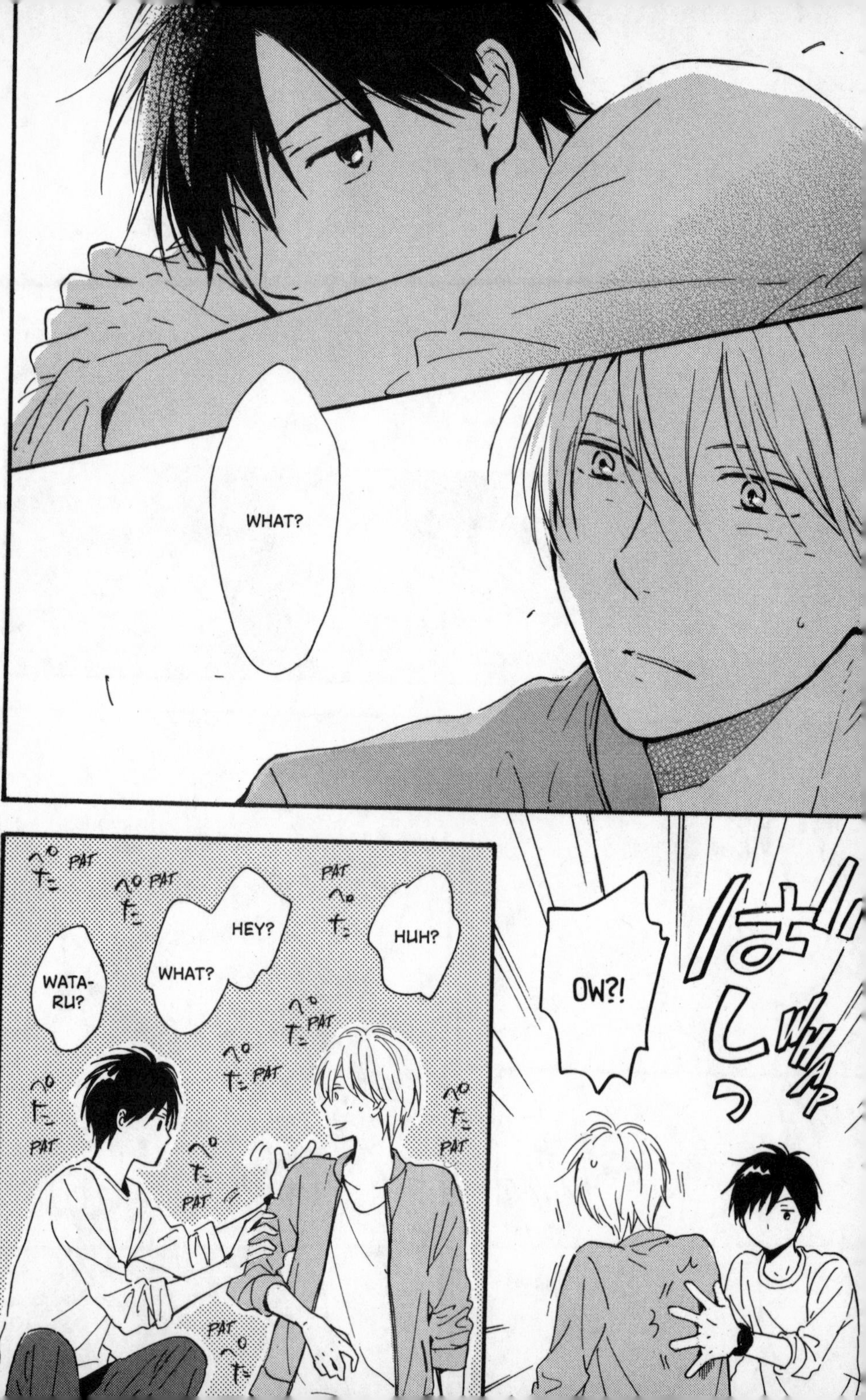
WHAT?
OW?!
はしっ
WHAP
HUH?
HEY?
WHAT?
WATA-RU?
PAT

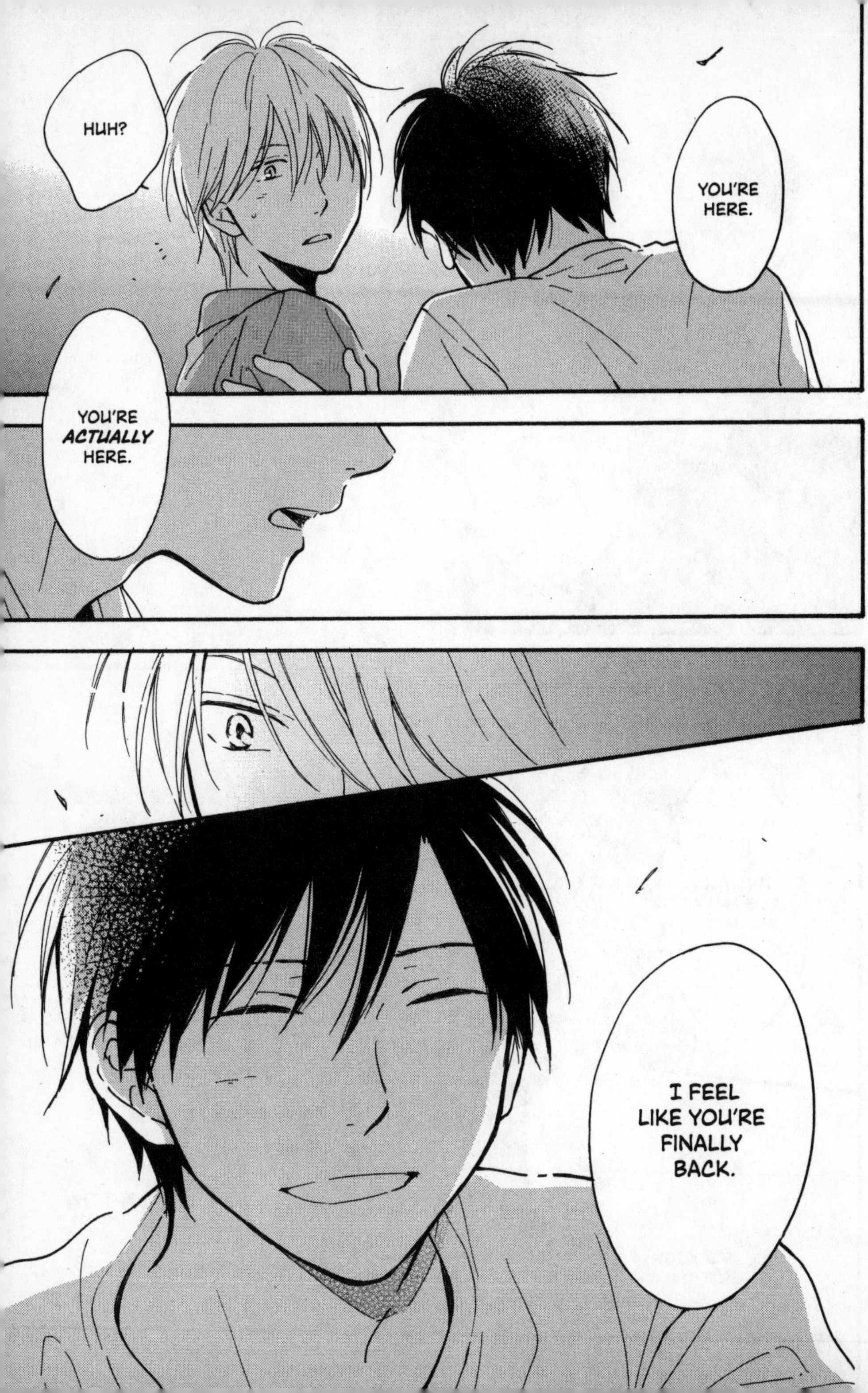
YOU'RE HERE.
HUH?
YOU'RE *ACTUALLY* HERE.
I FEEL LIKE YOU'RE FINALLY BACK.

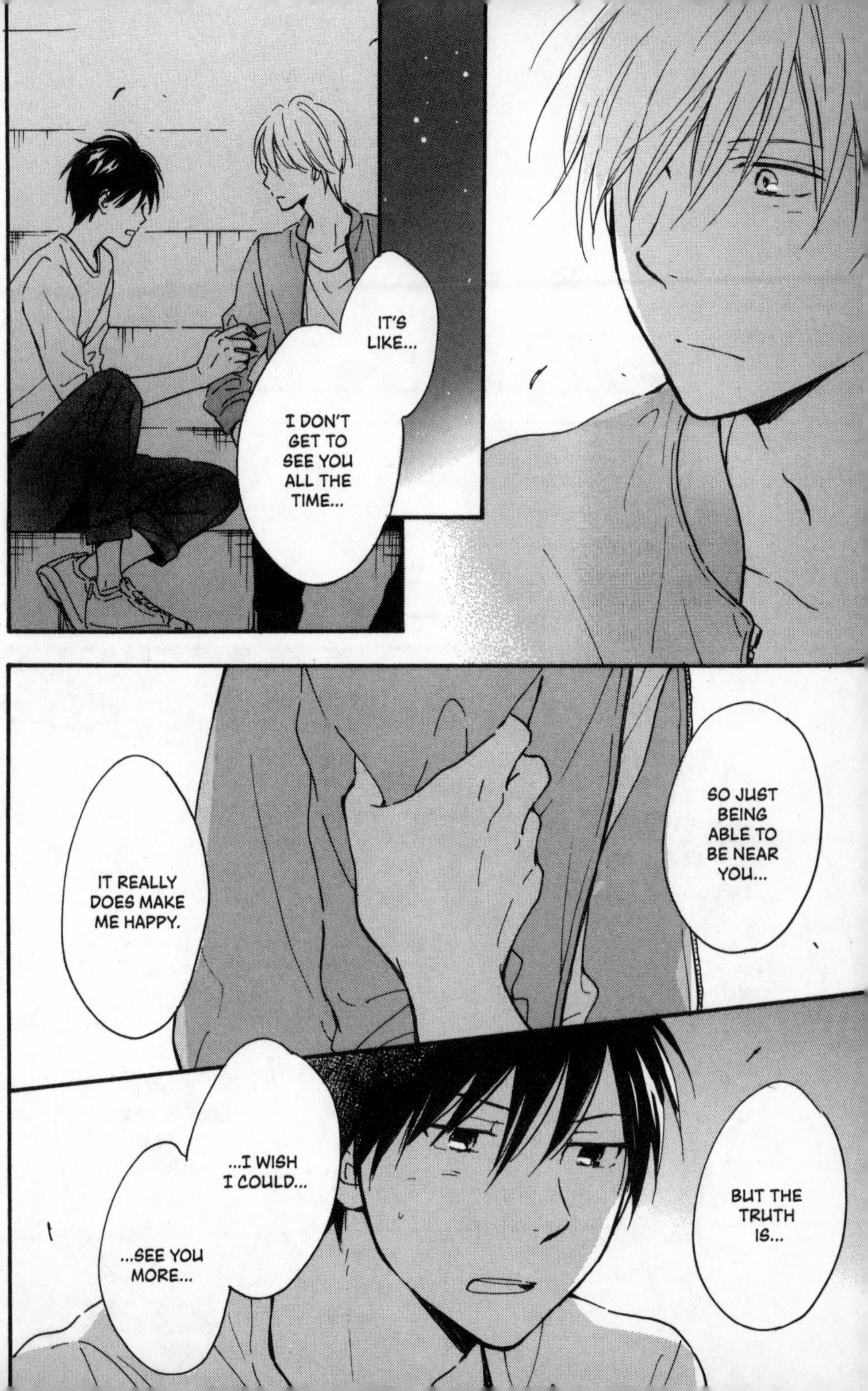
IT'S LIKE...
I DON'T GET TO SEE YOU ALL THE TIME...
SO JUST BEING ABLE TO BE NEAR YOU...
IT REALLY DOES MAKE ME HAPPY.
BUT THE TRUTH IS...
...I WISH I COULD...
...SEE YOU MORE...

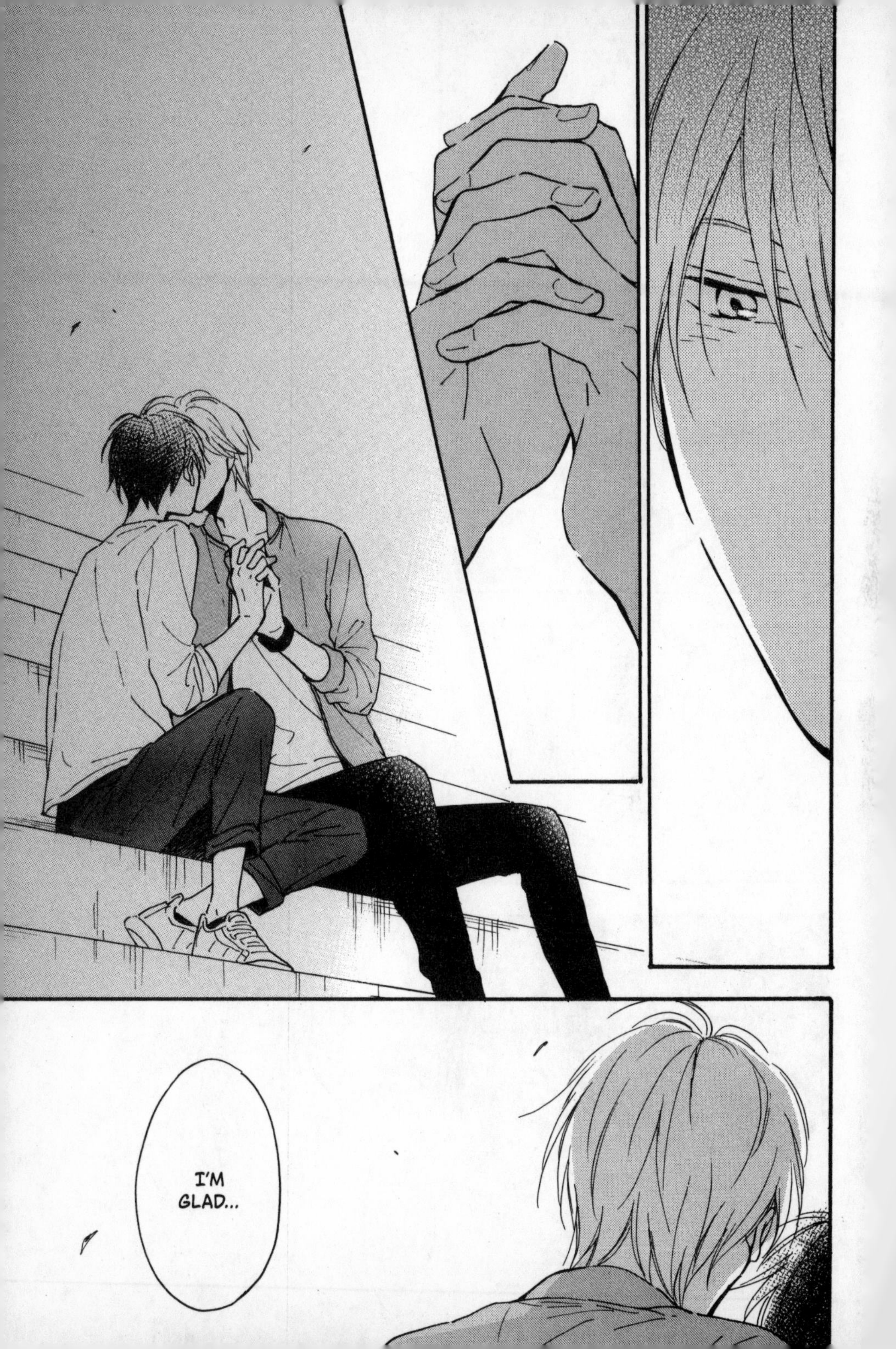
I'M GLAD...

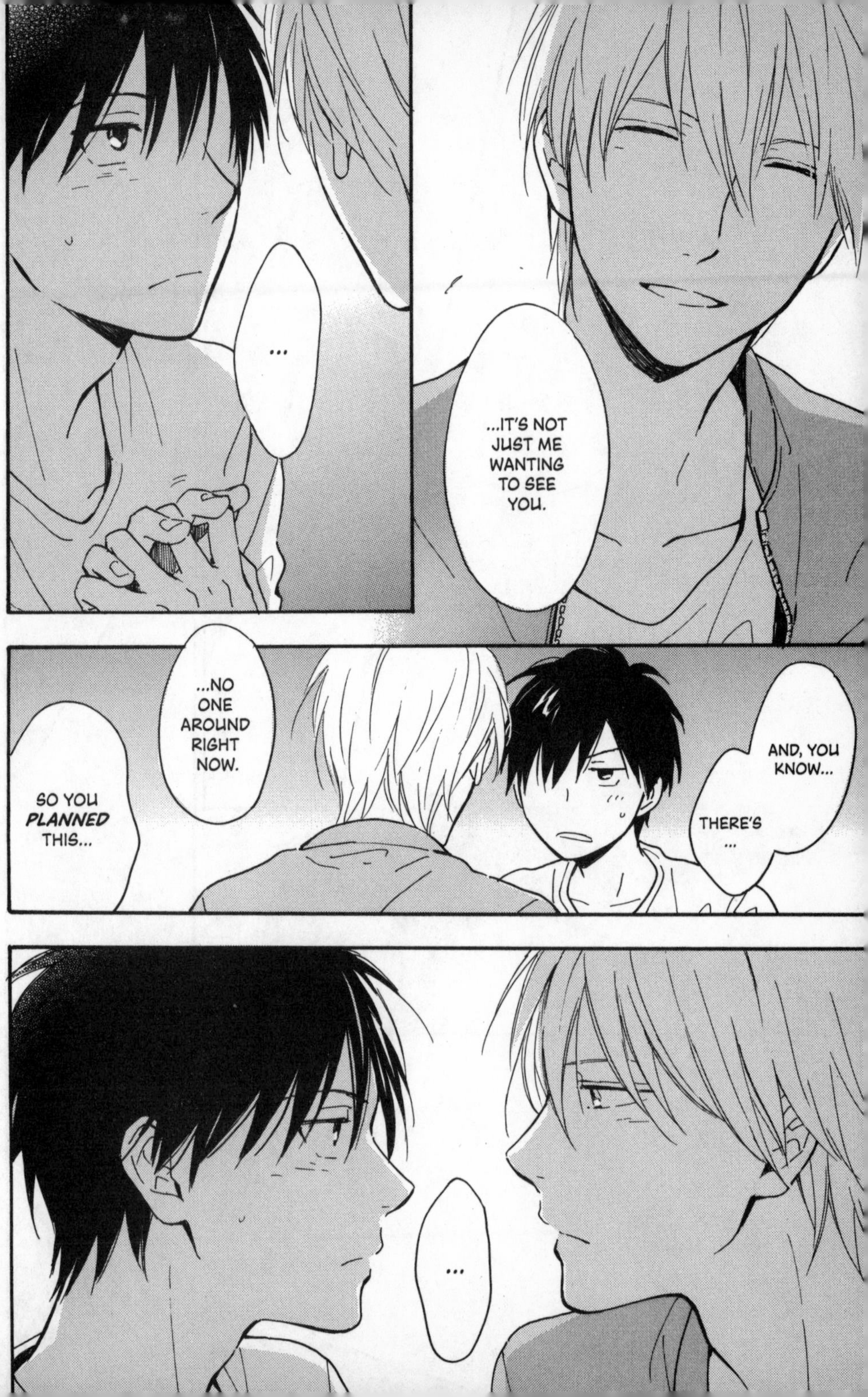
...IT'S NOT JUST ME WANTING TO SEE YOU.
...
AND, YOU KNOW... THERE'S ...
...NO ONE AROUND RIGHT NOW.
SO YOU *PLANNED* THIS...
...

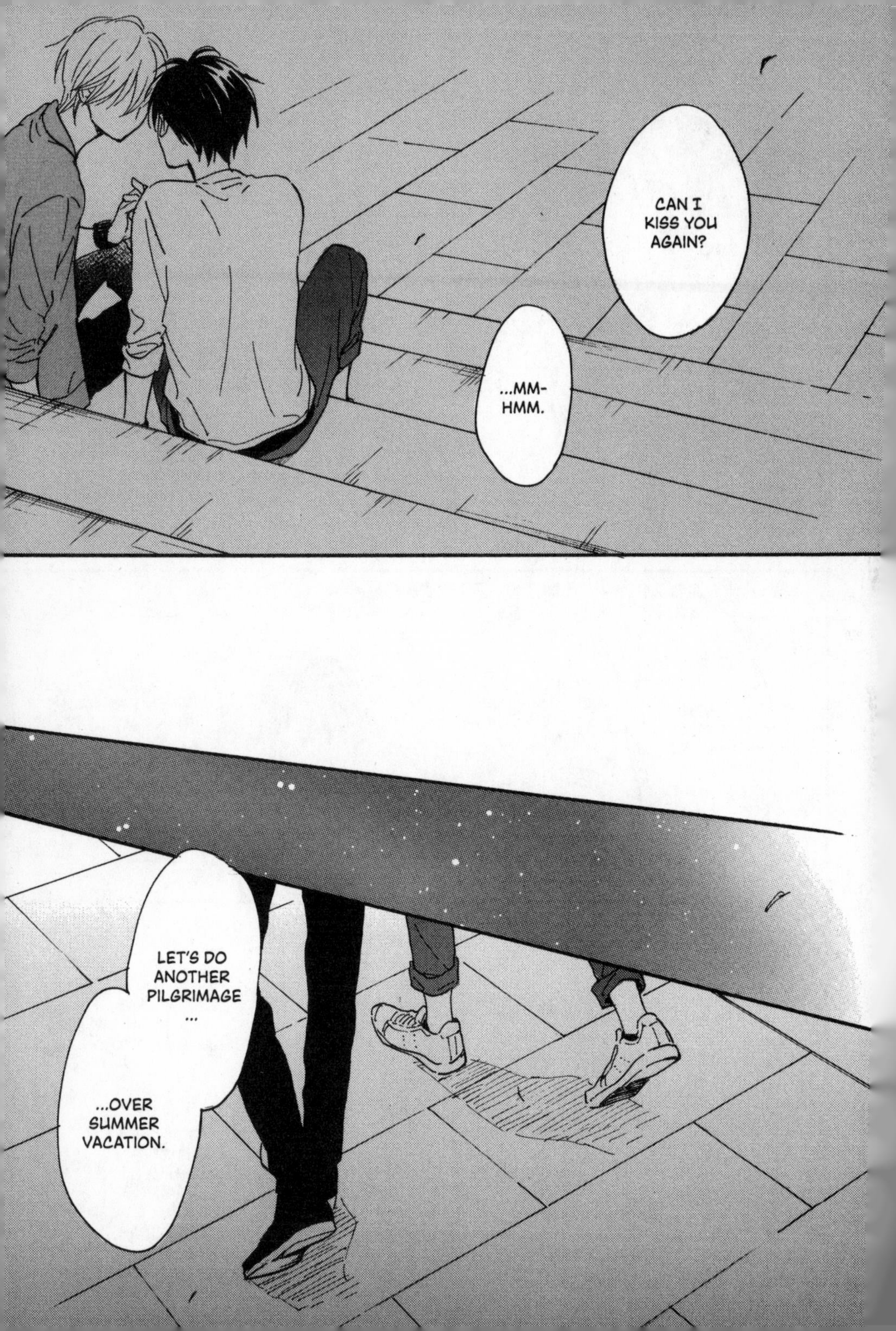
CAN I KISS YOU AGAIN?
...MM-HMM.
LET'S DO ANOTHER PILGRIMAGE ...
...OVER SUMMER VACATION.

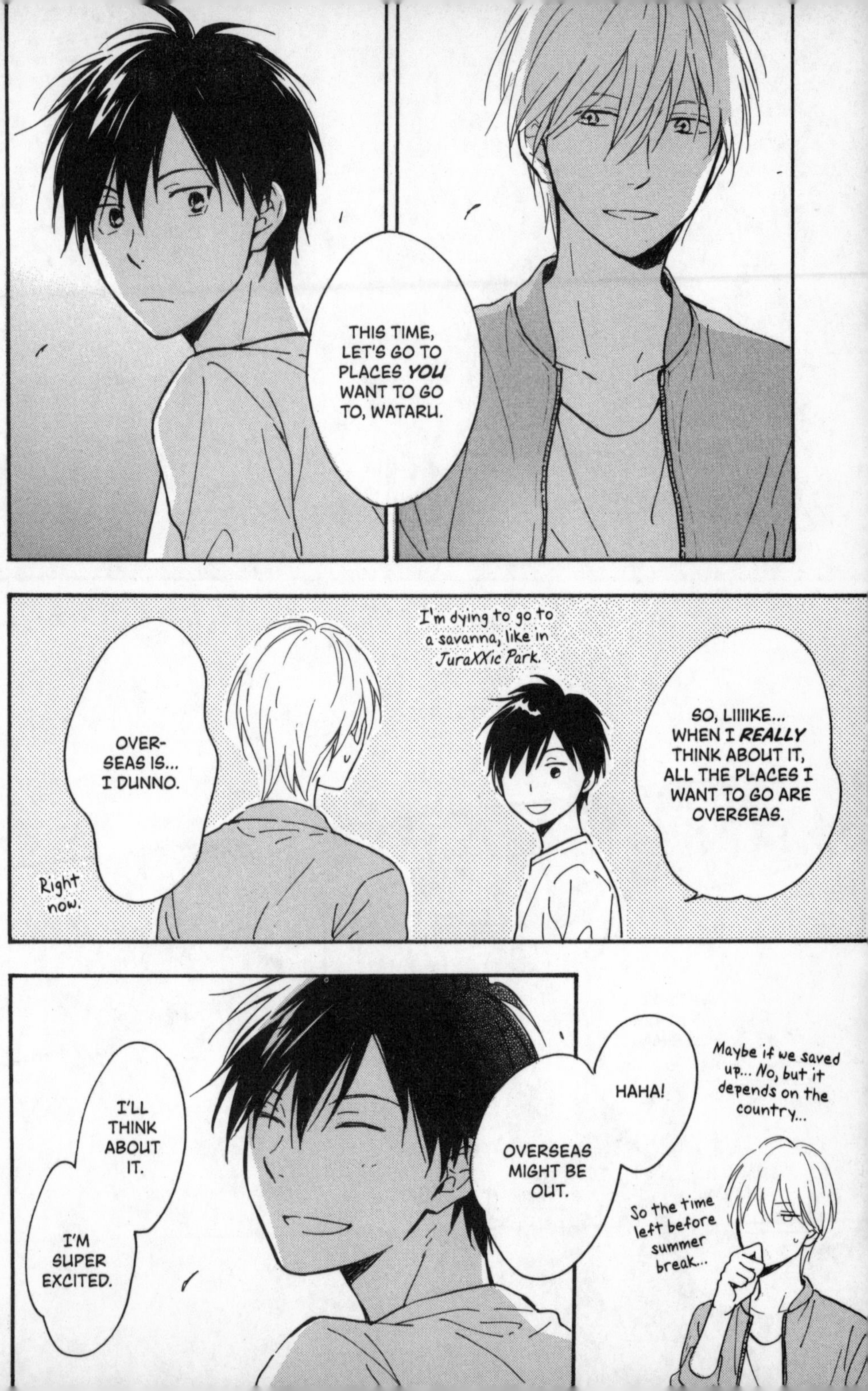
THIS TIME, LET'S GO TO PLACES YOU WANT TO GO TO, WATARU.
SO, LIIIIKE... WHEN I REALLY THINK ABOUT IT, ALL THE PLACES I WANT TO GO ARE OVERSEAS.
I'm dying to go to a savanna, like in JuraXXic Park.
OVER-SEAS IS... I DUNNO.
Right now.
Maybe if we saved up... No, but it depends on the country...
So the time left before summer break...
HAHA!
OVERSEAS MIGHT BE OUT.
I'LL THINK ABOUT IT.
I'M SUPER EXCITED.

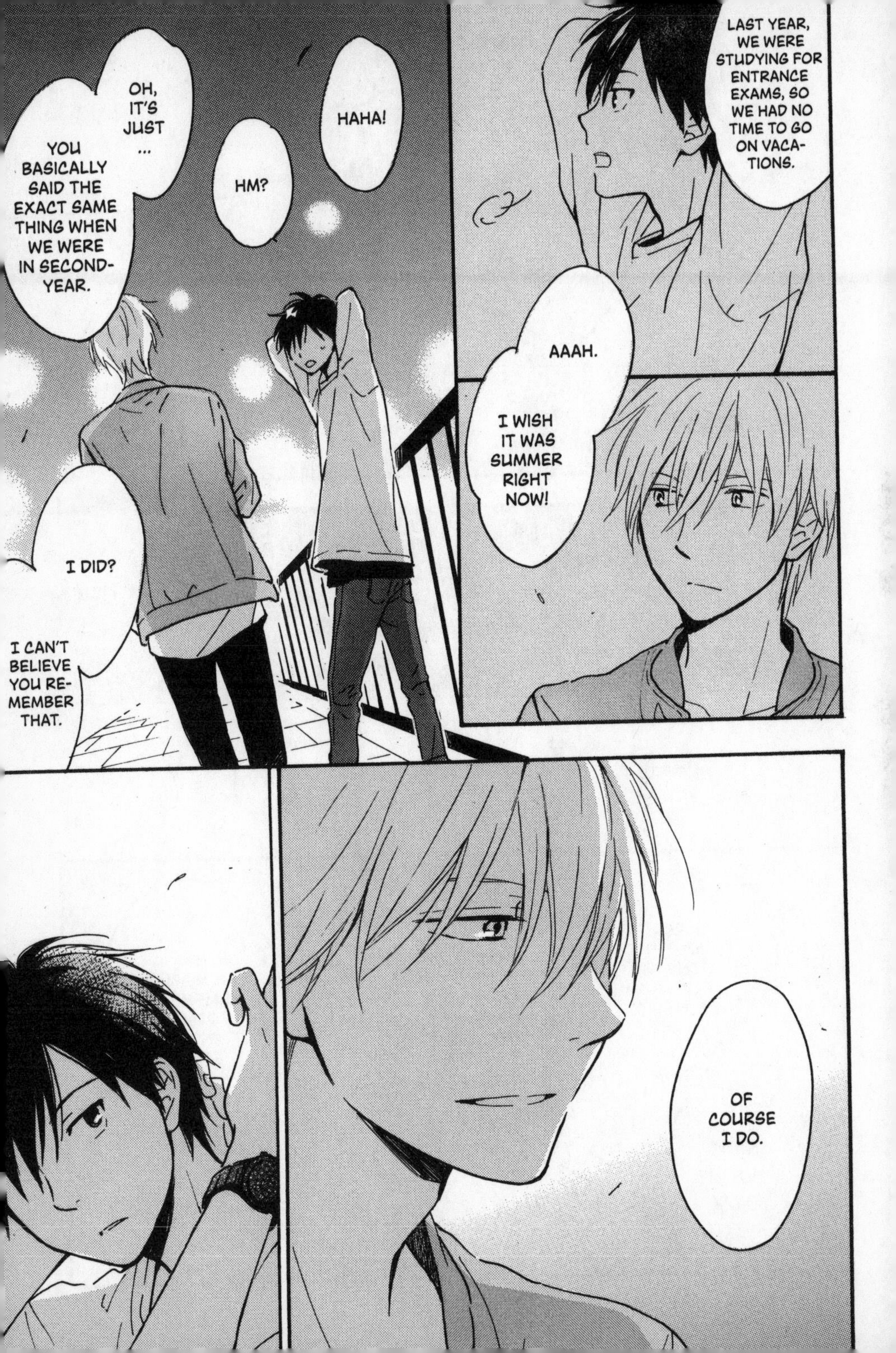
LAST YEAR, WE WERE STUDYING FOR ENTRANCE EXAMS, SO WE HAD NO TIME TO GO ON VACA-TIONS.
AAAH.
I WISH IT WAS SUMMER RIGHT NOW!
HAHA!
HM?
OH, IT'S JUST ...
YOU BASICALLY SAID THE EXACT SAME THING WHEN WE WERE IN SECOND-YEAR.
I DID?
I CAN'T BELIEVE YOU RE-MEMBER THAT.
OF COURSE I DO.

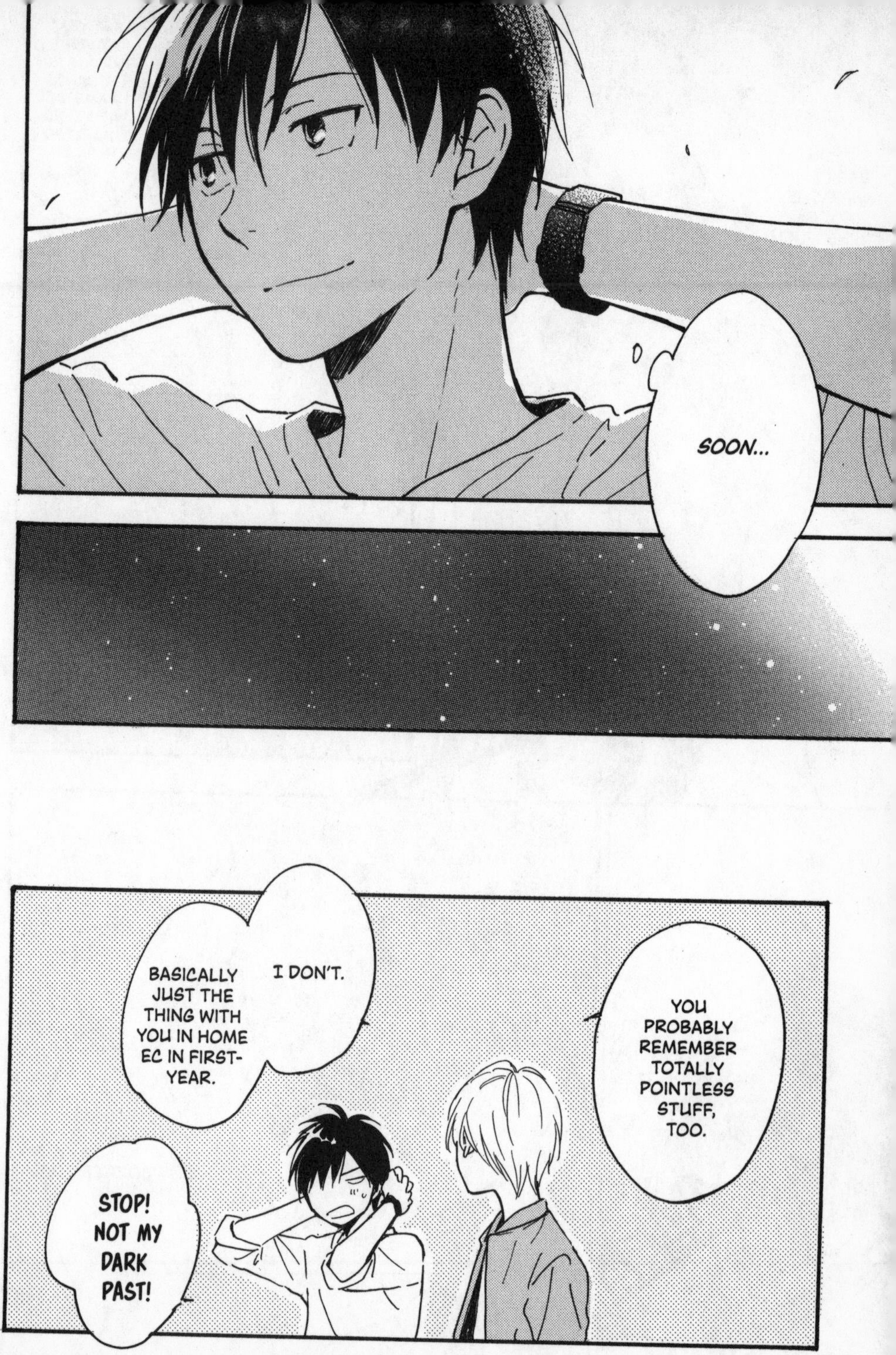
SOON...
YOU PROBABLY REMEMBER TOTALLY POINTLESS STUFF, TOO.
I DON'T.
BASICALLY JUST THE THING WITH YOU IN HOME EC IN FIRST-YEAR.
STOP! NOT MY DARK PAST!

MY SUMMER OF YOU

MY **SUMMER** OF **YOU**

MY SUMMER OF YOU

Chapter 2

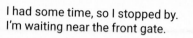

BEEBOOP

I had some time, so I stopped by.
I'm waiting near the front gate.

'SUP.

WATARU.

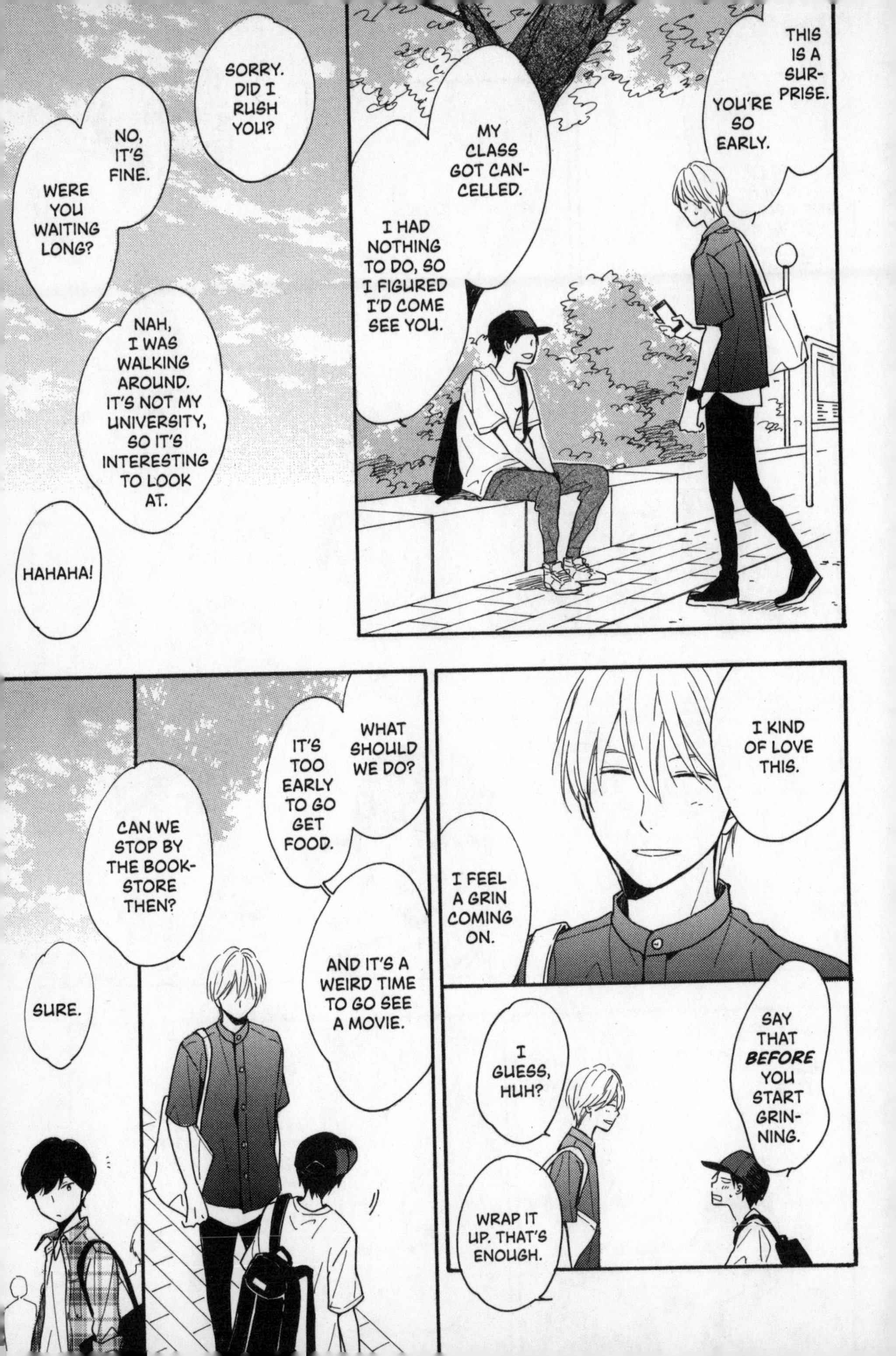
THIS IS A SURPRISE.
YOU'RE SO EARLY.
MY CLASS GOT CANCELLED.
I HAD NOTHING TO DO, SO I FIGURED I'D COME SEE YOU.
SORRY. DID I RUSH YOU?
NO, IT'S FINE.
WERE YOU WAITING LONG?
NAH, I WAS WALKING AROUND. IT'S NOT MY UNIVERSITY, SO IT'S INTERESTING TO LOOK AT.
HAHAHA!
I KIND OF LOVE THIS.
I FEEL A GRIN COMING ON.
SAY THAT ***BEFORE*** YOU START GRINNING.
I GUESS, HUH?
WRAP IT UP. THAT'S ENOUGH.
WHAT SHOULD WE DO?
IT'S TOO EARLY TO GO GET FOOD.
AND IT'S A WEIRD TIME TO GO SEE A MOVIE.
CAN WE STOP BY THE BOOKSTORE THEN?
SURE.

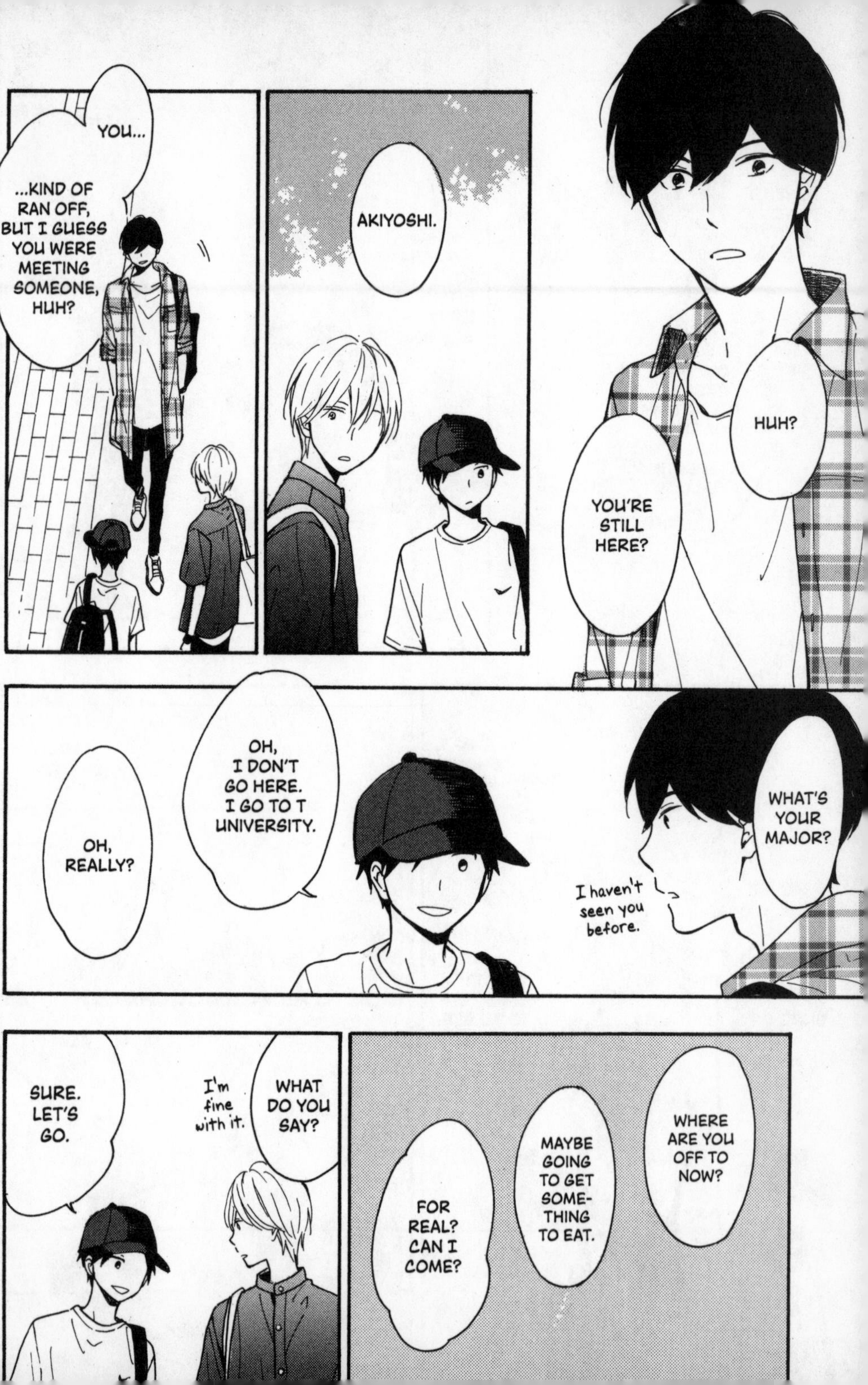
HUH?
YOU'RE STILL HERE?
AKIYOSHI.
YOU...
...KIND OF RAN OFF, BUT I GUESS YOU WERE MEETING SOMEONE, HUH?
WHAT'S YOUR MAJOR?
I haven't seen you before.
OH, I DON'T GO HERE. I GO TO T UNIVERSITY.
OH, REALLY?
WHERE ARE YOU OFF TO NOW?
MAYBE GOING TO GET SOME-THING TO EAT.
FOR REAL? CAN I COME?
WHAT DO YOU SAY?
I'm fine with it.
SURE. LET'S GO.

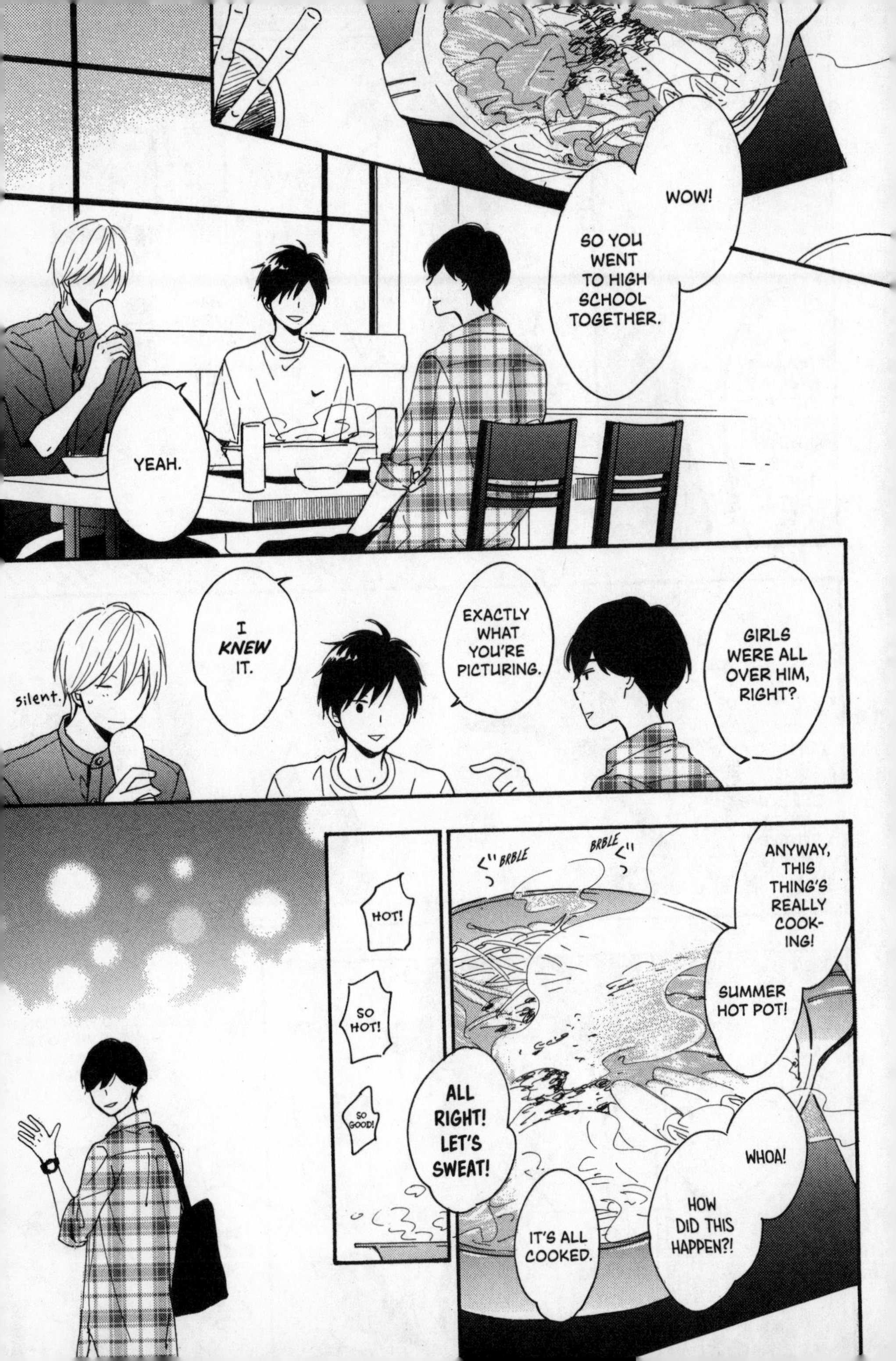
WOW!
SO YOU WENT TO HIGH SCHOOL TOGETHER.
YEAH.
GIRLS WERE ALL OVER HIM, RIGHT?
EXACTLY WHAT YOU'RE PICTURING.
I KNEW IT.
silent.
ANYWAY, THIS THING'S REALLY COOK-ING!
BRBLE
BRBLE
SUMMER HOT POT!
WHOA!
HOW DID THIS HAPPEN?!
IT'S ALL COOKED.
ALL RIGHT! LET'S SWEAT!
HOT!
SO HOT!
SO GOOD!

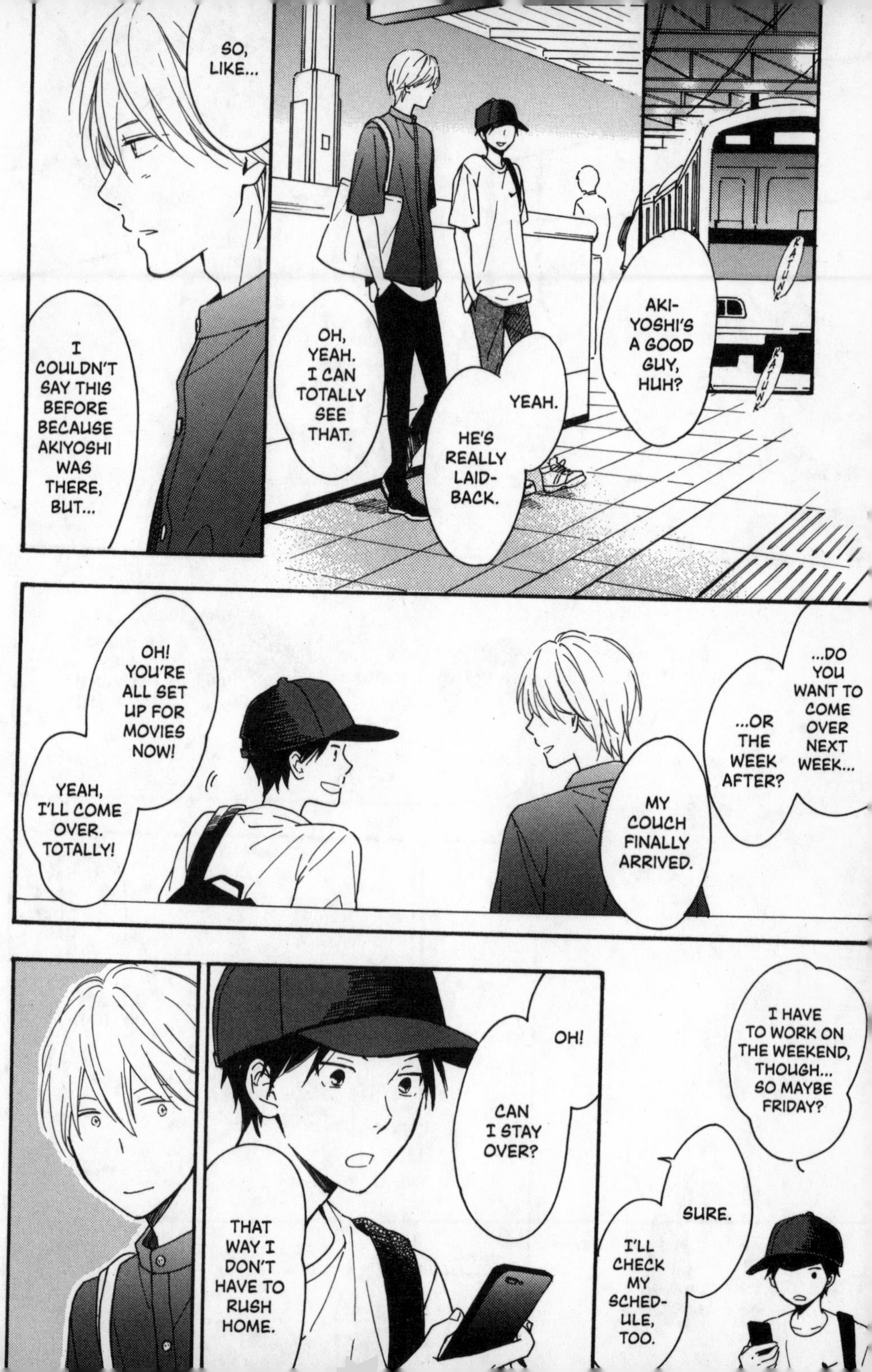
KATUNK
KATUNK
AKI-YOSHI'S A GOOD GUY, HUH?
YEAH.
HE'S REALLY LAID-BACK.
OH, YEAH. I CAN TOTALLY SEE THAT.
SO, LIKE...
I COULDN'T SAY THIS BEFORE BECAUSE AKIYOSHI WAS THERE, BUT...
...DO YOU WANT TO COME OVER NEXT WEEK...
...OR THE WEEK AFTER?
MY COUCH FINALLY ARRIVED.
OH! YOU'RE ALL SET UP FOR MOVIES NOW!
YEAH, I'LL COME OVER. TOTALLY!
I HAVE TO WORK ON THE WEEKEND, THOUGH... SO MAYBE FRIDAY?
SURE.
I'LL CHECK MY SCHEDULE, TOO.
OH!
CAN I STAY OVER?
THAT WAY I DON'T HAVE TO RUSH HOME.

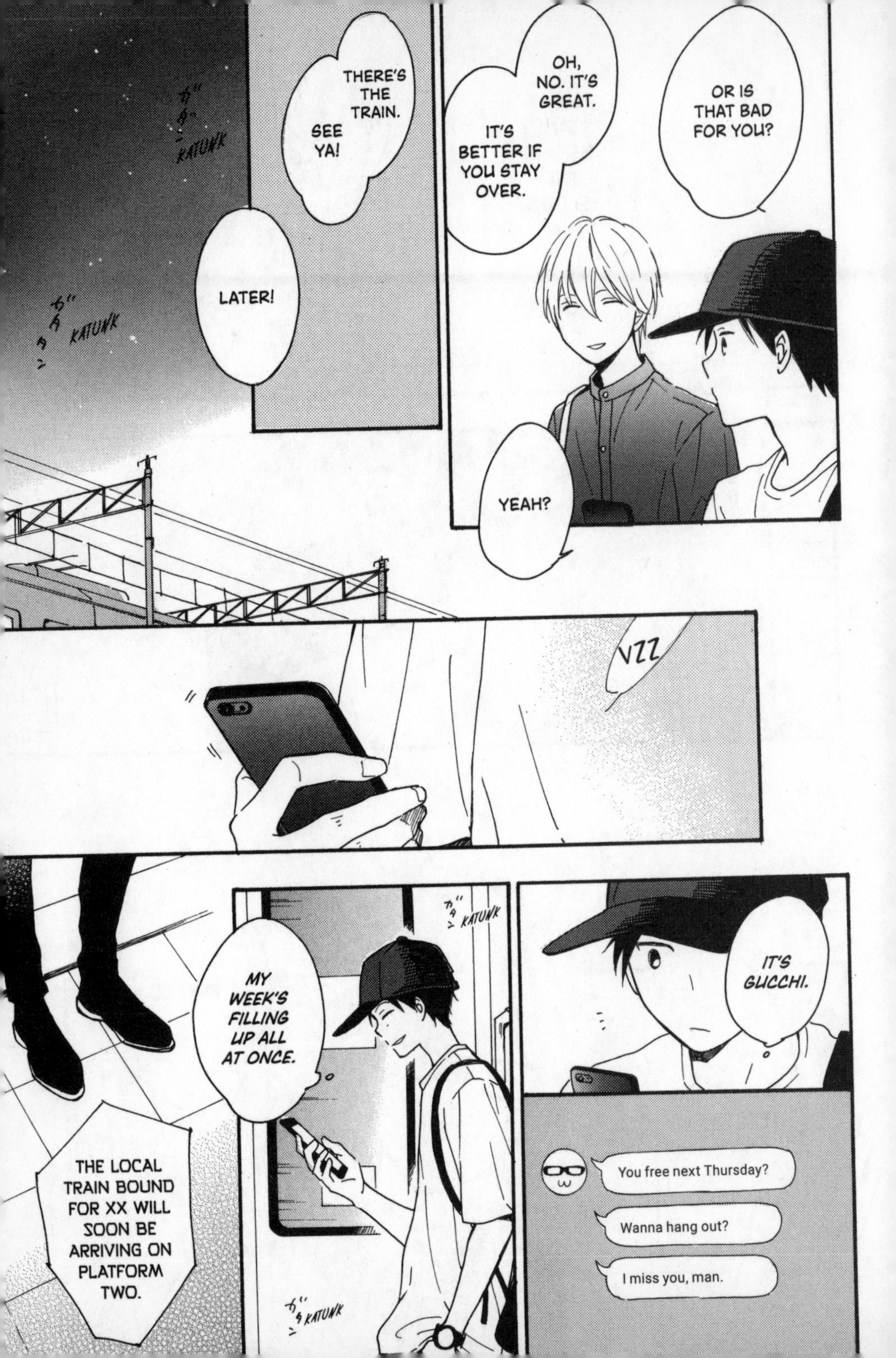

OR IS THAT BAD FOR YOU?
OH, NO. IT'S GREAT.
IT'S BETTER IF YOU STAY OVER.
YEAH?
THERE'S THE TRAIN.
SEE YA!
KATUNK
LATER!
KATUNK
VZZ
IT'S GUCCHI.
You free next Thursday?
Wanna hang out?
I miss you, man.
KATUNK
MY WEEK'S FILLING UP ALL AT ONCE.
THE LOCAL TRAIN BOUND FOR XX WILL SOON BE ARRIVING ON PLATFORM TWO.
KATUNK

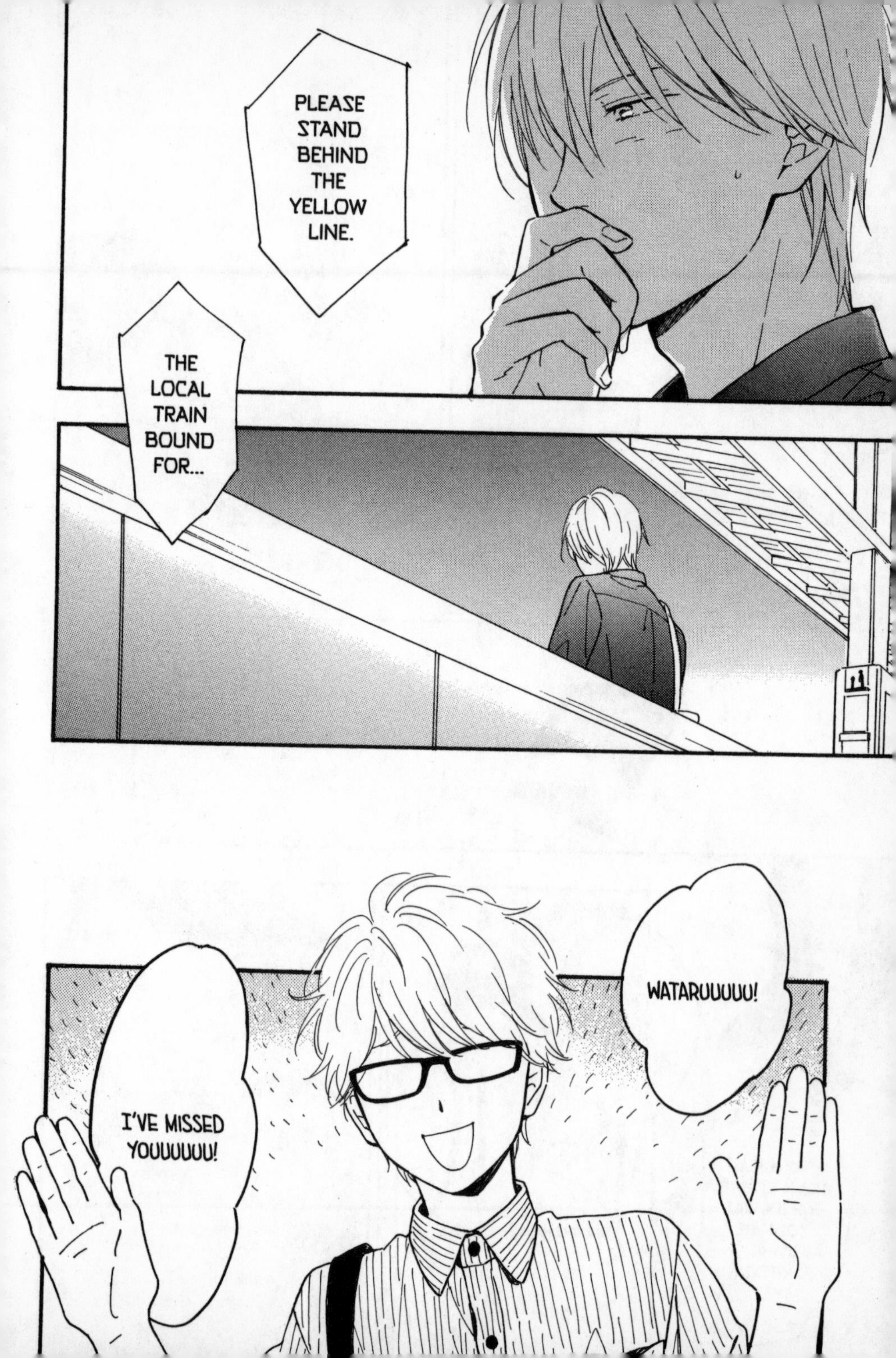
PLEASE STAND BEHIND THE YELLOW LINE.
THE LOCAL TRAIN BOUND FOR...
WATARUUUUU!
I'VE MISSED YOUUUUUU!

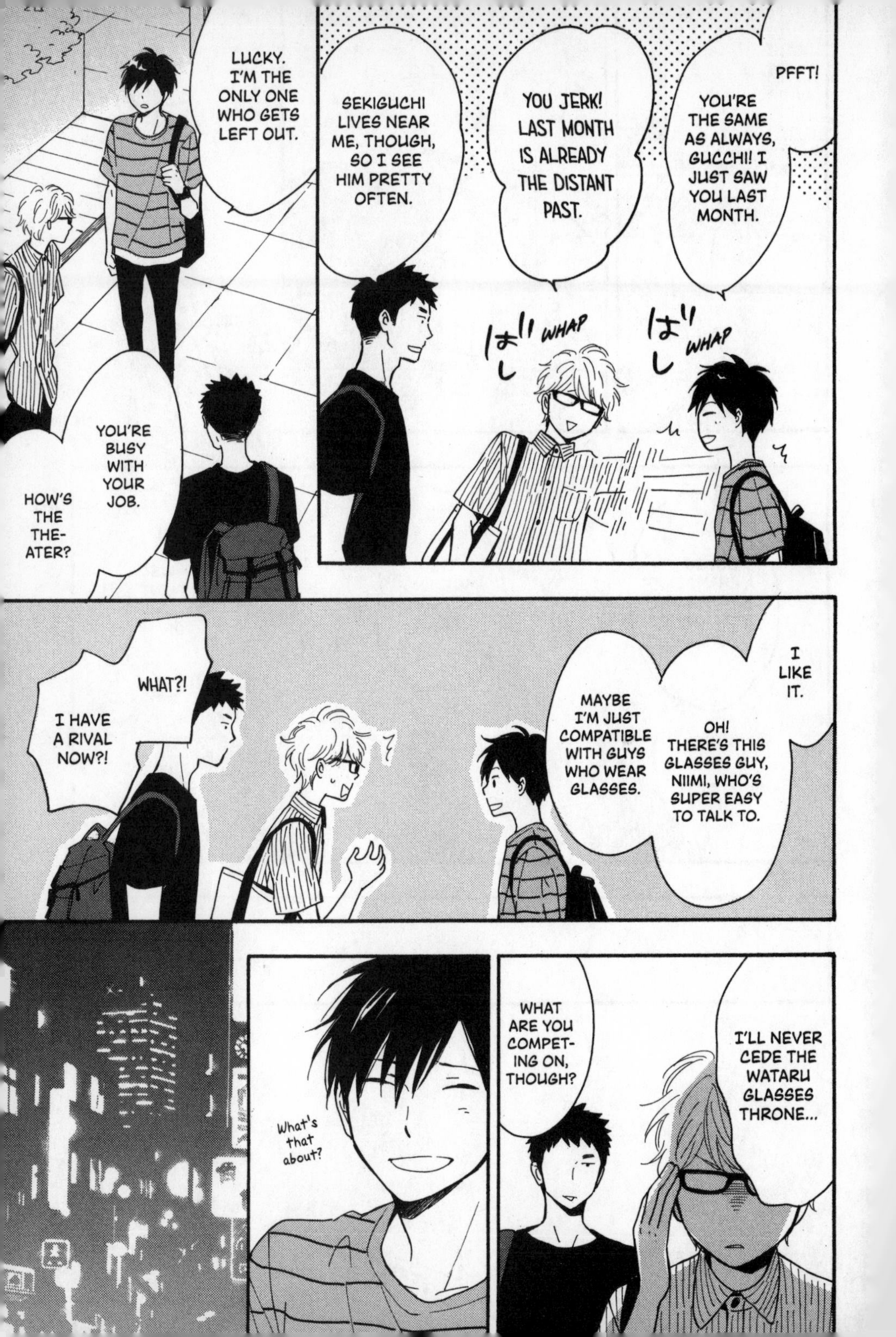
PFFT!
YOU'RE THE SAME AS ALWAYS, GUCCHI! I JUST SAW YOU LAST MONTH.
YOU JERK! LAST MONTH IS ALREADY THE DISTANT PAST.
SEKIGUCHI LIVES NEAR ME, THOUGH, SO I SEE HIM PRETTY OFTEN.
ばし WHAP
ばし WHAP
LUCKY. I'M THE ONLY ONE WHO GETS LEFT OUT.
YOU'RE BUSY WITH YOUR JOB.
HOW'S THE THE-ATER?
I LIKE IT.
OH! THERE'S THIS GLASSES GUY, NIIMI, WHO'S SUPER EASY TO TALK TO.
MAYBE I'M JUST COMPATIBLE WITH GUYS WHO WEAR GLASSES.
WHAT?!
I HAVE A RIVAL NOW?!
I'LL NEVER CEDE THE WATARU GLASSES THRONE...
WHAT ARE YOU COMPET-ING ON, THOUGH?
What's that about?

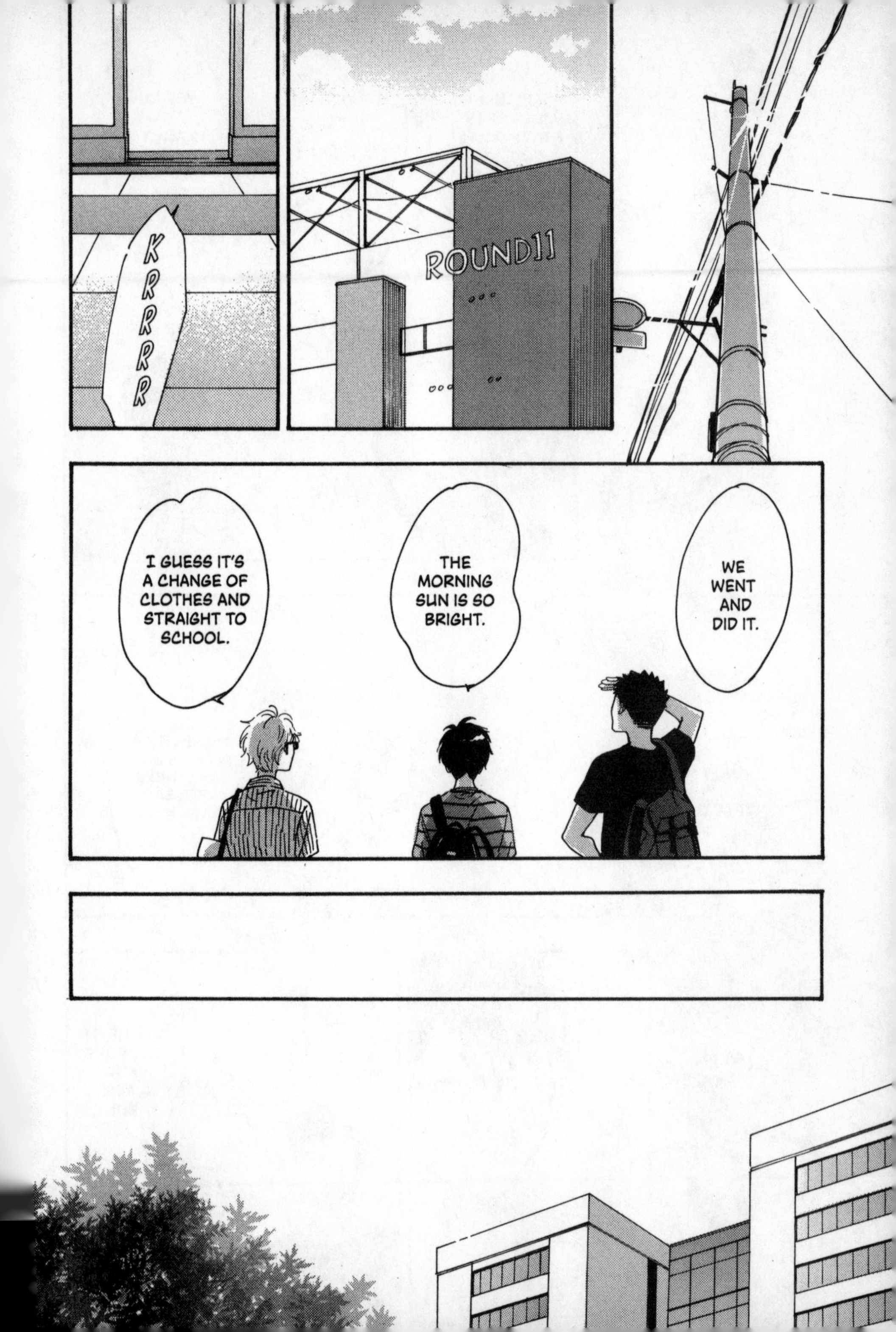
ROUND11
KRRRR
WE WENT AND DID IT.
THE MORNING SUN IS SO BRIGHT.
I GUESS IT'S A CHANGE OF CLOTHES AND STRAIGHT TO SCHOOL.

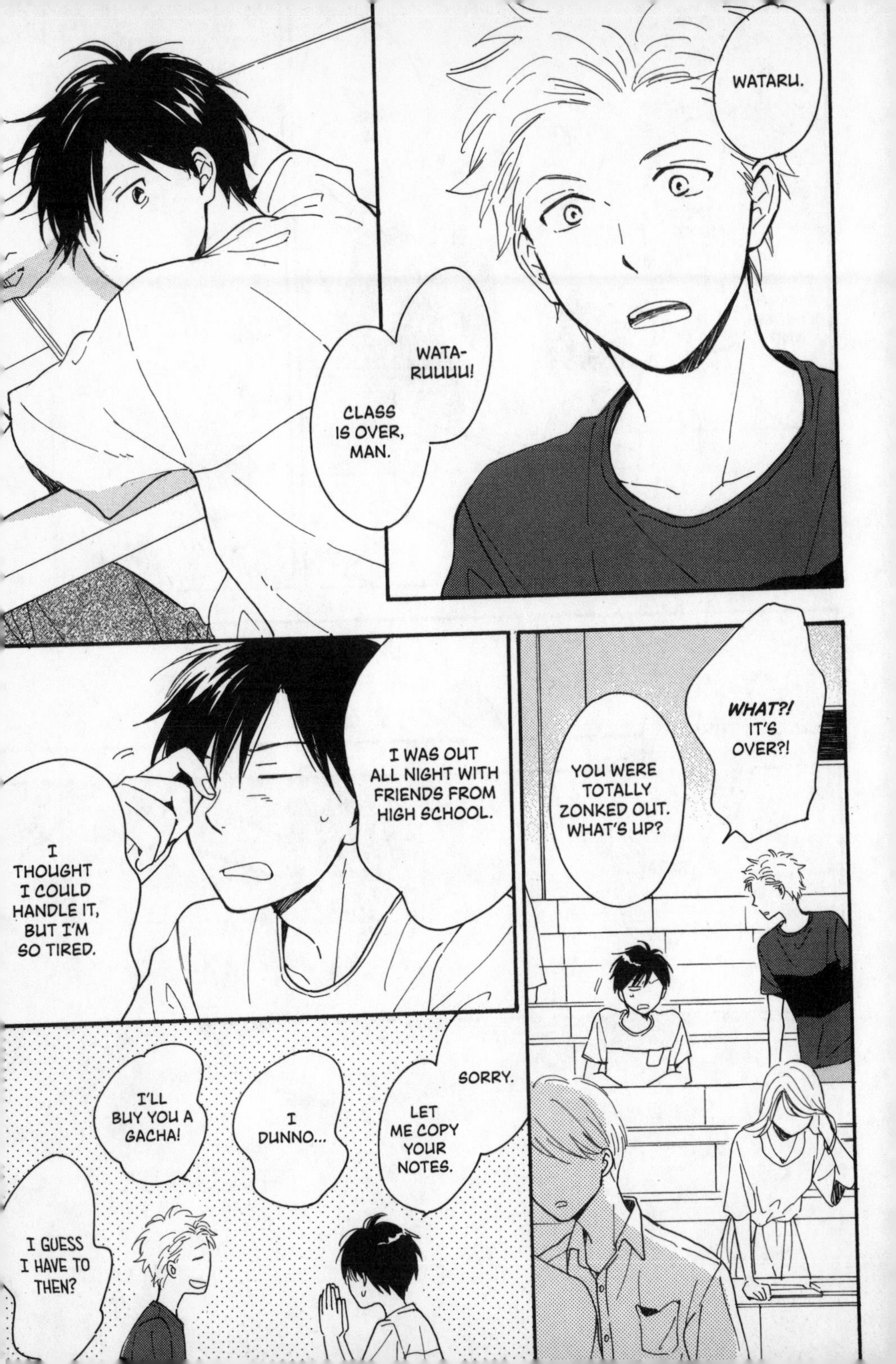
WATARU.
WATA-RUUUU!
CLASS IS OVER, MAN.
WHAT?! IT'S OVER?!
YOU WERE TOTALLY ZONKED OUT. WHAT'S UP?
I WAS OUT ALL NIGHT WITH FRIENDS FROM HIGH SCHOOL.
I THOUGHT I COULD HANDLE IT, BUT I'M SO TIRED.
SORRY.
LET ME COPY YOUR NOTES.
I DUNNO...
I'LL BUY YOU A GACHA!
I GUESS I HAVE TO THEN?

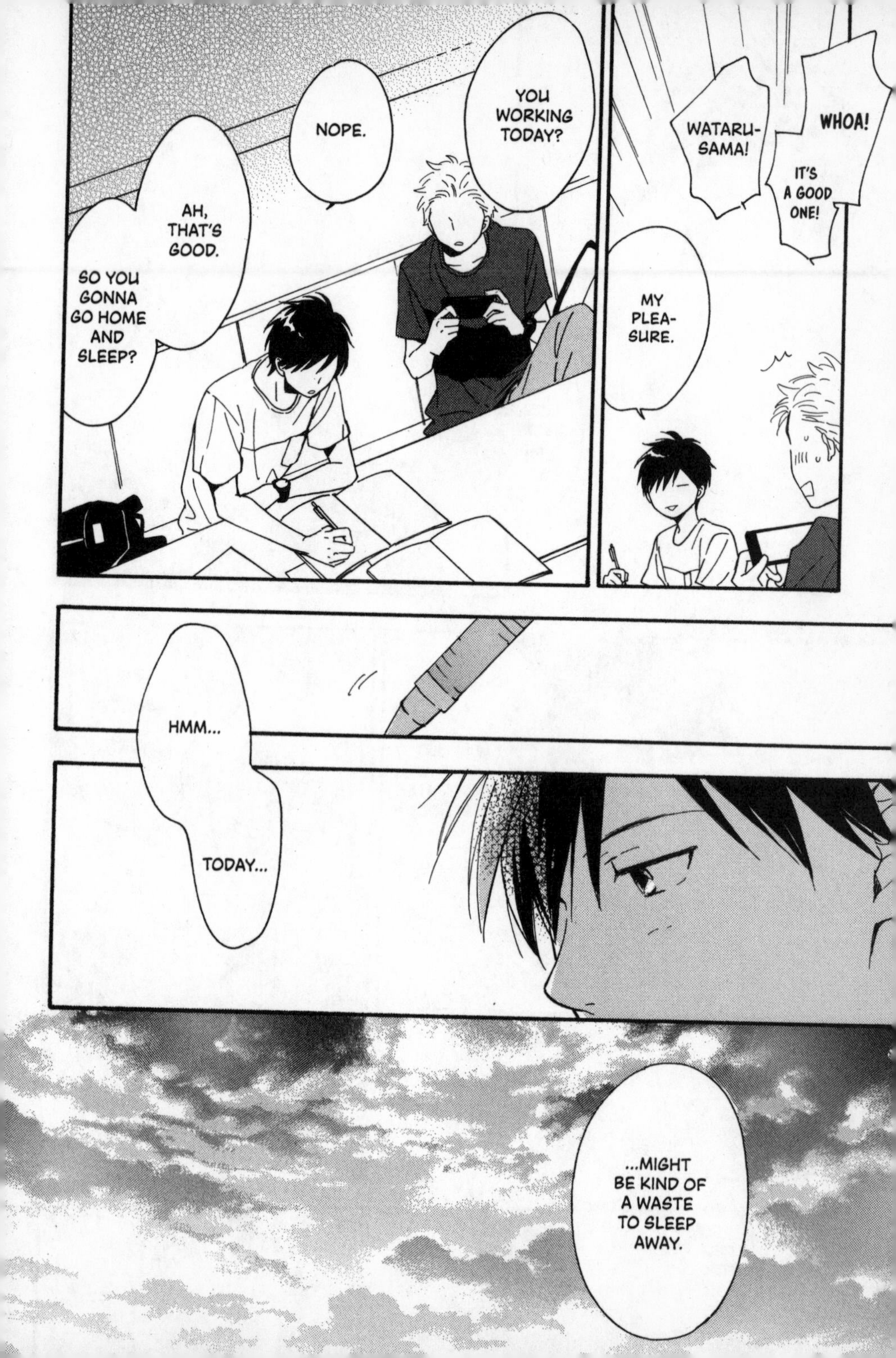
WHOA!
IT'S A GOOD ONE!
WATARU-SAMA!
MY PLEASURE.
YOU WORKING TODAY?
NOPE.
AH, THAT'S GOOD.
SO YOU GONNA GO HOME AND SLEEP?
HMM...
TODAY...
...MIGHT BE KIND OF A WASTE TO SLEEP AWAY.

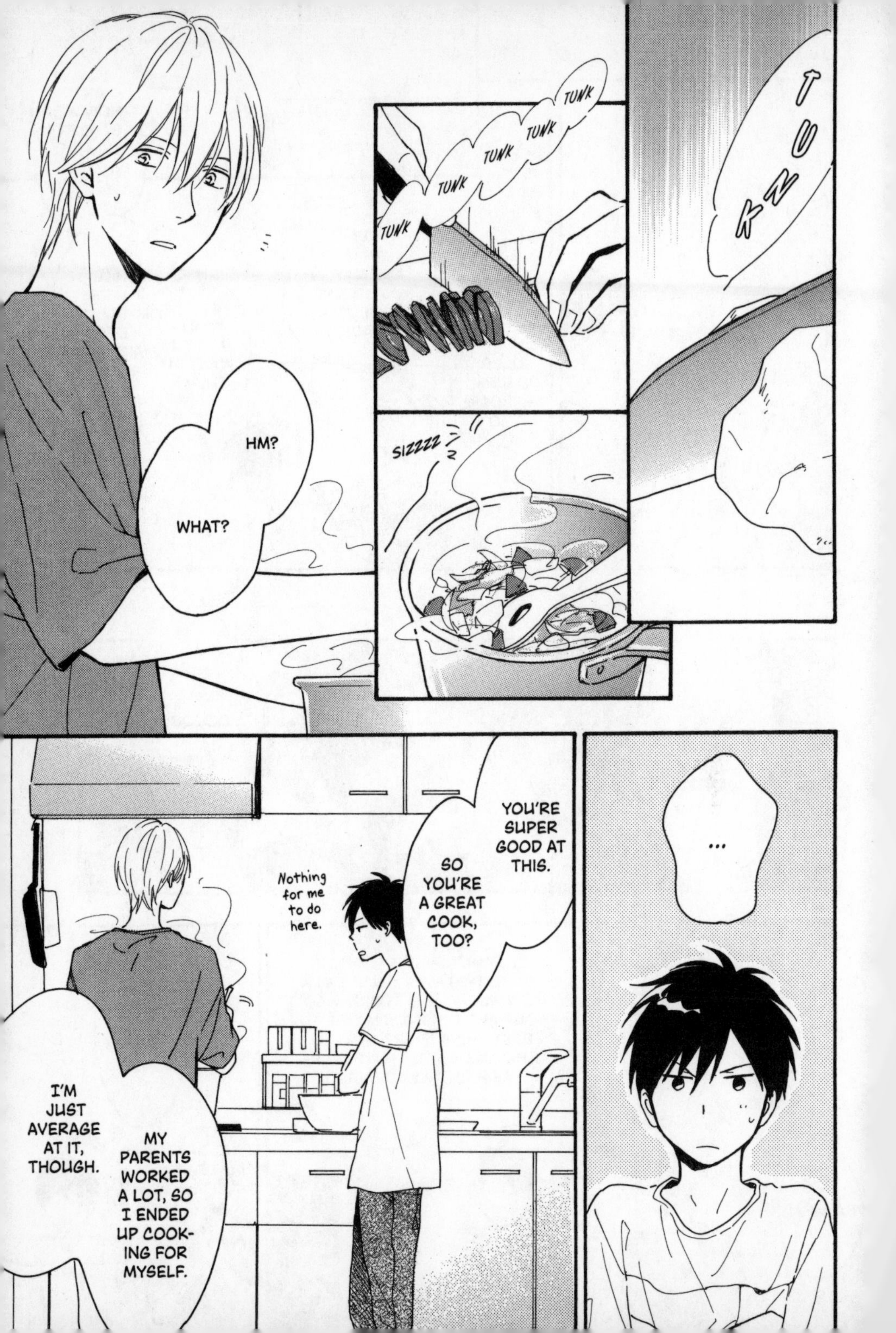
TUNK
TUNK
TUNK
TUNK
TUNK
TUNK
SIZZZZ
HM?
WHAT?
...
YOU'RE SUPER GOOD AT THIS.
SO YOU'RE A GREAT COOK, TOO?
Nothing for me to do here.
I'M JUST AVERAGE AT IT, THOUGH.
MY PARENTS WORKED A LOT, SO I ENDED UP COOKING FOR MYSELF.

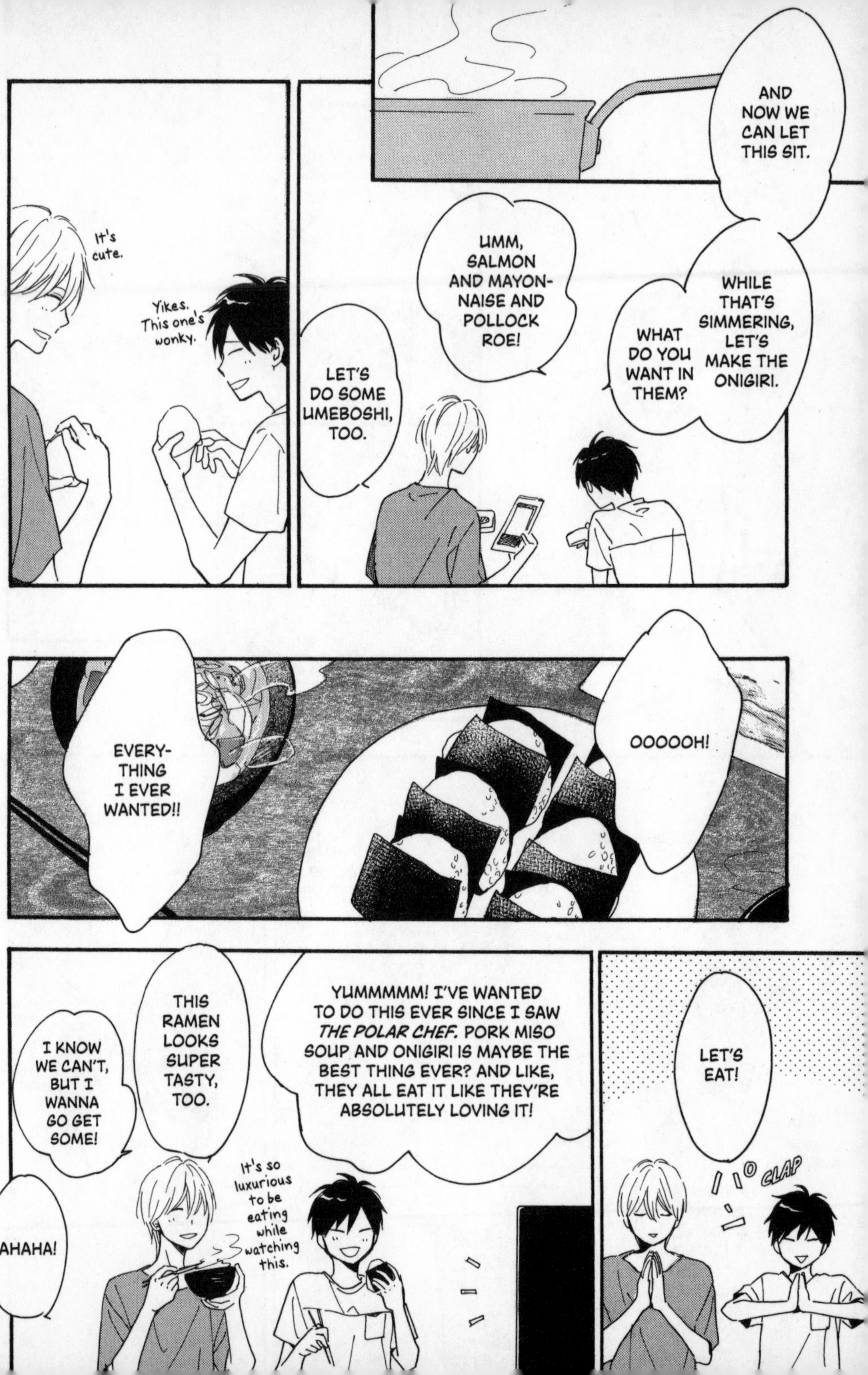
AND NOW WE CAN LET THIS SIT.
WHILE THAT'S SIMMERING, LET'S MAKE THE ONIGIRI.
WHAT DO YOU WANT IN THEM?
UMM, SALMON AND MAYON-NAISE AND POLLOCK ROE!
LET'S DO SOME UMEBOSHI, TOO.
Yikes. This one's wonky.
It's cute.
OOOOOH!
EVERY-THING I EVER WANTED!!
LET'S EAT!
CLAP
YUMMMMM! I'VE WANTED TO DO THIS EVER SINCE I SAW *THE POLAR CHEF.* PORK MISO SOUP AND ONIGIRI IS MAYBE THE BEST THING EVER? AND LIKE, THEY ALL EAT IT LIKE THEY'RE ABSOLUTELY LOVING IT!
THIS RAMEN LOOKS SUPER TASTY, TOO.
I KNOW WE CAN'T, BUT I WANNA GO GET SOME!
It's so luxurious to be eating while watching this.
HAHAHA!

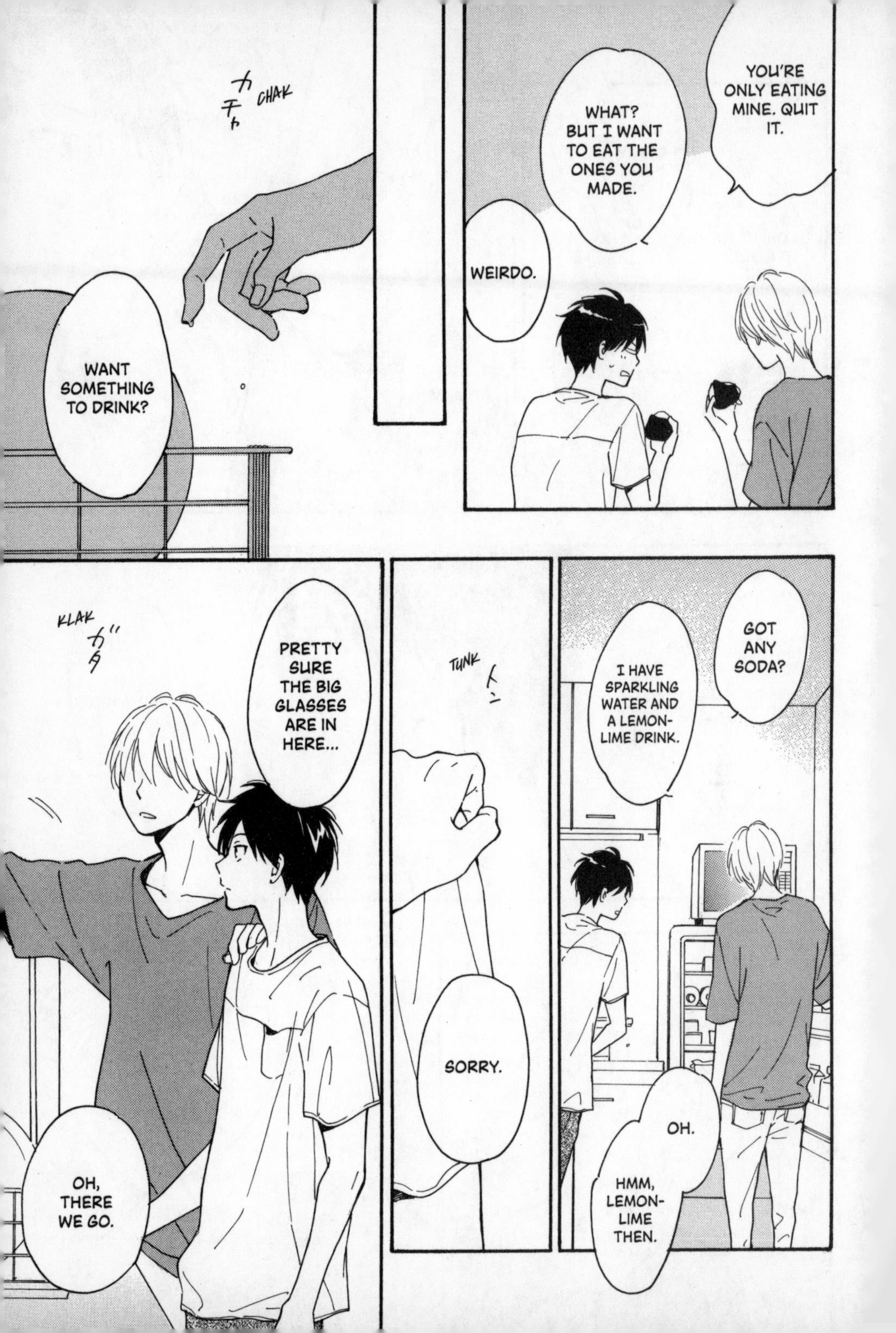

YOU'RE ONLY EATING MINE. QUIT IT.
WHAT? BUT I WANT TO EAT THE ONES YOU MADE.
WEIRDO.
カチャ
CHAK
WANT SOMETHING TO DRINK?
GOT ANY SODA?
I HAVE SPARKLING WATER AND A LEMON-LIME DRINK.
OH.
HMM, LEMON-LIME THEN.
TUNK
SORRY.
KLAK
ガタ
PRETTY SURE THE BIG GLASSES ARE IN HERE...
OH, THERE WE GO.

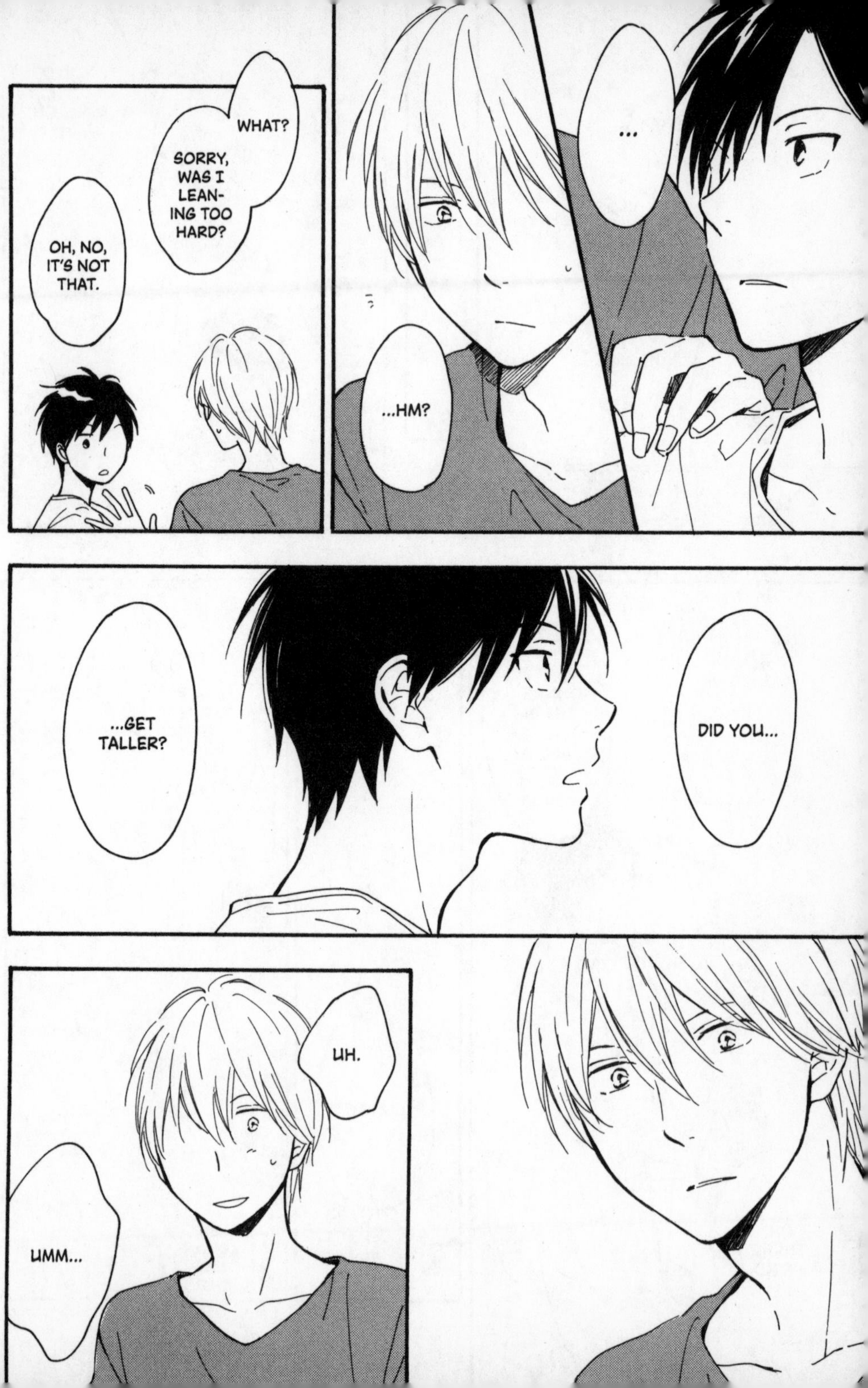
...
...HM?
WHAT?
SORRY, WAS I LEANING TOO HARD?
OH, NO, IT'S NOT THAT.
DID YOU...
...GET TALLER?
UH.
UMM...

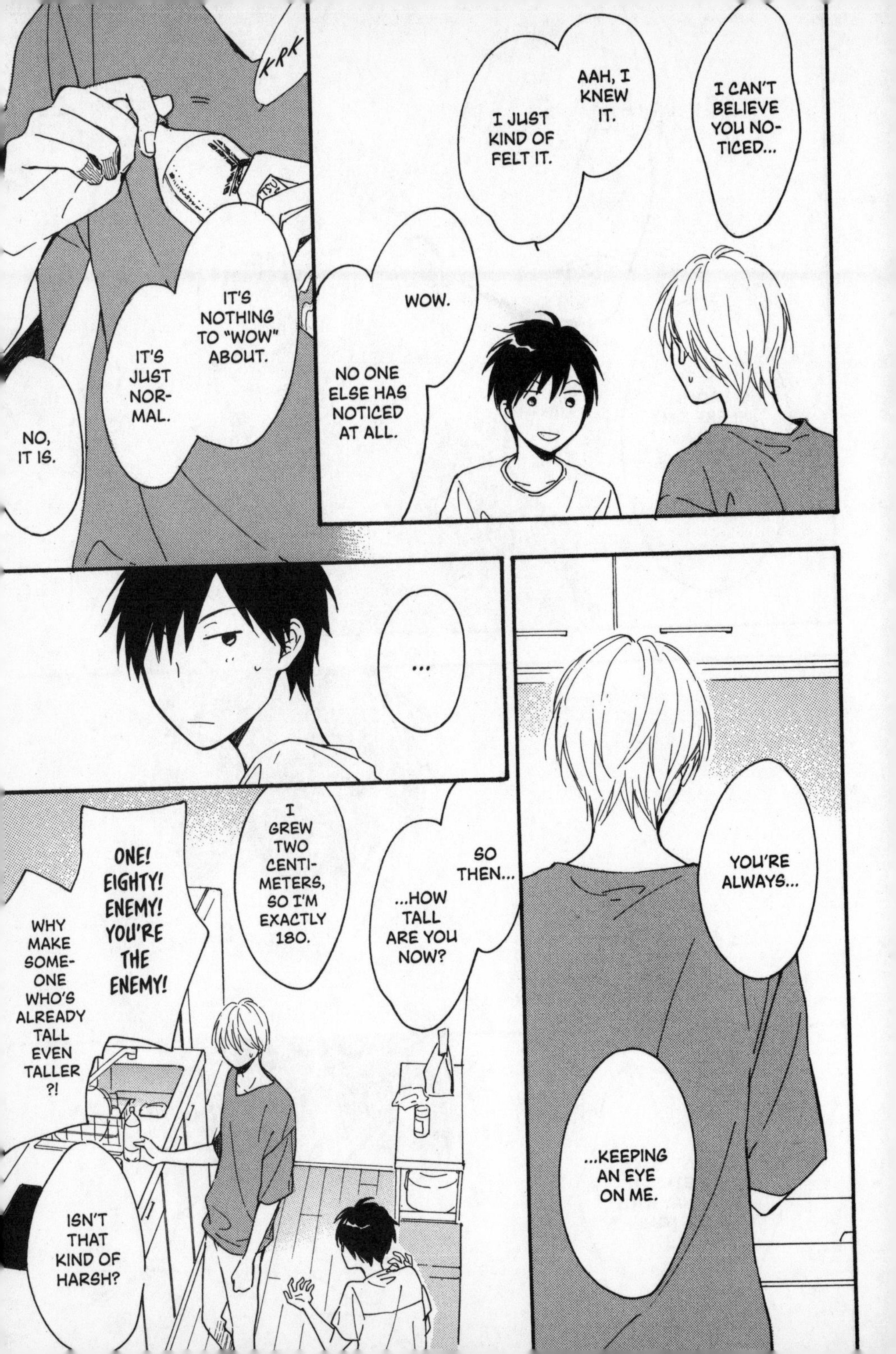
I CAN'T BELIEVE YOU NO-TICED...
AAH, I KNEW IT.
I JUST KIND OF FELT IT.
WOW.
NO ONE ELSE HAS NOTICED AT ALL.
KRK
IT'S NOTHING TO "WOW" ABOUT.
IT'S JUST NOR-MAL.
NO, IT IS.
YOU'RE ALWAYS...
...KEEPING AN EYE ON ME.
...
SO THEN...
...HOW TALL ARE YOU NOW?
I GREW TWO CENTI-METERS, SO I'M EXACTLY 180.
ONE! EIGHTY! ENEMY! YOU'RE THE ENEMY!
WHY MAKE SOME-ONE WHO'S ALREADY TALL EVEN TALLER ?!
ISN'T THAT KIND OF HARSH?

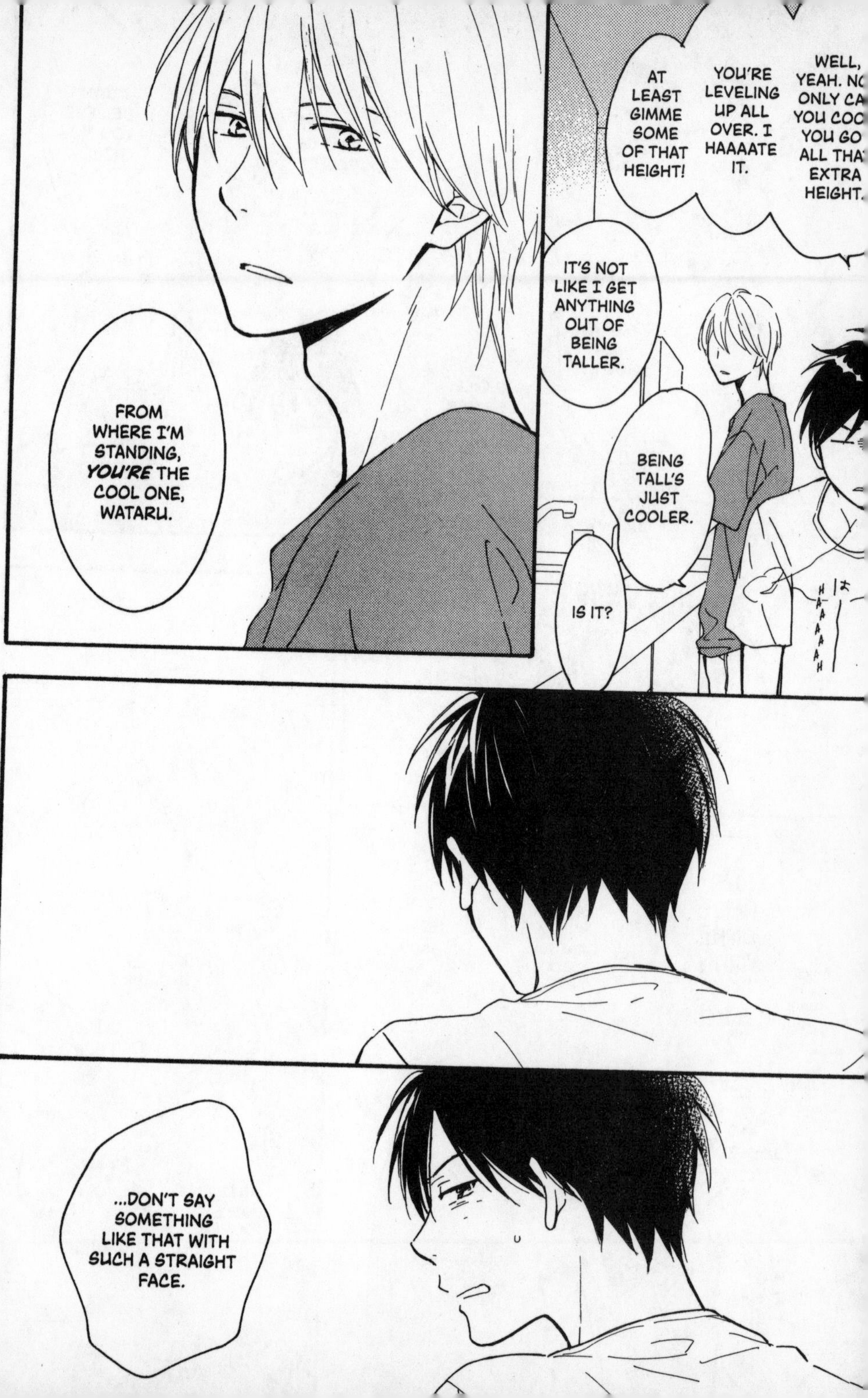
WELL, YEAH. NO ONLY CA YOU COO YOU GO ALL THA EXTRA HEIGHT.
YOU'RE LEVELING UP ALL OVER. I HAAAATE IT.
AT LEAST GIMME SOME OF THAT HEIGHT!
HAAAAAH
IT'S NOT LIKE I GET ANYTHING OUT OF BEING TALLER.
BEING TALL'S JUST COOLER.
IS IT?
FROM WHERE I'M STANDING, *YOU'RE* THE COOL ONE, WATARU.
...DON'T SAY SOMETHING LIKE THAT WITH SUCH A STRAIGHT FACE.

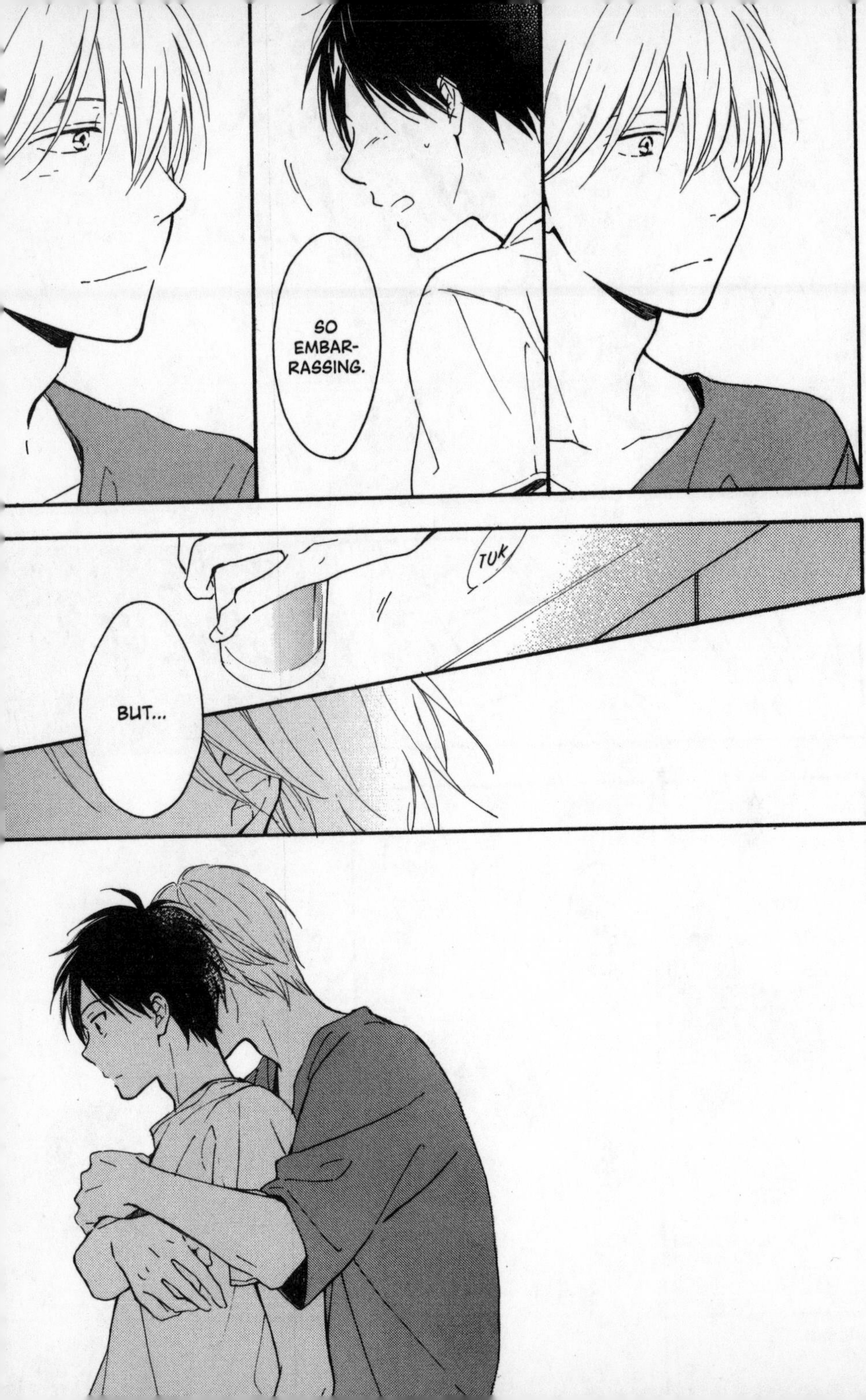
SO EMBAR-RASSING.
TUK
BUT...

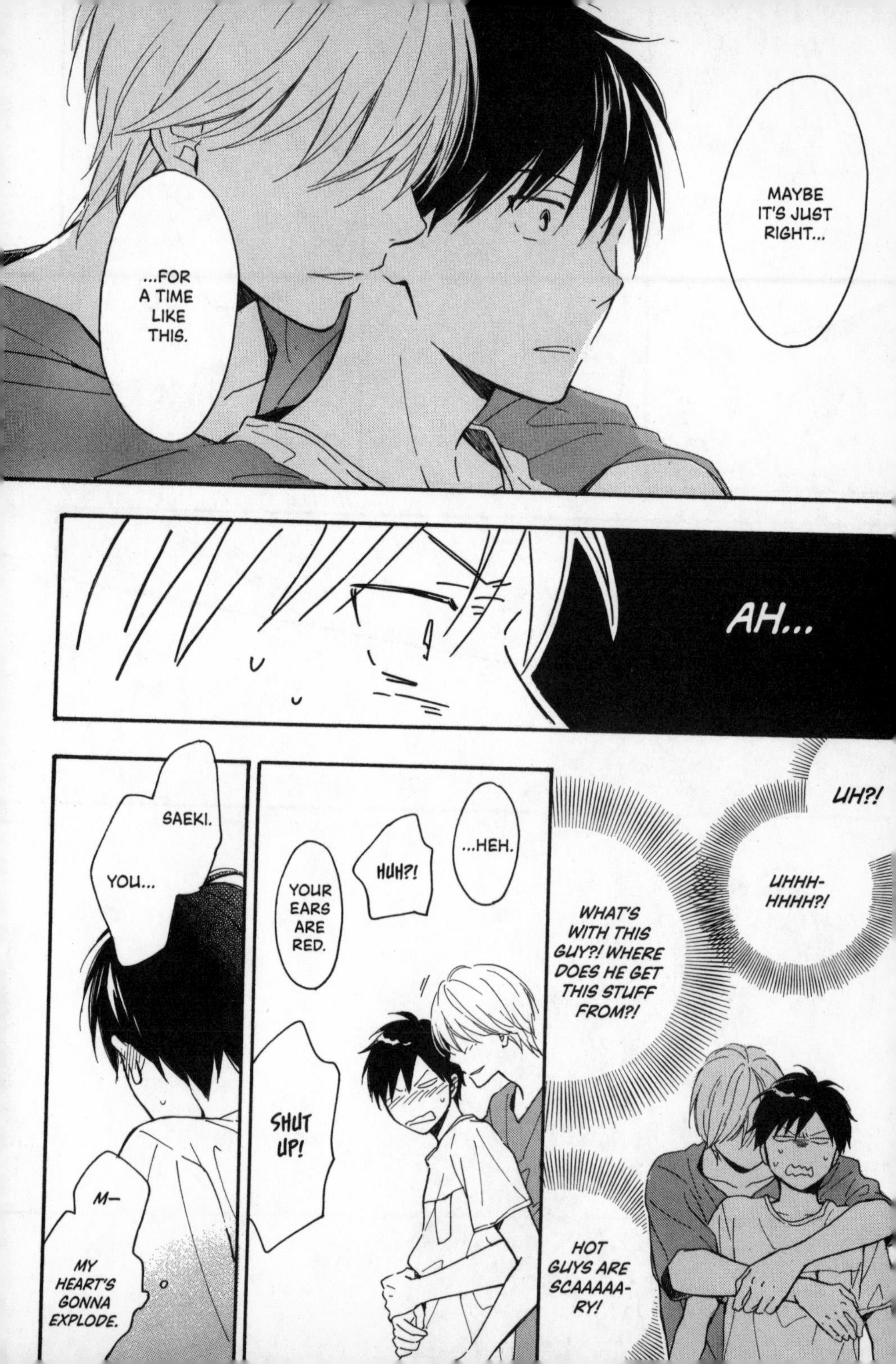

MAYBE IT'S JUST RIGHT...
...FOR A TIME LIKE THIS.
AH...
UH?!
UHHH-HHHH?!
WHAT'S WITH THIS GUY?! WHERE DOES HE GET THIS STUFF FROM?!
HOT GUYS ARE SCAAAAAA-RY!
...HEH.
HUH?!
YOUR EARS ARE RED.
SHUT UP!
SAEKI.
YOU...
M—
MY HEART'S GONNA EXPLODE.

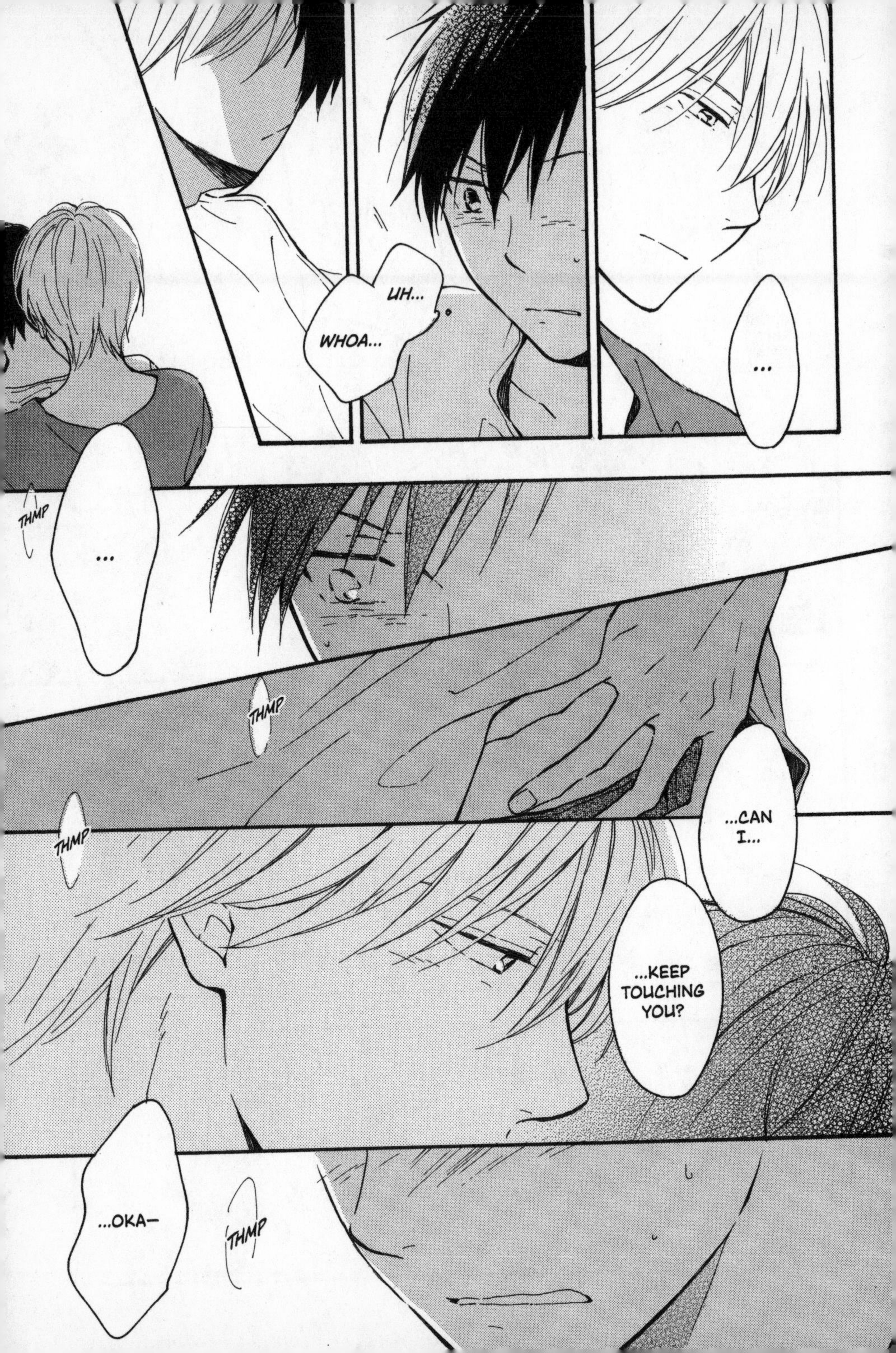
...
UH...
WHOA...
...
THMP
THMP
...CAN I...
...KEEP TOUCHING YOU?
THMP
THMP
...OKA-

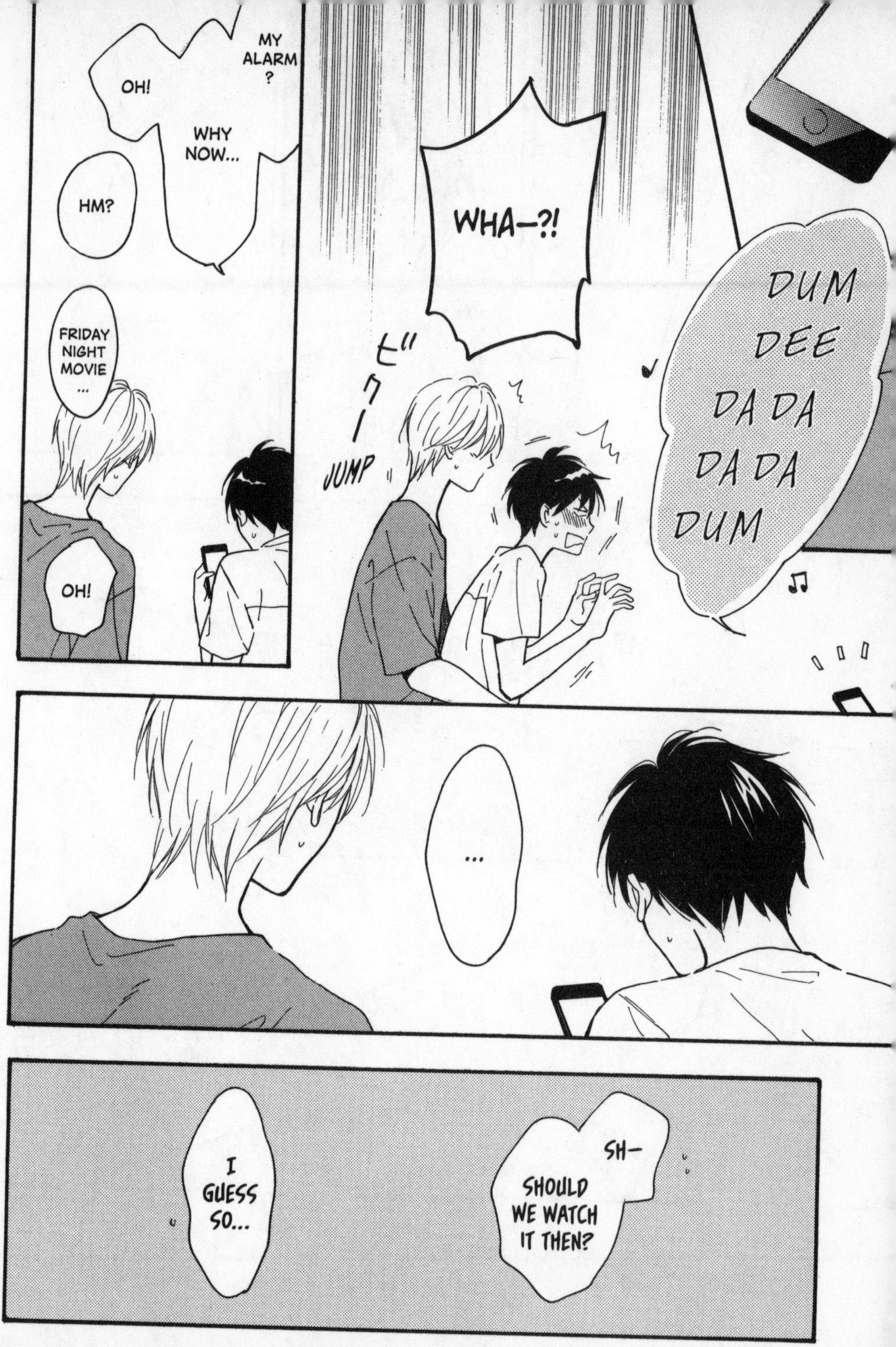
DUM DEE DA DA DA DA DUM
WHA-?!
JUMP
MY ALARM ?
OH!
WHY NOW...
HM?
FRIDAY NIGHT MOVIE ...
OH!
...
SH-
SHOULD WE WATCH IT THEN?
I GUESS SO...

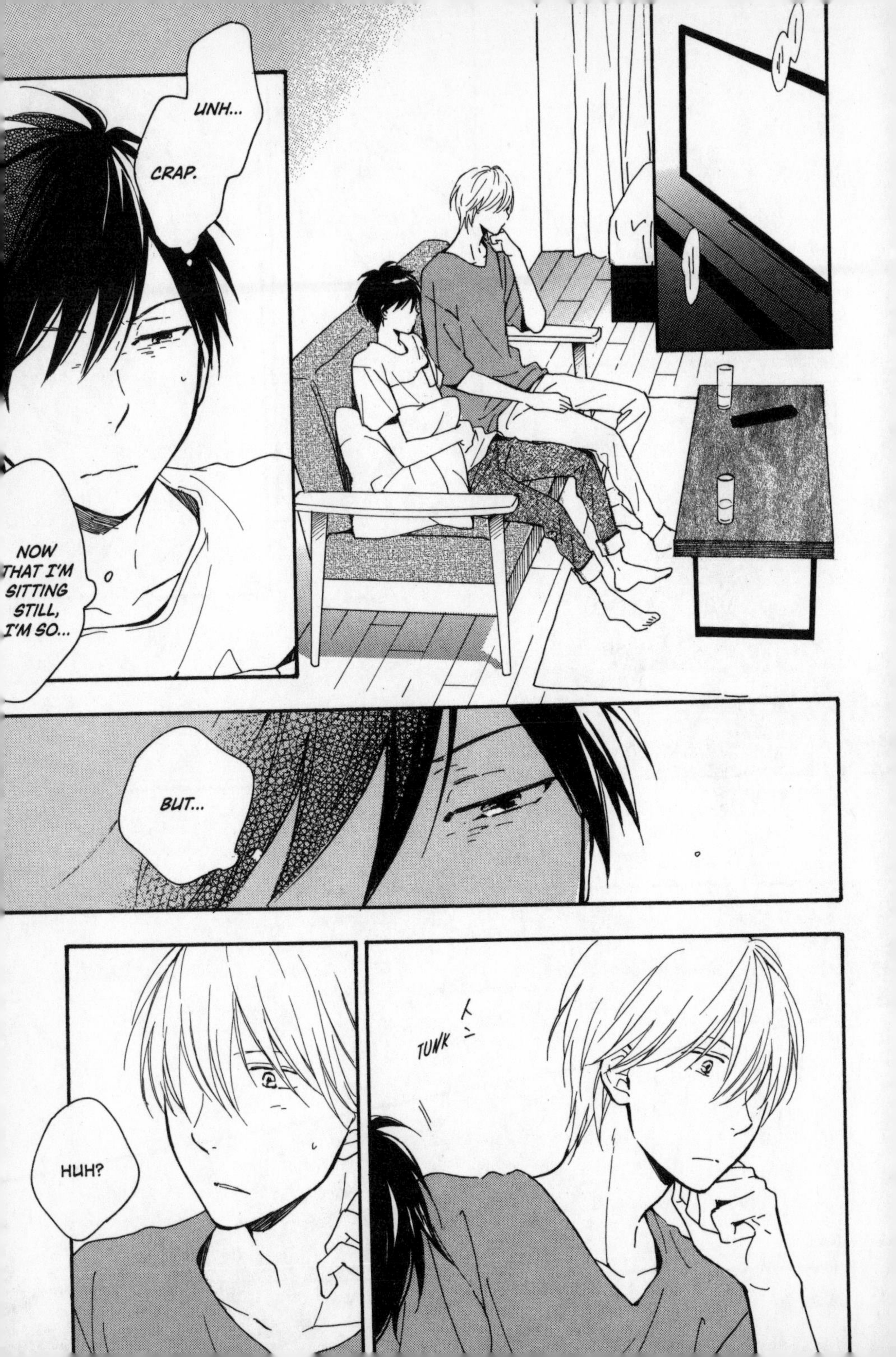
UNH...
CRAP.
NOW THAT I'M SITTING STILL, I'M SO...
BUT...
TUNK
HUH?

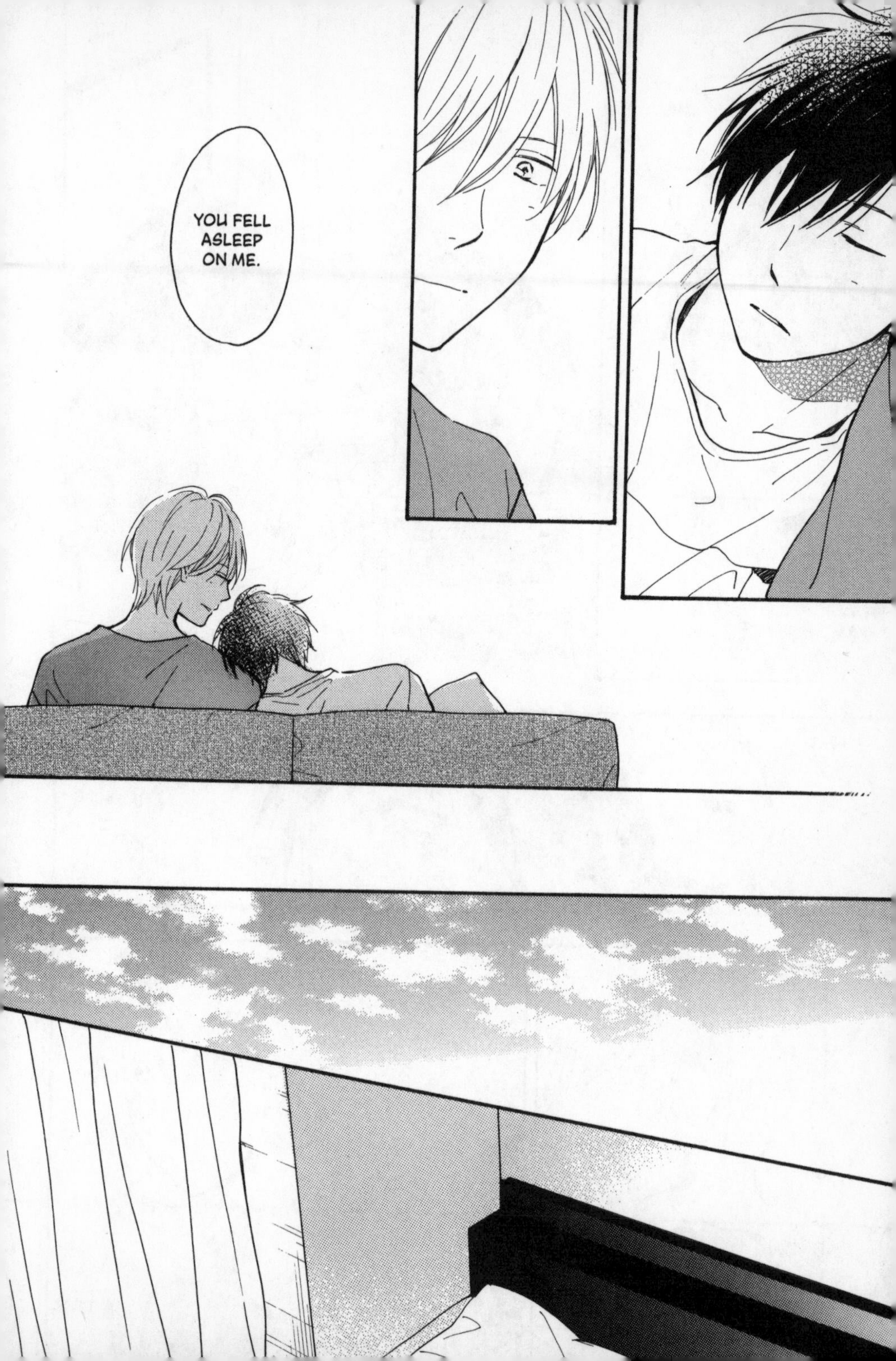
YOU FELL ASLEEP ON ME.

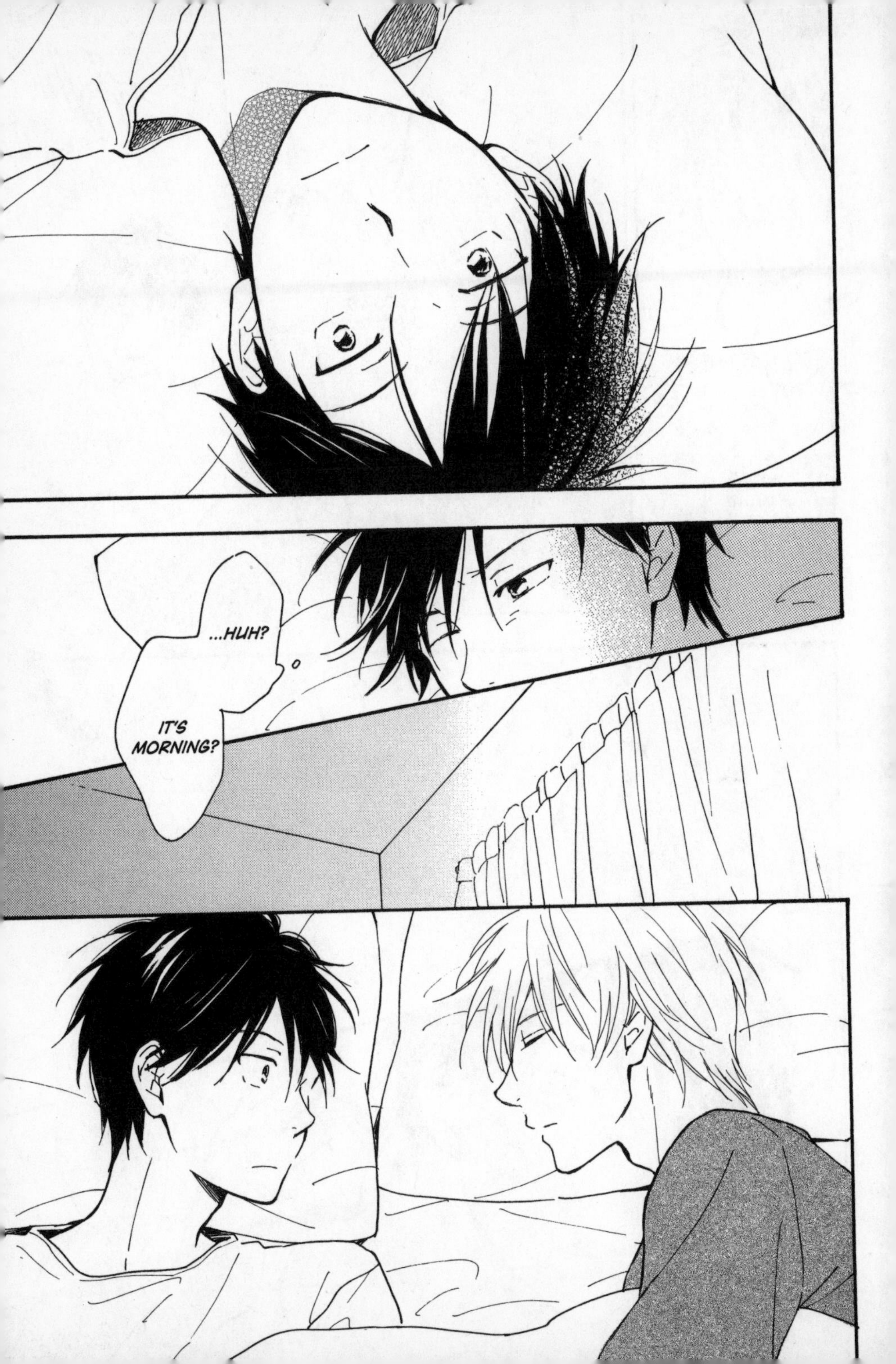
...HUH?
IT'S MORNING?

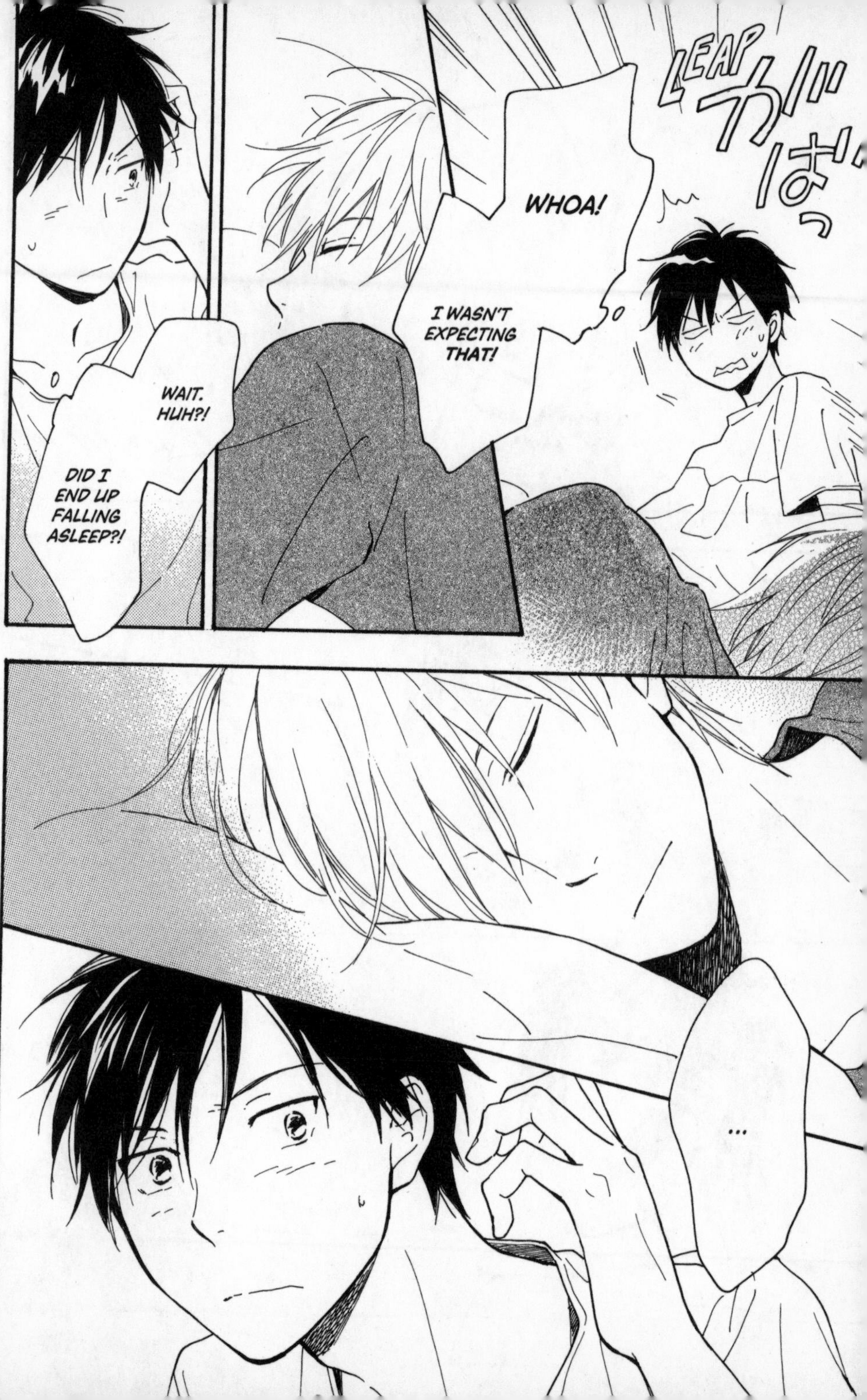
LEAP
がばっ
WHOA!
I WASN'T EXPECTING THAT!
WAIT. HUH?!
DID I END UP FALLING ASLEEP?!
...

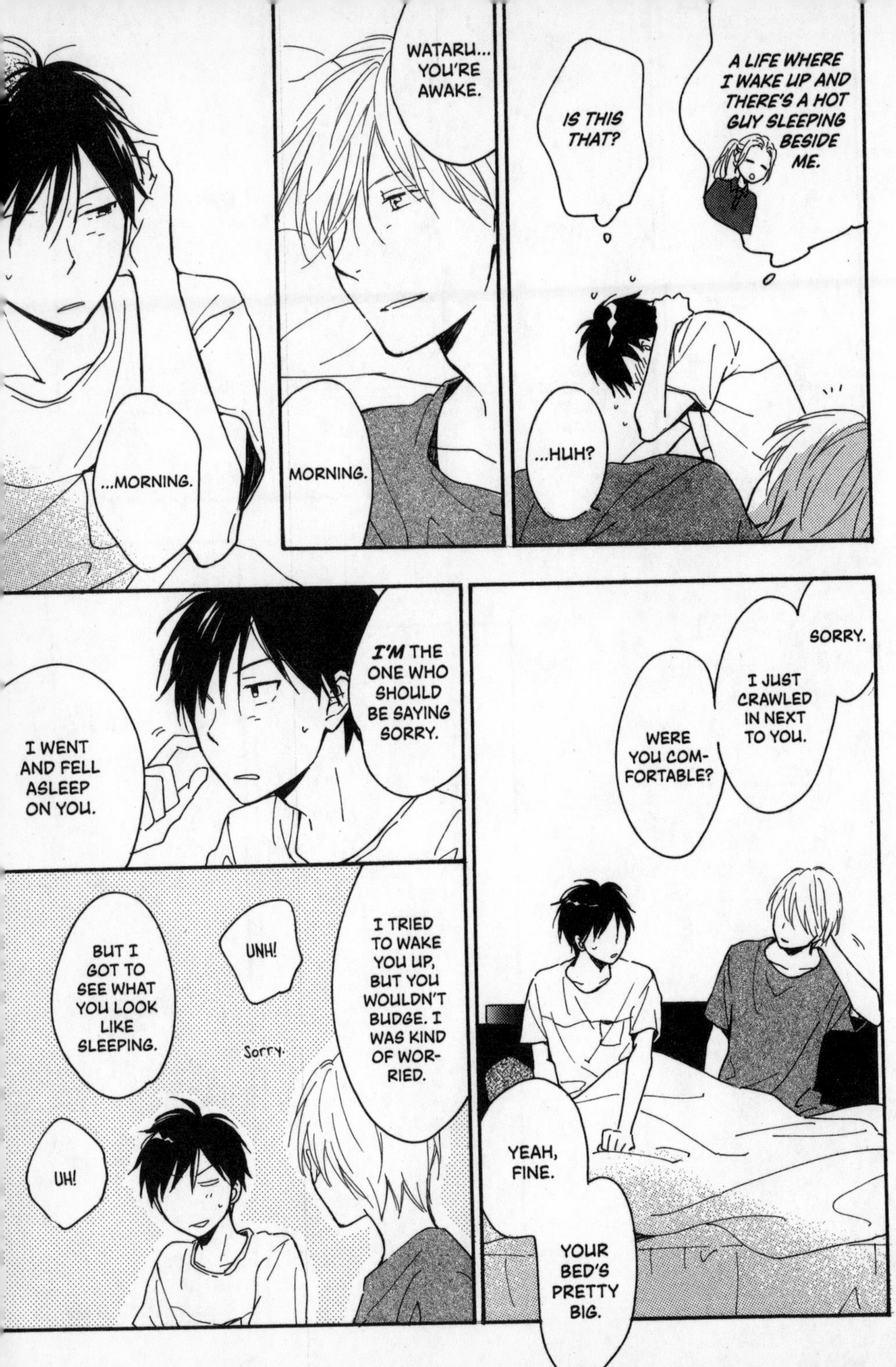

A LIFE WHERE I WAKE UP AND THERE'S A HOT GUY SLEEPING BESIDE ME.
IS THIS THAT?
...HUH?
WATARU... YOU'RE AWAKE.
MORNING.
...MORNING.
SORRY.
I JUST CRAWLED IN NEXT TO YOU.
WERE YOU COMFORTABLE?
YEAH, FINE.
YOUR BED'S PRETTY BIG.
I'M THE ONE WHO SHOULD BE SAYING SORRY.
I WENT AND FELL ASLEEP ON YOU.
I TRIED TO WAKE YOU UP, BUT YOU WOULDN'T BUDGE. I WAS KIND OF WORRIED.
UNH!
BUT I GOT TO SEE WHAT YOU LOOK LIKE SLEEPING.
Sorry.
UH!

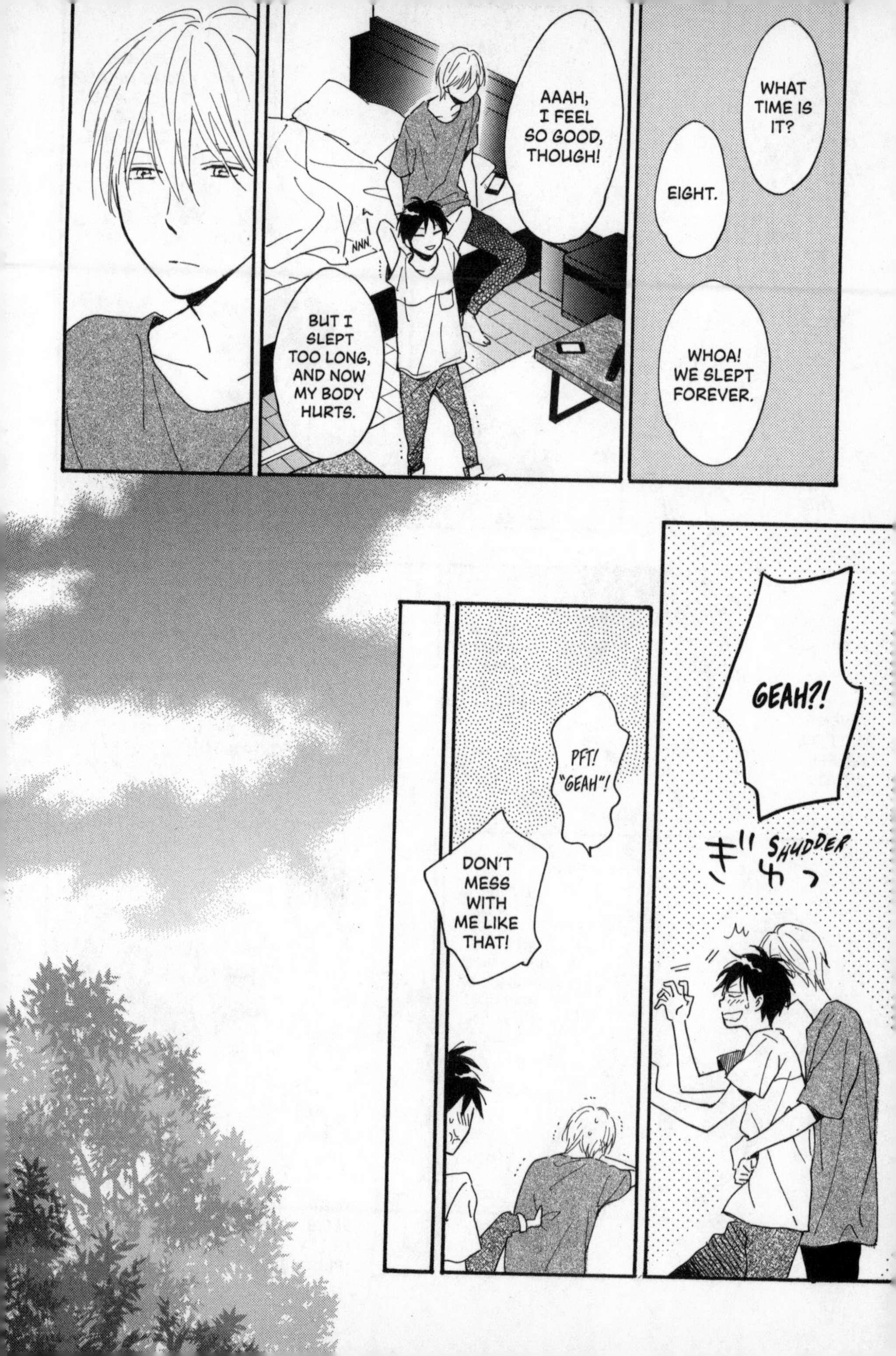
WHAT TIME IS IT?
EIGHT.
WHOA! WE SLEPT FOREVER.
AAAH, I FEEL SO GOOD, THOUGH!
NNN
BUT I SLEPT TOO LONG, AND NOW MY BODY HURTS.
GEAH?!
ぎゅっ
SHUDDER
PFT! "GEAH"!
DON'T MESS WITH ME LIKE THAT!

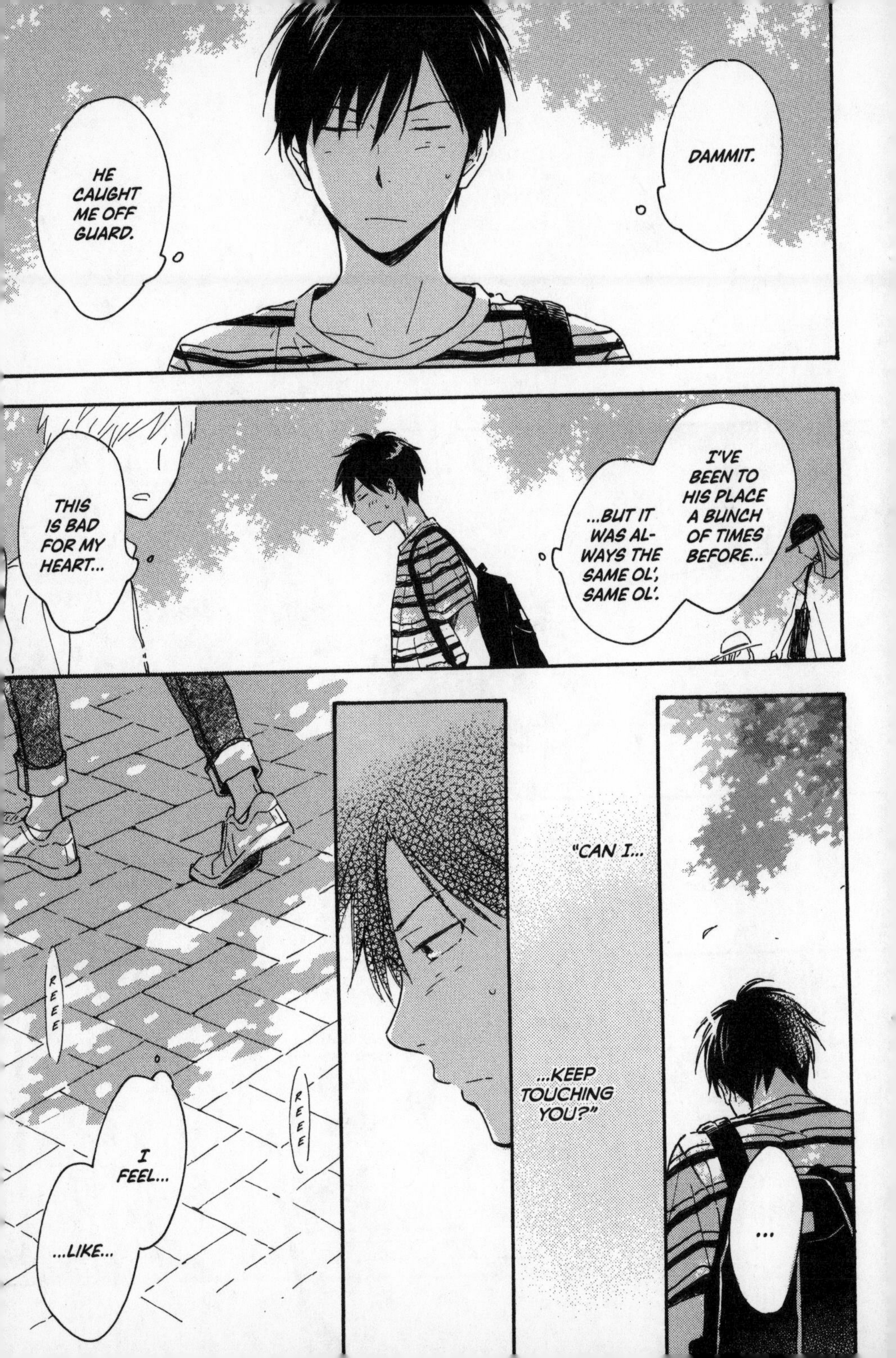
DAMMIT.
HE CAUGHT ME OFF GUARD.
I'VE BEEN TO HIS PLACE A BUNCH OF TIMES BEFORE...
...BUT IT WAS AL-WAYS THE SAME OL', SAME OL'.
THIS IS BAD FOR MY HEART...
...
"CAN I...
...KEEP TOUCHING YOU?"
REEE
REEE
I FEEL...
...LIKE...

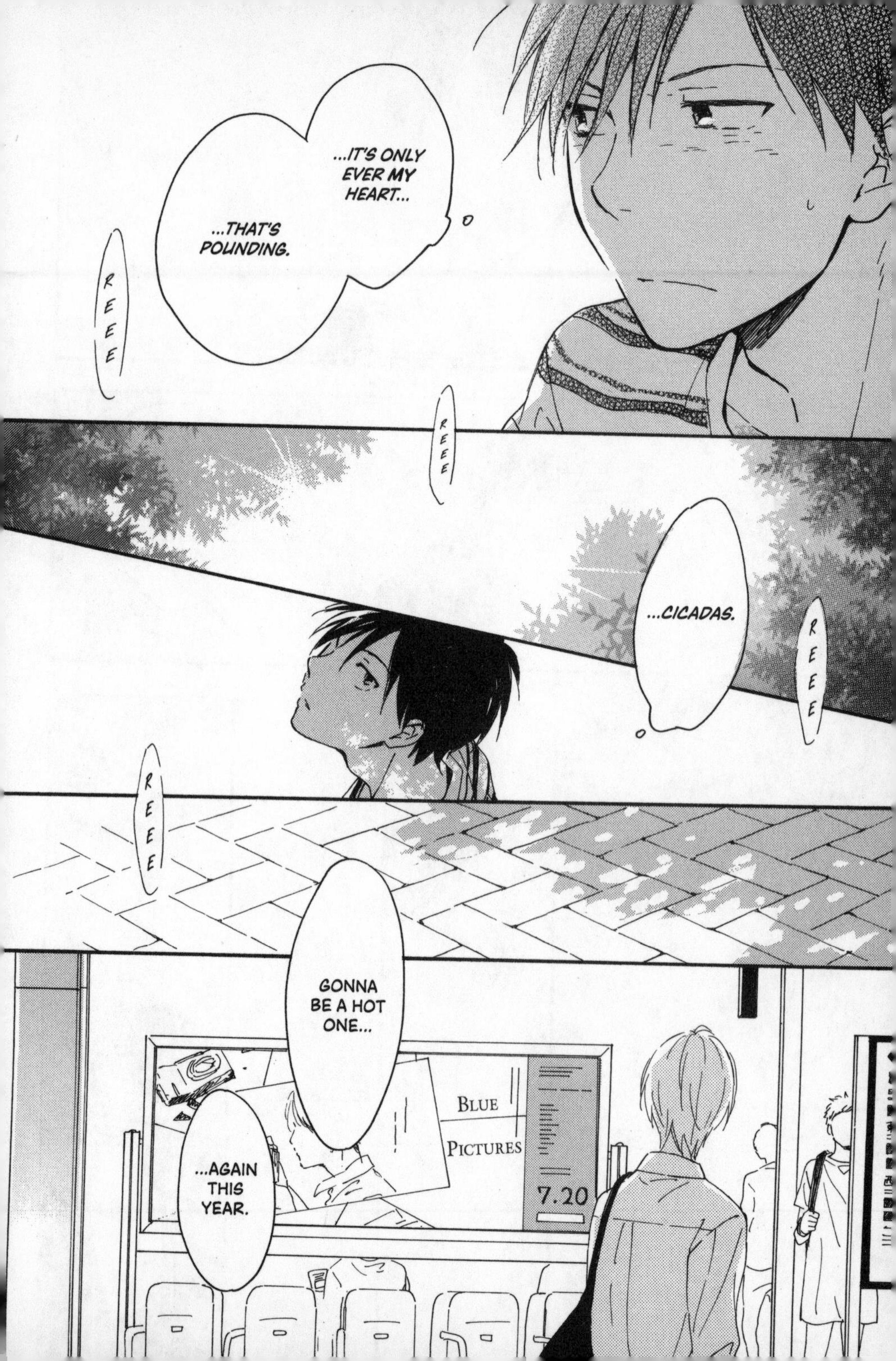
...IT'S ONLY EVER MY HEART...
...THAT'S POUNDING.
REEE
REEE
REEE
...CICADAS.
REEE
GONNA BE A HOT ONE...
...AGAIN THIS YEAR.
BLUE PICTURES
7.20

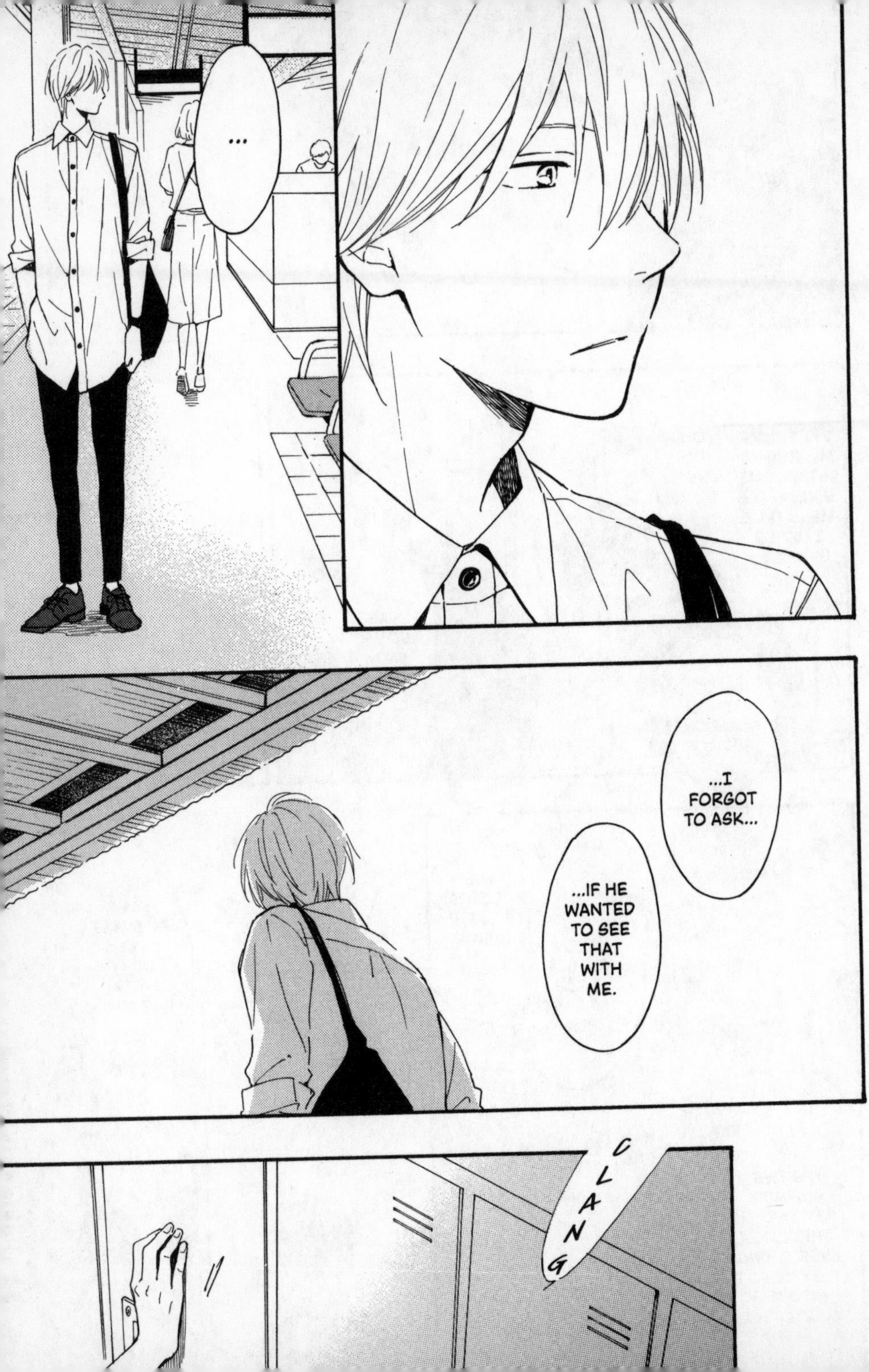
...
...I FORGOT TO ASK...
...IF HE WANTED TO SEE THAT WITH ME.
CLANG

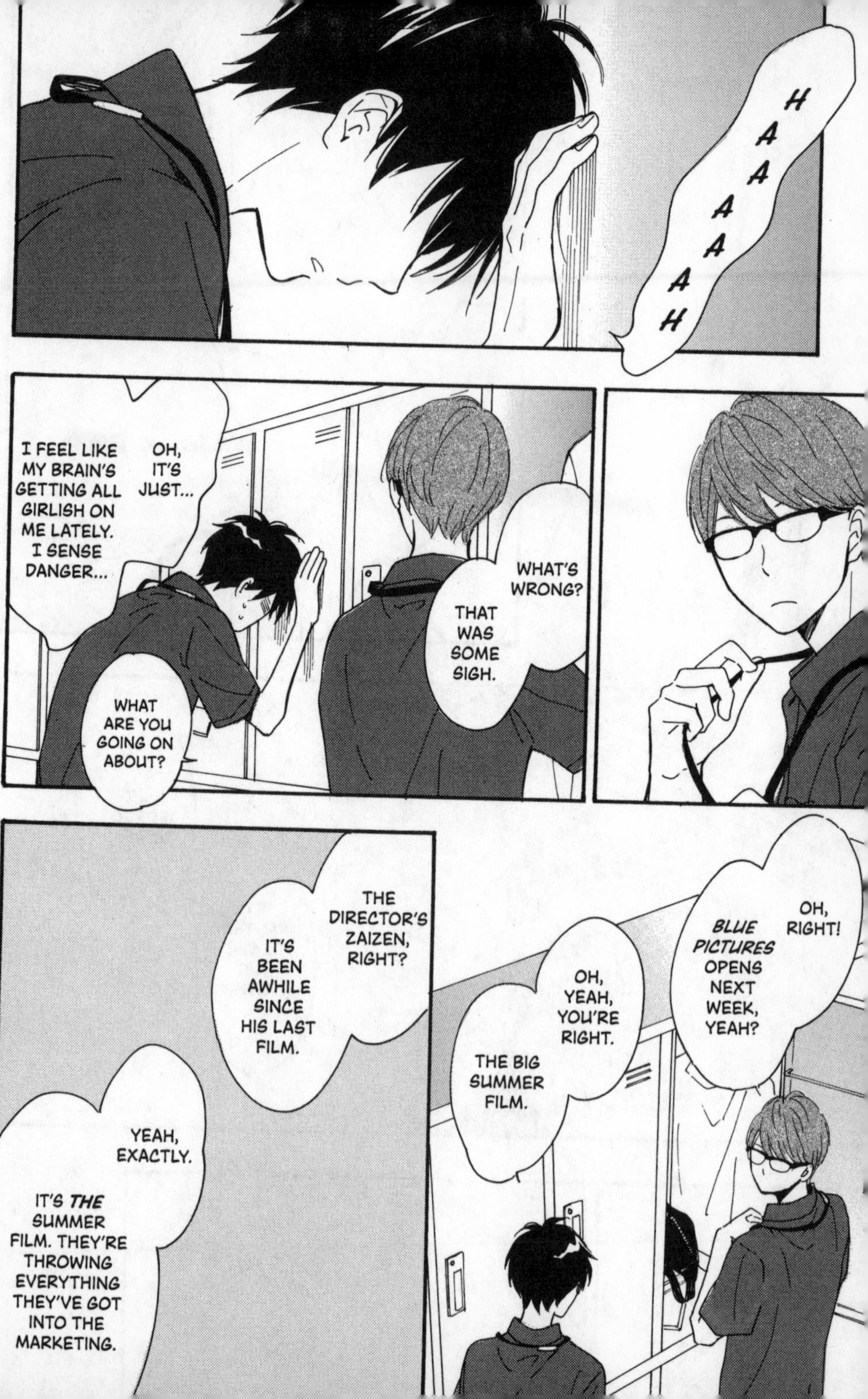
HAAAAAH
WHAT'S WRONG? THAT WAS SOME SIGH.
OH, IT'S JUST... I FEEL LIKE MY BRAIN'S GETTING ALL GIRLISH ON ME LATELY. I SENSE DANGER...
WHAT ARE YOU GOING ON ABOUT?
OH, RIGHT! *BLUE PICTURES* OPENS NEXT WEEK, YEAH?
OH, YEAH, YOU'RE RIGHT. THE BIG SUMMER FILM.
THE DIRECTOR'S ZAIZEN, RIGHT? IT'S BEEN AWHILE SINCE HIS LAST FILM.
YEAH, EXACTLY. IT'S ***THE*** SUMMER FILM. THEY'RE THROWING EVERYTHING THEY'VE GOT INTO THE MARKETING.

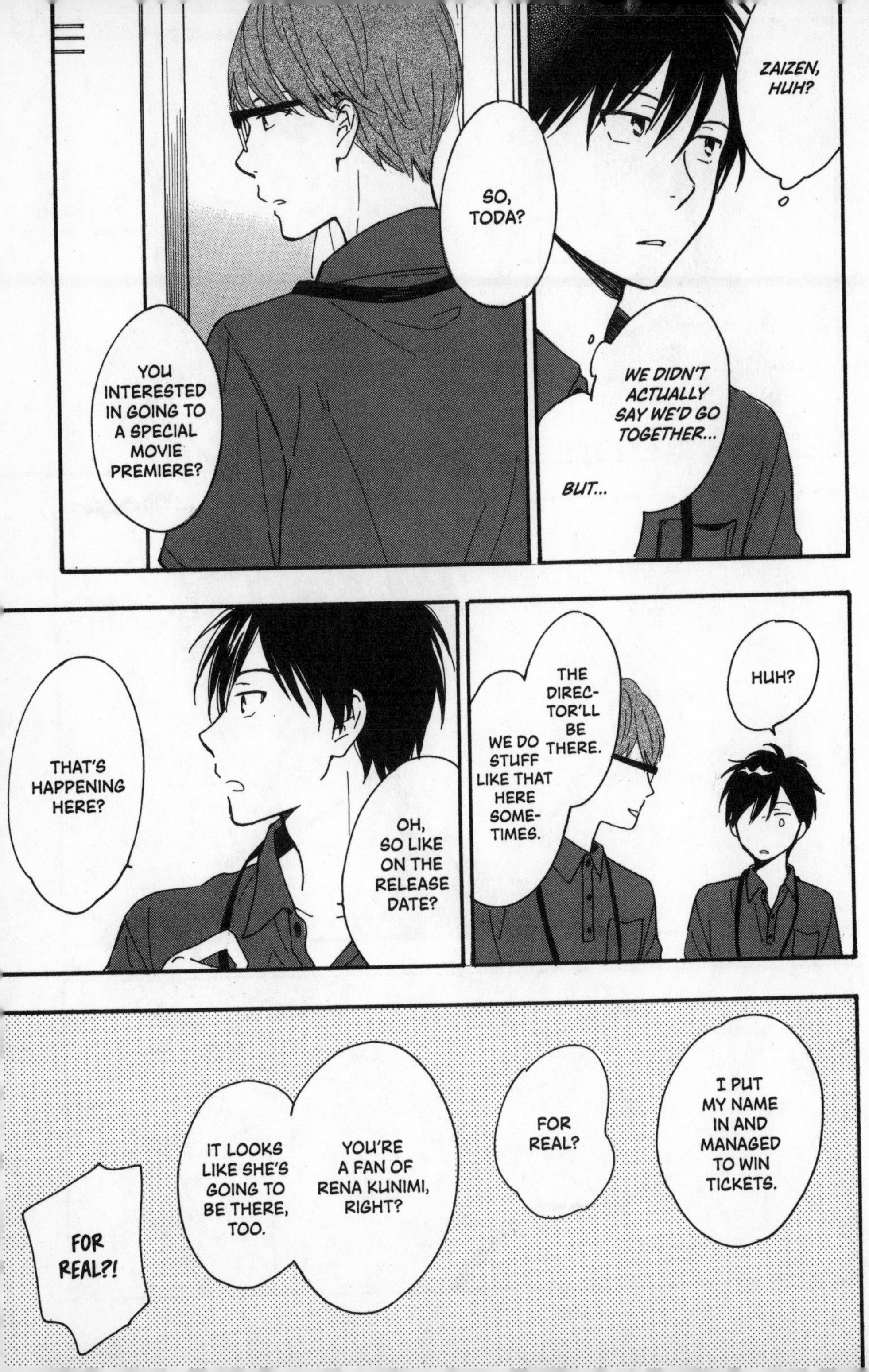
ZAIZEN, HUH?
WE DIDN'T ACTUALLY SAY WE'D GO TOGETHER...
BUT...
SO, TODA?
YOU INTERESTED IN GOING TO A SPECIAL MOVIE PREMIERE?
HUH?
THE DIRECTOR'LL BE THERE.
WE DO STUFF LIKE THAT HERE SOMETIMES.
OH, SO LIKE ON THE RELEASE DATE?
THAT'S HAPPENING HERE?
I PUT MY NAME IN AND MANAGED TO WIN TICKETS.
FOR REAL?
YOU'RE A FAN OF RENA KUNIMI, RIGHT?
IT LOOKS LIKE SHE'S GOING TO BE THERE, TOO.
FOR REAL?!

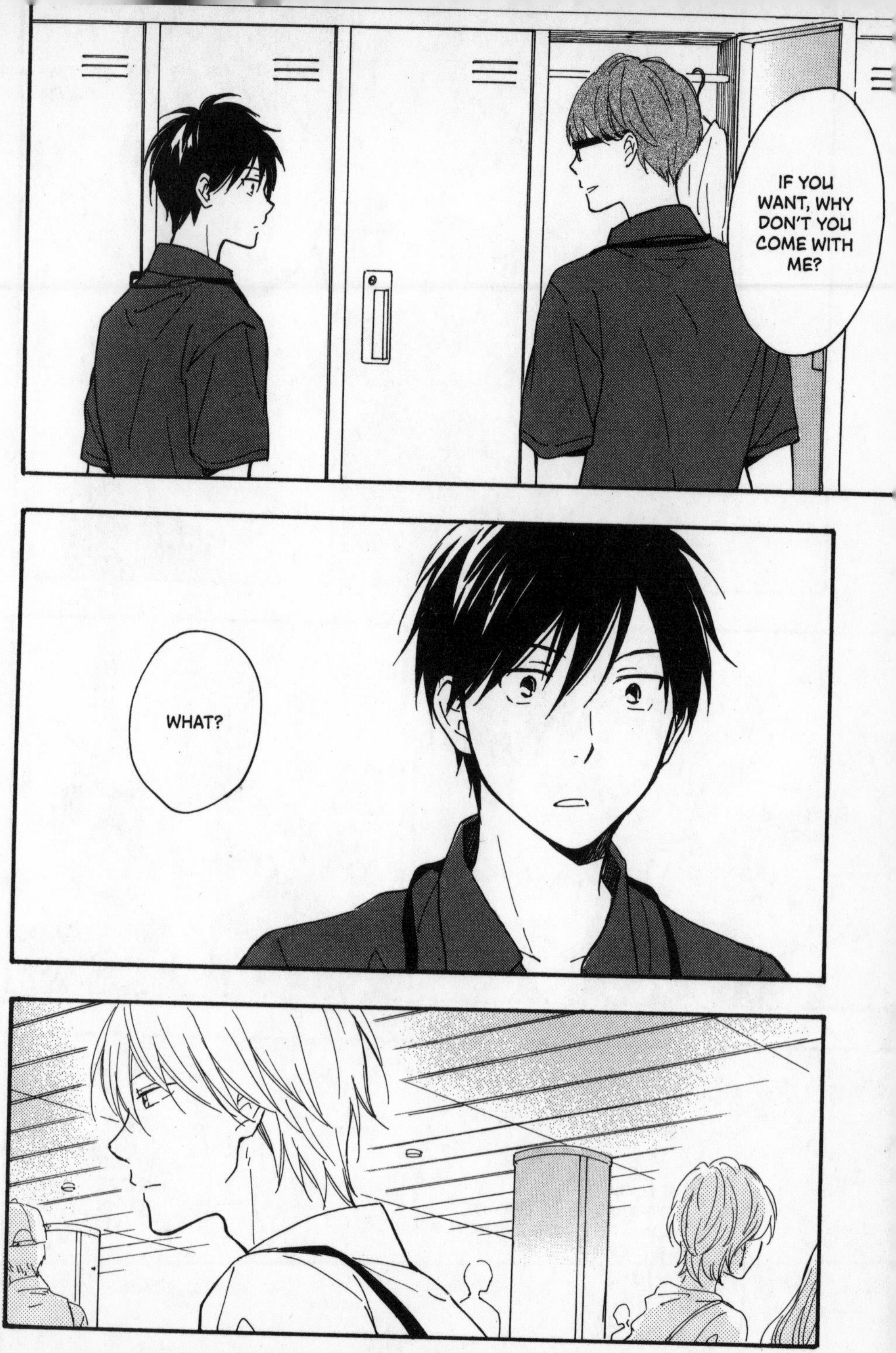
IF YOU WANT, WHY DON'T YOU COME WITH ME?
WHAT?

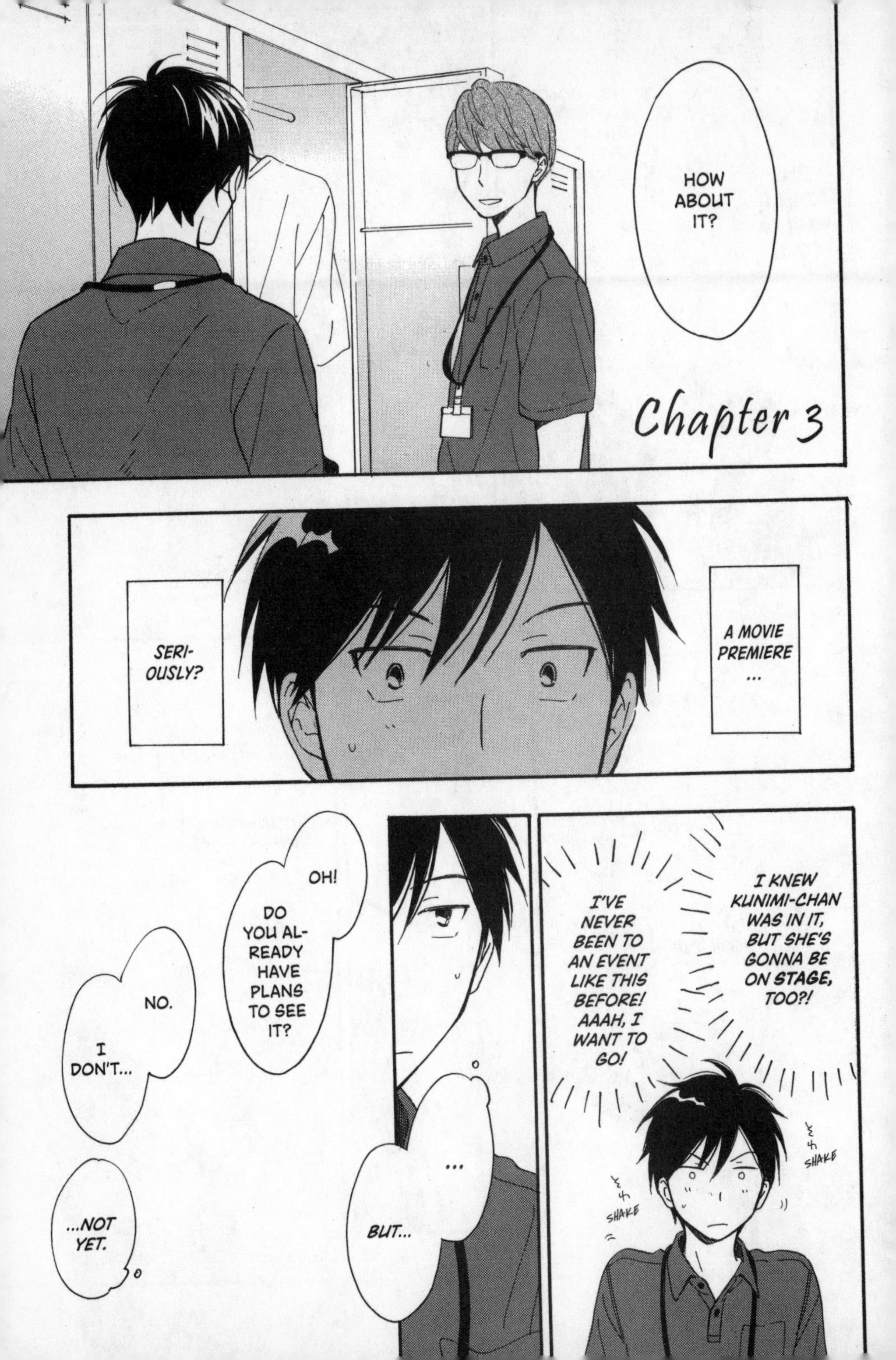
HOW ABOUT IT?
Chapter 3
A MOVIE PREMIERE ...
SERI-OUSLY?
I KNEW KUNIMI-CHAN WAS IN IT, BUT SHE'S GONNA BE ON STAGE, TOO?!
I'VE NEVER BEEN TO AN EVENT LIKE THIS BEFORE! AAAH, I WANT TO GO!
SHAKE
SHAKE
OH! DO YOU AL-READY HAVE PLANS TO SEE IT?
NO. I DON'T...
...
BUT...
...NOT YET.

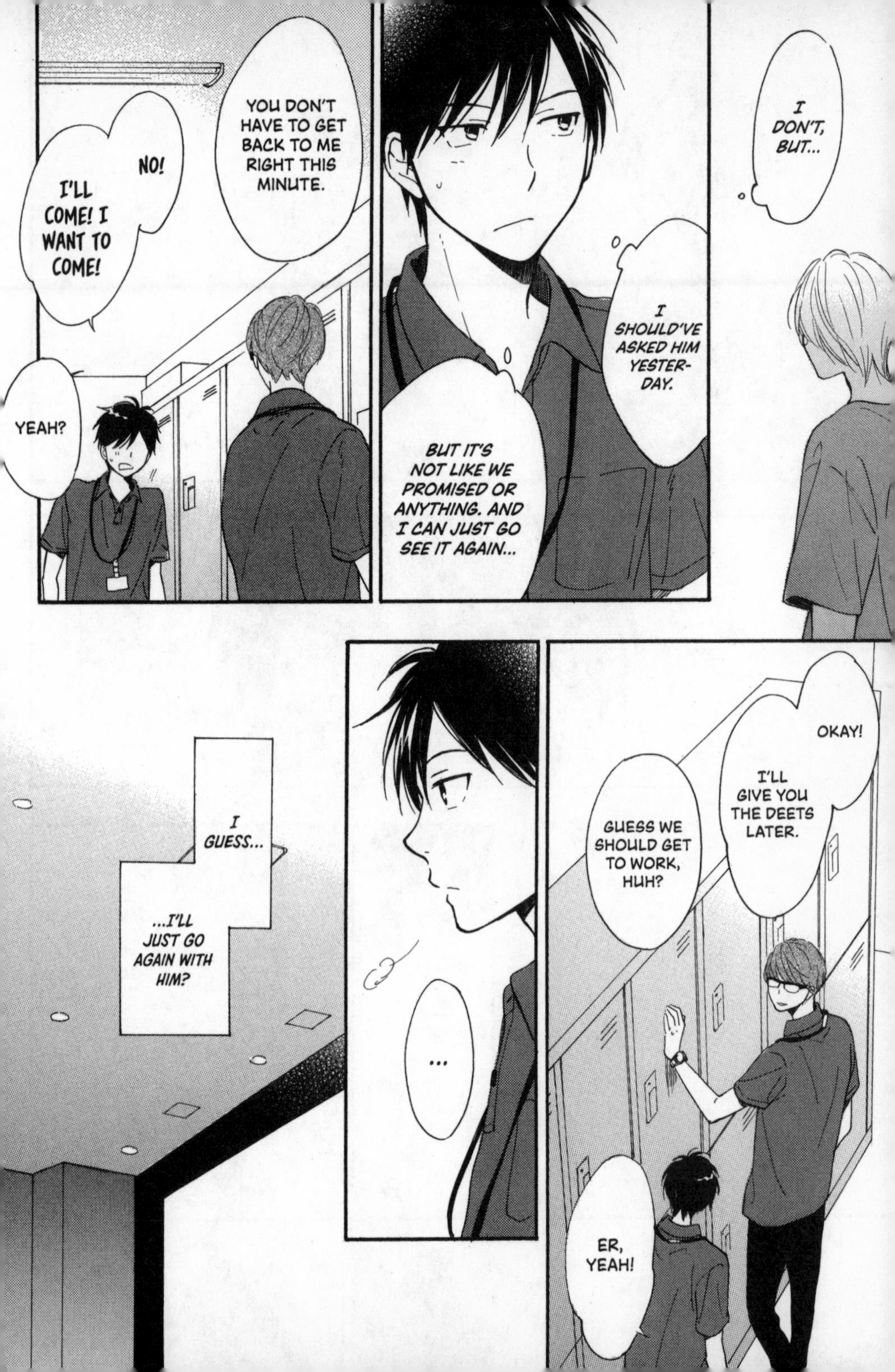
I DON'T, BUT...
I SHOULD'VE ASKED HIM YESTER-DAY.
BUT IT'S NOT LIKE WE PROMISED OR ANYTHING. AND I CAN JUST GO SEE IT AGAIN...
YOU DON'T HAVE TO GET BACK TO ME RIGHT THIS MINUTE.
NO! I'LL COME! I WANT TO COME!
YEAH?
OKAY! I'LL GIVE YOU THE DEETS LATER.
GUESS WE SHOULD GET TO WORK, HUH?
ER, YEAH!
...
I GUESS...
...I'LL JUST GO AGAIN WITH HIM?

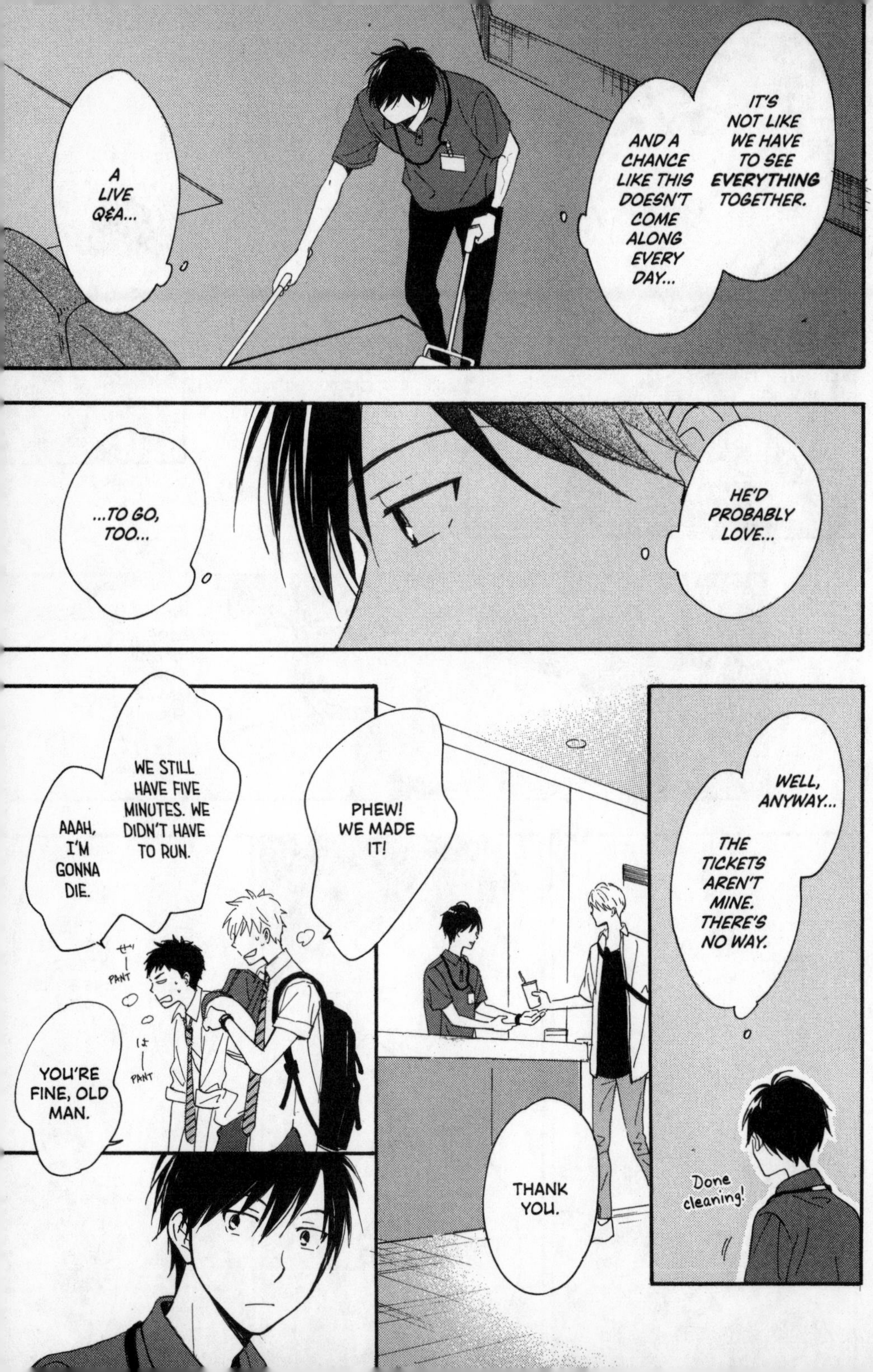
IT'S NOT LIKE WE HAVE TO SEE EVERYTHING TOGETHER.
AND A CHANCE LIKE THIS DOESN'T COME ALONG EVERY DAY...
A LIVE Q&A...
HE'D PROBABLY LOVE...
...TO GO, TOO...
WELL, ANYWAY...
THE TICKETS AREN'T MINE. THERE'S NO WAY.
Done cleaning!
THANK YOU.
PHEW! WE MADE IT!
WE STILL HAVE FIVE MINUTES. WE DIDN'T HAVE TO RUN.
AAAH, I'M GONNA DIE.
PANT
PANT
YOU'RE FINE, OLD MAN.

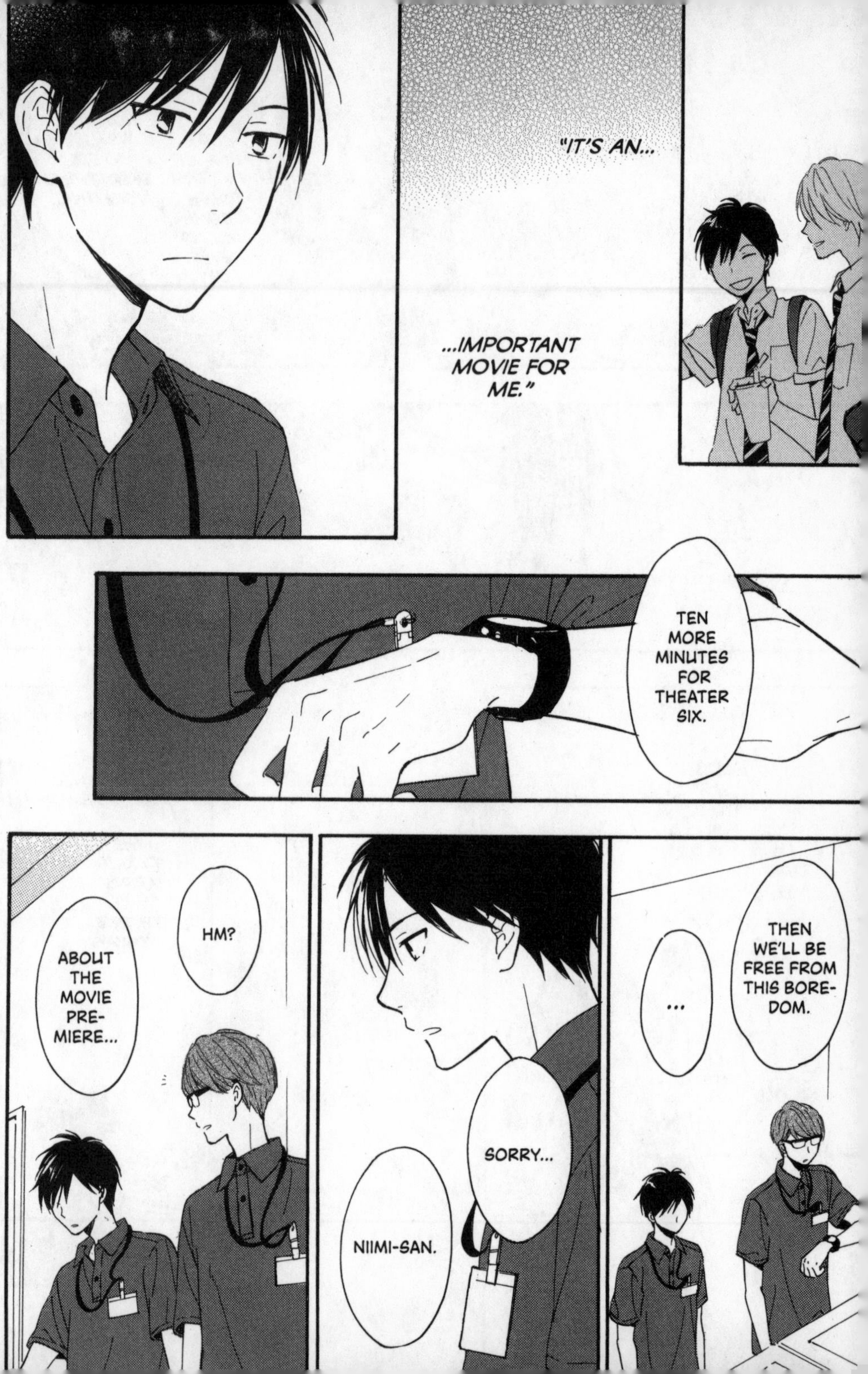
"IT'S AN...
...IMPORTANT MOVIE FOR ME."
TEN MORE MINUTES FOR THEATER SIX.
THEN WE'LL BE FREE FROM THIS BORE-DOM.
...
SORRY...
NIIMI-SAN.
HM?
ABOUT THE MOVIE PRE-MIERE...

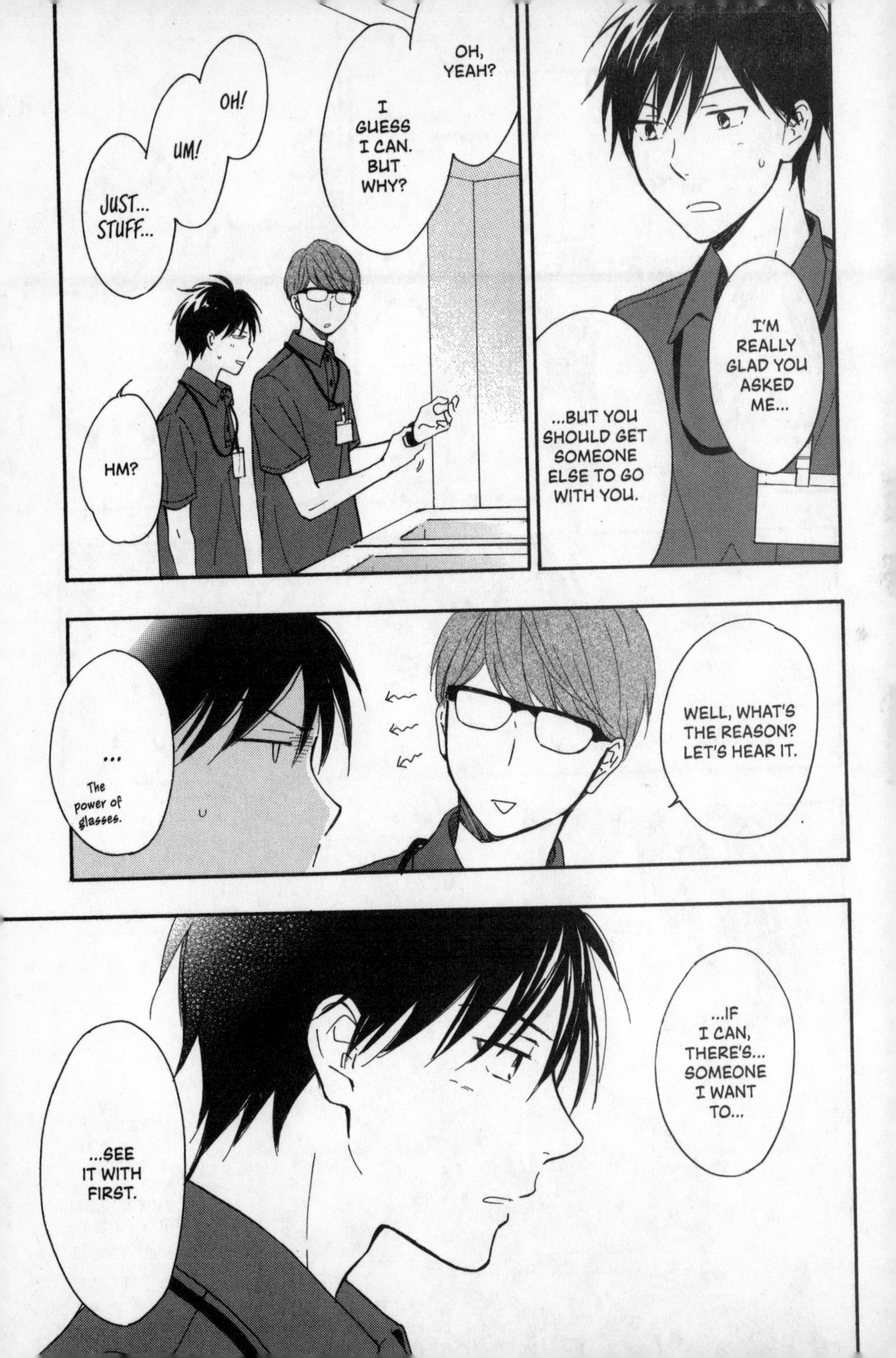
I'M REALLY GLAD YOU ASKED ME...
...BUT YOU SHOULD GET SOMEONE ELSE TO GO WITH YOU.
OH, YEAH?
I GUESS I CAN. BUT WHY?
OH!
UM!
JUST... STUFF...
HM?
WELL, WHAT'S THE REASON? LET'S HEAR IT.
...
The power of glasses.
...IF I CAN, THERE'S... SOMEONE I WANT TO...
...SEE IT WITH FIRST.

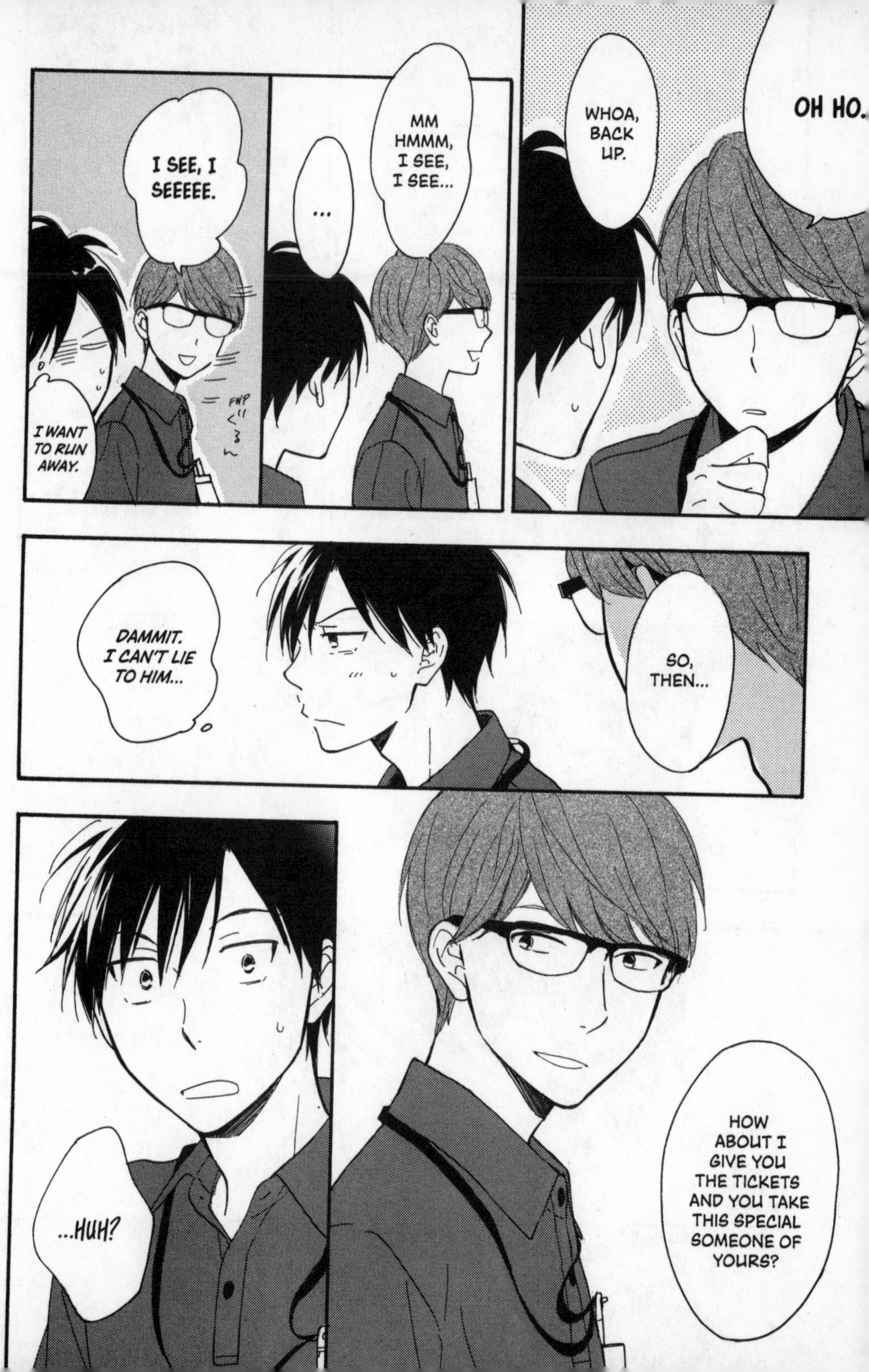
OH HO.
WHOA, BACK UP.
MM HMMM, I SEE, I SEE...
...
I SEE, I SEEEEE.
FWP
I WANT TO RUN AWAY.
SO, THEN...
DAMMIT. I CAN'T LIE TO HIM...
HOW ABOUT I GIVE YOU THE TICKETS AND YOU TAKE THIS SPECIAL SOMEONE OF YOURS?
...HUH?

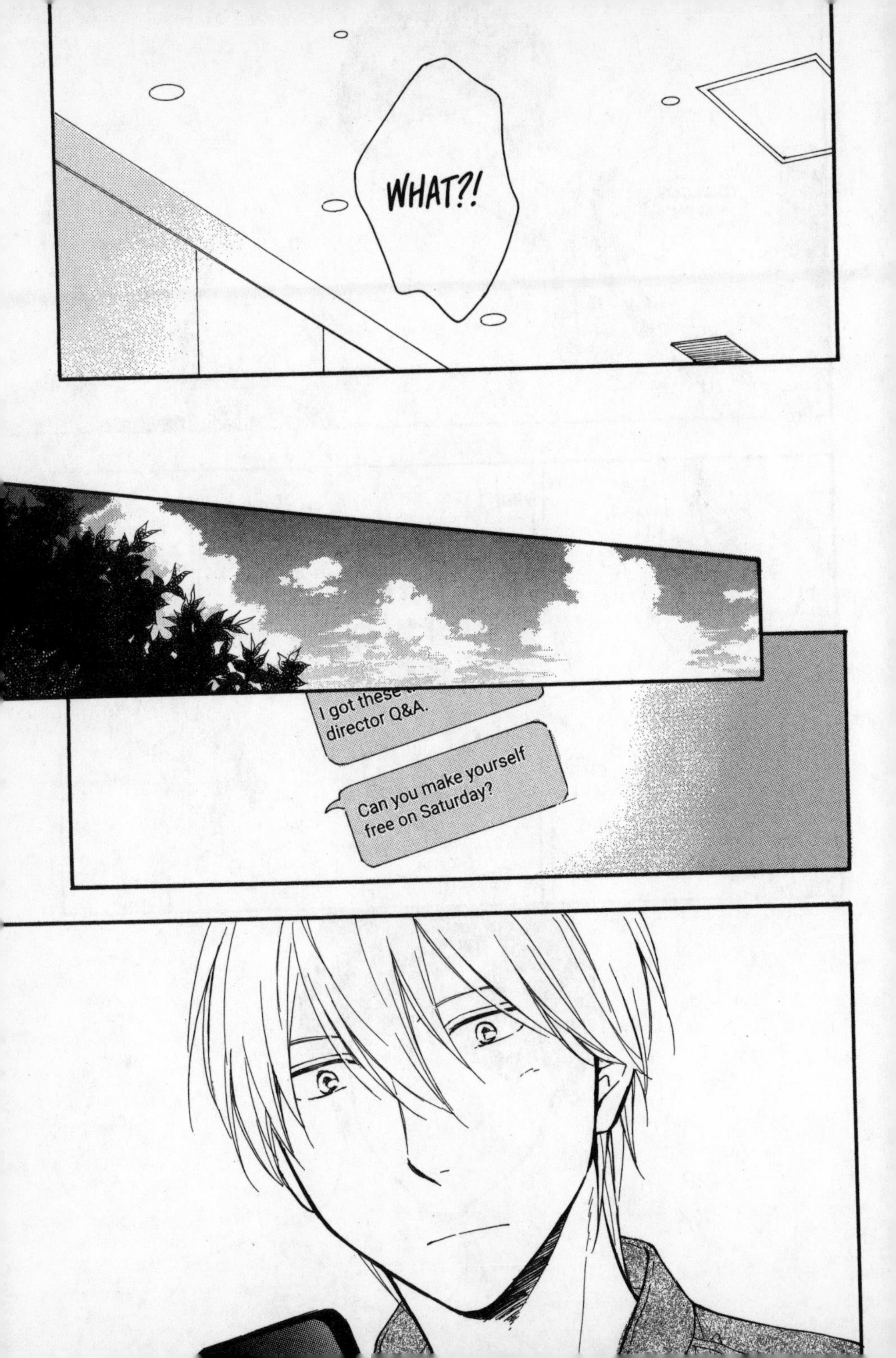
WHAT?!
I got these
director Q&A.
Can you make yourself free on Saturday?

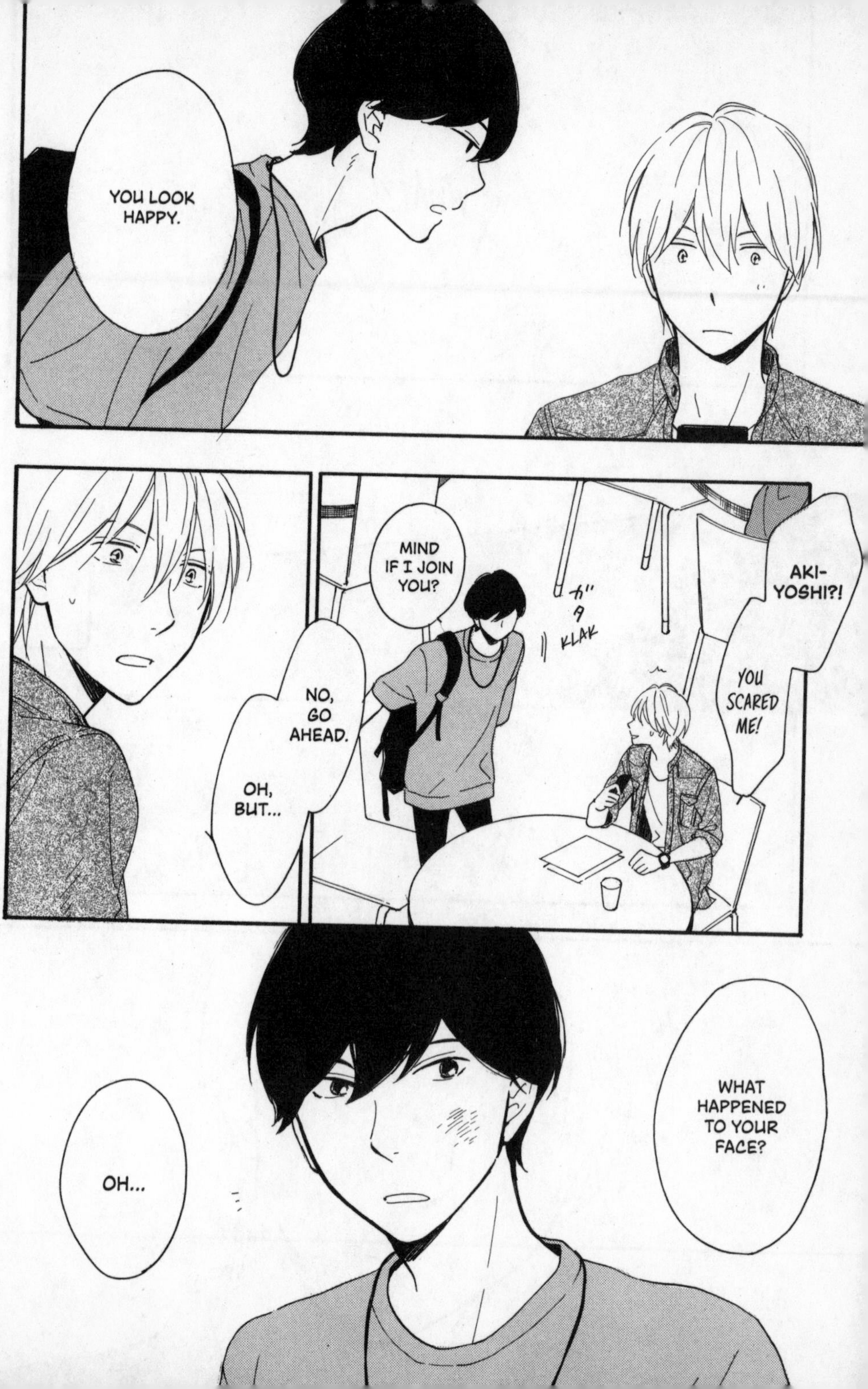
YOU LOOK HAPPY.
AKI-YOSHI?!
YOU SCARED ME!
ガタ KLAK
MIND IF I JOIN YOU?
NO, GO AHEAD.
OH, BUT...
WHAT HAPPENED TO YOUR FACE?
OH...

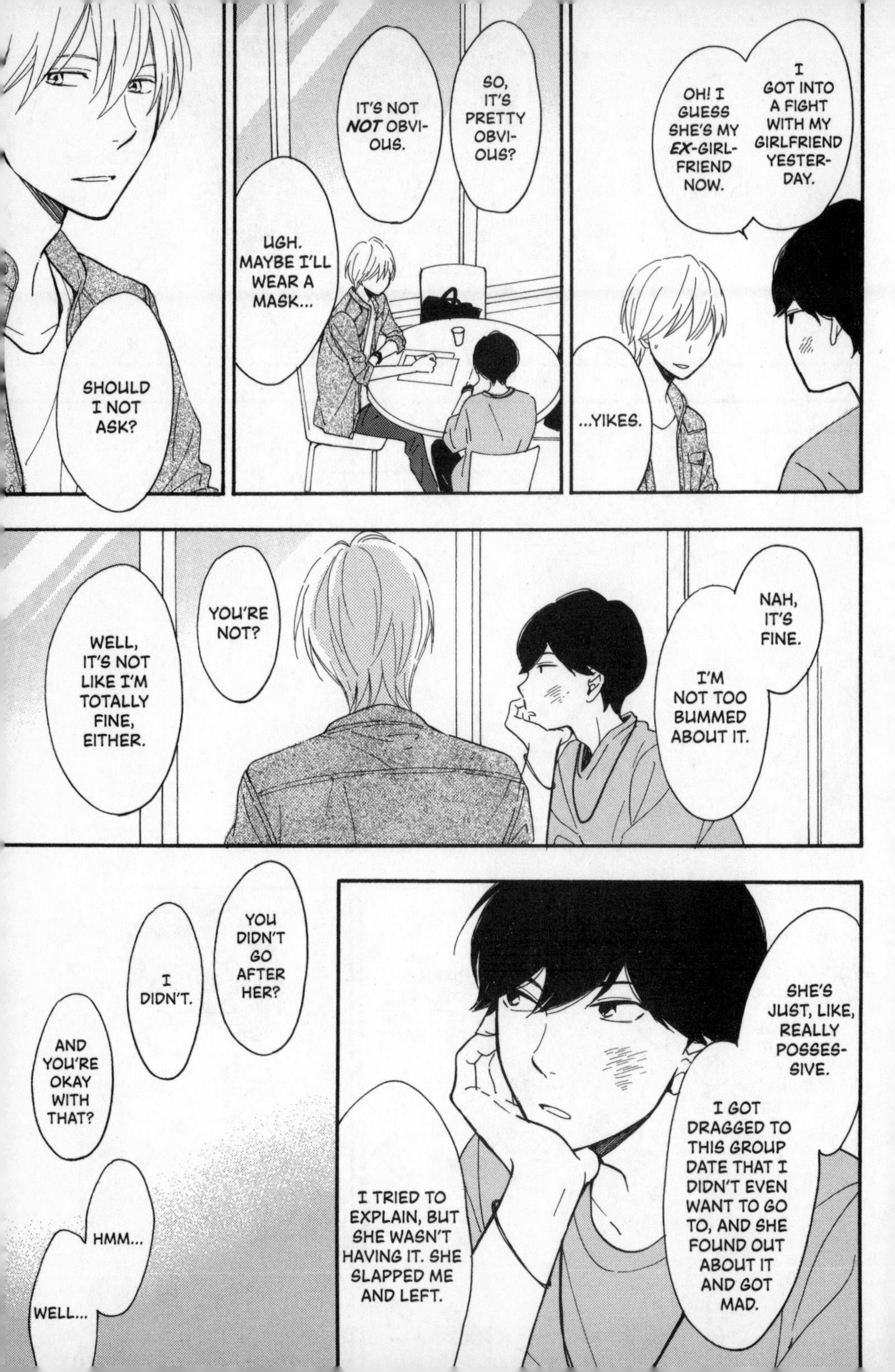
I GOT INTO A FIGHT WITH MY GIRLFRIEND YESTERDAY.
OH! I GUESS SHE'S MY *EX*-GIRLFRIEND NOW.
...YIKES.
SO, IT'S PRETTY OBVIOUS?
IT'S NOT *NOT* OBVIOUS.
UGH. MAYBE I'LL WEAR A MASK...
SHOULD I NOT ASK?
NAH, IT'S FINE.
I'M NOT TOO BUMMED ABOUT IT.
YOU'RE NOT?
WELL, IT'S NOT LIKE I'M TOTALLY FINE, EITHER.
SHE'S JUST, LIKE, REALLY POSSESSIVE.
I GOT DRAGGED TO THIS GROUP DATE THAT I DIDN'T EVEN WANT TO GO TO, AND SHE FOUND OUT ABOUT IT AND GOT MAD.
I TRIED TO EXPLAIN, BUT SHE WASN'T HAVING IT. SHE SLAPPED ME AND LEFT.
YOU DIDN'T GO AFTER HER?
I DIDN'T.
AND YOU'RE OKAY WITH THAT?
HMM...
WELL...

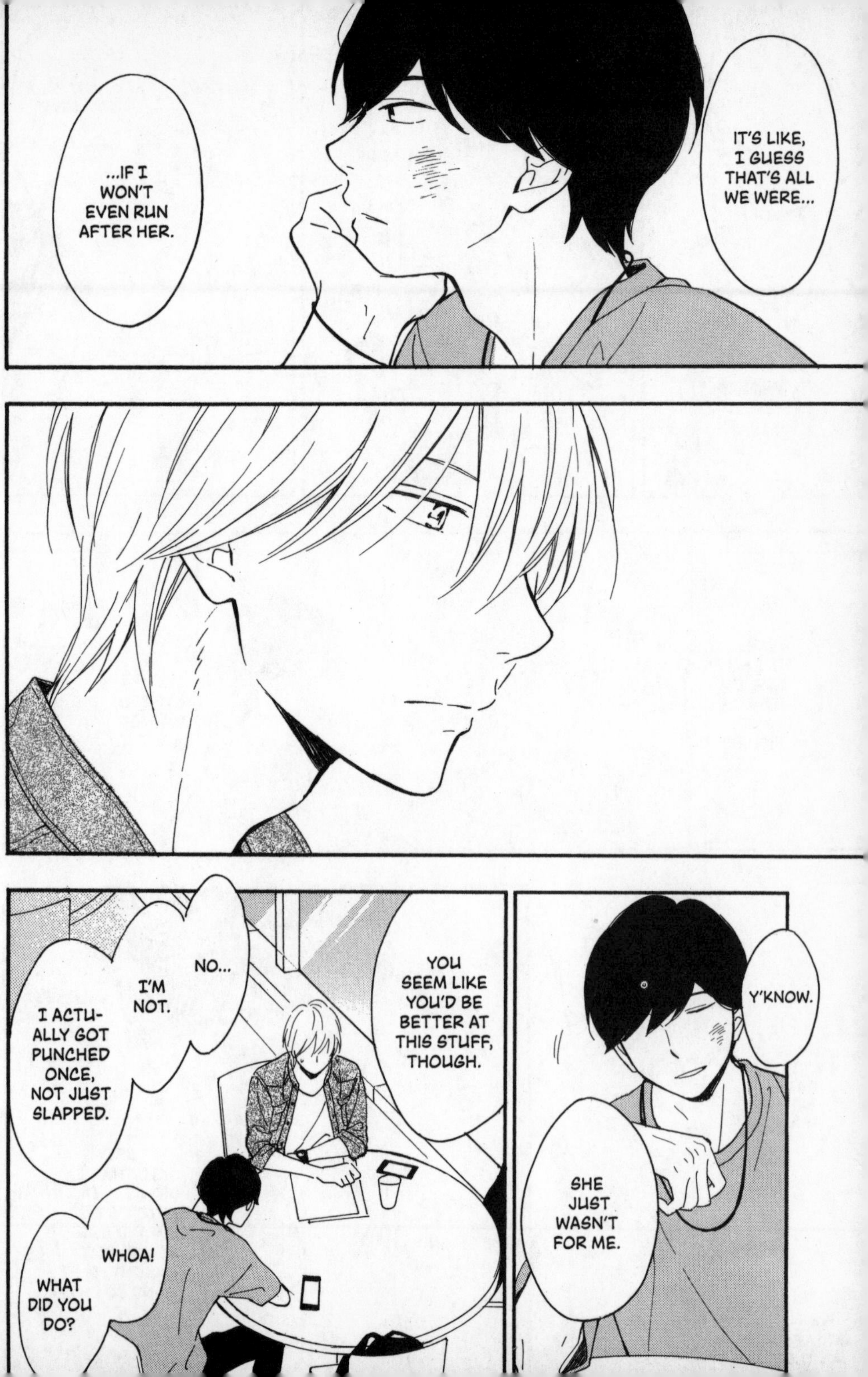
IT'S LIKE, I GUESS THAT'S ALL WE WERE...
...IF I WON'T EVEN RUN AFTER HER.
Y'KNOW.
SHE JUST WASN'T FOR ME.
YOU SEEM LIKE YOU'D BE BETTER AT THIS STUFF, THOUGH.
NO...
I'M NOT.
I ACTU-ALLY GOT PUNCHED ONCE, NOT JUST SLAPPED.
WHOA!
WHAT DID YOU DO?

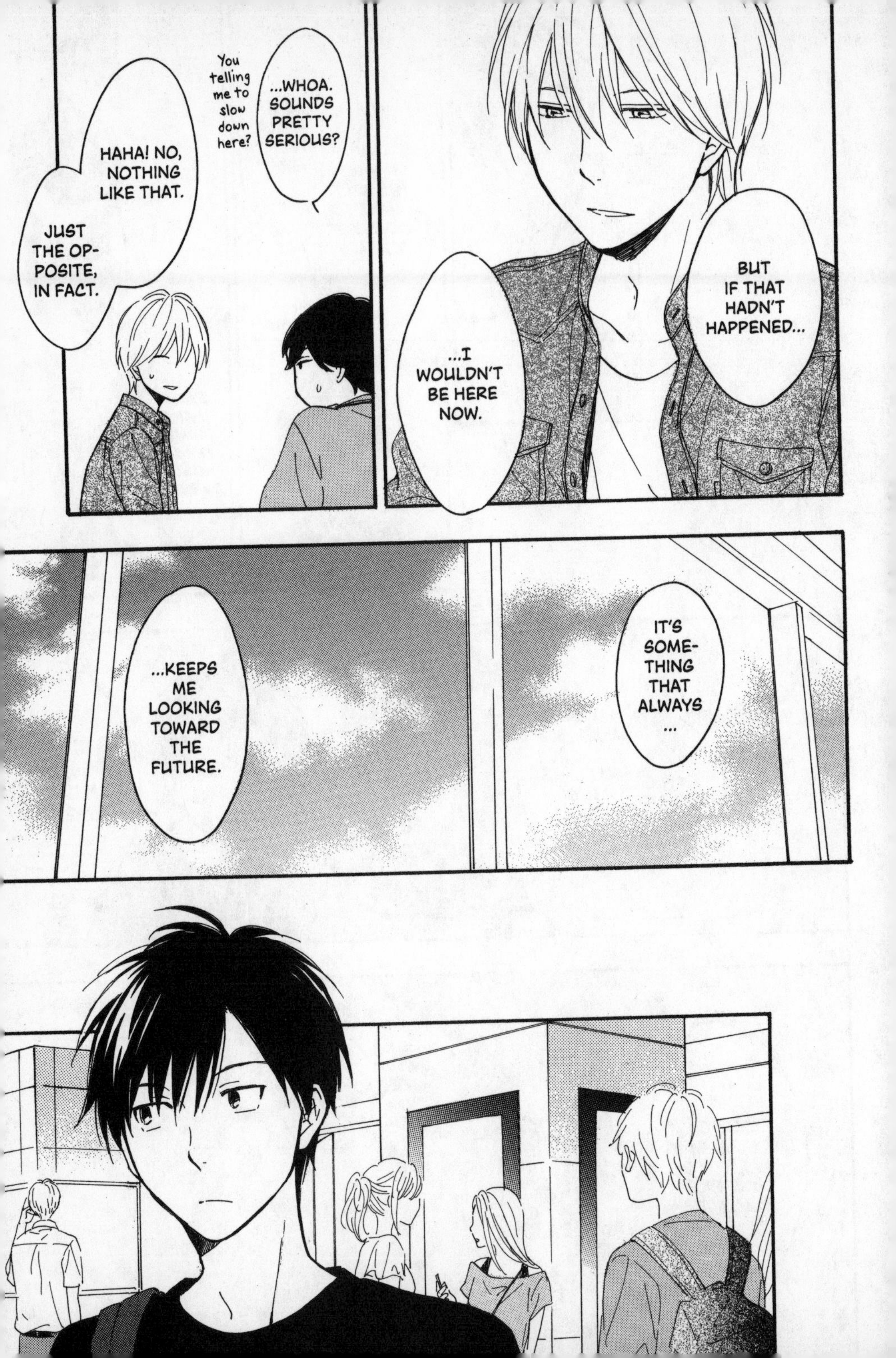
BUT IF THAT HADN'T HAPPENED...
...I WOULDN'T BE HERE NOW.
...WHOA. SOUNDS PRETTY SERIOUS?
You telling me to slow down here?
HAHA! NO, NOTHING LIKE THAT.
JUST THE OP-POSITE, IN FACT.
IT'S SOME-THING THAT ALWAYS...
...KEEPS ME LOOKING TOWARD THE FUTURE.

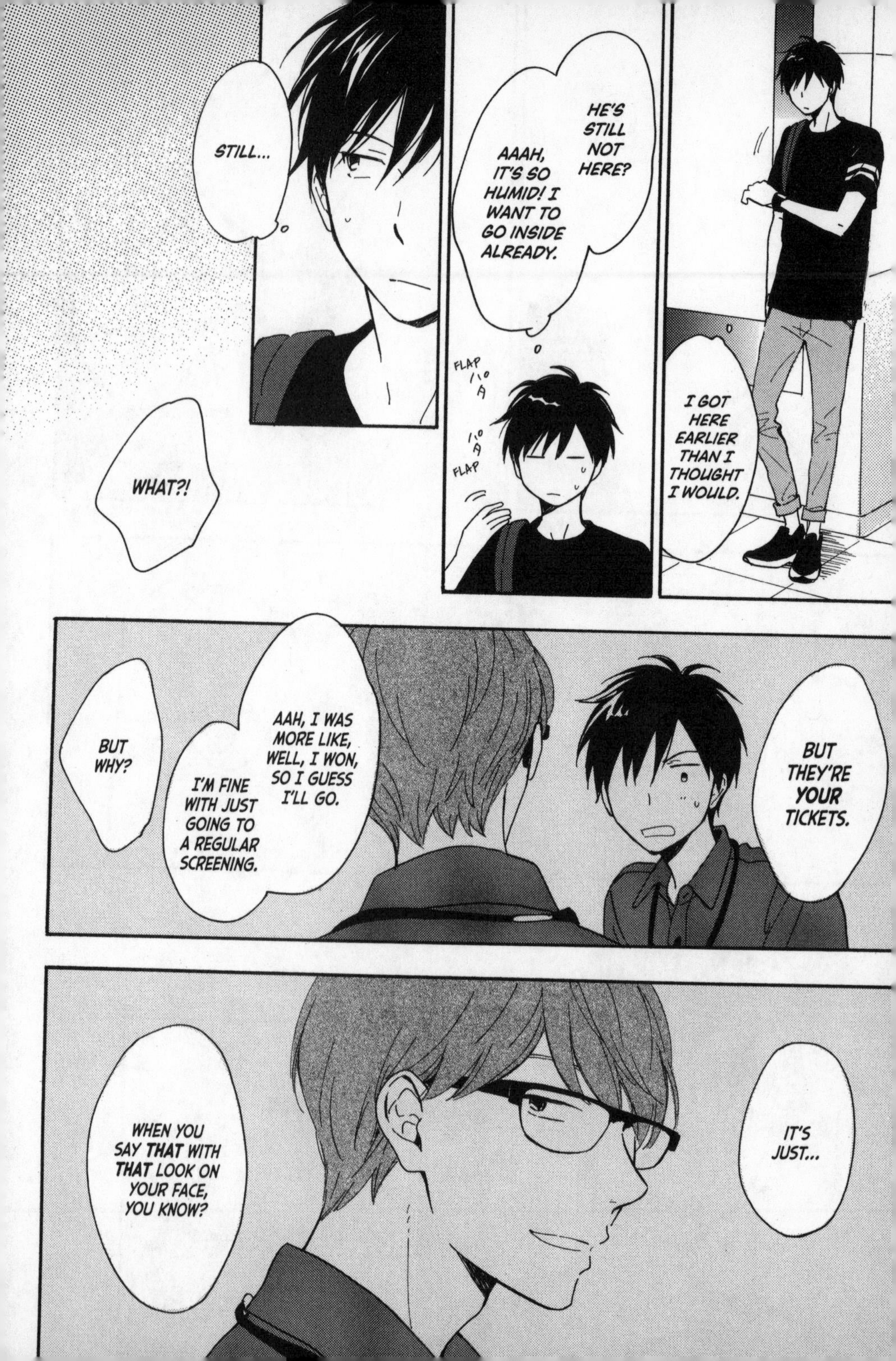
I GOT HERE EARLIER THAN I THOUGHT I WOULD.
HE'S STILL NOT HERE?
AAAH, IT'S SO HUMID! I WANT TO GO INSIDE ALREADY.
FLAP
FLAP
STILL...
WHAT?!
BUT THEY'RE YOUR TICKETS.
AAH, I WAS MORE LIKE, WELL, I WON, SO I GUESS I'LL GO.
I'M FINE WITH JUST GOING TO A REGULAR SCREENING.
BUT WHY?
IT'S JUST...
WHEN YOU SAY THAT WITH THAT LOOK ON YOUR FACE, YOU KNOW?

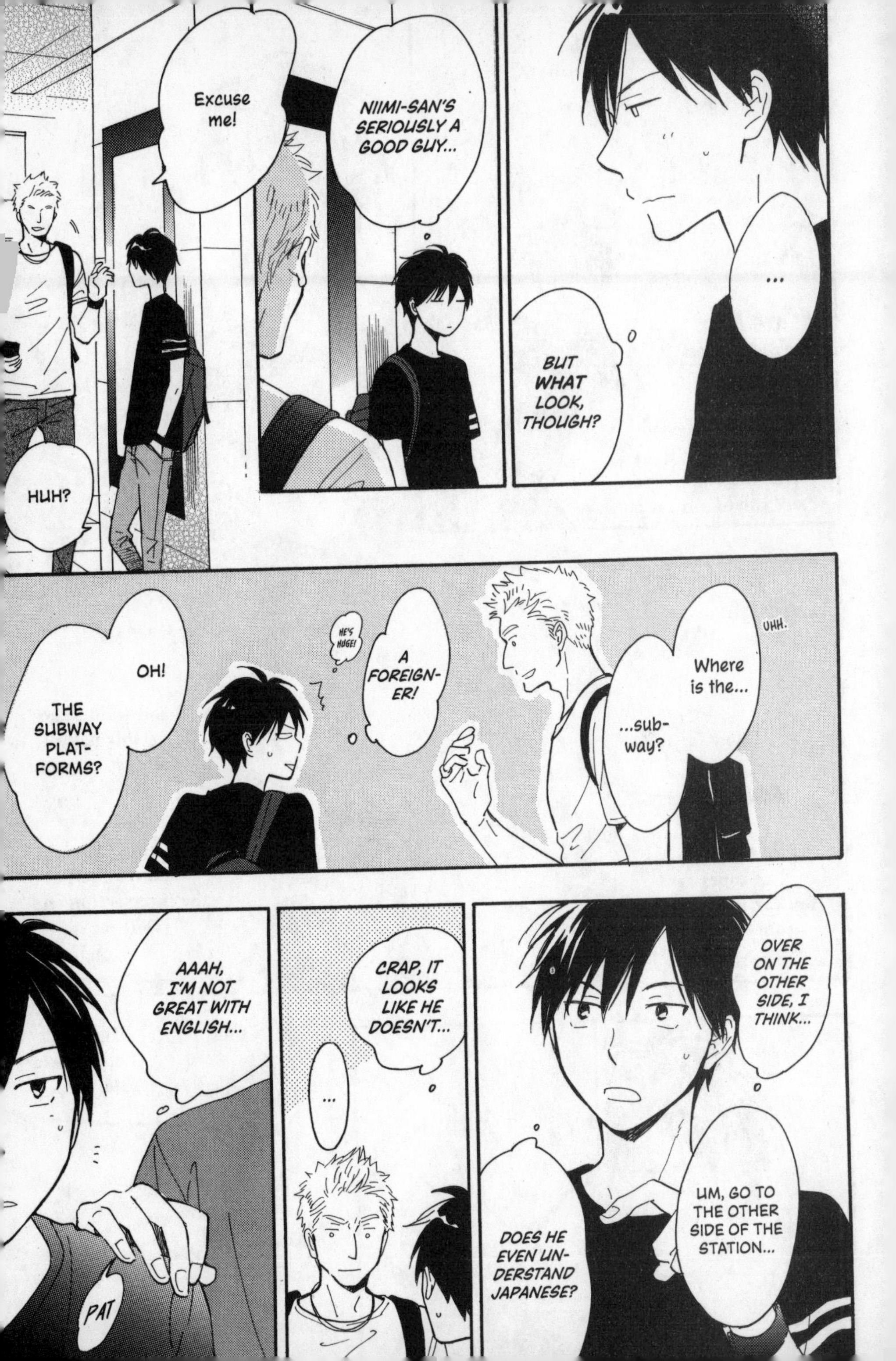
...
BUT WHAT LOOK, THOUGH?
NIIMI-SAN'S SERIOUSLY A GOOD GUY...
Excuse me!
HUH?
UHH.
Where is the...
...sub-way?
A FOREIGN-ER!
HE'S HUGE!
OH!
THE SUBWAY PLAT-FORMS?
OVER ON THE OTHER SIDE, I THINK...
UM, GO TO THE OTHER SIDE OF THE STATION...
DOES HE EVEN UN-DERSTAND JAPANESE?
CRAP, IT LOOKS LIKE HE DOESN'T...
...
AAAH, I'M NOT GREAT WITH ENGLISH...
PAT

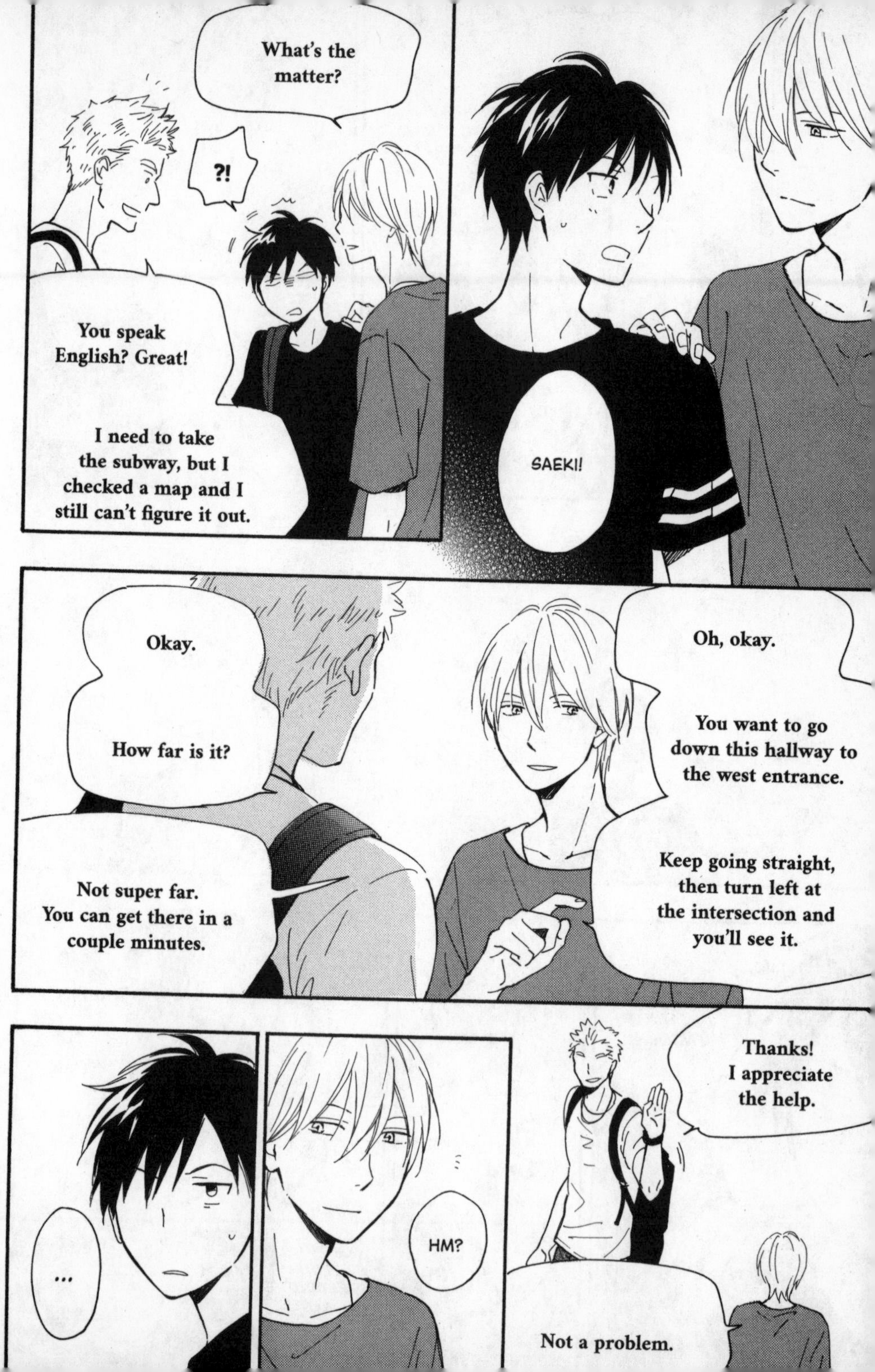
SAEKI!
What's the matter?
?!
You speak English? Great!
I need to take the subway, but I checked a map and I still can't figure it out.
Oh, okay.
You want to go down this hallway to the west entrance.
Keep going straight, then turn left at the intersection and you'll see it.
Okay.
How far is it?
Not super far. You can get there in a couple minutes.
Thanks! I appreciate the help.
Not a problem.
HM?
...

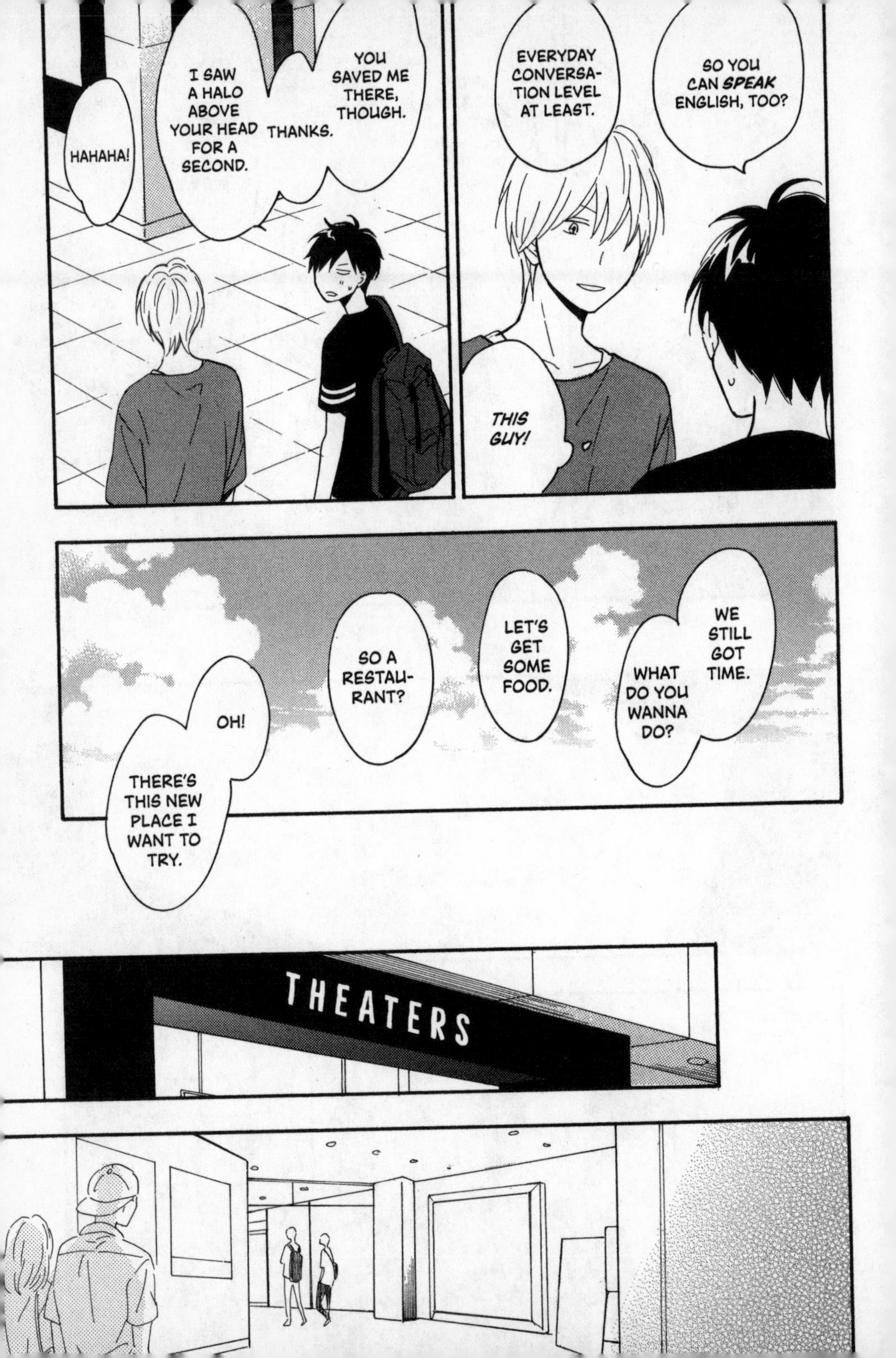
SO YOU CAN SPEAK ENGLISH, TOO?
EVERYDAY CONVERSATION LEVEL AT LEAST.
THIS GUY!
YOU SAVED ME THERE, THOUGH.
THANKS.
I SAW A HALO ABOVE YOUR HEAD FOR A SECOND.
HAHAHA!
WE STILL GOT TIME.
WHAT DO YOU WANNA DO?
LET'S GET SOME FOOD.
SO A RESTAURANT?
OH!
THERE'S THIS NEW PLACE I WANT TO TRY.
THEATERS

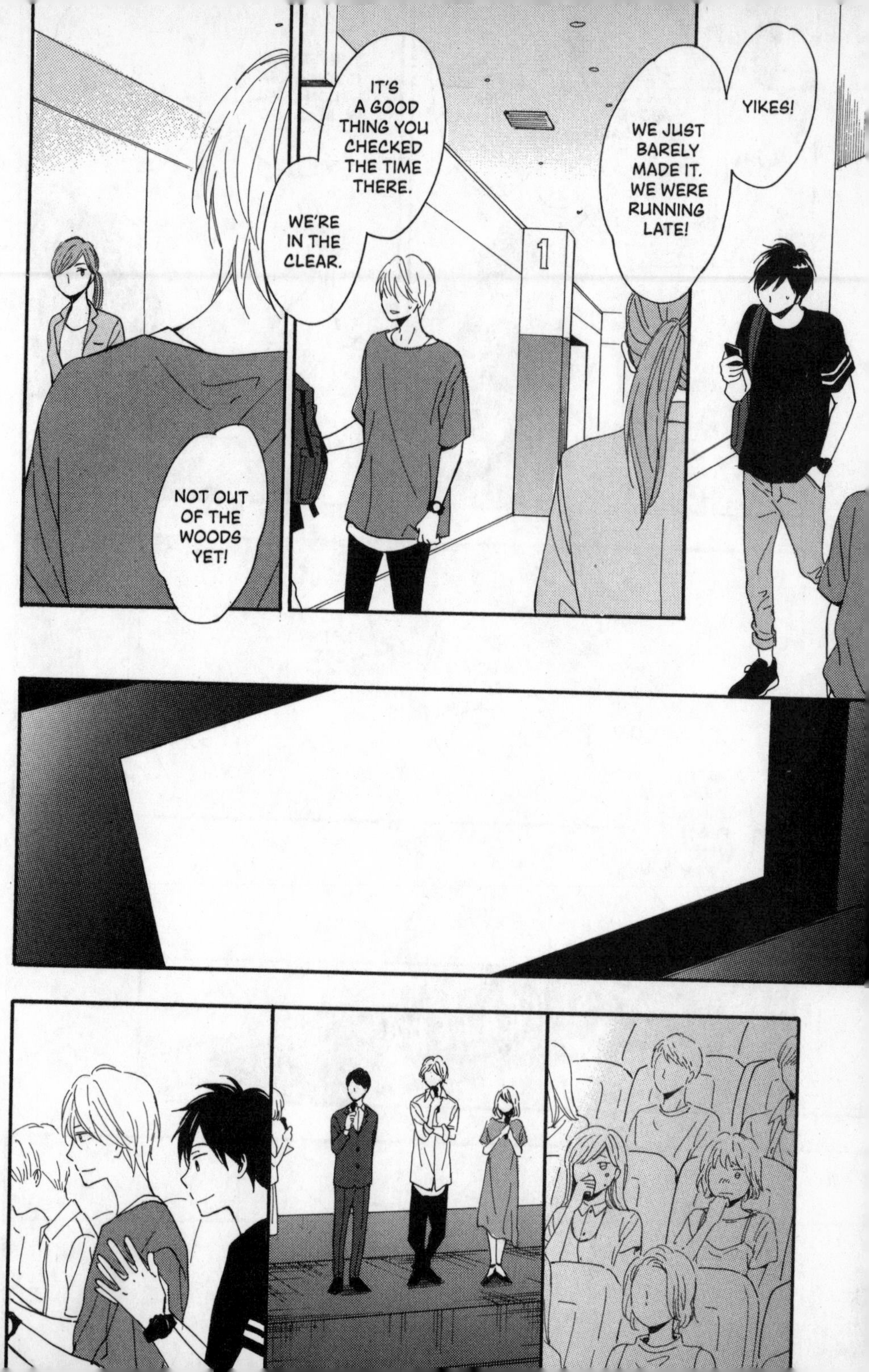
YIKES!
WE JUST BARELY MADE IT. WE WERE RUNNING LATE!
IT'S A GOOD THING YOU CHECKED THE TIME THERE.
WE'RE IN THE CLEAR.
NOT OUT OF THE WOODS YET!

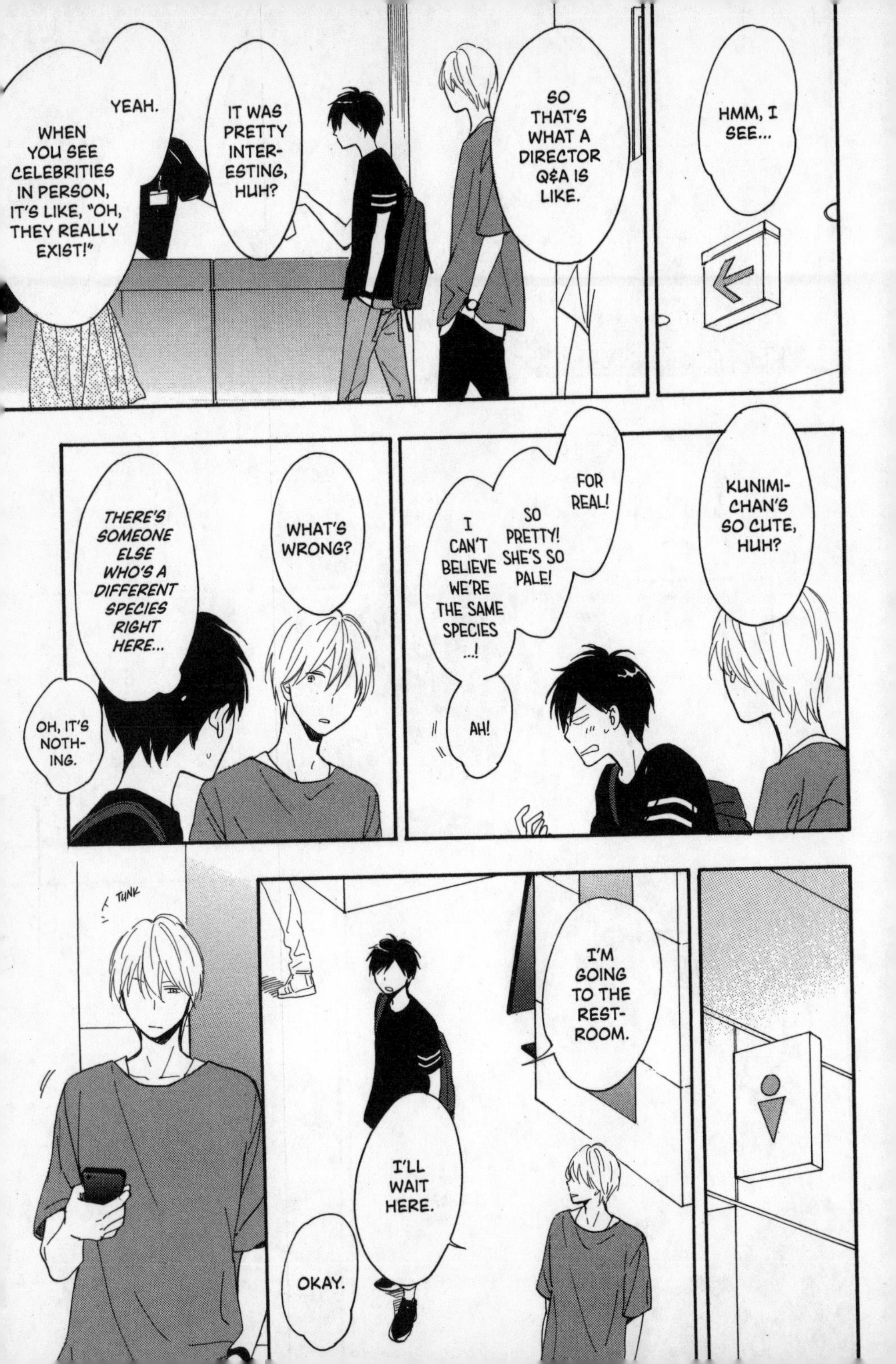
HMM, I SEE...
SO THAT'S WHAT A DIRECTOR Q&A IS LIKE.
IT WAS PRETTY INTERESTING, HUH?
YEAH.
WHEN YOU SEE CELEBRITIES IN PERSON, IT'S LIKE, "OH, THEY REALLY EXIST!"
KUNIMI-CHAN'S SO CUTE, HUH?
FOR REAL!
SO PRETTY! SHE'S SO PALE!
I CAN'T BELIEVE WE'RE THE SAME SPECIES...!
AH!
WHAT'S WRONG?
THERE'S SOMEONE ELSE WHO'S A DIFFERENT SPECIES RIGHT HERE...
OH, IT'S NOTHING.
I'M GOING TO THE RESTROOM.
I'LL WAIT HERE.
OKAY.
TUNK

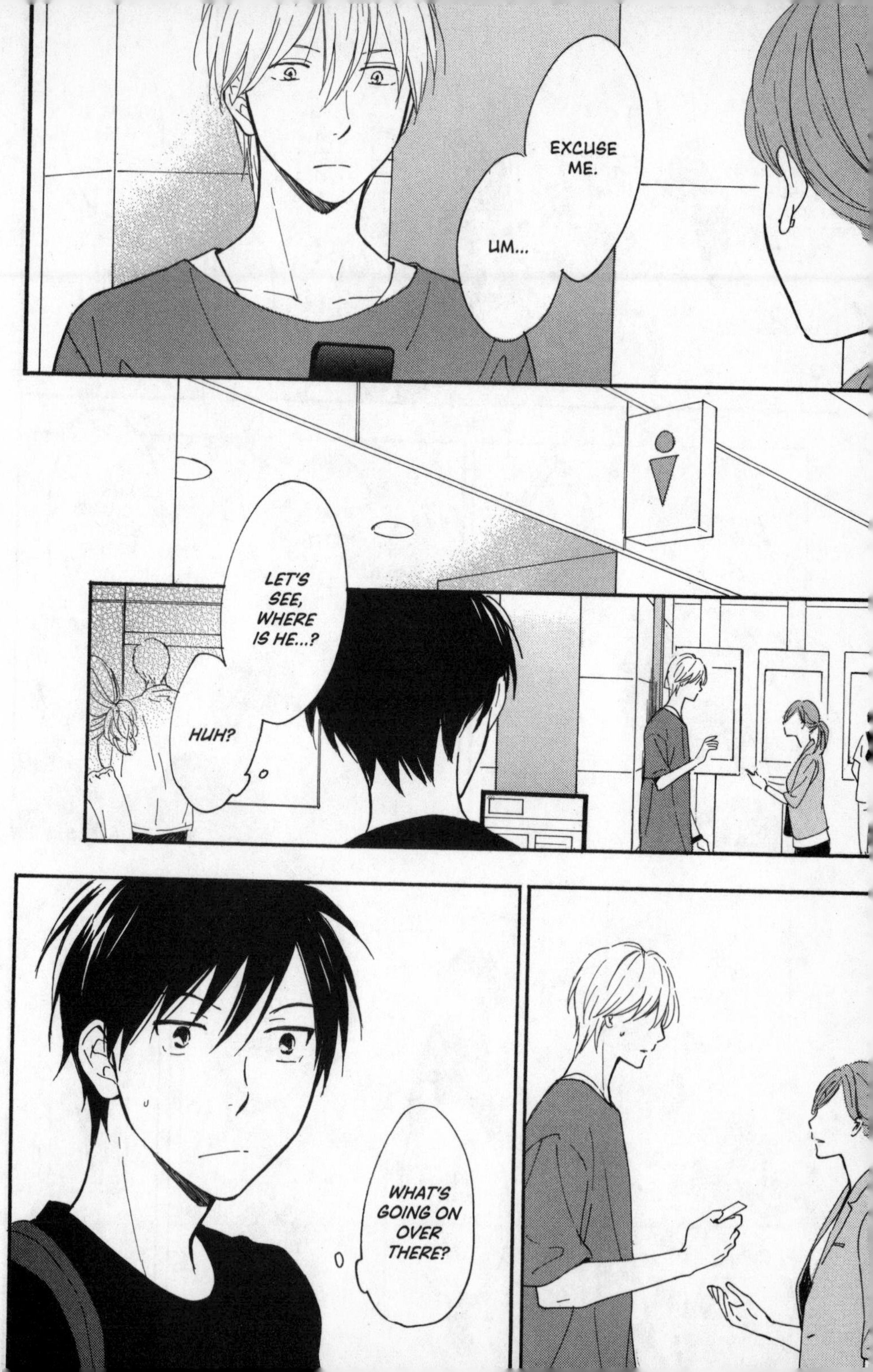
EXCUSE ME.
UM...
LET'S SEE, WHERE IS HE...?
HUH?
WHAT'S GOING ON OVER THERE?

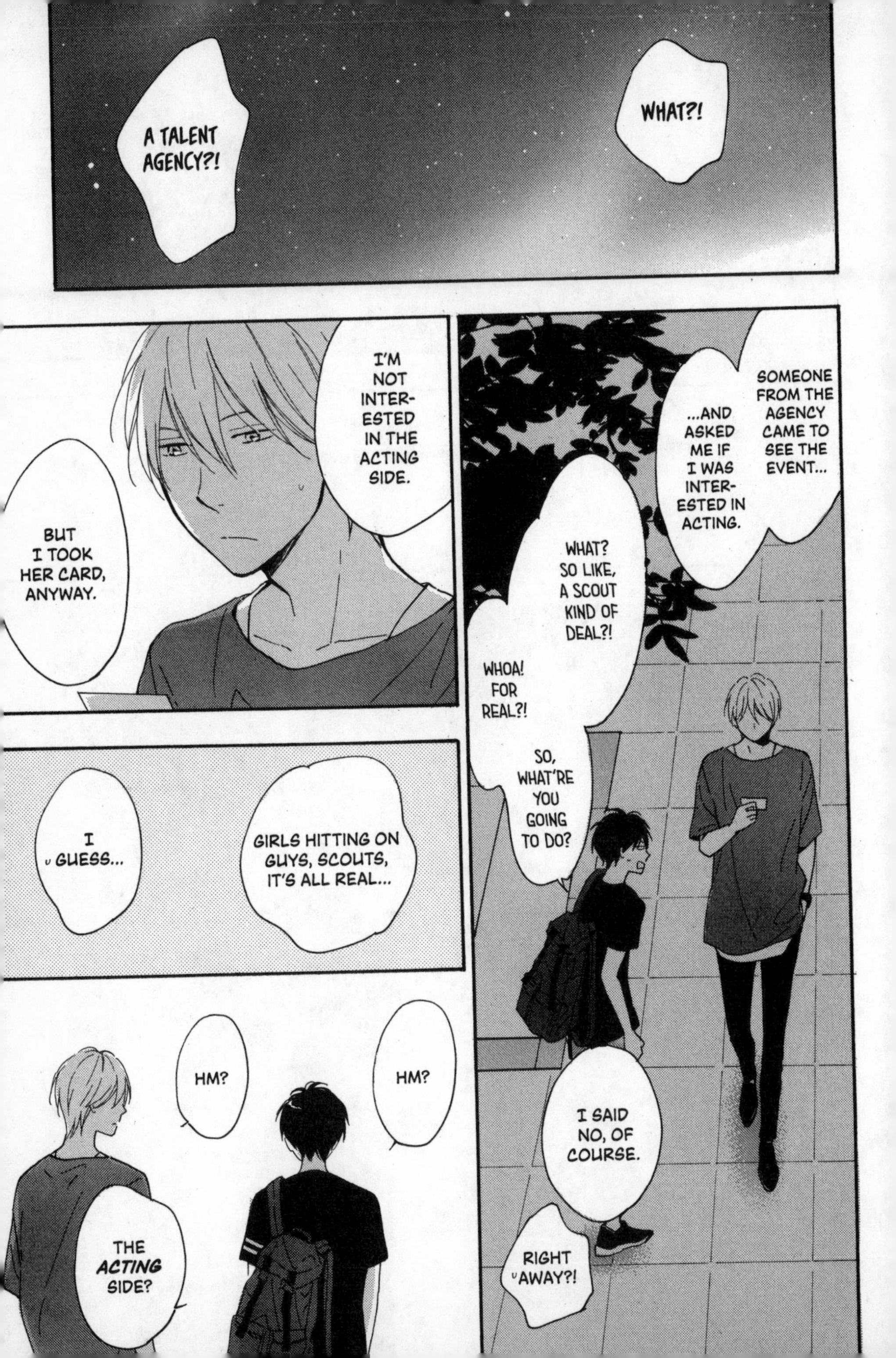
WHAT?!
A TALENT AGENCY?!
SOMEONE FROM THE AGENCY CAME TO SEE THE EVENT...
...AND ASKED ME IF I WAS INTERESTED IN ACTING.
WHAT? SO LIKE, A SCOUT KIND OF DEAL?!
WHOA! FOR REAL?!
SO, WHAT'RE YOU GOING TO DO?
I SAID NO, OF COURSE.
RIGHT AWAY?!
I'M NOT INTERESTED IN THE ACTING SIDE.
BUT I TOOK HER CARD, ANYWAY.
GIRLS HITTING ON GUYS, SCOUTS, IT'S ALL REAL...
I GUESS...
HM?
HM?
THE *ACTING* SIDE?

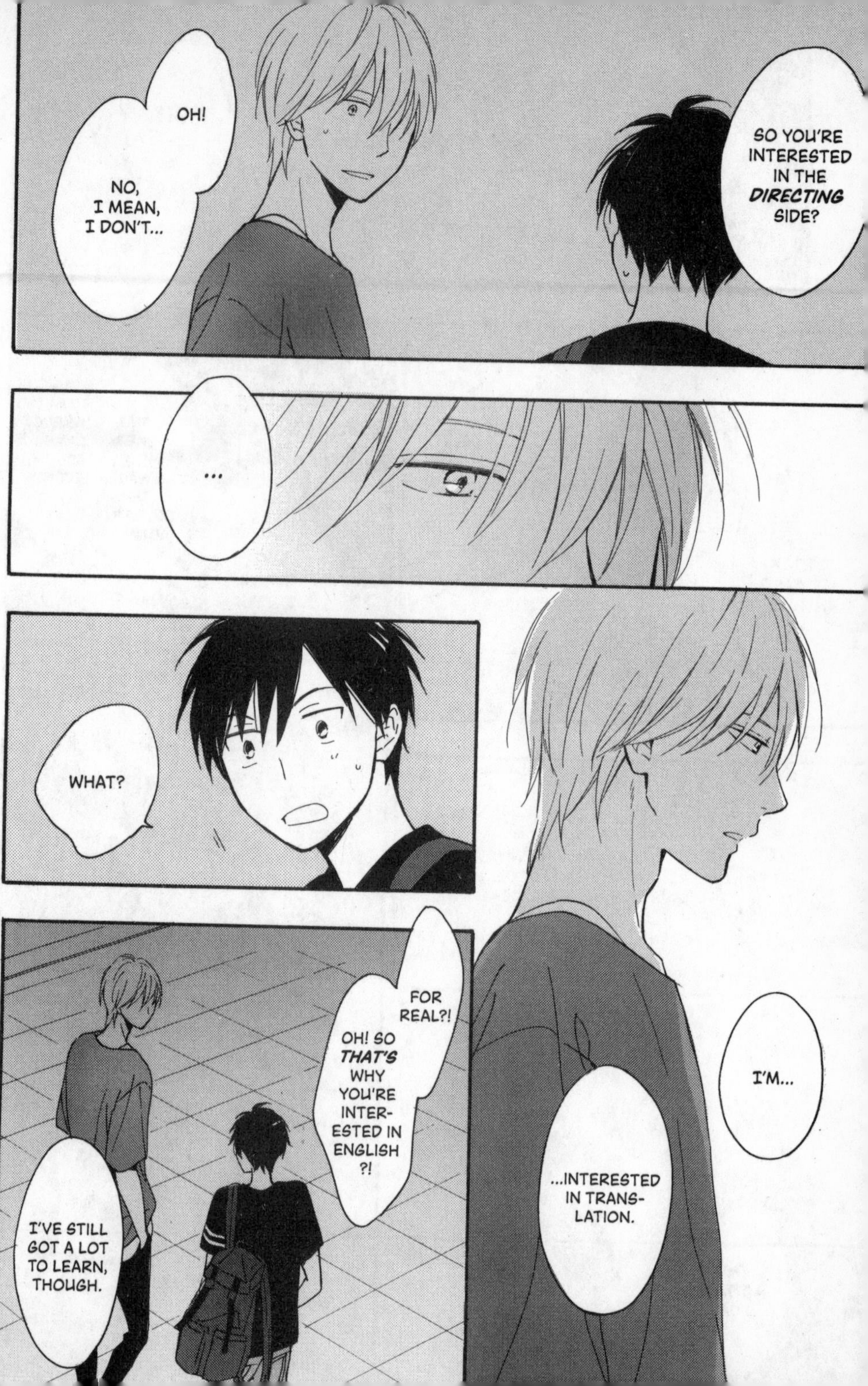
SO YOU'RE INTERESTED IN THE *DIRECTING* SIDE?
OH!
NO, I MEAN, I DON'T...
...
I'M...
...INTERESTED IN TRANSLATION.
WHAT?
FOR REAL?!
OH! SO *THAT'S* WHY YOU'RE INTERESTED IN ENGLISH?!
I'VE STILL GOT A LOT TO LEARN, THOUGH.

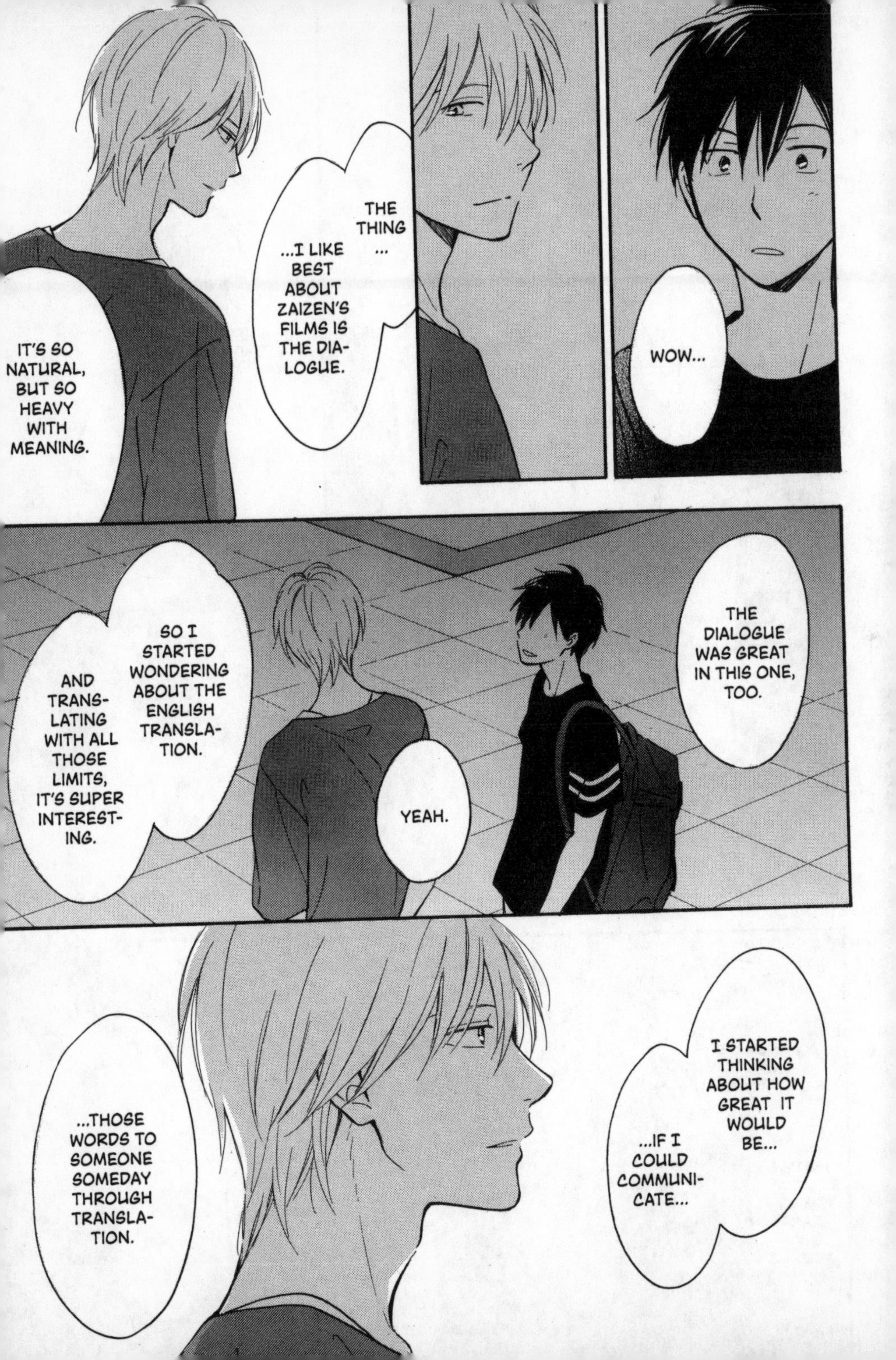
WOW...
THE THING ...
...I LIKE BEST ABOUT ZAIZEN'S FILMS IS THE DIA-LOGUE.
IT'S SO NATURAL, BUT SO HEAVY WITH MEANING.
THE DIALOGUE WAS GREAT IN THIS ONE, TOO.
YEAH.
SO I STARTED WONDERING ABOUT THE ENGLISH TRANSLA-TION.
AND TRANS-LATING WITH ALL THOSE LIMITS, IT'S SUPER INTEREST-ING.
I STARTED THINKING ABOUT HOW GREAT IT WOULD BE...
...IF I COULD COMMUNI-CATE...
...THOSE WORDS TO SOMEONE SOMEDAY THROUGH TRANSLA-TION.

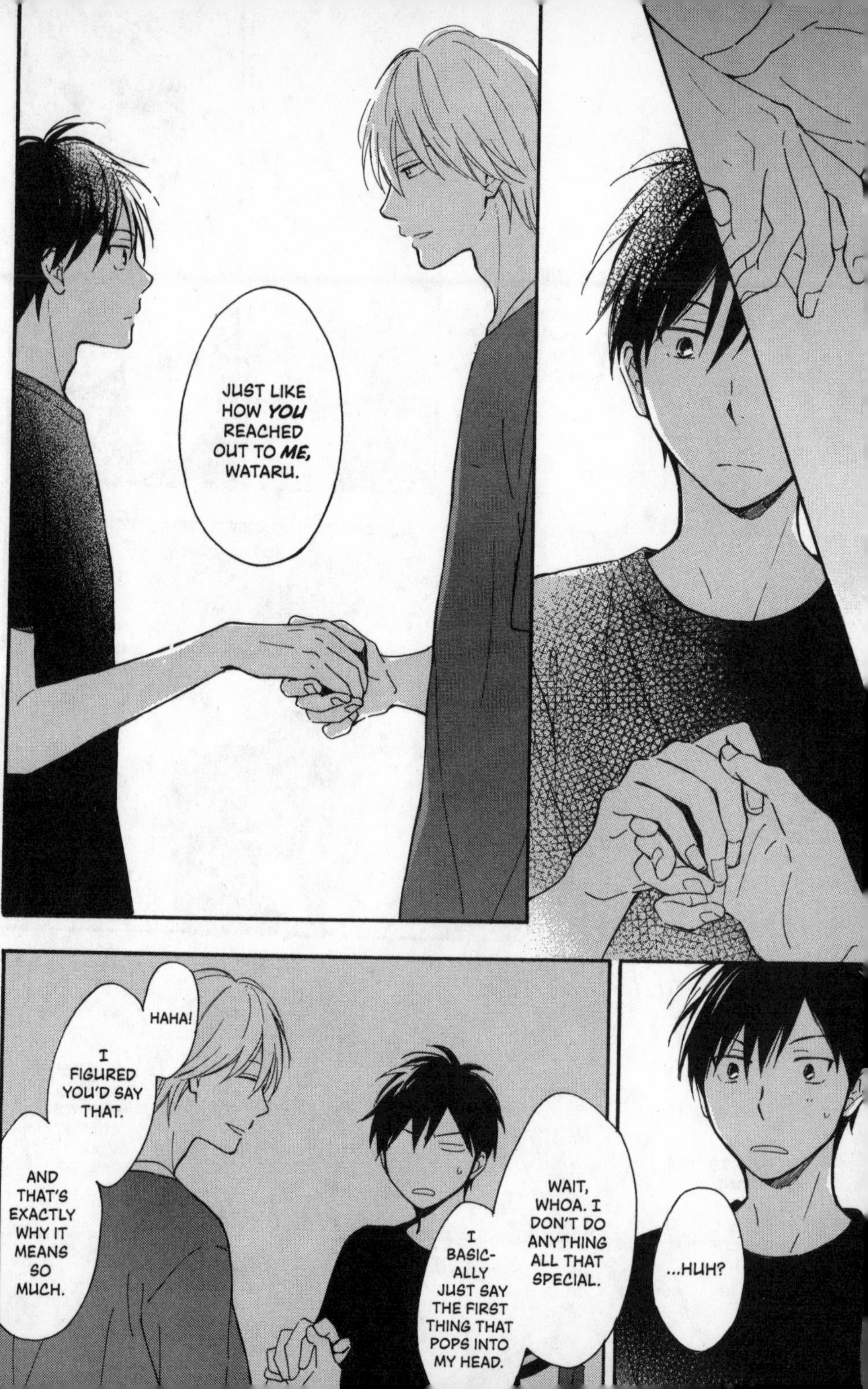
JUST LIKE HOW *YOU* REACHED OUT TO *ME,* WATARU.
...HUH?
WAIT, WHOA. I DON'T DO ANYTHING ALL THAT SPECIAL.
I BASIC-ALLY JUST SAY THE FIRST THING THAT POPS INTO MY HEAD.
HAHA!
I FIGURED YOU'D SAY THAT.
AND THAT'S EXACTLY WHY IT MEANS SO MUCH.

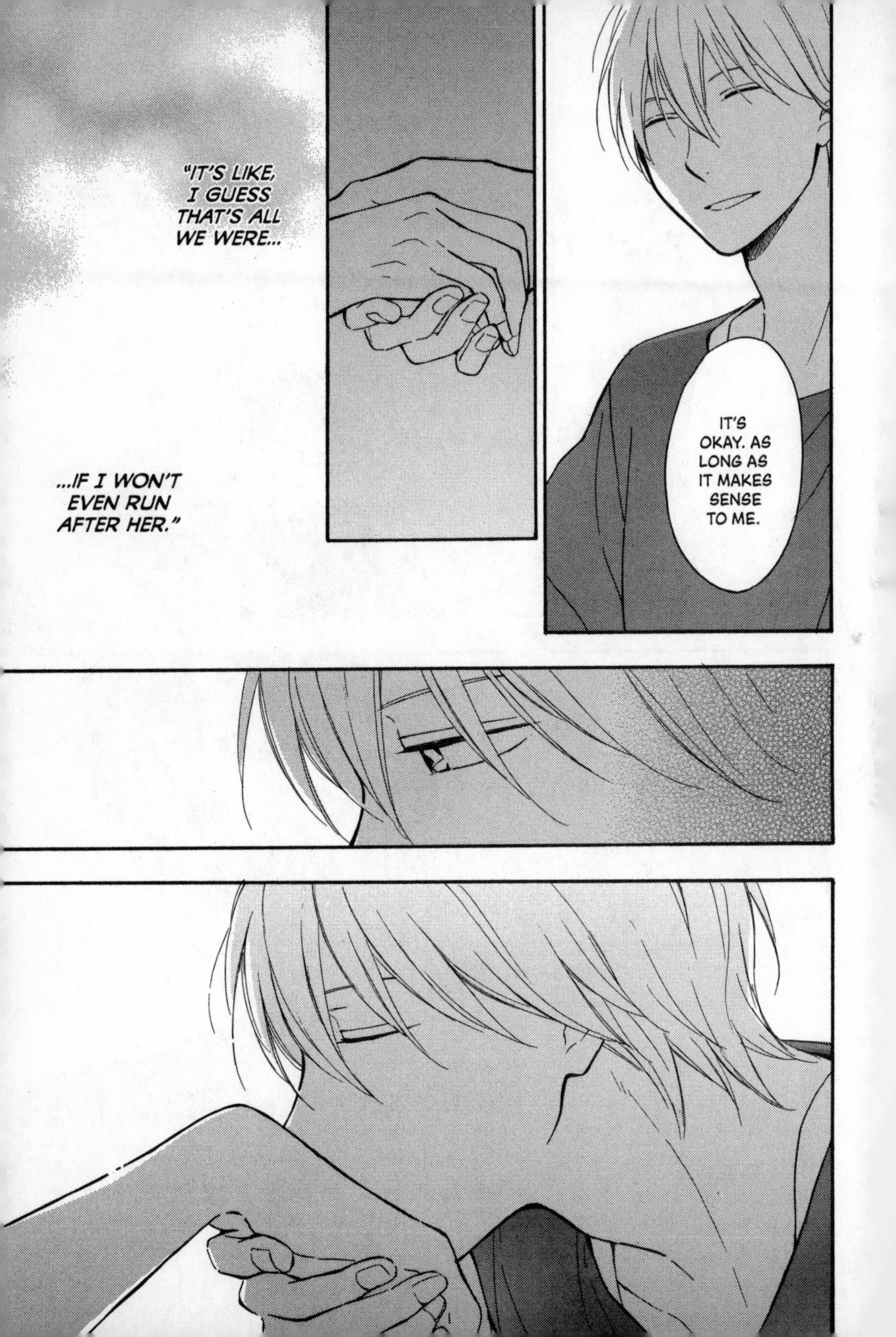
IT'S OKAY. AS LONG AS IT MAKES SENSE TO ME.
"IT'S LIKE, I GUESS THAT'S ALL WE WERE...
...IF I WON'T EVEN RUN AFTER HER."

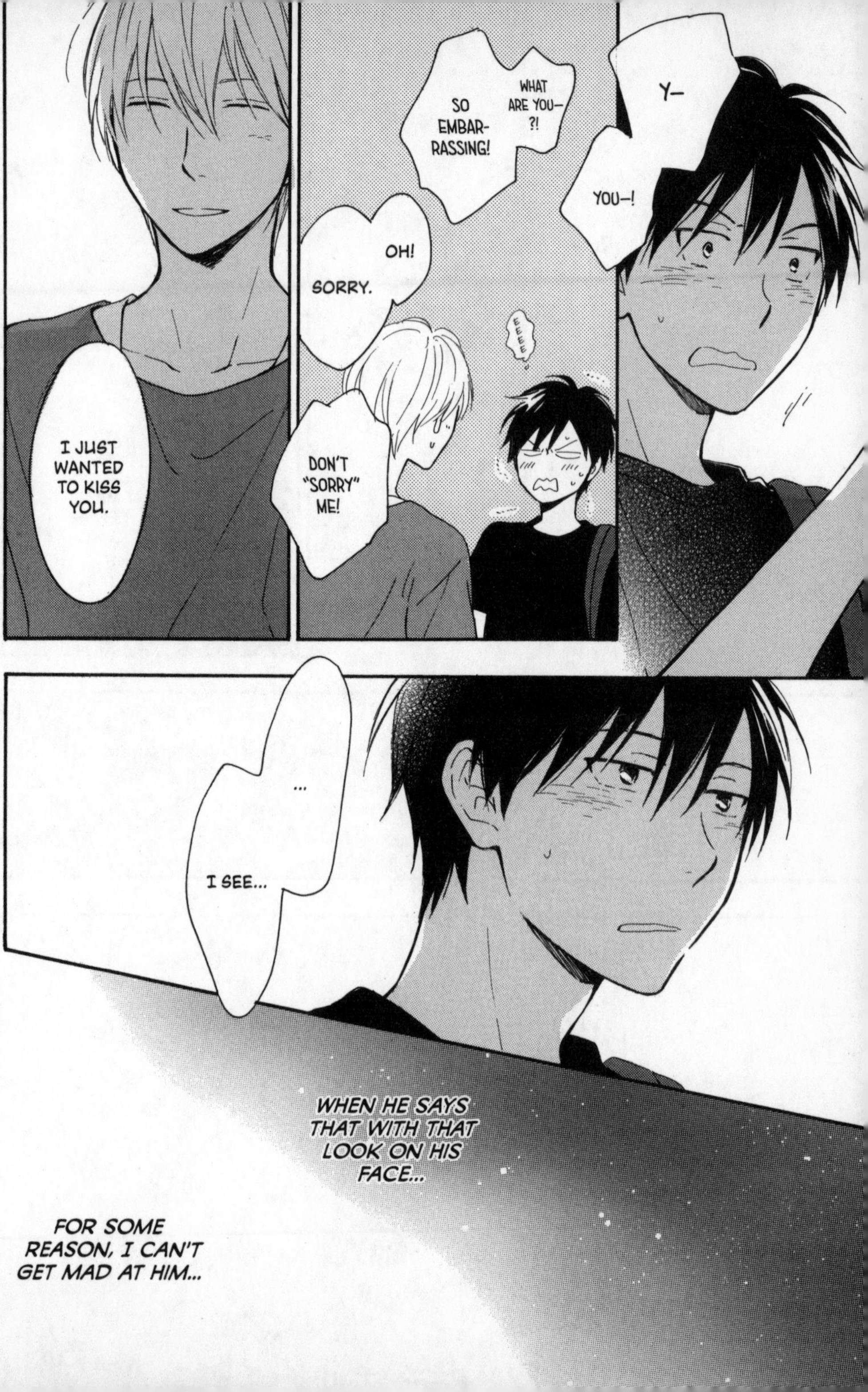
Y—
YOU—!
WHAT ARE YOU—?!
SO EMBARRASSING!
OH!
SORRY.
DON'T "SORRY" ME!
I JUST WANTED TO KISS YOU.
...
I SEE...
WHEN HE SAYS THAT WITH THAT LOOK ON HIS FACE...
FOR SOME REASON, I CAN'T GET MAD AT HIM...

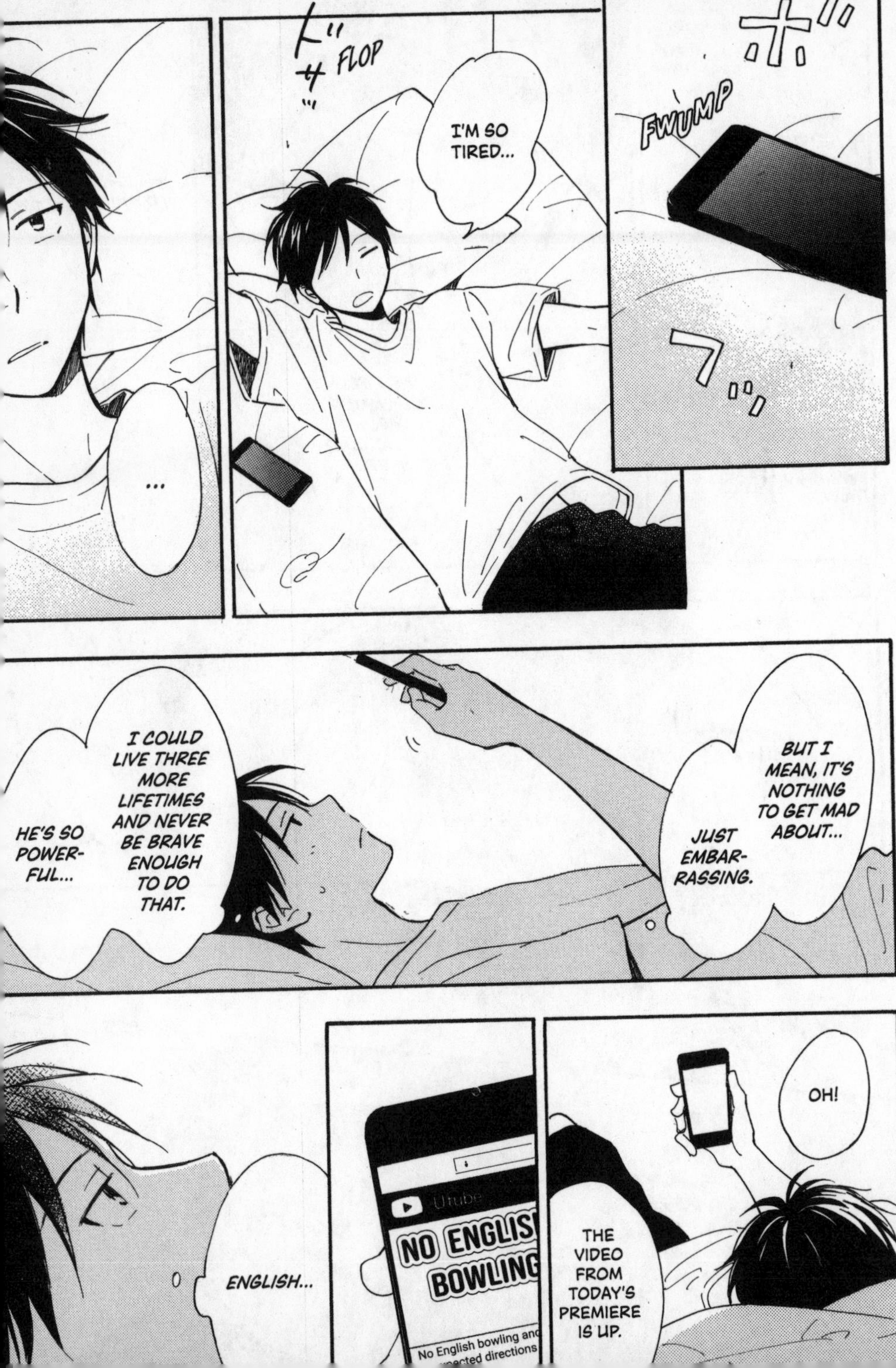
ポフッ
FWUMP
ドサッ
FLOP
I'M SO TIRED...
...
BUT I MEAN, IT'S NOTHING TO GET MAD ABOUT...
JUST EMBARRASSING.
I COULD LIVE THREE MORE LIFETIMES AND NEVER BE BRAVE ENOUGH TO DO THAT.
HE'S SO POWERFUL...
OH!
THE VIDEO FROM TODAY'S PREMIERE IS UP.
Utube
BOWLING
No English bowling and
ENGLISH...

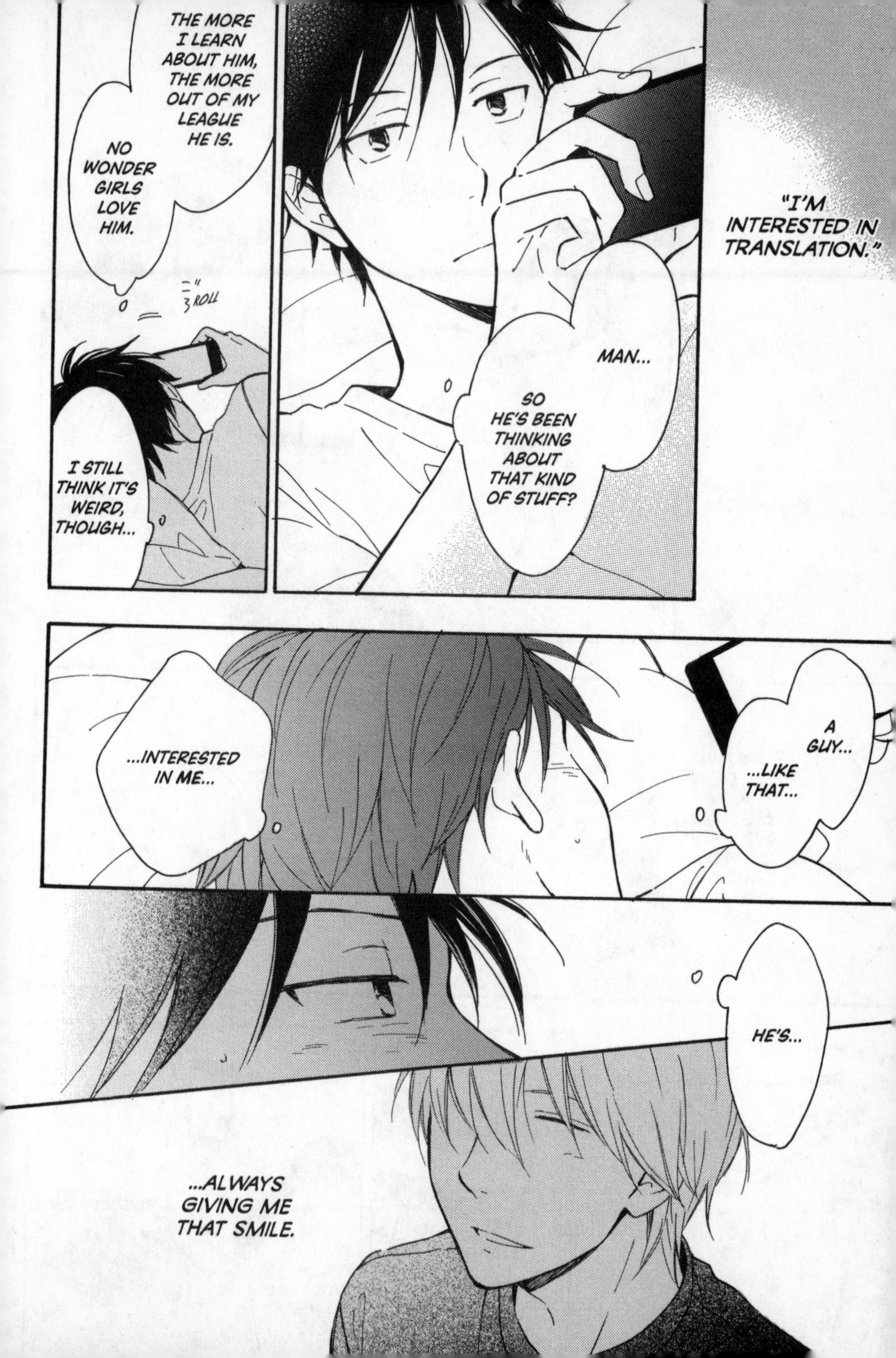
"I'M INTERESTED IN TRANSLATION."
MAN...
SO HE'S BEEN THINKING ABOUT THAT KIND OF STUFF?
THE MORE I LEARN ABOUT HIM, THE MORE OUT OF MY LEAGUE HE IS.
NO WONDER GIRLS LOVE HIM.
ROLL
I STILL THINK IT'S WEIRD, THOUGH...
A GUY...
...LIKE THAT...
...INTERESTED IN ME...
HE'S...
...ALWAYS GIVING ME THAT SMILE.

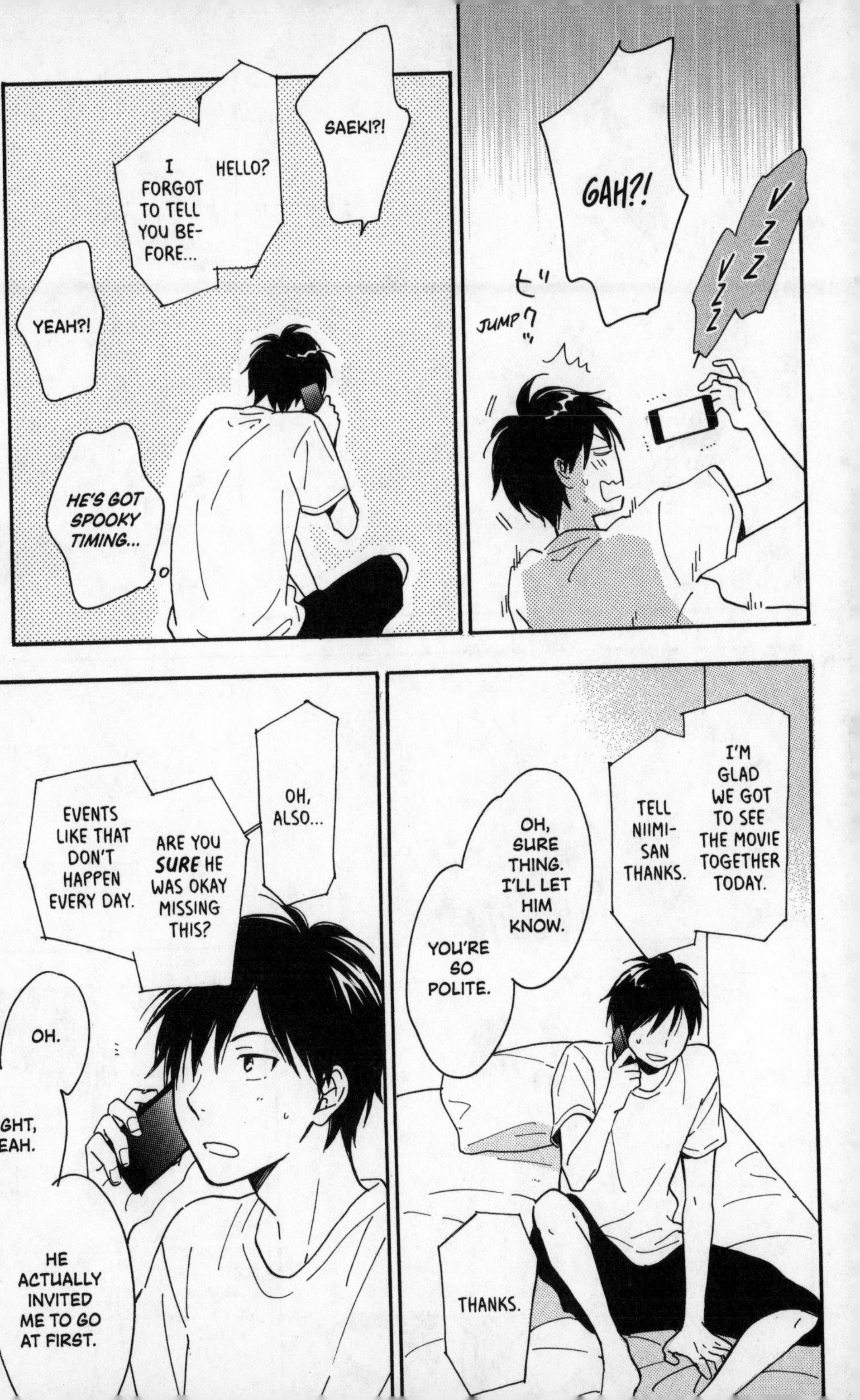
VZZ
VZZ
GAH?!
ビ
JUMP
SAEKI?!
HELLO?
I FORGOT TO TELL YOU BE-FORE...
YEAH?!
HE'S GOT SPOOKY TIMING...
I'M GLAD WE GOT TO SEE THE MOVIE TOGETHER TODAY.
TELL NIIMI-SAN THANKS.
OH, SURE THING. I'LL LET HIM KNOW.
YOU'RE SO POLITE.
THANKS.
OH, ALSO...
ARE YOU SURE HE WAS OKAY MISSING THIS?
EVENTS LIKE THAT DON'T HAPPEN EVERY DAY.
OH.
RIGHT, YEAH.
HE ACTUALLY INVITED ME TO GO AT FIRST.

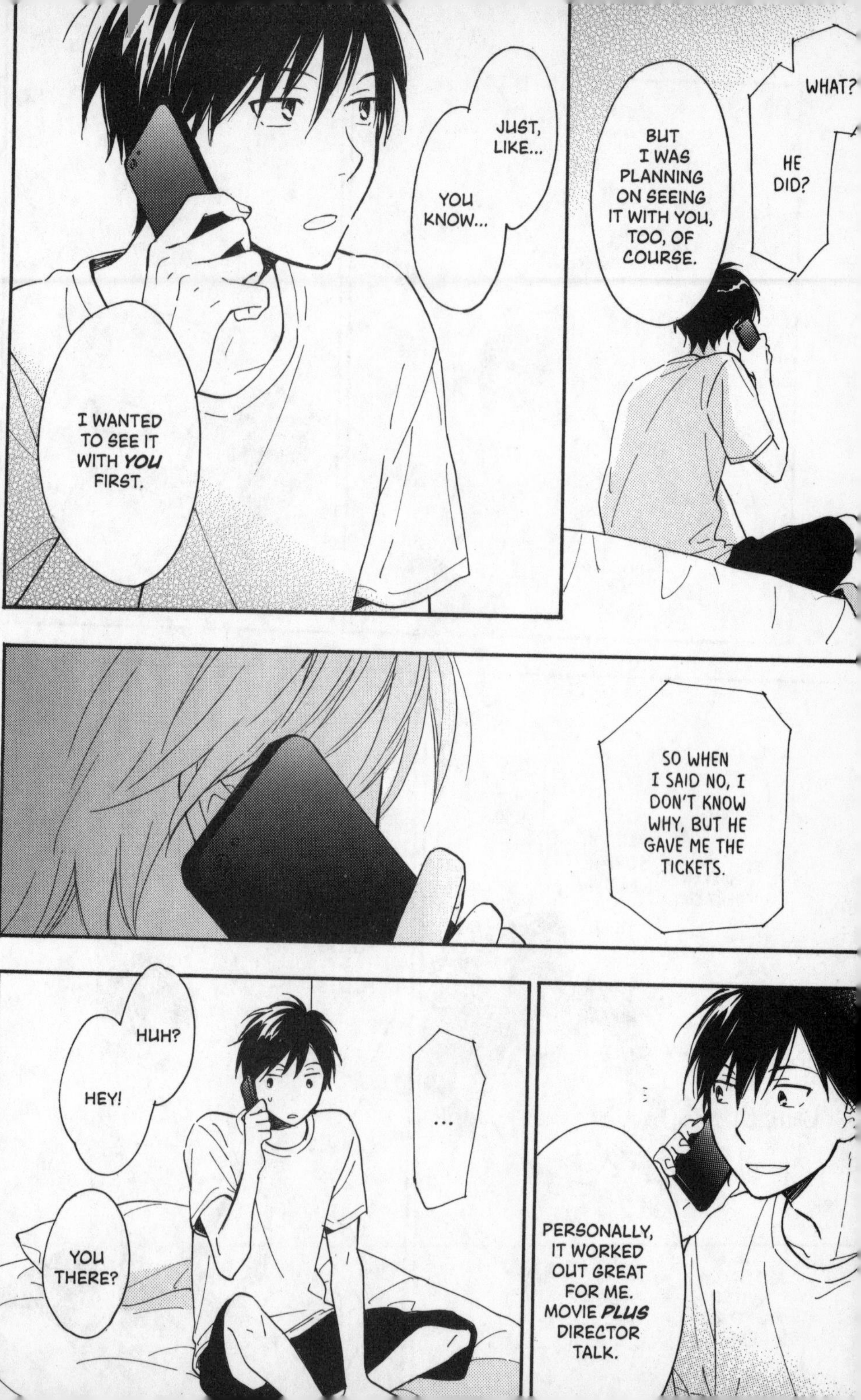
WHAT?
HE DID?
BUT I WAS PLANNING ON SEEING IT WITH YOU, TOO, OF COURSE.
JUST, LIKE...
YOU KNOW...
I WANTED TO SEE IT WITH *YOU* FIRST.
SO WHEN I SAID NO, I DON'T KNOW WHY, BUT HE GAVE ME THE TICKETS.
PERSONALLY, IT WORKED OUT GREAT FOR ME. MOVIE *PLUS* DIRECTOR TALK.
...
HUH?
HEY!
YOU THERE?

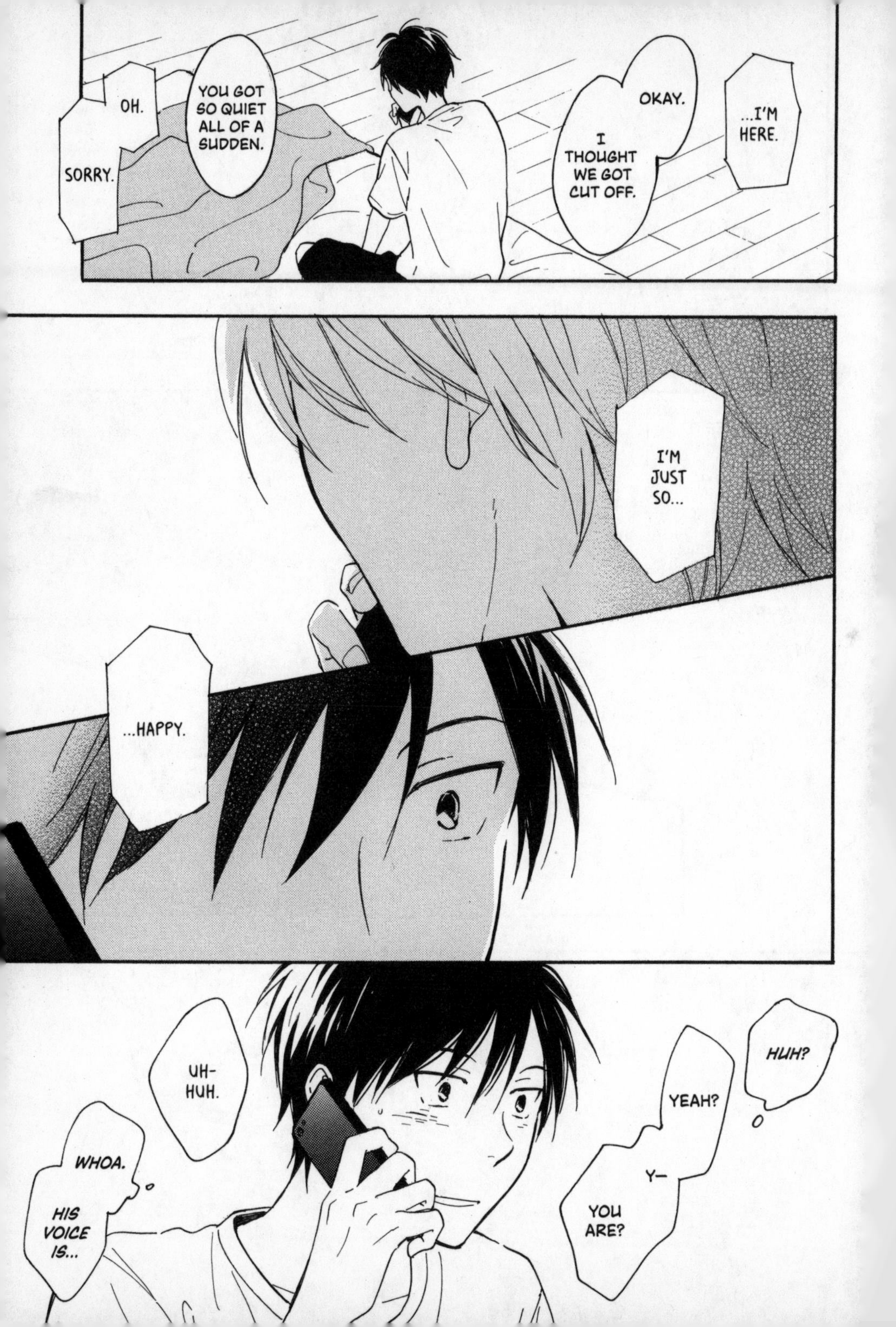
...I'M HERE.
OKAY.
I THOUGHT WE GOT CUT OFF.
YOU GOT SO QUIET ALL OF A SUDDEN.
OH.
SORRY.
I'M JUST SO...
...HAPPY.
HUH?
YEAH?
Y—
YOU ARE?
UH-HUH.
WHOA.
HIS VOICE IS...

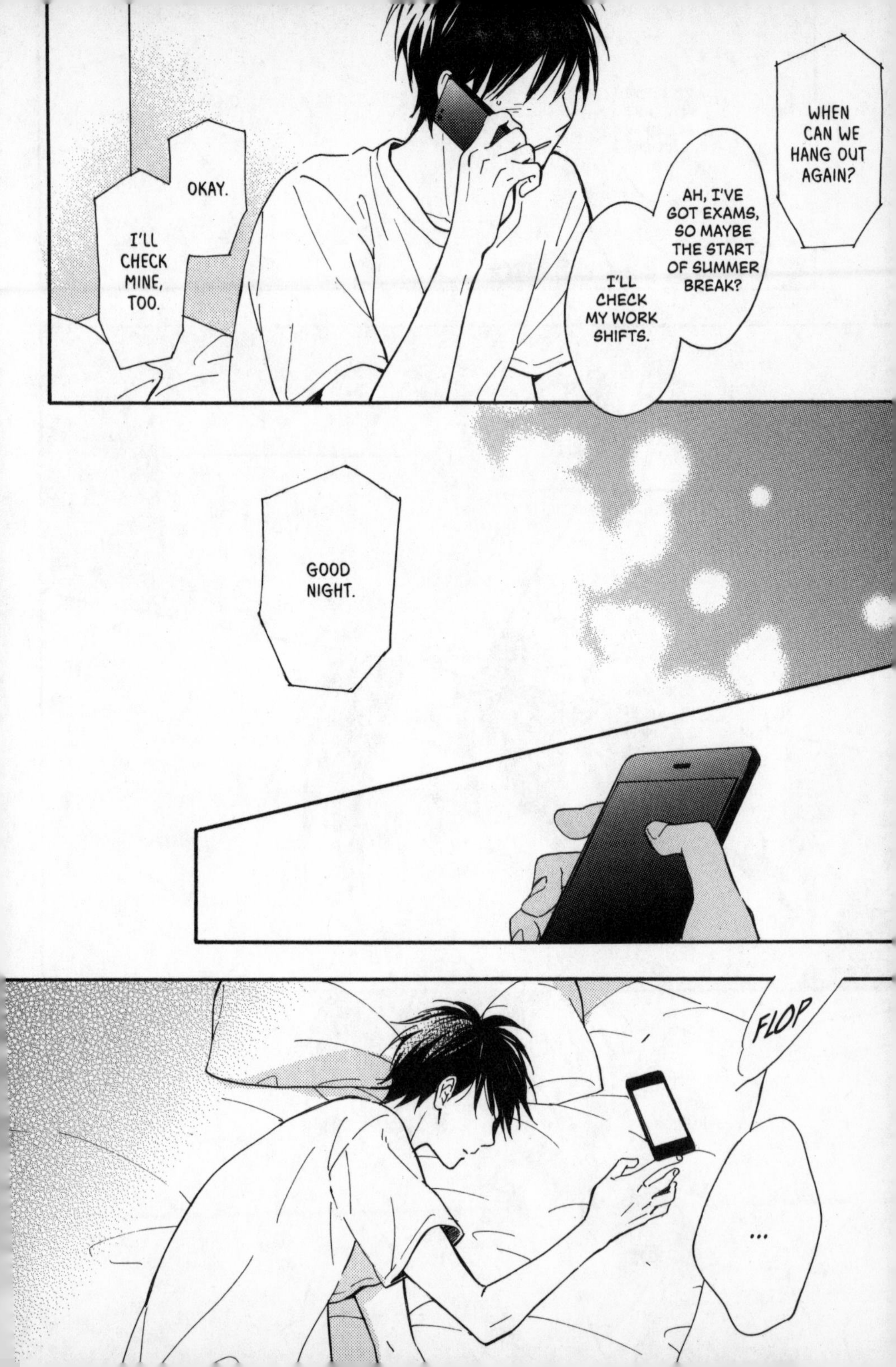
WHEN CAN WE HANG OUT AGAIN?
AH, I'VE GOT EXAMS, SO MAYBE THE START OF SUMMER BREAK?
I'LL CHECK MY WORK SHIFTS.
OKAY.
I'LL CHECK MINE, TOO.
GOOD NIGHT.
FLOP
...

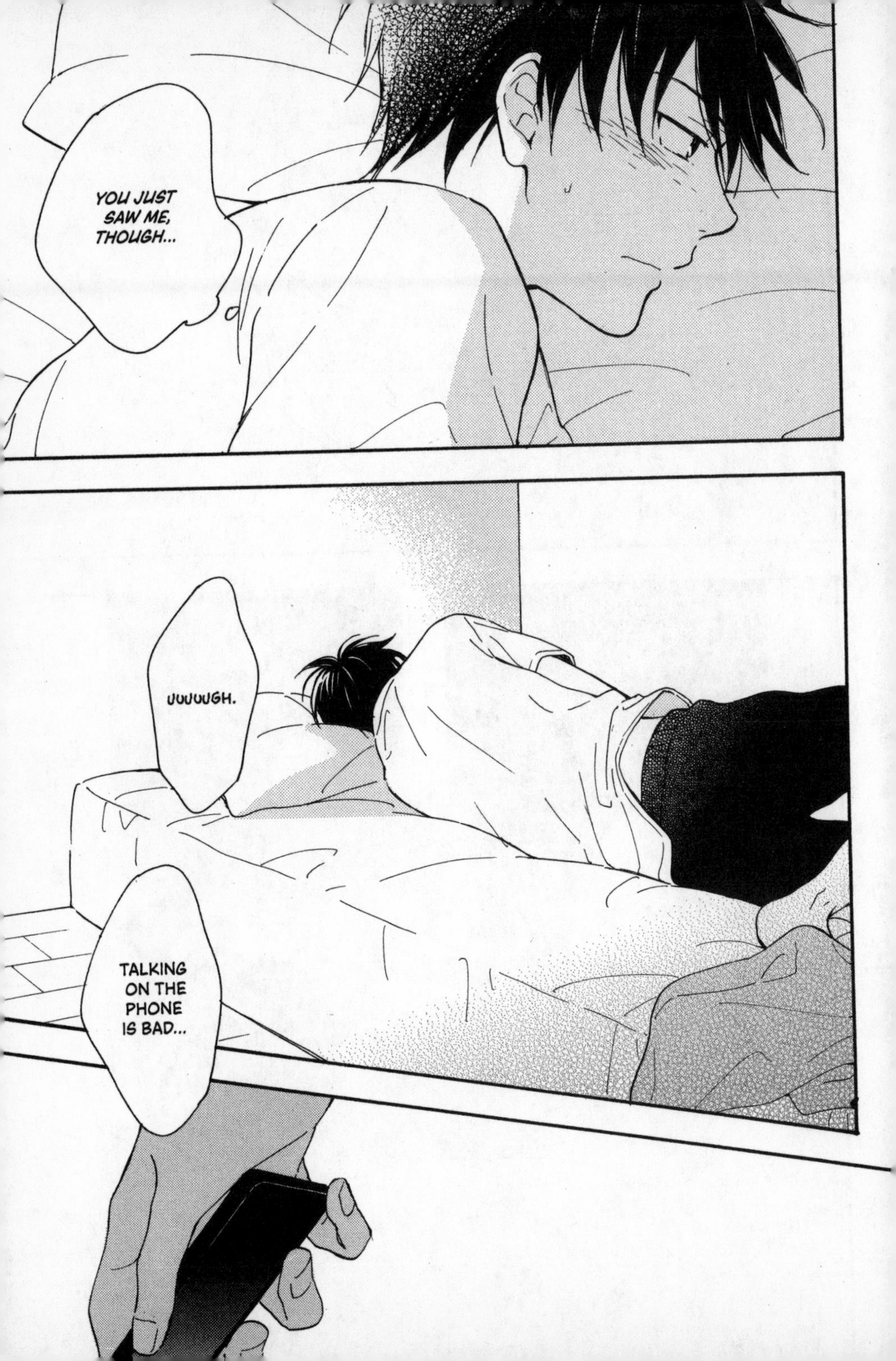
YOU JUST SAW ME, THOUGH...
UUUUUGH.
TALKING ON THE PHONE IS BAD...

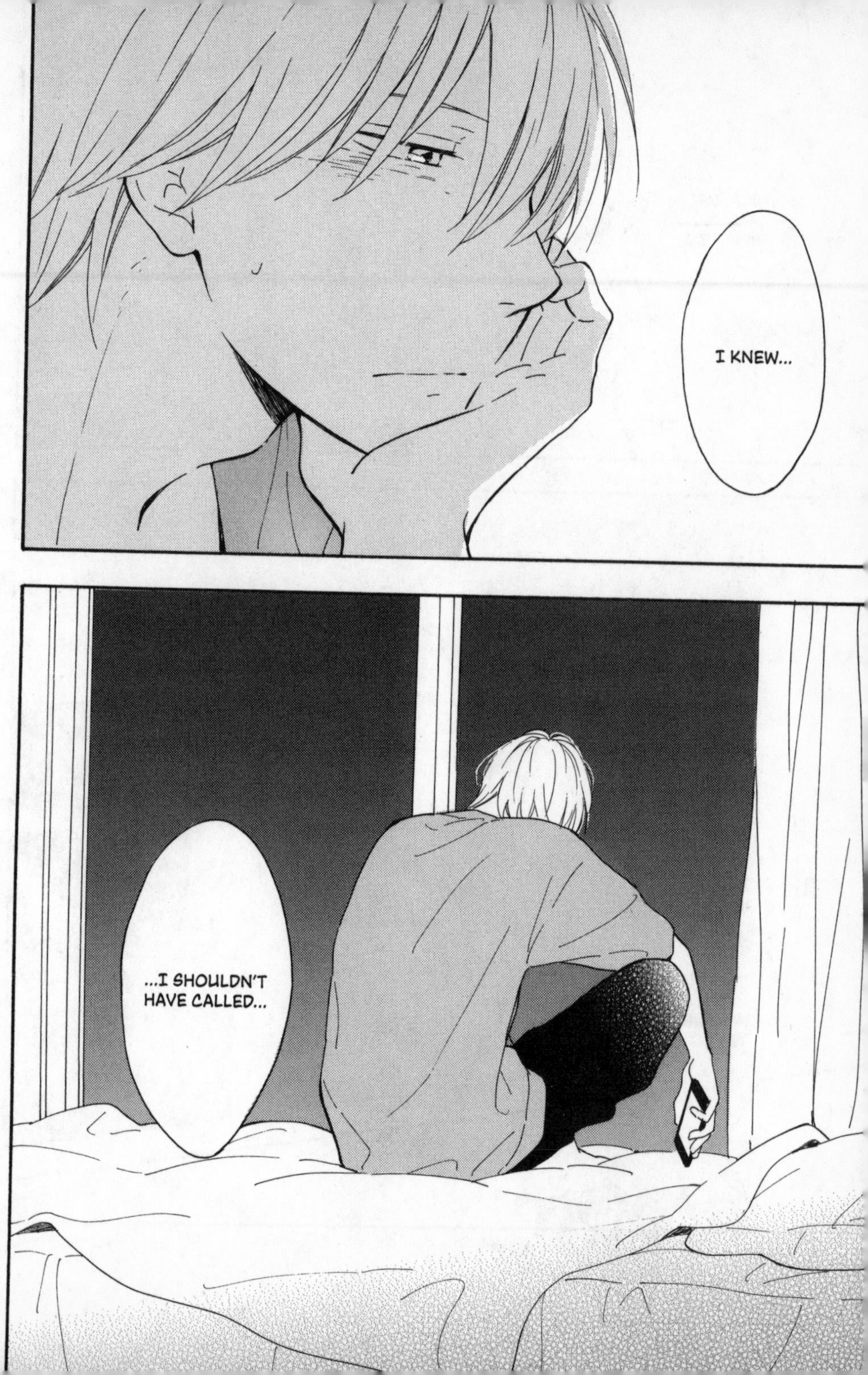
I KNEW...
...I SHOULDN'T HAVE CALLED...

MY SUMMER OF YOU

VOL.2: THE SUMMER WITH YOU

MY SUMMER OF YOU

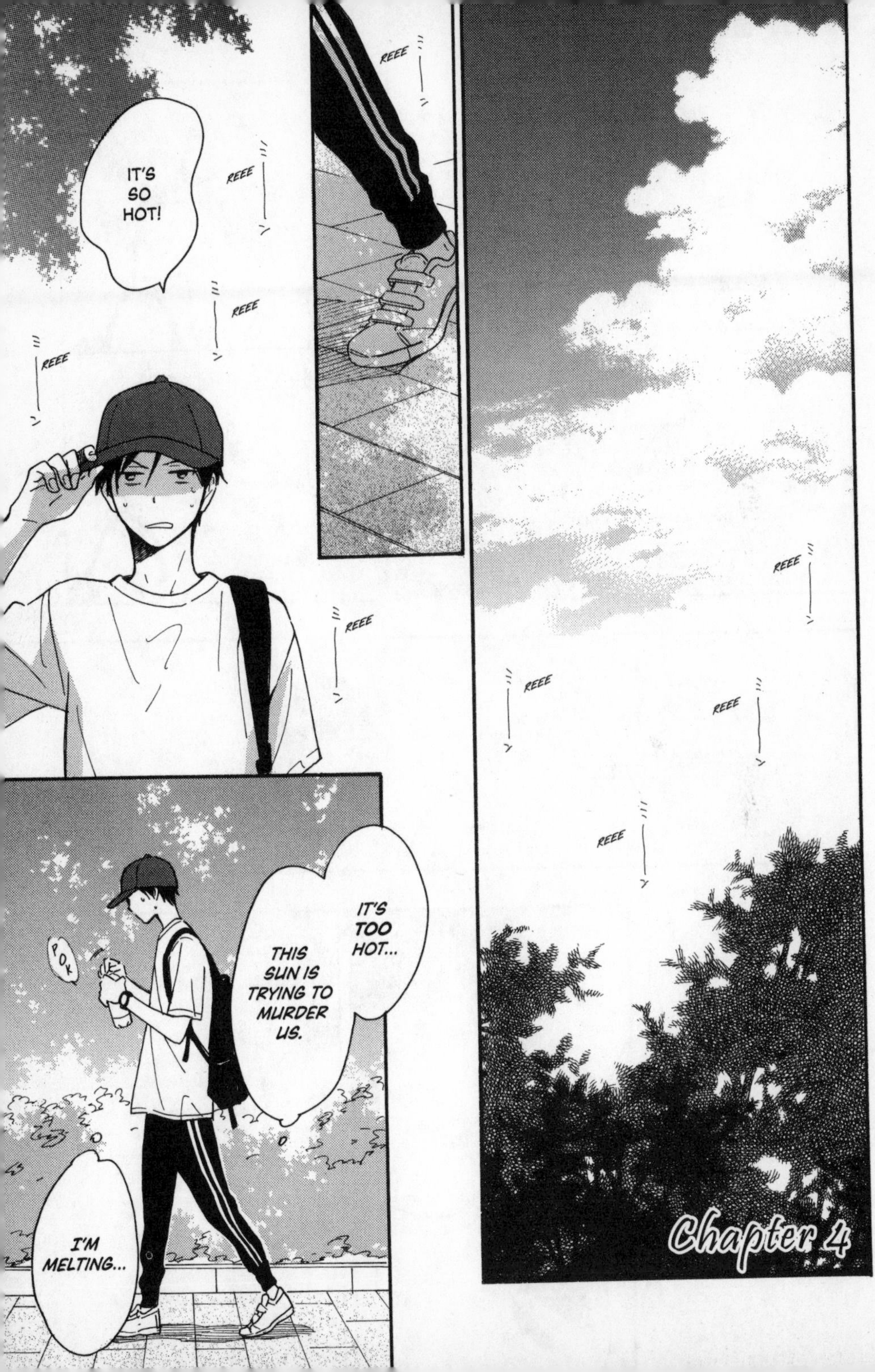

REEE
REEE
REEE
REEE
REEE
Chapter 4
REEE
REEE
IT'S SO HOT!
REEE
REEE
REEE
IT'S TOO HOT...
THIS SUN IS TRYING TO MURDER US.
POK
I'M MELTING...

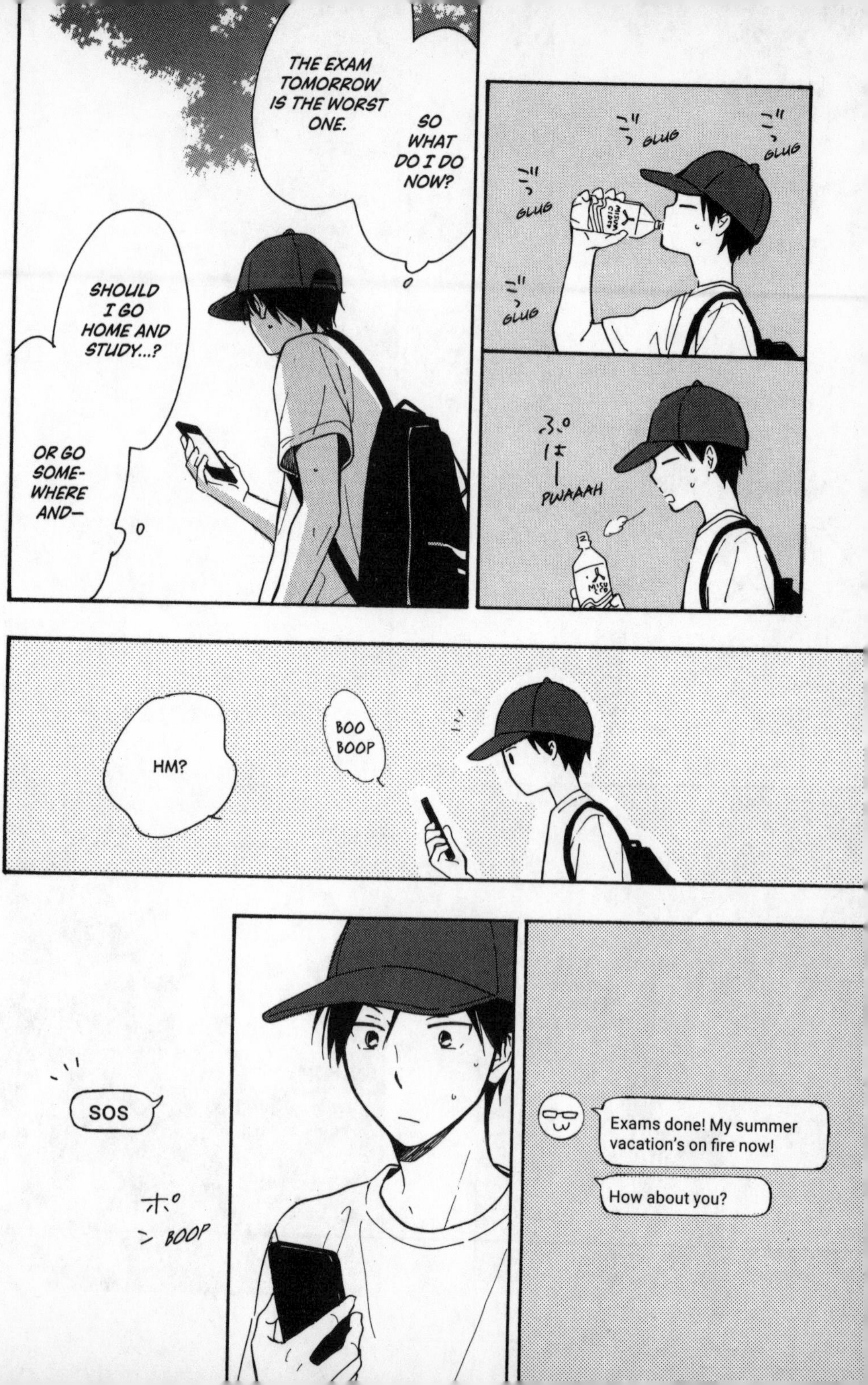
ごっ GLUG
ごっ GLUG
ごっ GLUG
ごっ GLUG
ぷはー PWAAAH
THE EXAM TOMORROW IS THE WORST ONE.
SO WHAT DO I DO NOW?
SHOULD I GO HOME AND STUDY...?
OR GO SOME-WHERE AND—
BOO BOOP
HM?
Exams done! My summer vacation's on fire now!
How about you?
SOS
ポ BOOP

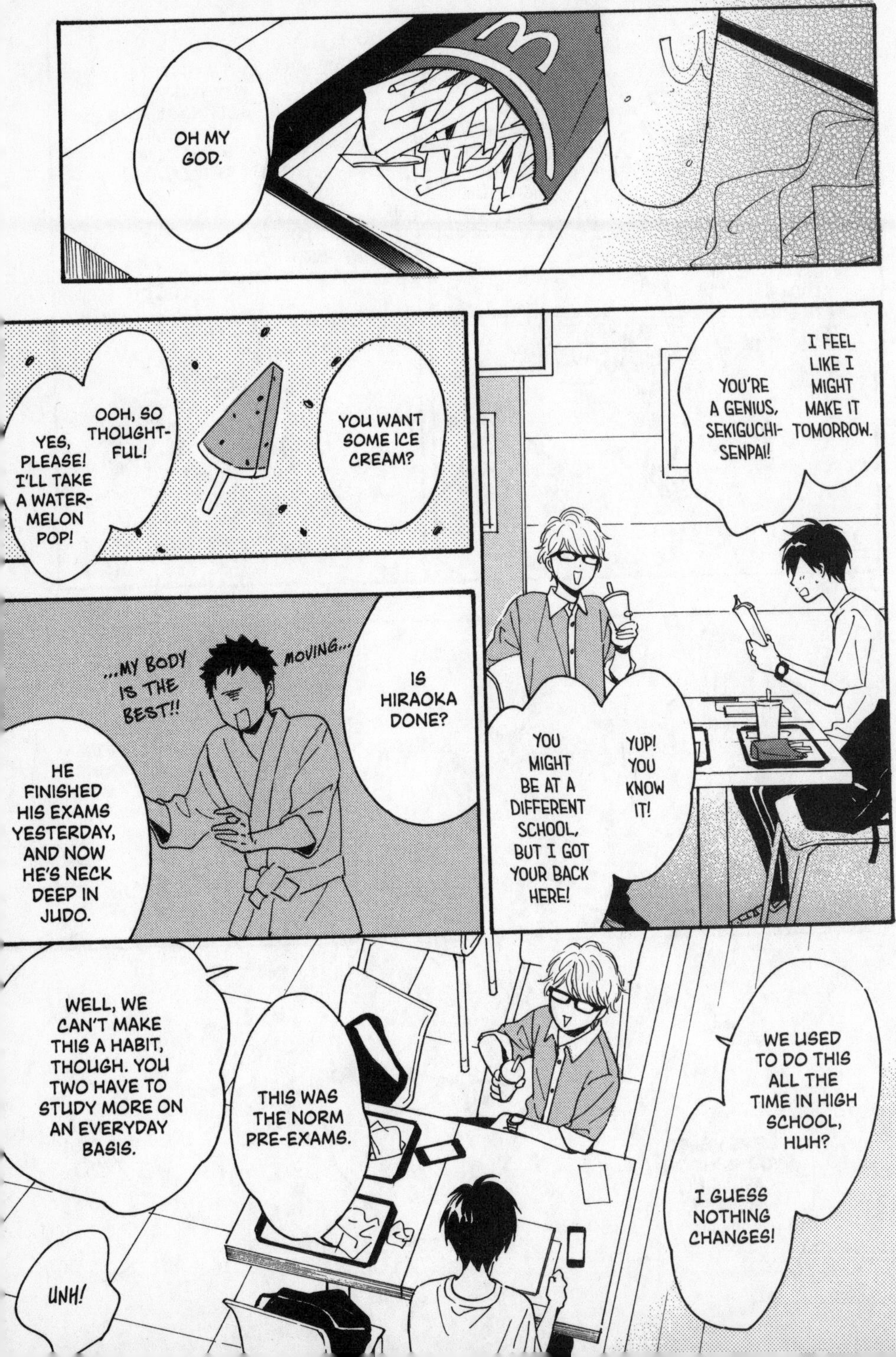

OH MY GOD.
I FEEL LIKE I MIGHT MAKE IT TOMORROW.
YOU'RE A GENIUS, SEKIGUCHI-SENPAI!
YUP! YOU KNOW IT!
YOU MIGHT BE AT A DIFFERENT SCHOOL, BUT I GOT YOUR BACK HERE!
YOU WANT SOME ICE CREAM?
OOH, SO THOUGHTFUL!
YES, PLEASE! I'LL TAKE A WATERMELON POP!
IS HIRAOKA DONE?
MOVING...
...MY BODY IS THE BEST!!
HE FINISHED HIS EXAMS YESTERDAY, AND NOW HE'S NECK DEEP IN JUDO.
WE USED TO DO THIS ALL THE TIME IN HIGH SCHOOL, HUH?
I GUESS NOTHING CHANGES!
THIS WAS THE NORM PRE-EXAMS.
WELL, WE CAN'T MAKE THIS A HABIT, THOUGH. YOU TWO HAVE TO STUDY MORE ON AN EVERYDAY BASIS.
UNH!

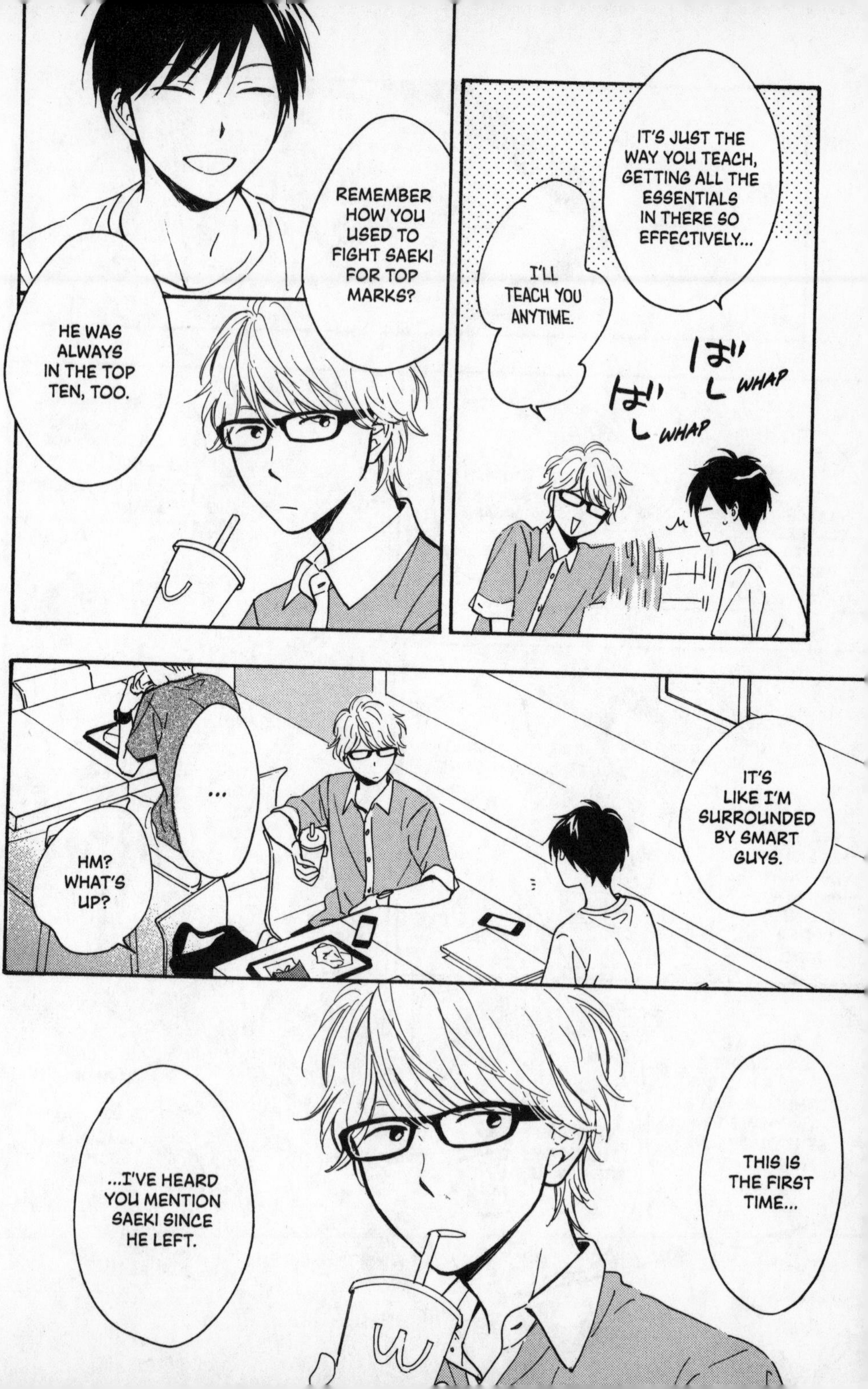
IT'S JUST THE WAY YOU TEACH, GETTING ALL THE ESSENTIALS IN THERE SO EFFECTIVELY...
I'LL TEACH YOU ANYTIME.
ばし WHAP
ばし WHAP
REMEMBER HOW YOU USED TO FIGHT SAEKI FOR TOP MARKS?
HE WAS ALWAYS IN THE TOP TEN, TOO.
IT'S LIKE I'M SURROUNDED BY SMART GUYS.
...
HM? WHAT'S UP?
THIS IS THE FIRST TIME...
...I'VE HEARD YOU MENTION SAEKI SINCE HE LEFT.

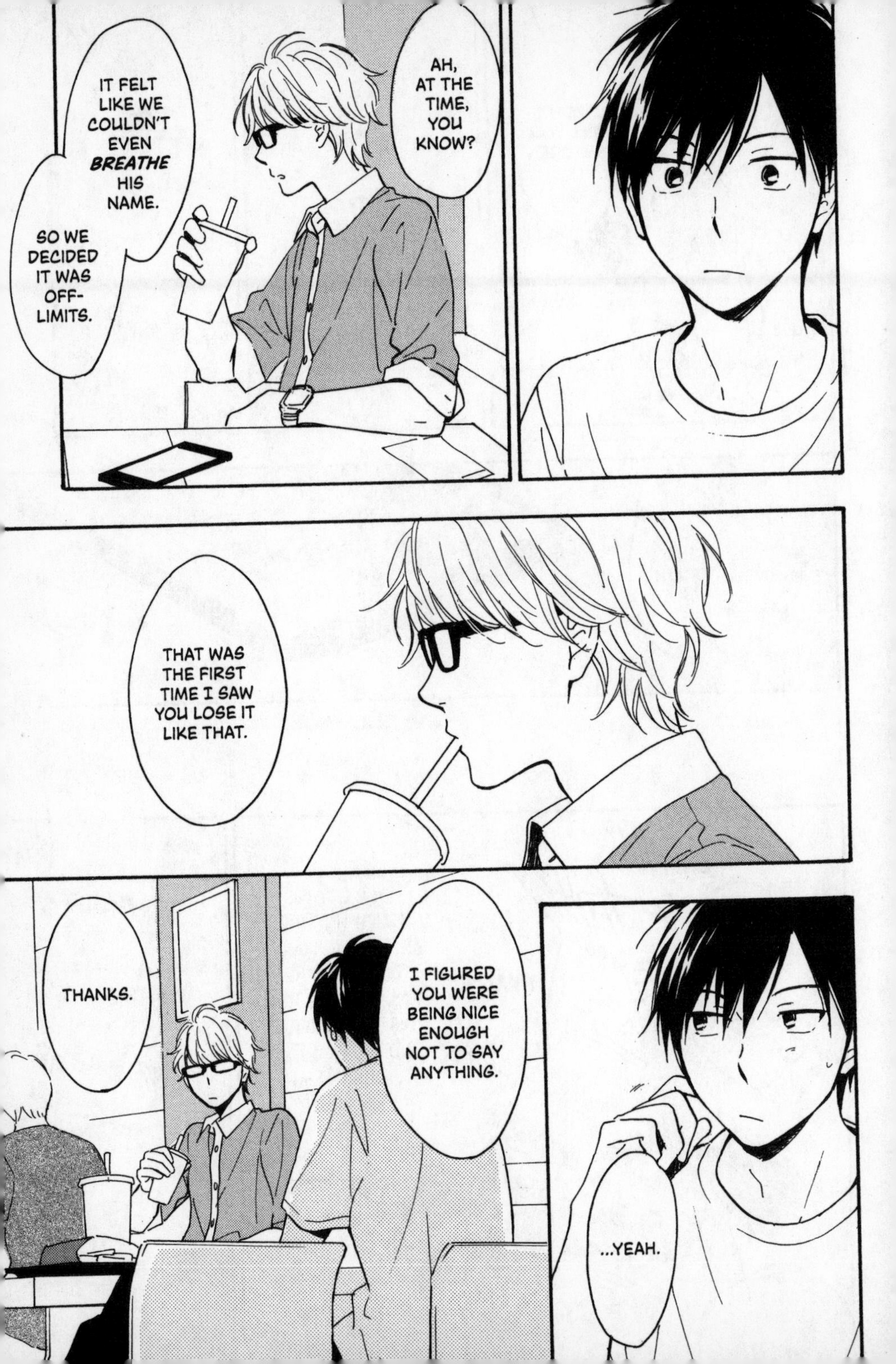
AH, AT THE TIME, YOU KNOW?
IT FELT LIKE WE COULDN'T EVEN BREATHE HIS NAME.
SO WE DECIDED IT WAS OFF-LIMITS.
THAT WAS THE FIRST TIME I SAW YOU LOSE IT LIKE THAT.
...YEAH.
I FIGURED YOU WERE BEING NICE ENOUGH NOT TO SAY ANYTHING.
THANKS.

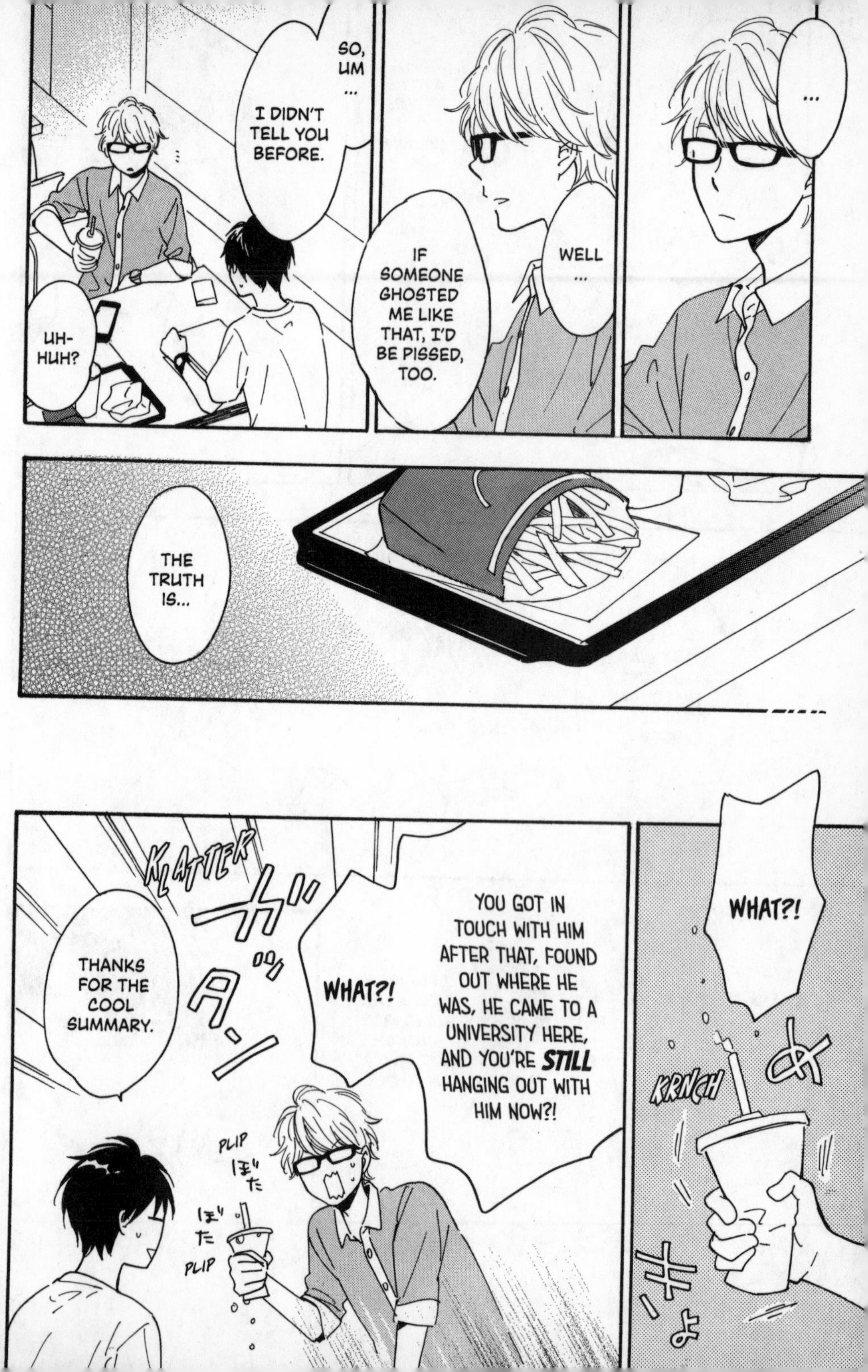
...
WELL ...
IF SOMEONE GHOSTED ME LIKE THAT, I'D BE PISSED, TOO.
SO, UM ...
I DIDN'T TELL YOU BEFORE.
UH-HUH?
THE TRUTH IS...
WHAT?!
KRNCH
YOU GOT IN TOUCH WITH HIM AFTER THAT, FOUND OUT WHERE HE WAS, HE CAME TO A UNIVERSITY HERE, AND YOU'RE **STILL** HANGING OUT WITH HIM NOW?!
WHAT?!
KLATTER
THANKS FOR THE COOL SUMMARY.
PLIP
PLIP

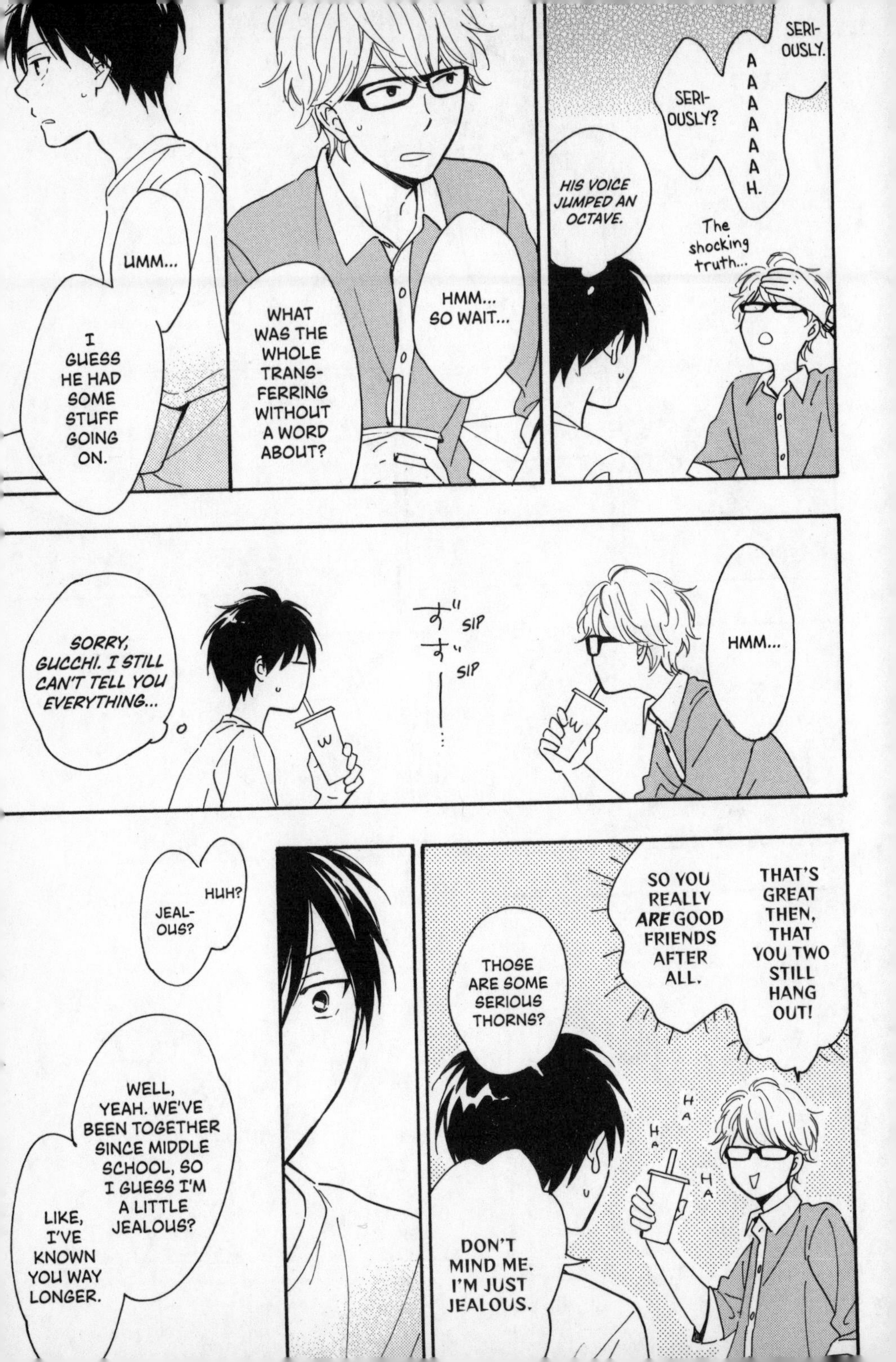
SERI-OUSLY.
SERI-OUSLY?
AAAAAAAH.
HIS VOICE JUMPED AN OCTAVE.
The shocking truth...
HMM... SO WAIT...
WHAT WAS THE WHOLE TRANS-FERRING WITHOUT A WORD ABOUT?
UMM...
I GUESS HE HAD SOME STUFF GOING ON.
HMM...
ず SIP
ず SIP
SORRY, GUCCHI. I STILL CAN'T TELL YOU EVERYTHING...
THAT'S GREAT THEN, THAT YOU TWO STILL HANG OUT!
SO YOU REALLY *ARE* GOOD FRIENDS AFTER ALL.
THOSE ARE SOME SERIOUS THORNS?
HA HA HA HA
DON'T MIND ME. I'M JUST JEALOUS.
HUH? JEAL-OUS?
WELL, YEAH. WE'VE BEEN TOGETHER SINCE MIDDLE SCHOOL, SO I GUESS I'M A LITTLE JEALOUS?
LIKE, I'VE KNOWN YOU WAY LONGER.

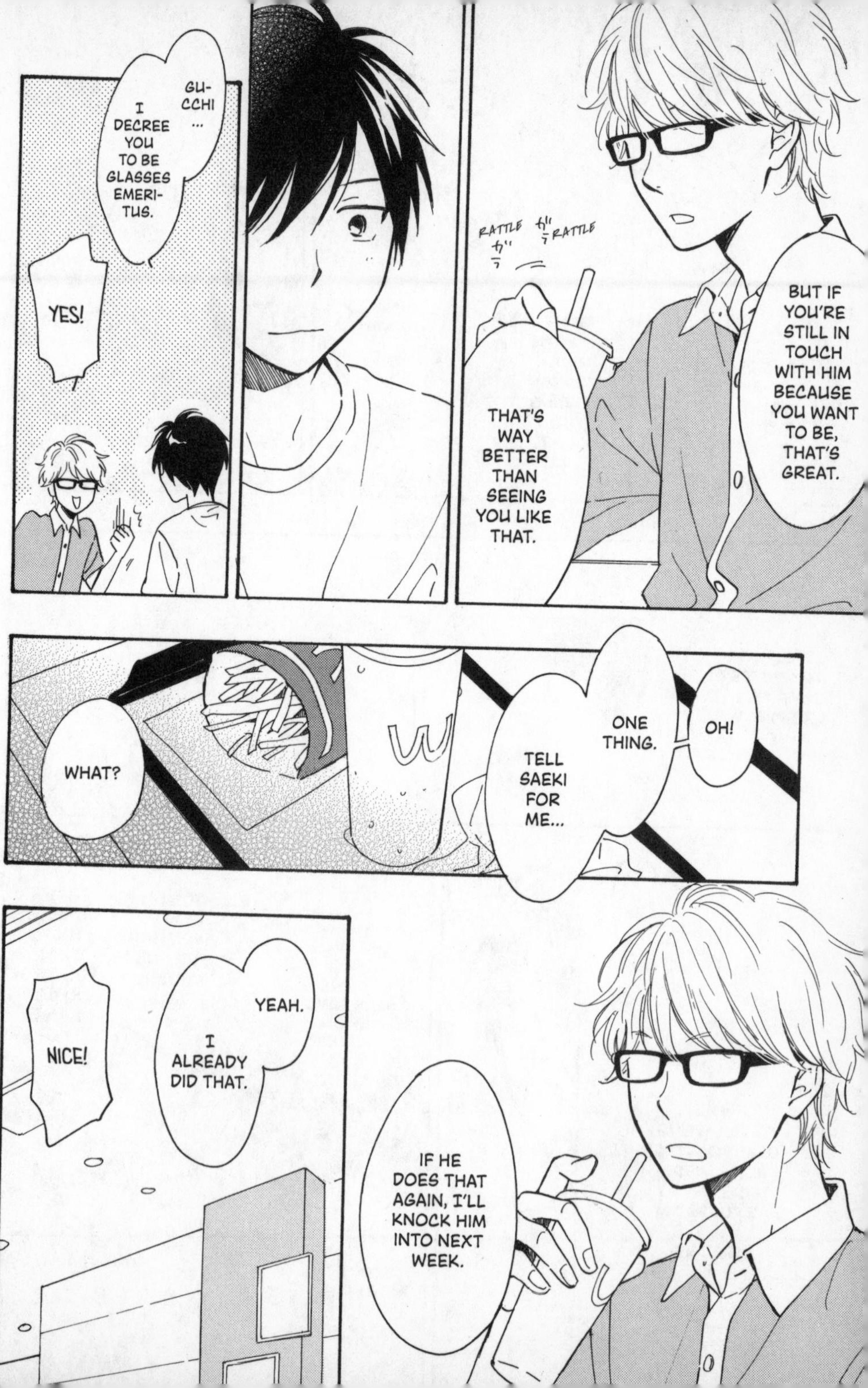
BUT IF YOU'RE STILL IN TOUCH WITH HIM BECAUSE YOU WANT TO BE, THAT'S GREAT.
RATTLE RATTLE
THAT'S WAY BETTER THAN SEEING YOU LIKE THAT.
GU-CCHI...
I DECREE YOU TO BE GLASSES EMERITUS.
YES!
OH!
ONE THING.
TELL SAEKI FOR ME...
WHAT?
IF HE DOES THAT AGAIN, I'LL KNOCK HIM INTO NEXT WEEK.
YEAH.
I ALREADY DID THAT.
NICE!

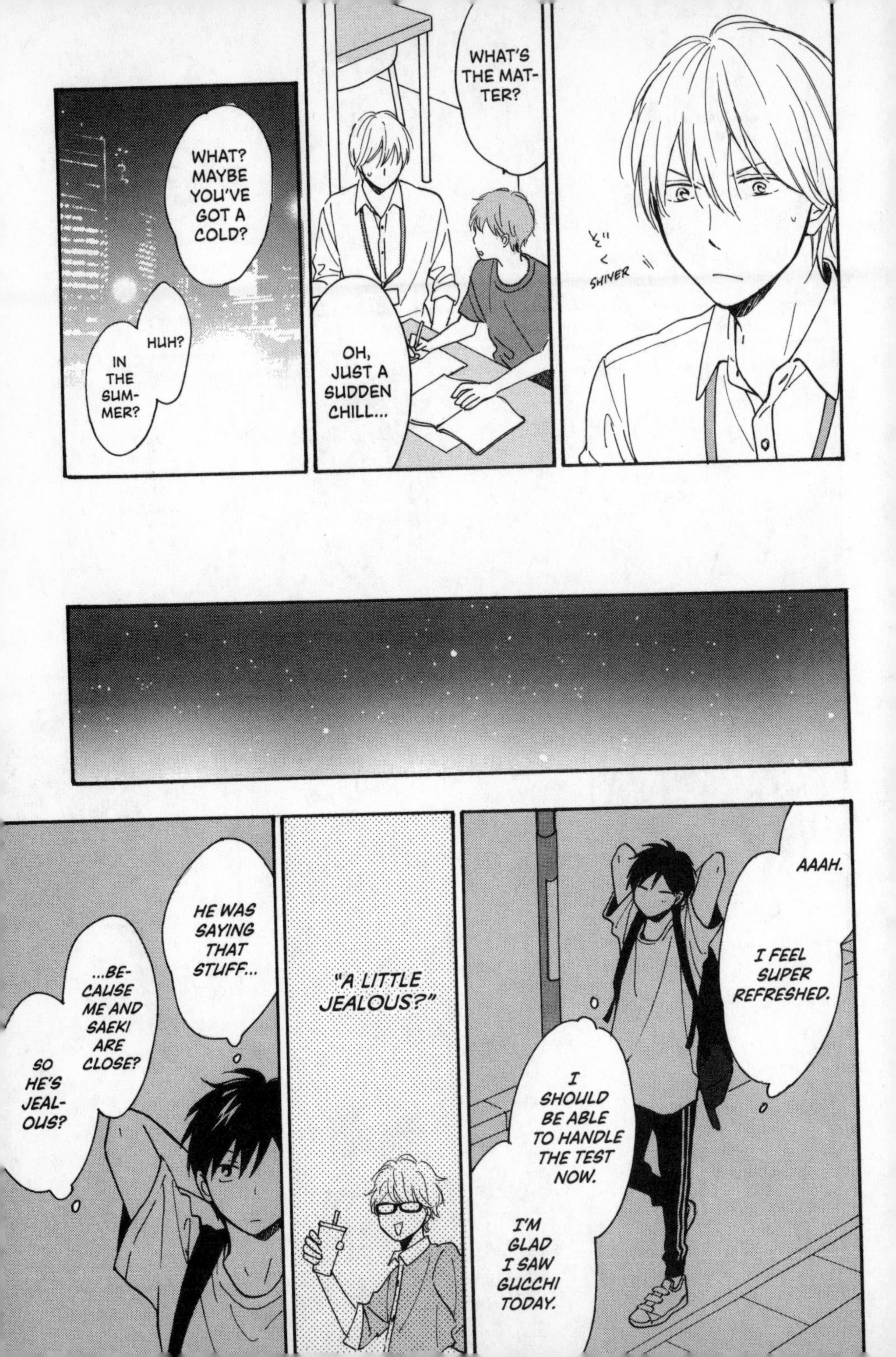
SHIVER
WHAT'S THE MATTER?
OH, JUST A SUDDEN CHILL...
WHAT? MAYBE YOU'VE GOT A COLD?
HUH? IN THE SUMMER?
AAAH.
I FEEL SUPER REFRESHED.
I SHOULD BE ABLE TO HANDLE THE TEST NOW.
I'M GLAD I SAW GUCCHI TODAY.
"A LITTLE JEALOUS?"
HE WAS SAYING THAT STUFF...
...BECAUSE ME AND SAEKI ARE CLOSE?
SO HE'S JEALOUS?

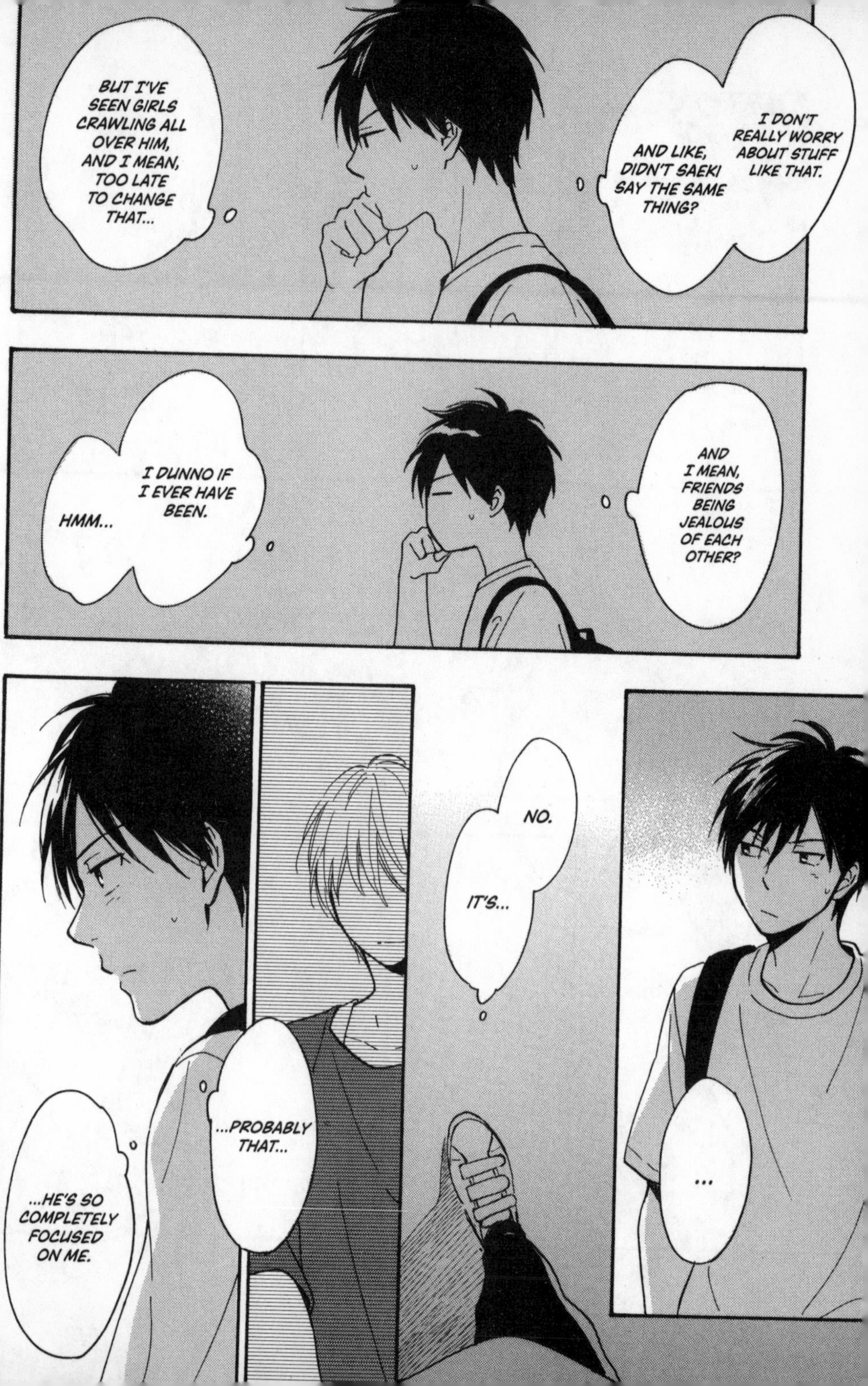
I DON'T REALLY WORRY ABOUT STUFF LIKE THAT.
AND LIKE, DIDN'T SAEKI SAY THE SAME THING?
BUT I'VE SEEN GIRLS CRAWLING ALL OVER HIM, AND I MEAN, TOO LATE TO CHANGE THAT...
AND I MEAN, FRIENDS BEING JEALOUS OF EACH OTHER?
I DUNNO IF I EVER HAVE BEEN.
HMM...
...
NO.
IT'S...
...PROBABLY THAT...
...HE'S SO COMPLETELY FOCUSED ON ME.

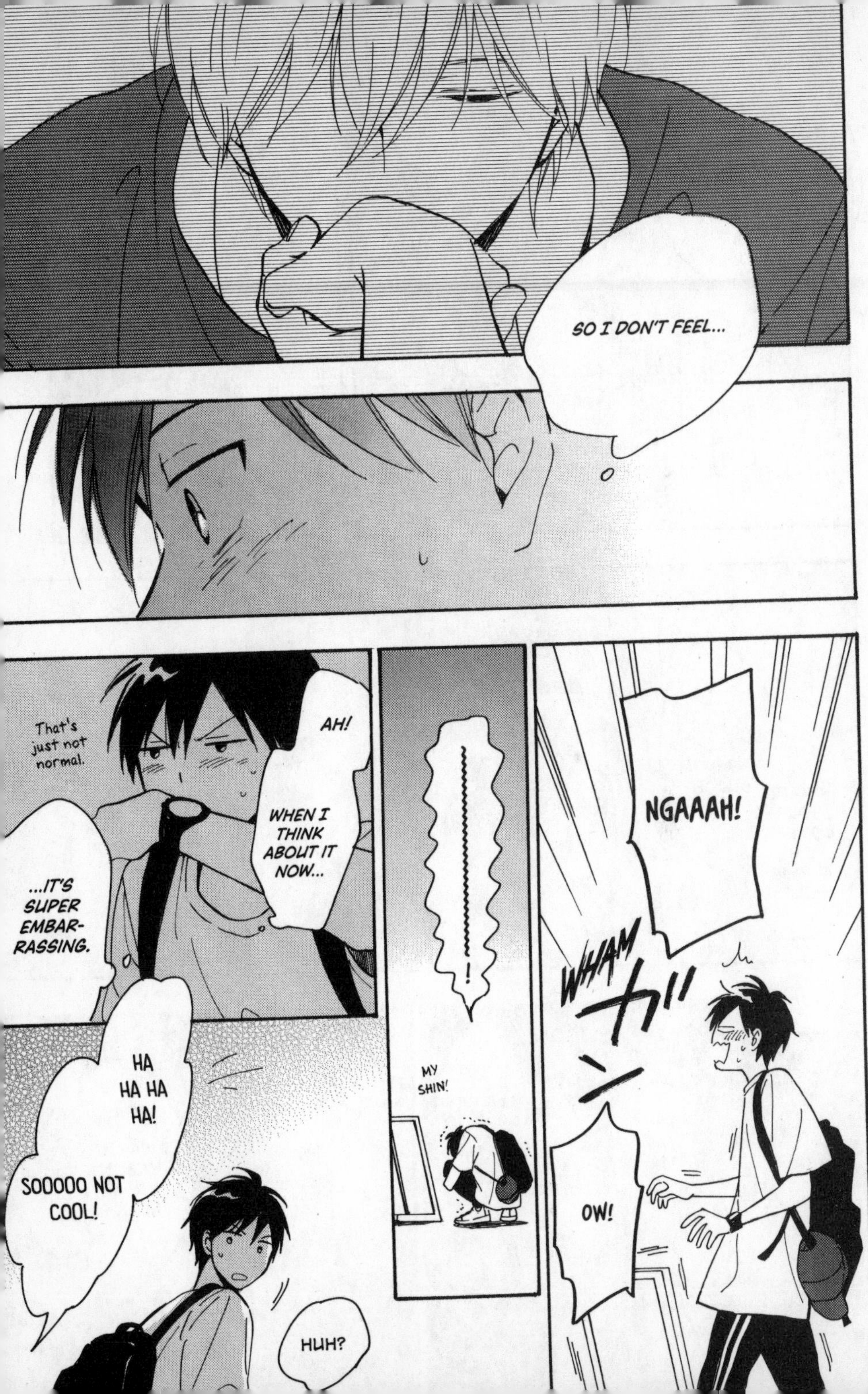

SO I DON'T FEEL...
NGAAAH!
WHAM
OW!
—!
MY SHIN!
AH!
WHEN I THINK ABOUT IT NOW...
...IT'S SUPER EMBARRASSING.
That's just not normal.
HA HA HA HA!
SOOOOO NOT COOL!
HUH?

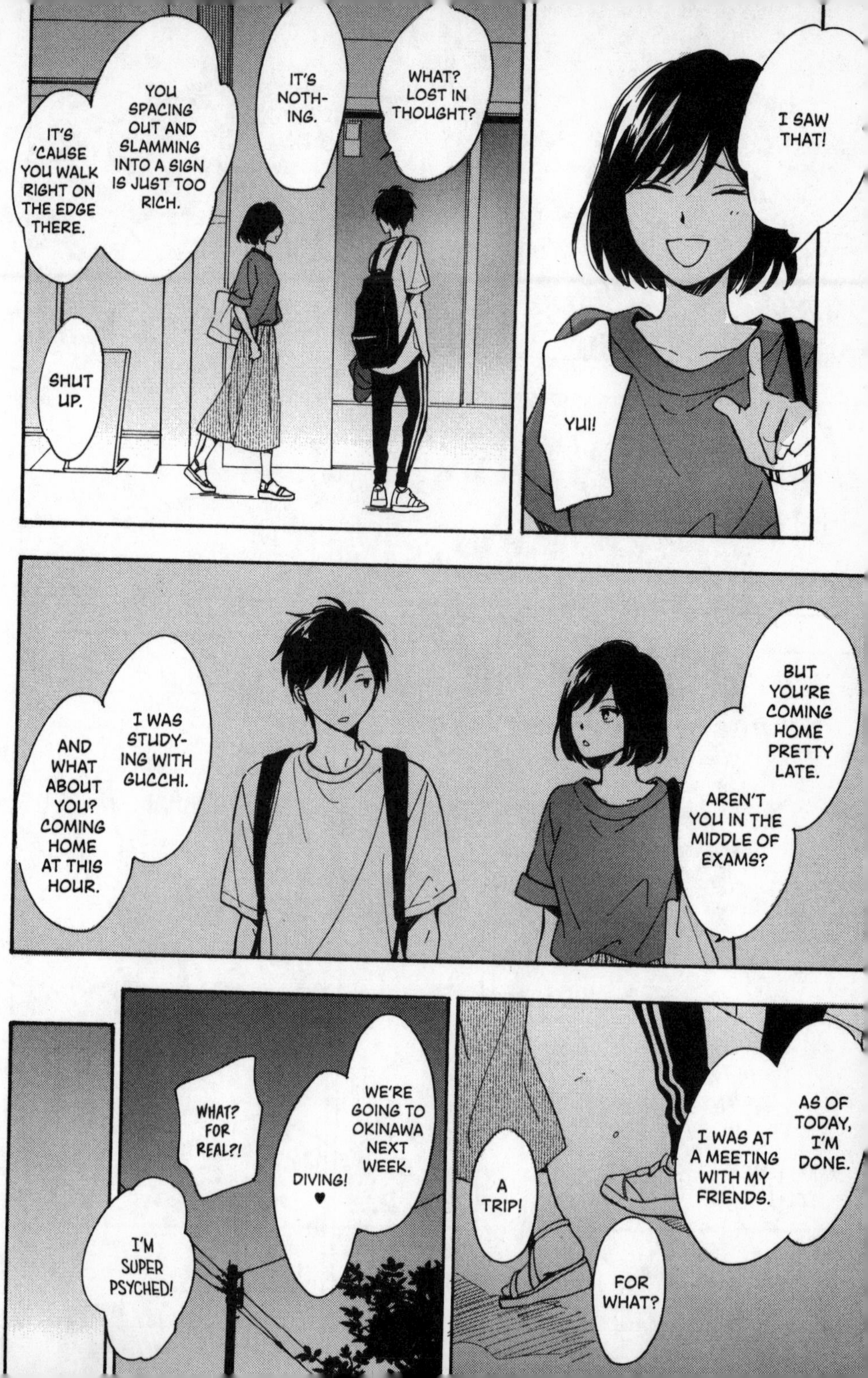
I SAW THAT!
YUI!
WHAT? LOST IN THOUGHT?
IT'S NOTHING.
YOU SPACING OUT AND SLAMMING INTO A SIGN IS JUST TOO RICH.
IT'S 'CAUSE YOU WALK RIGHT ON THE EDGE THERE.
SHUT UP.
BUT YOU'RE COMING HOME PRETTY LATE.
AREN'T YOU IN THE MIDDLE OF EXAMS?
I WAS STUDYING WITH GUCCHI.
AND WHAT ABOUT YOU? COMING HOME AT THIS HOUR.
AS OF TODAY, I'M DONE.
I WAS AT A MEETING WITH MY FRIENDS.
FOR WHAT?
A TRIP!
WE'RE GOING TO OKINAWA NEXT WEEK.
DIVING! ♥
WHAT? FOR REAL?!
I'M SUPER PSYCHED!

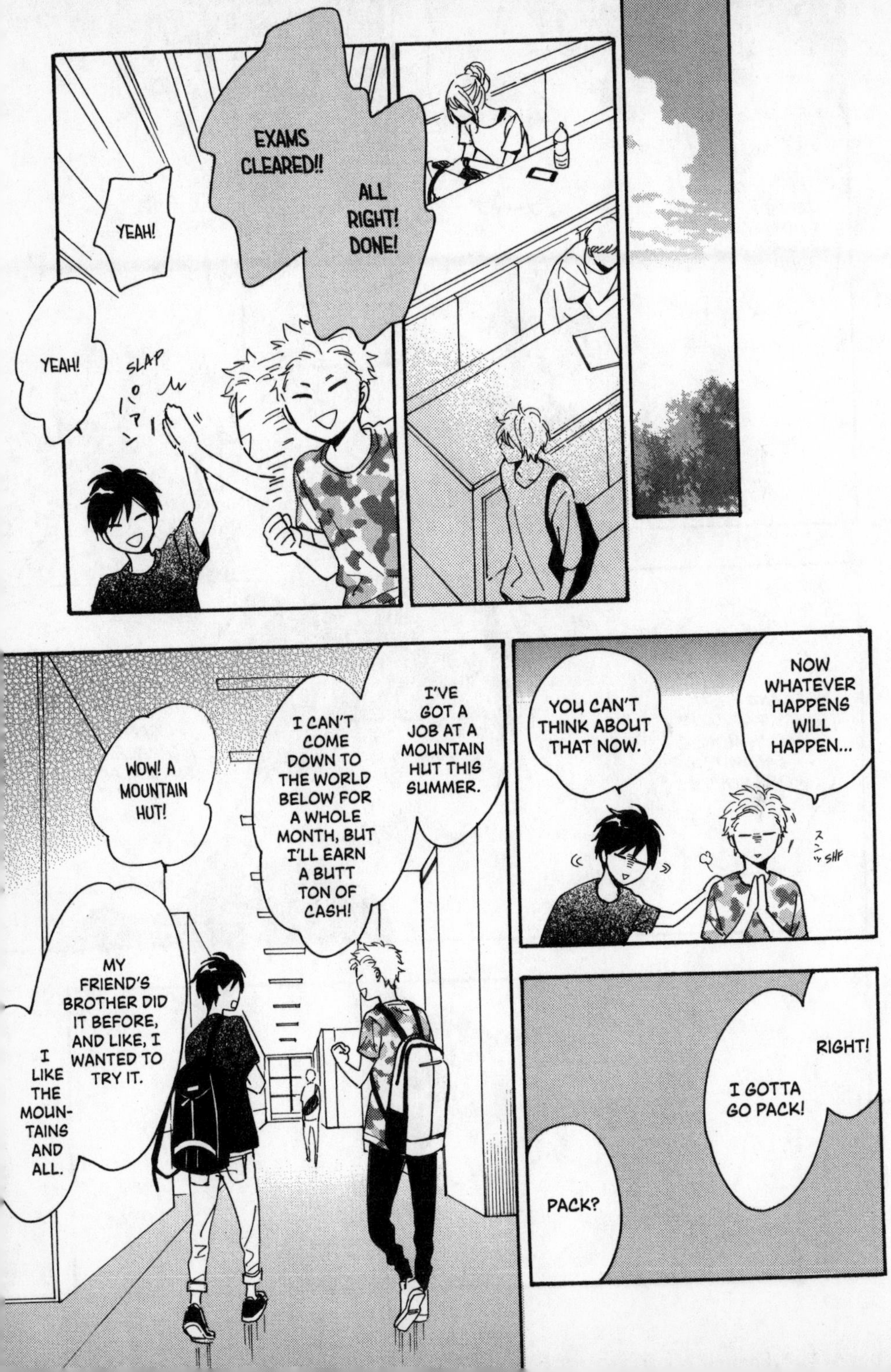
EXAMS CLEARED!!
ALL RIGHT! DONE!
YEAH!
YEAH!
SLAP
NOW WHATEVER HAPPENS WILL HAPPEN...
YOU CAN'T THINK ABOUT THAT NOW.
SHF
RIGHT!
I GOTTA GO PACK!
PACK?
I'VE GOT A JOB AT A MOUNTAIN HUT THIS SUMMER.
I CAN'T COME DOWN TO THE WORLD BELOW FOR A WHOLE MONTH, BUT I'LL EARN A BUTT TON OF CASH!
WOW! A MOUNTAIN HUT!
MY FRIEND'S BROTHER DID IT BEFORE, AND LIKE, I WANTED TO TRY IT.
I LIKE THE MOUN-TAINS AND ALL.

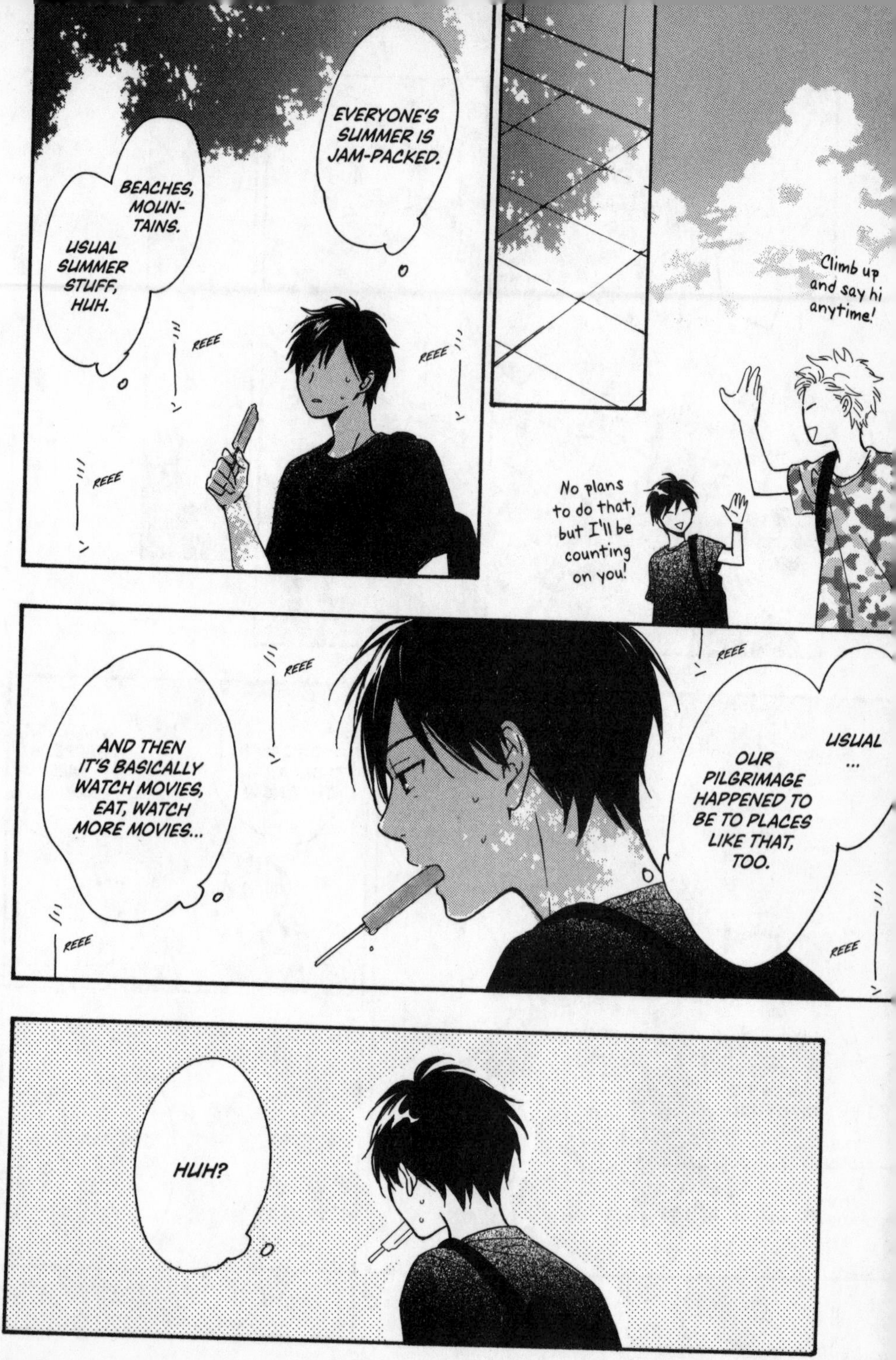

Climb up and say hi anytime!
No plans to do that, but I'll be counting on you!
EVERYONE'S SUMMER IS JAM-PACKED.
BEACHES, MOUN-TAINS.
USUAL SUMMER STUFF, HUH.
REEE
REEE
REEE
REEE
USUAL ...
OUR PILGRIMAGE HAPPENED TO BE TO PLACES LIKE THAT, TOO.
REEE
REEE
AND THEN IT'S BASICALLY WATCH MOVIES, EAT, WATCH MORE MOVIES...
REEE
HUH?

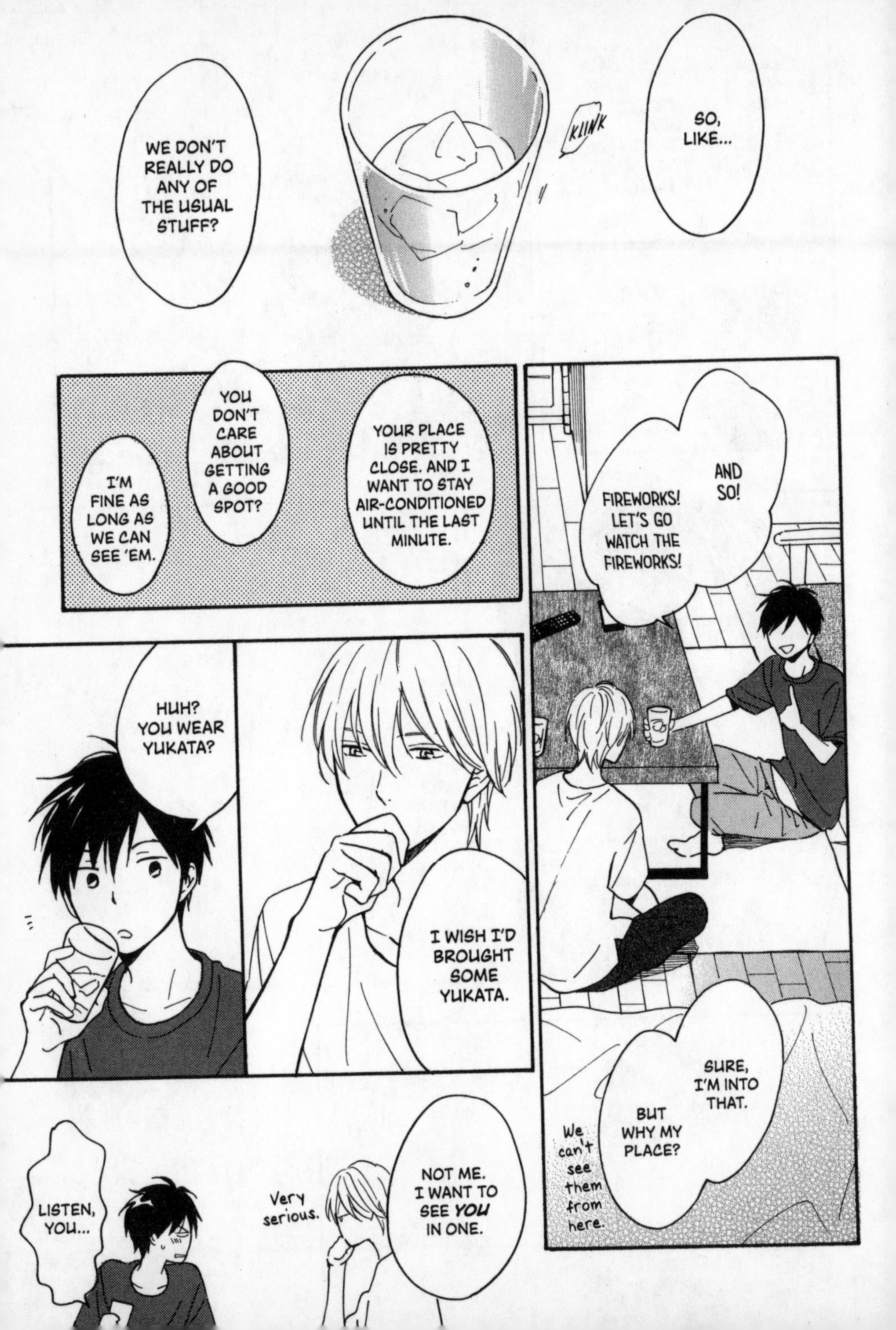
SO, LIKE...
KLINK
WE DON'T REALLY DO ANY OF THE USUAL STUFF?
AND SO!
FIREWORKS! LET'S GO WATCH THE FIREWORKS!
SURE, I'M INTO THAT.
BUT WHY MY PLACE?
We can't see them from here.
YOUR PLACE IS PRETTY CLOSE. AND I WANT TO STAY AIR-CONDITIONED UNTIL THE LAST MINUTE.
YOU DON'T CARE ABOUT GETTING A GOOD SPOT?
I'M FINE AS LONG AS WE CAN SEE 'EM.
I WISH I'D BROUGHT SOME YUKATA.
HUH? YOU WEAR YUKATA?
NOT ME. I WANT TO SEE ***YOU*** IN ONE.
Very serious.
LISTEN, YOU...

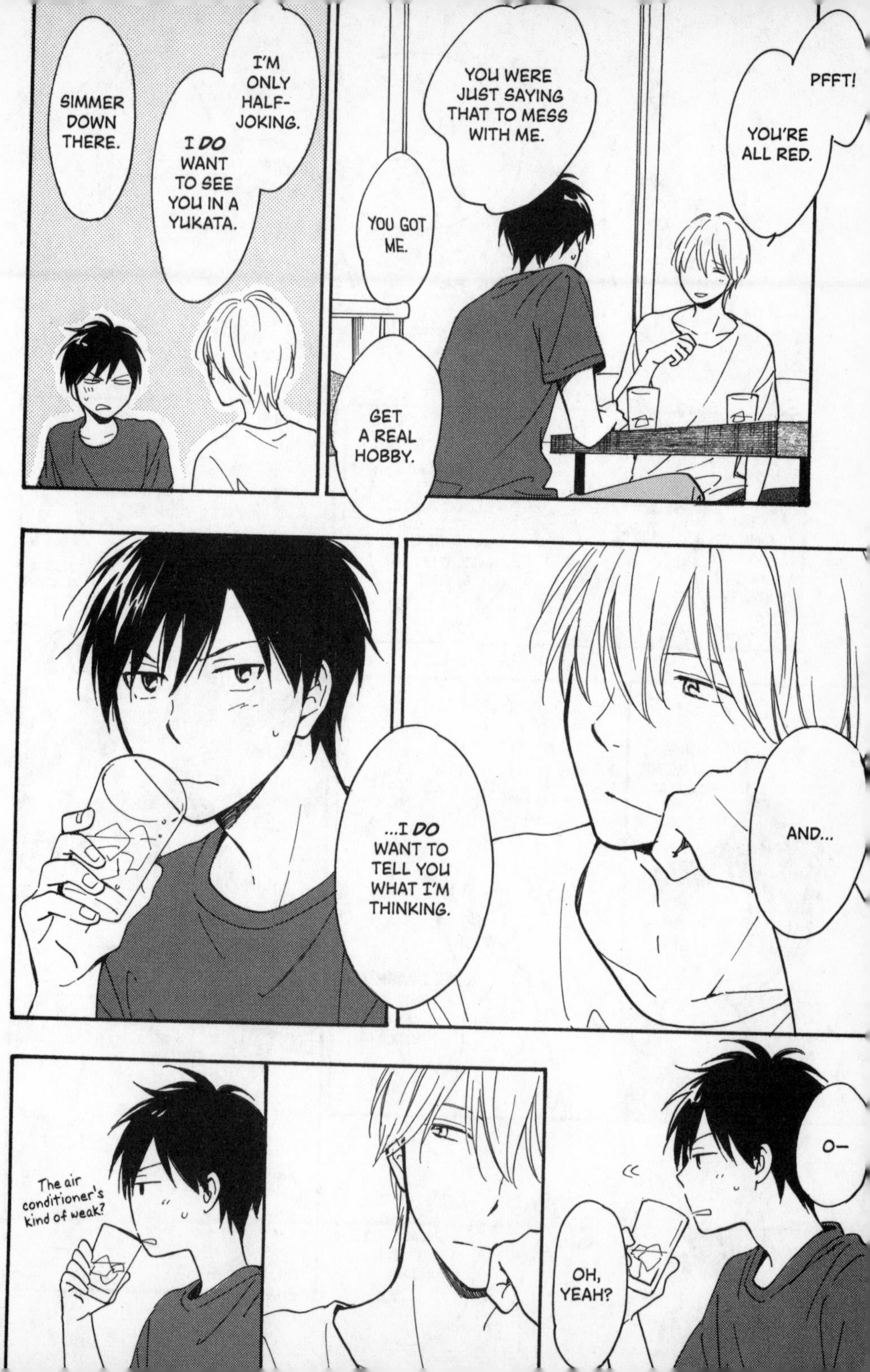
PFFT!
YOU'RE ALL RED.
YOU WERE JUST SAYING THAT TO MESS WITH ME.
YOU GOT ME.
GET A REAL HOBBY.
I'M ONLY HALF-JOKING.
I *DO* WANT TO SEE YOU IN A YUKATA.
SIMMER DOWN THERE.
AND...
...I *DO* WANT TO TELL YOU WHAT I'M THINKING.
O—
OH, YEAH?
The air conditioner's kind of weak?

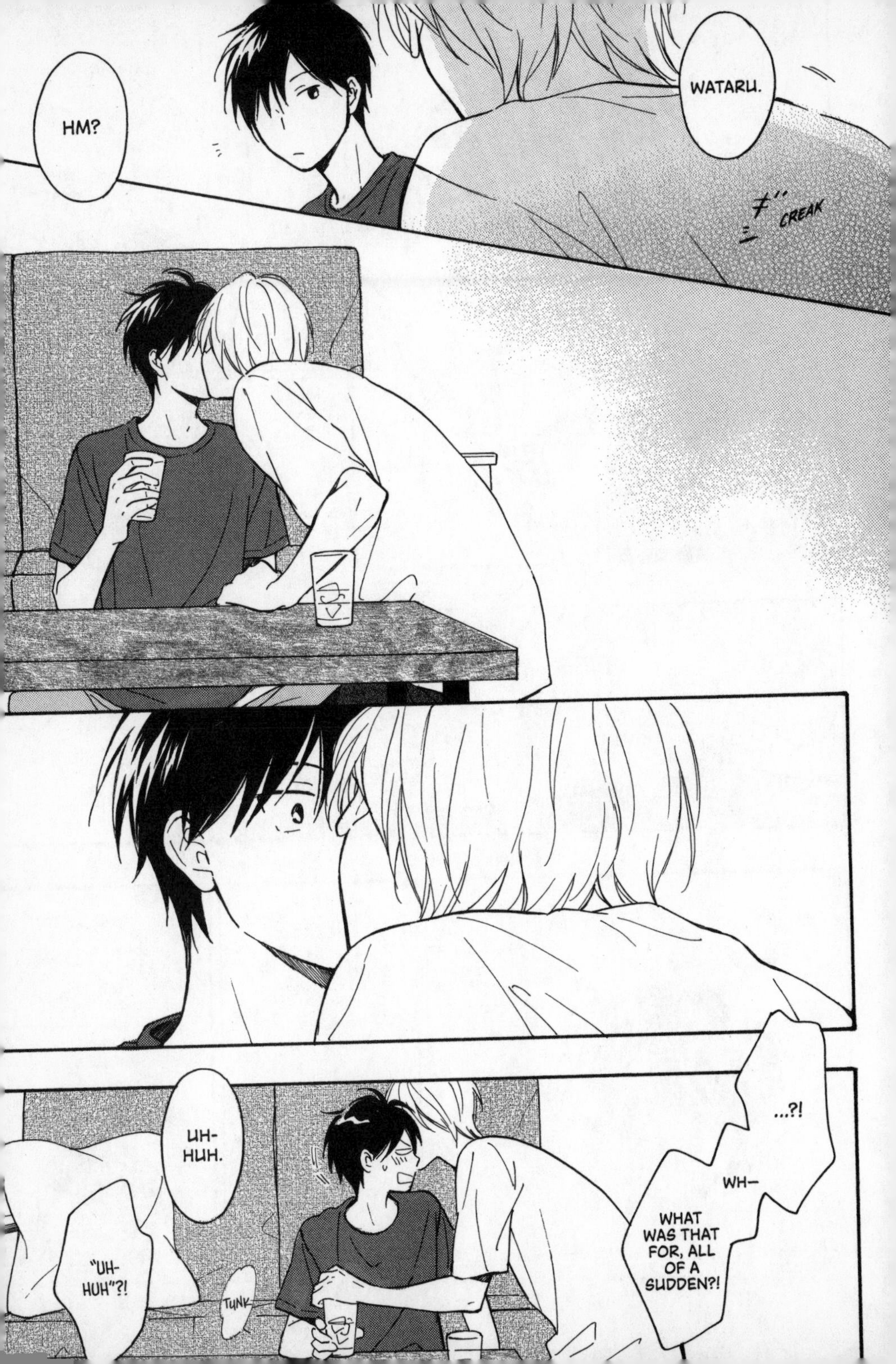
WATARU.
CREAK
HM?
...?!
WH—
WHAT WAS THAT FOR, ALL OF A SUDDEN?!
UH-HUH.
"UH-HUH"?!
TUNK

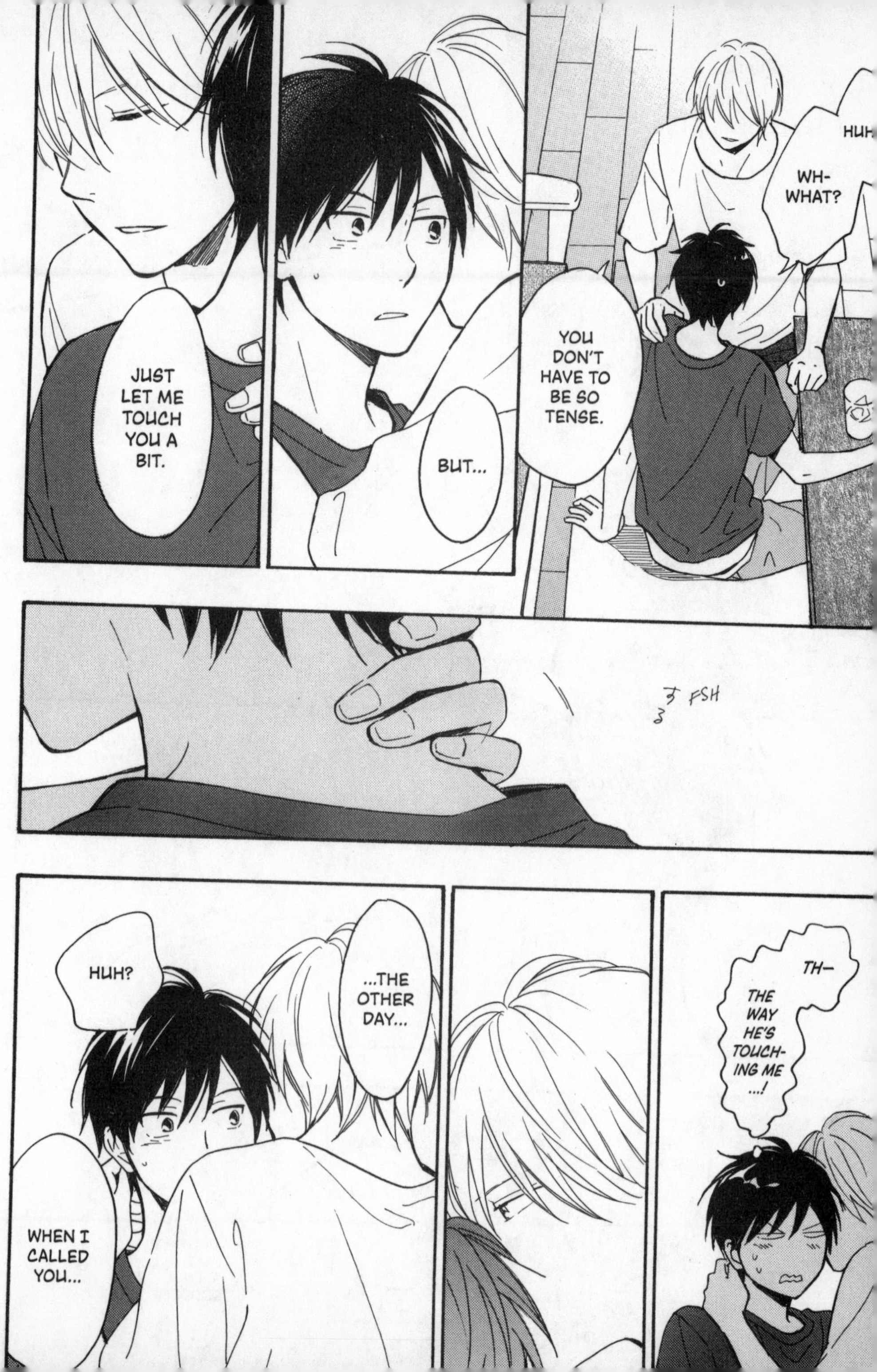

HUH
WH- WHAT?
YOU DON'T HAVE TO BE SO TENSE.
BUT...
JUST LET ME TOUCH YOU A BIT.
する FSH
TH— THE WAY HE'S TOUCH-ING ME ...!
...THE OTHER DAY...
HUH?
WHEN I CALLED YOU...

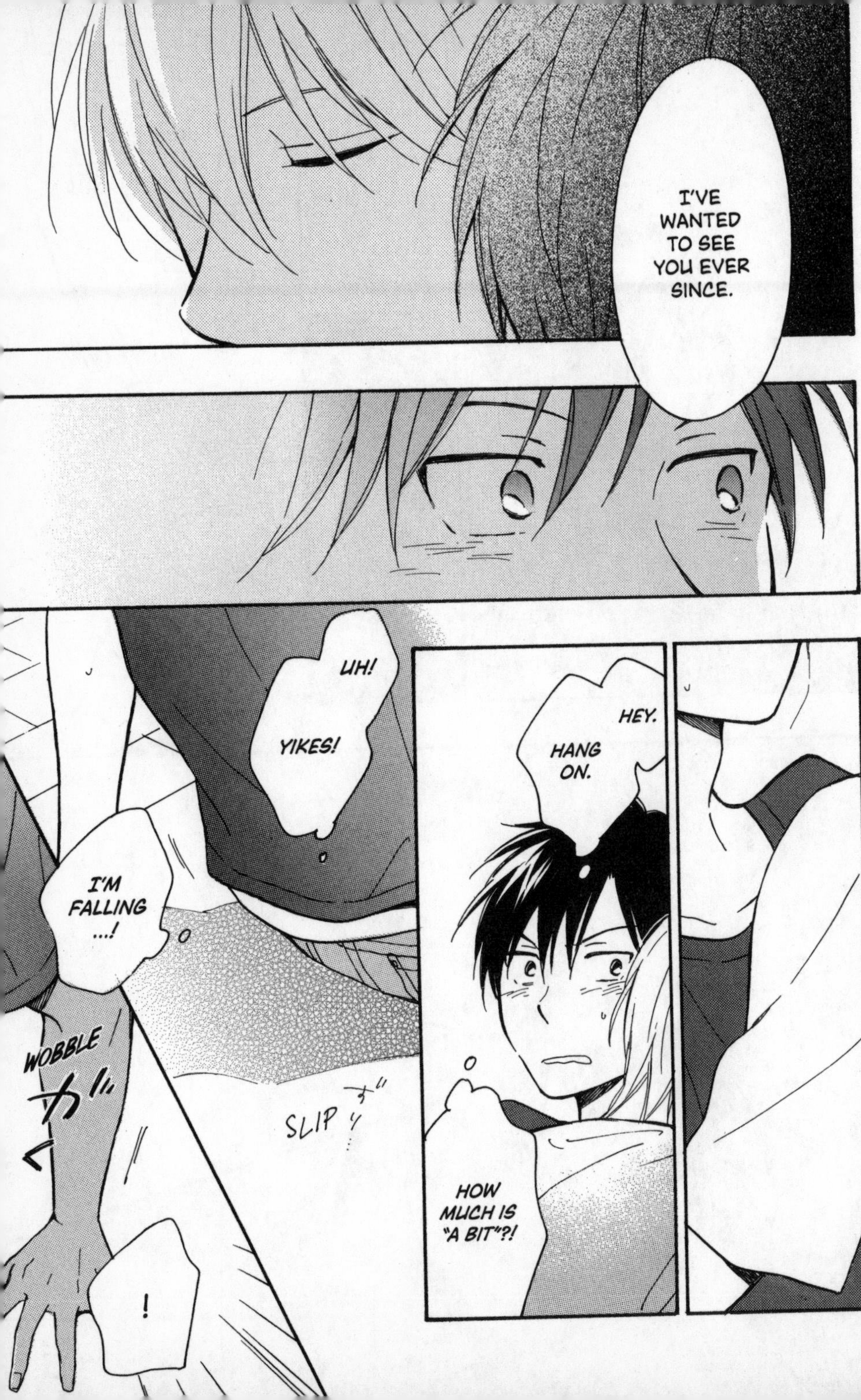
I'VE WANTED TO SEE YOU EVER SINCE.
HEY.
HANG ON.
HOW MUCH IS "A BIT"?!
UH!
YIKES!
I'M FALLING ...!
WOBBLE
SLIP
!

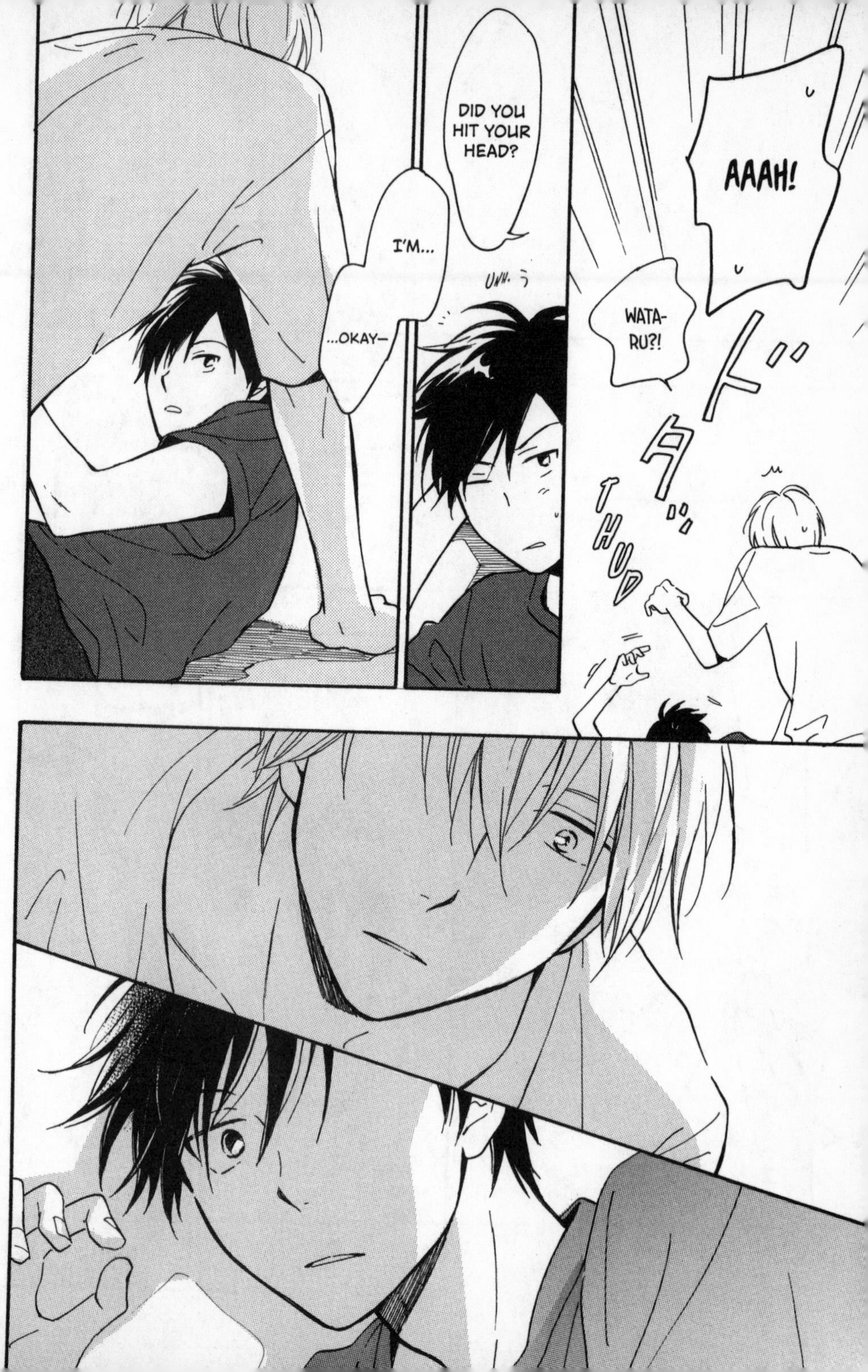
AAAH!
WATA-RU?!
ドタ
THUD
DID YOU HIT YOUR HEAD?
UNH. う
I'M...
...OKAY—

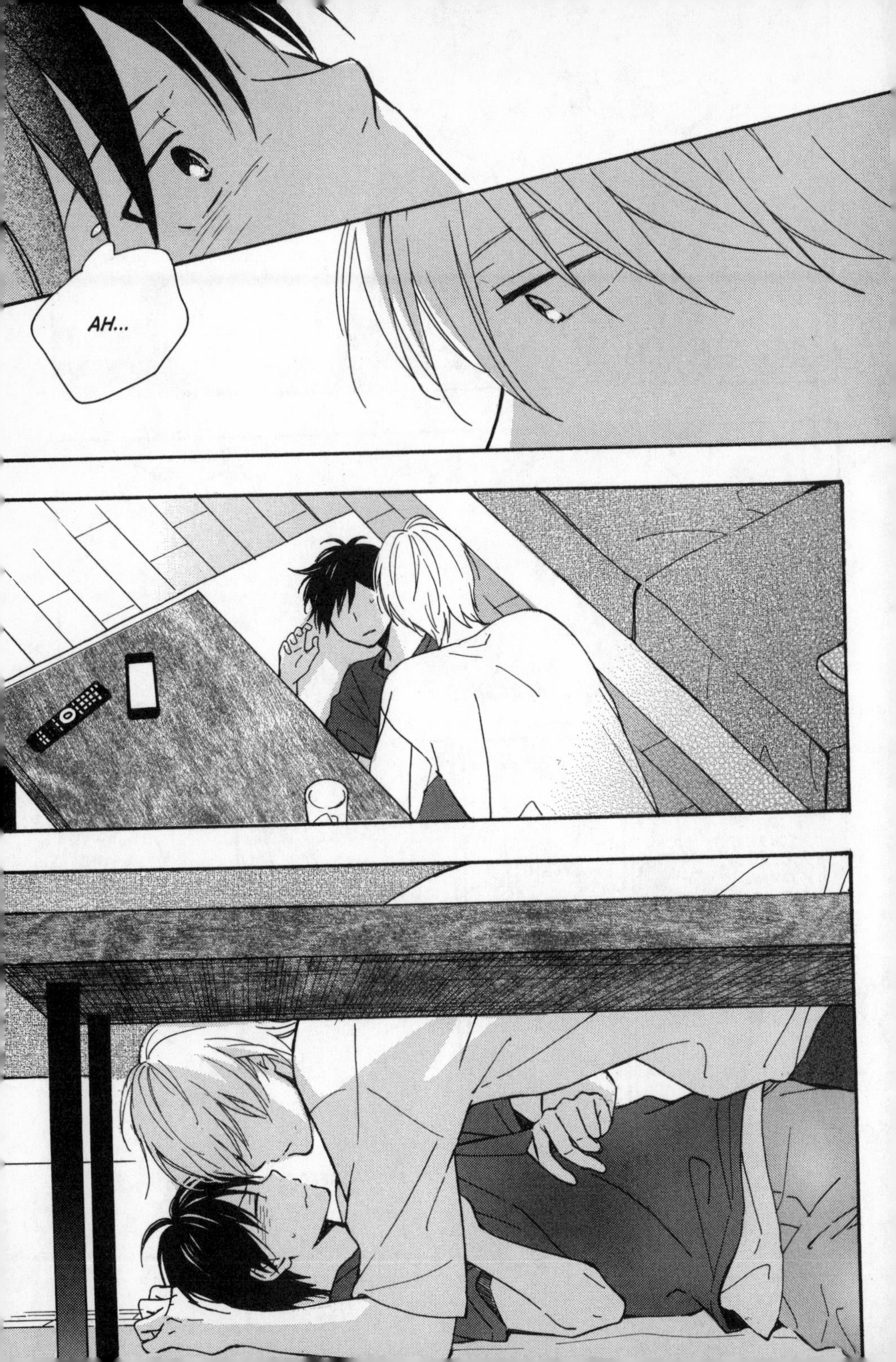
AH...

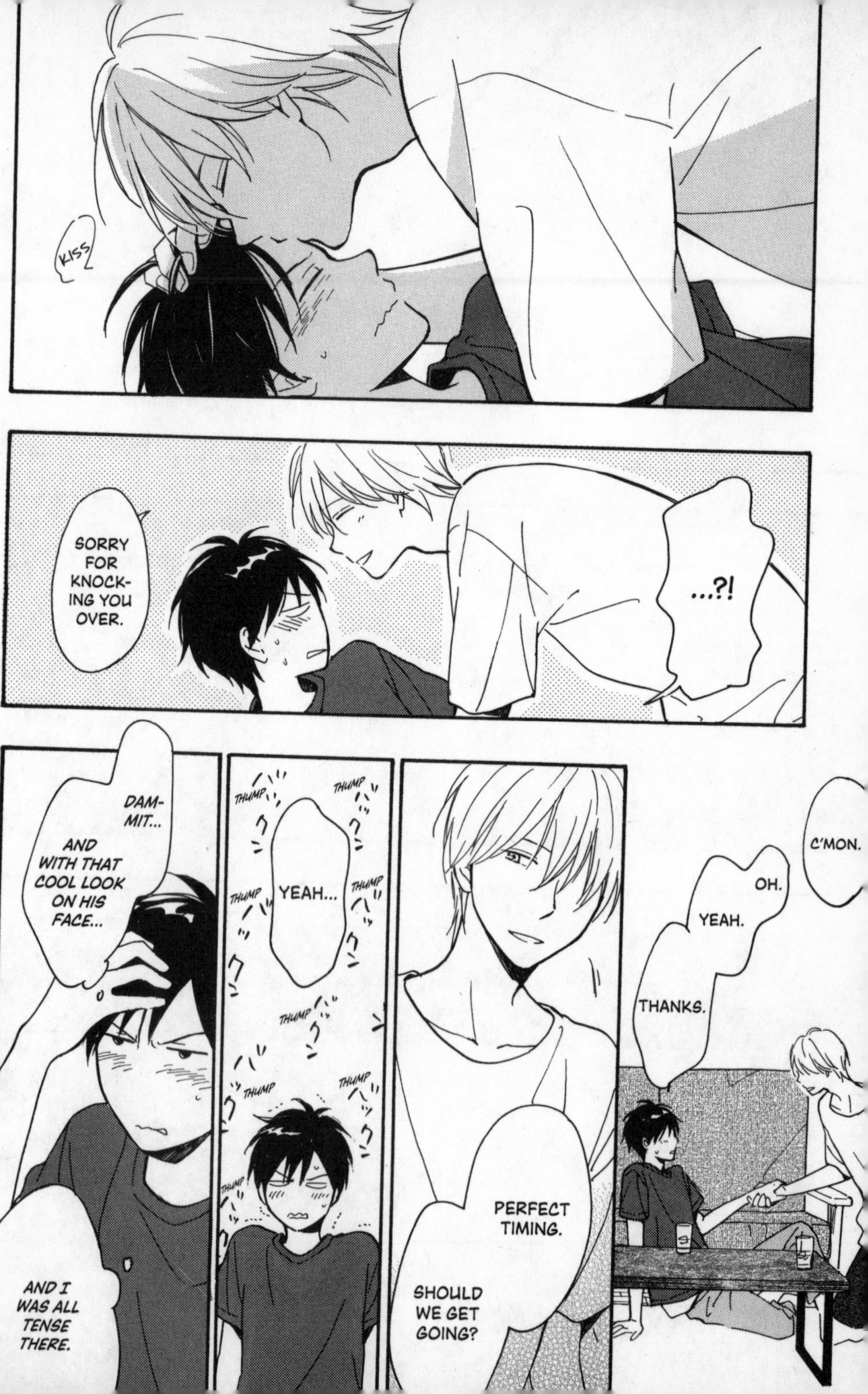
KISS
...?!
SORRY FOR KNOCKING YOU OVER.
C'MON.
OH.
YEAH.
THANKS.
PERFECT TIMING.
SHOULD WE GET GOING?
THUMP THUMP
YEAH...
THUMP THUMP THUMP THUMP THUMP THUMP
DAMMIT... AND WITH THAT COOL LOOK ON HIS FACE...
AND I WAS ALL TENSE THERE.

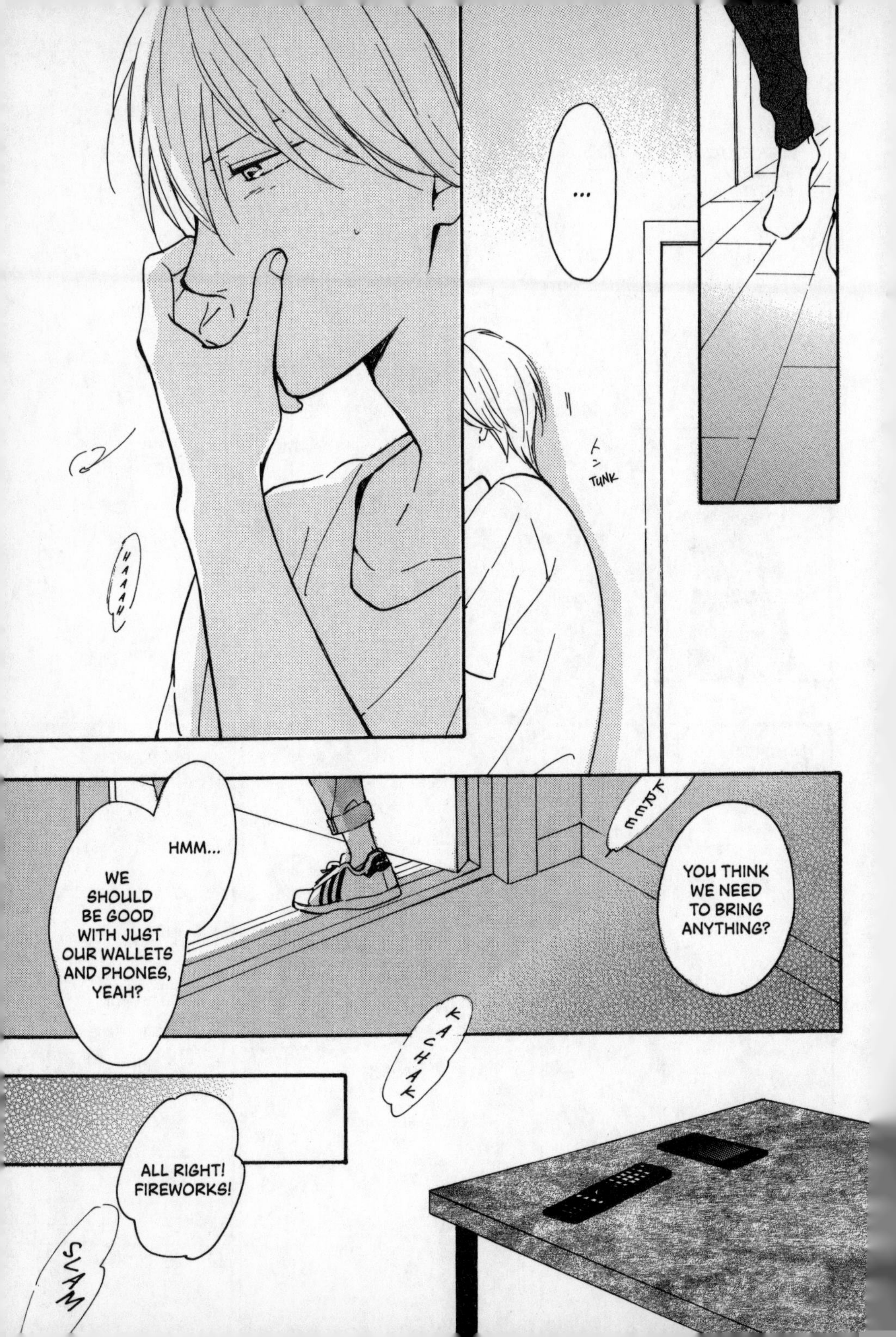
...
TUNK
HAAAH
KREE
YOU THINK WE NEED TO BRING ANYTHING?
HMM...
WE SHOULD BE GOOD WITH JUST OUR WALLETS AND PHONES, YEAH?
KACHAK
ALL RIGHT! FIREWORKS!
SLAM

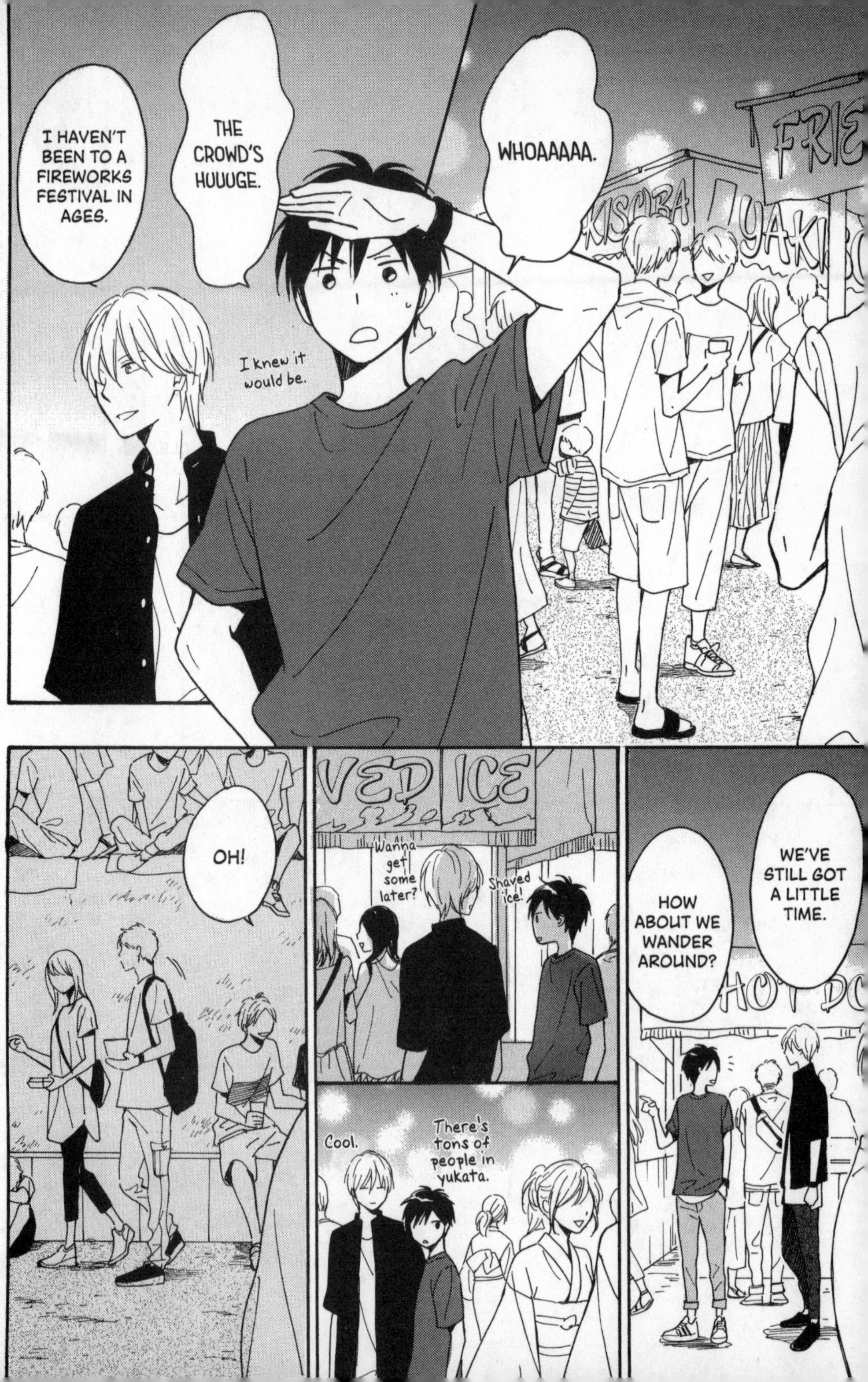
WHOAAAAA.
THE CROWD'S HUUUGE.
I HAVEN'T BEEN TO A FIREWORKS FESTIVAL IN AGES.
I knew it would be.
WE'VE STILL GOT A LITTLE TIME.
HOW ABOUT WE WANDER AROUND?
Shaved ice!
Wanna get some later?
There's tons of people in yukata.
Cool.
OH!

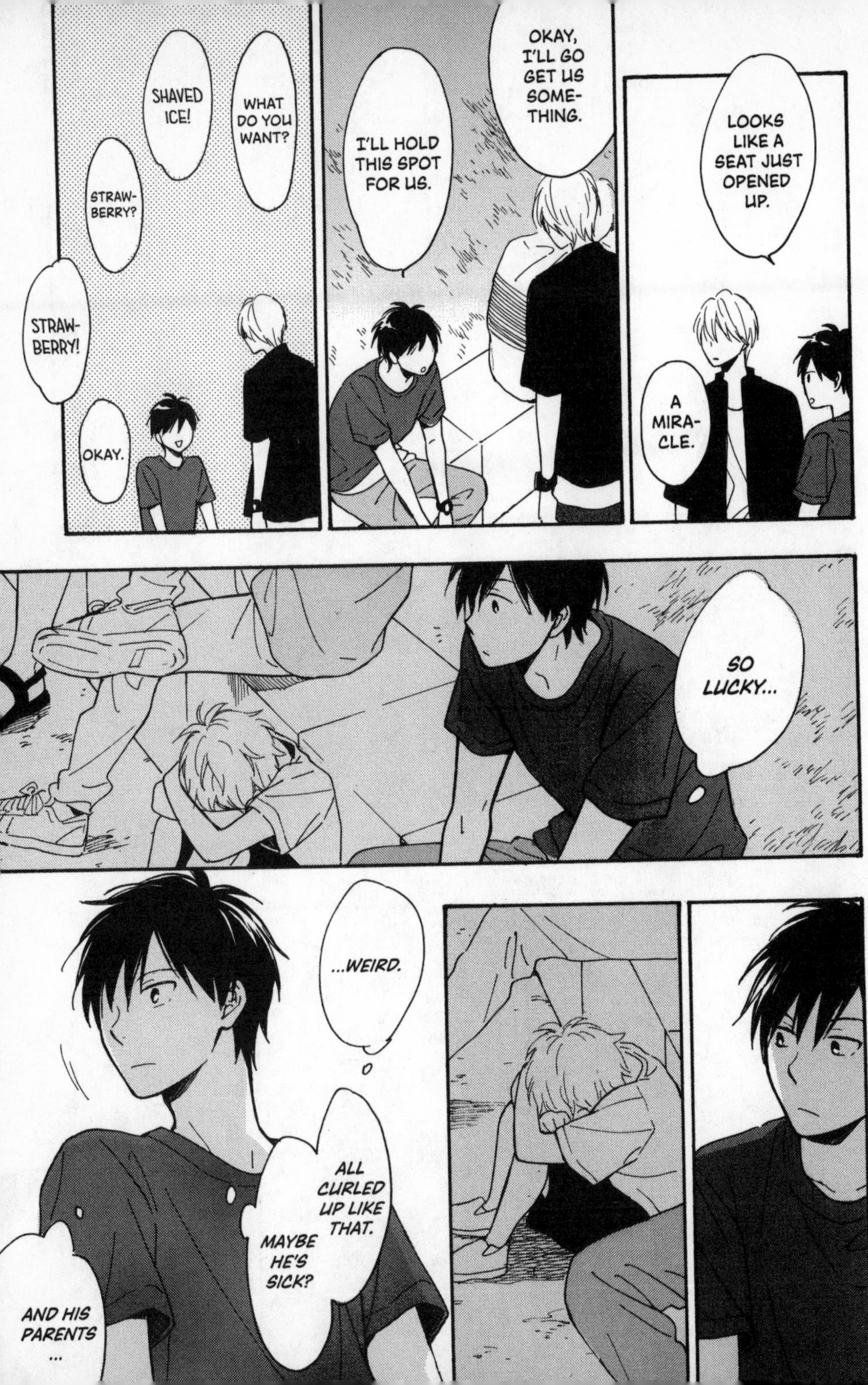
LOOKS LIKE A SEAT JUST OPENED UP.
A MIRACLE.
OKAY, I'LL GO GET US SOMETHING.
I'LL HOLD THIS SPOT FOR US.
WHAT DO YOU WANT?
SHAVED ICE!
STRAWBERRY?
STRAWBERRY!
OKAY.
SO LUCKY...
...WEIRD.
ALL CURLED UP LIKE THAT.
MAYBE HE'S SICK?
AND HIS PARENTS ...

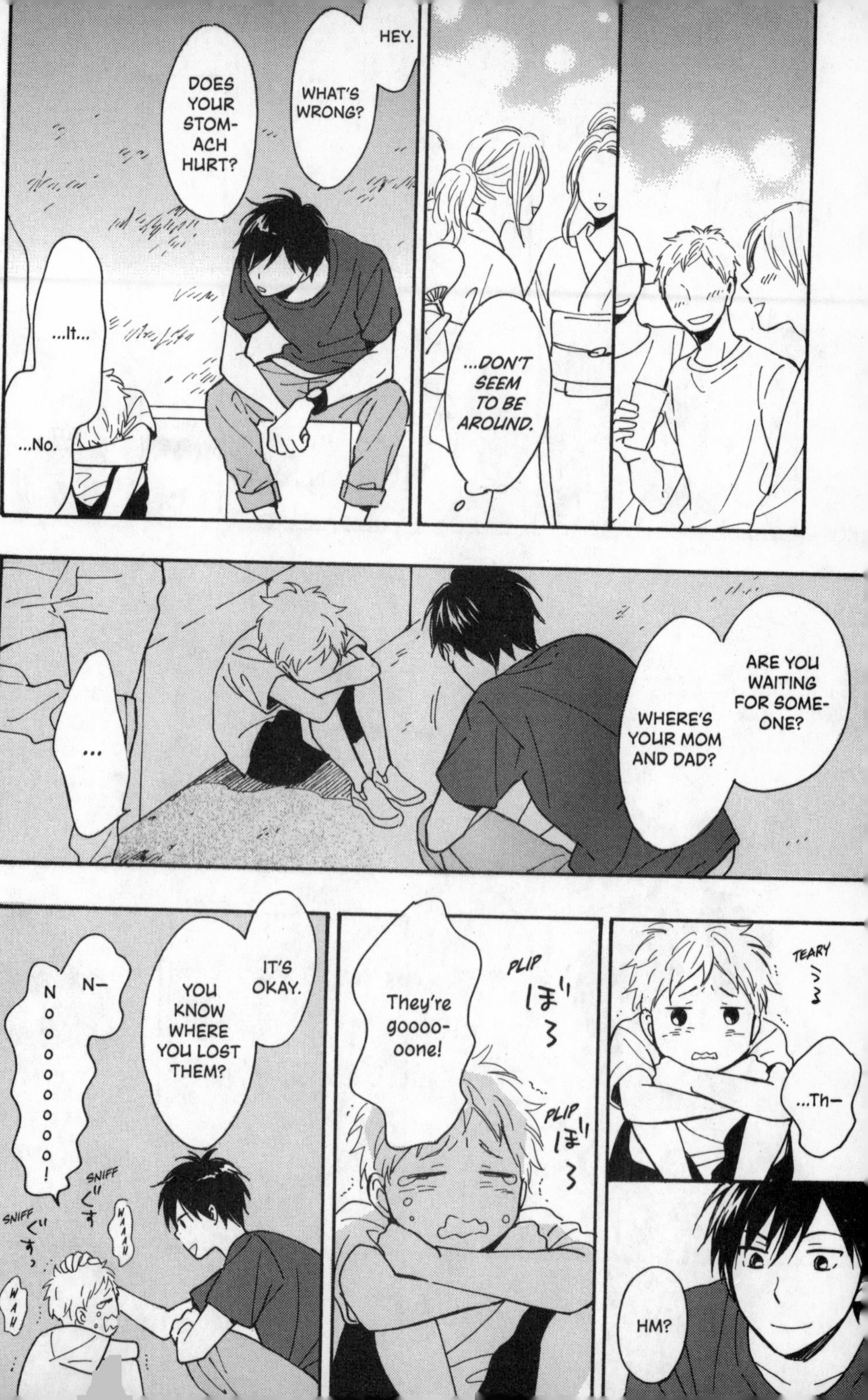
...DON'T SEEM TO BE AROUND.
HEY.
WHAT'S WRONG?
DOES YOUR STOMACH HURT?
...It...
...No.
ARE YOU WAITING FOR SOME-ONE?
WHERE'S YOUR MOM AND DAD?
...
TEARY
...Th-
HM?
PLIP ぼろ
They're goooo-oone!
PLIP ぼろ
IT'S OKAY.
YOU KNOW WHERE YOU LOST THEM?
N-
Nooooooooooo!
SNIFF ぐす
WAAAAH
SNIFF ぐすっ
WAH

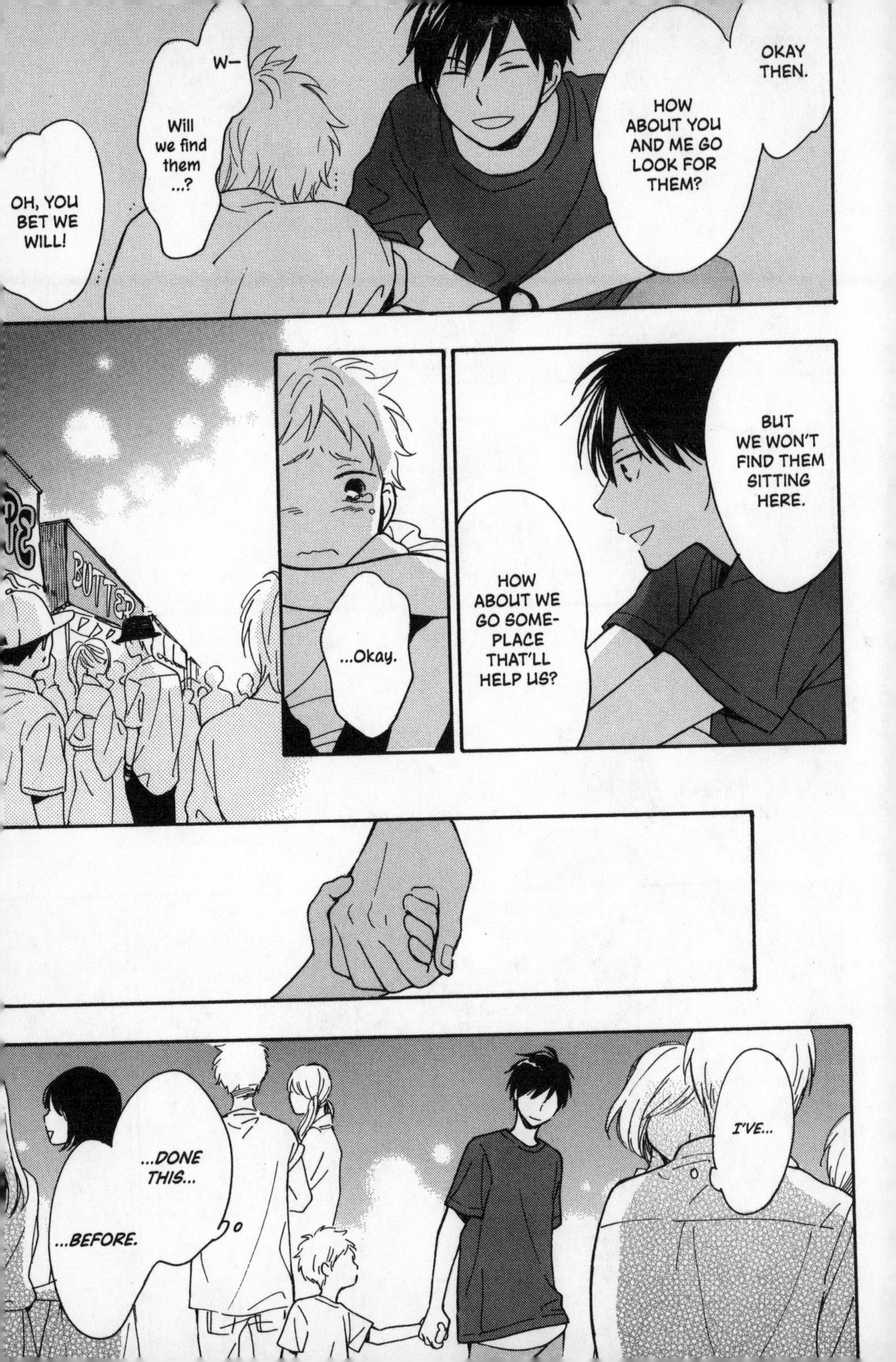

OKAY THEN.
HOW ABOUT YOU AND ME GO LOOK FOR THEM?
W—
Will we find them ...?
OH, YOU BET WE WILL!
BUT WE WON'T FIND THEM SITTING HERE.
HOW ABOUT WE GO SOME-PLACE THAT'LL HELP US?
...Okay.
I'VE...
...DONE THIS...
...BEFORE.

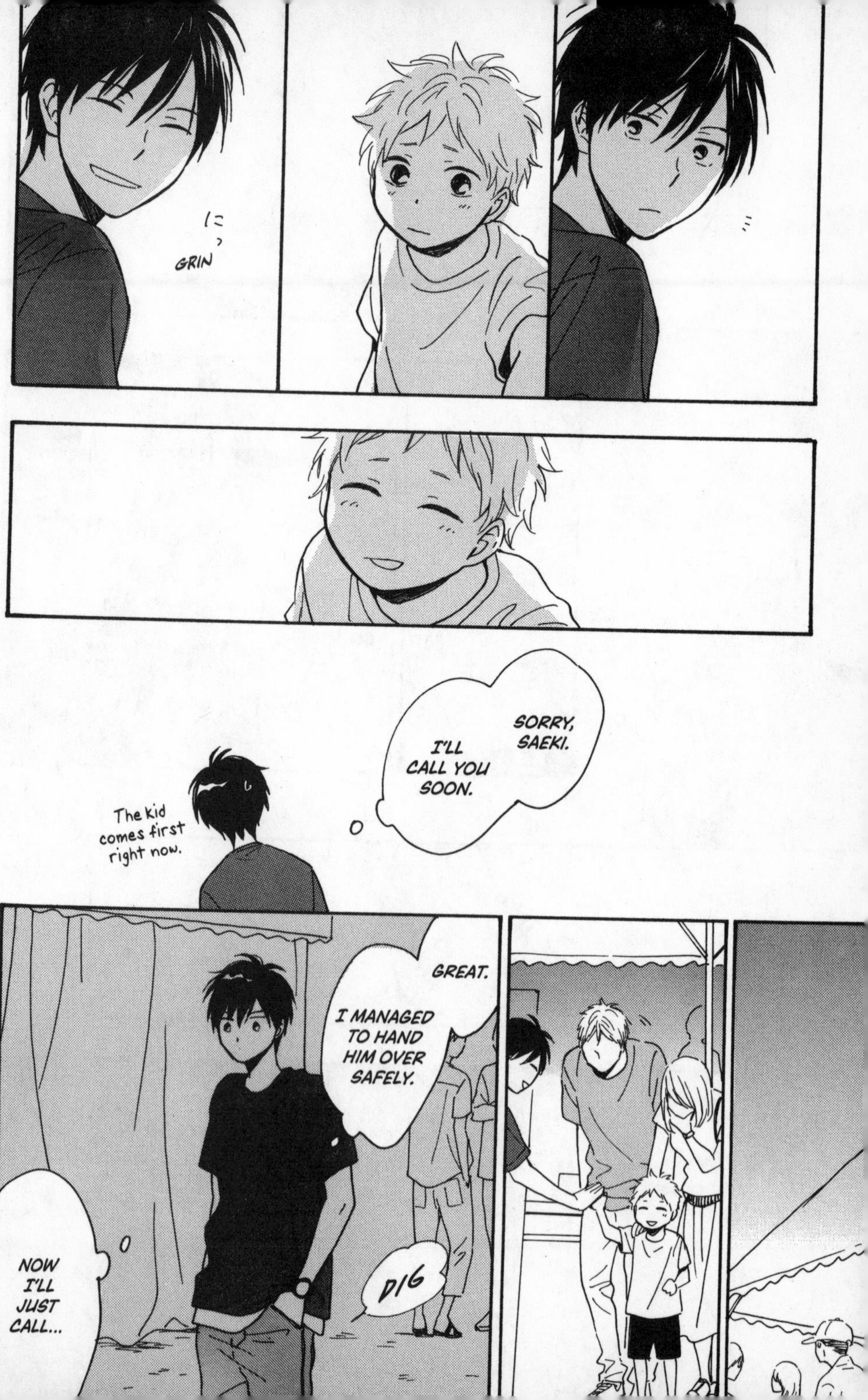
に
GRIN
SORRY, SAEKI.
I'LL CALL YOU SOON.
The kid comes first right now.
GREAT.
I MANAGED TO HAND HIM OVER SAFELY.
DIG
NOW I'LL JUST CALL...

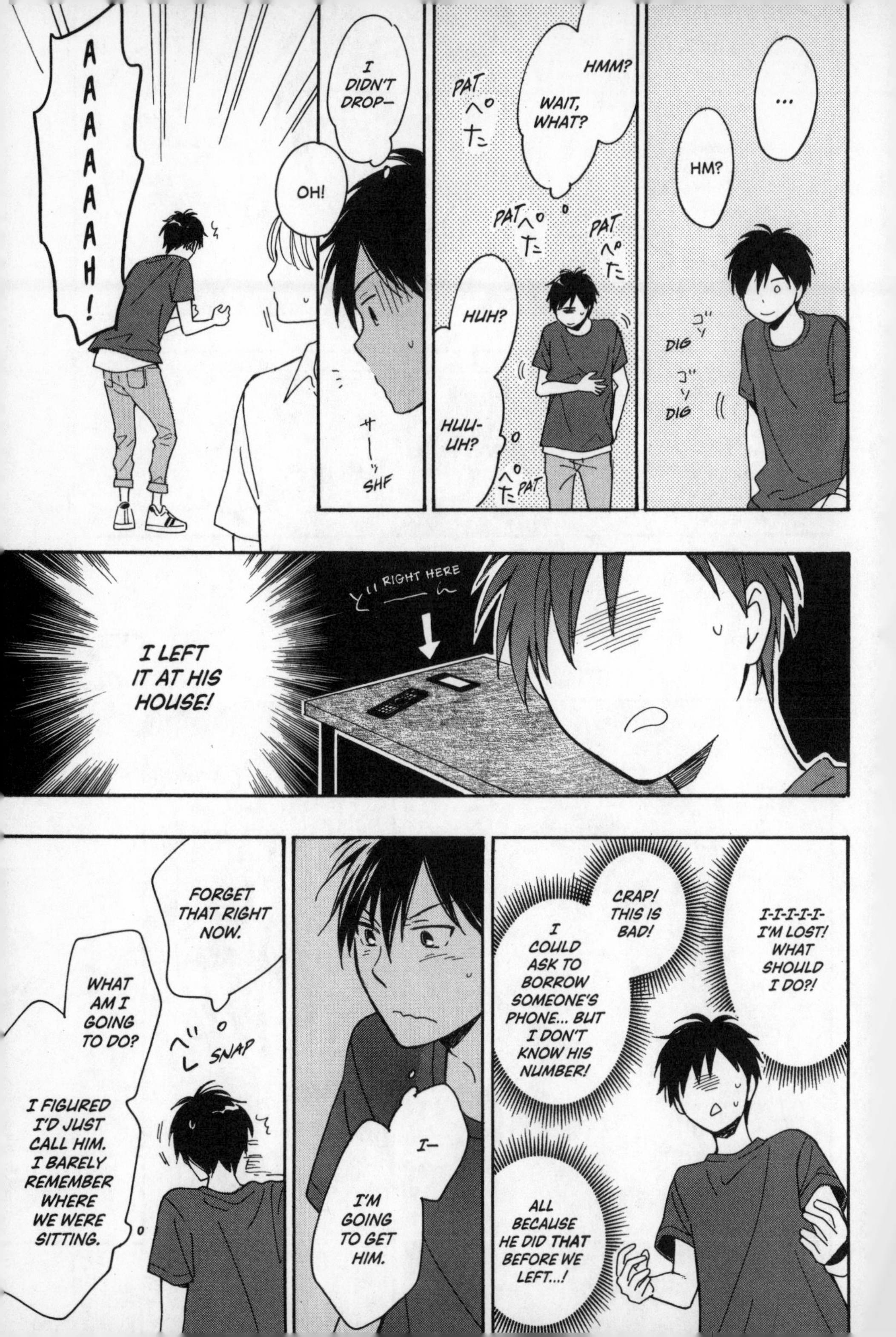
...
HM?
DIG
DIG
HMM?
WAIT, WHAT?
PAT
PAT
PAT
HUH?
HUUU-UH?
PAT
I DIDN'T DROP—
OH!
SHF
AAAAAAAAH!
RIGHT HERE
I LEFT IT AT HIS HOUSE!
I-I-I-I-I'M LOST! WHAT SHOULD I DO?!
CRAP! THIS IS BAD!
I COULD ASK TO BORROW SOMEONE'S PHONE... BUT I DON'T KNOW HIS NUMBER!
ALL BECAUSE HE DID THAT BEFORE WE LEFT...!
I—
I'M GOING TO GET HIM.
FORGET THAT RIGHT NOW.
WHAT AM I GOING TO DO?
SNAP
I FIGURED I'D JUST CALL HIM. I BARELY REMEMBER WHERE WE WERE SITTING.

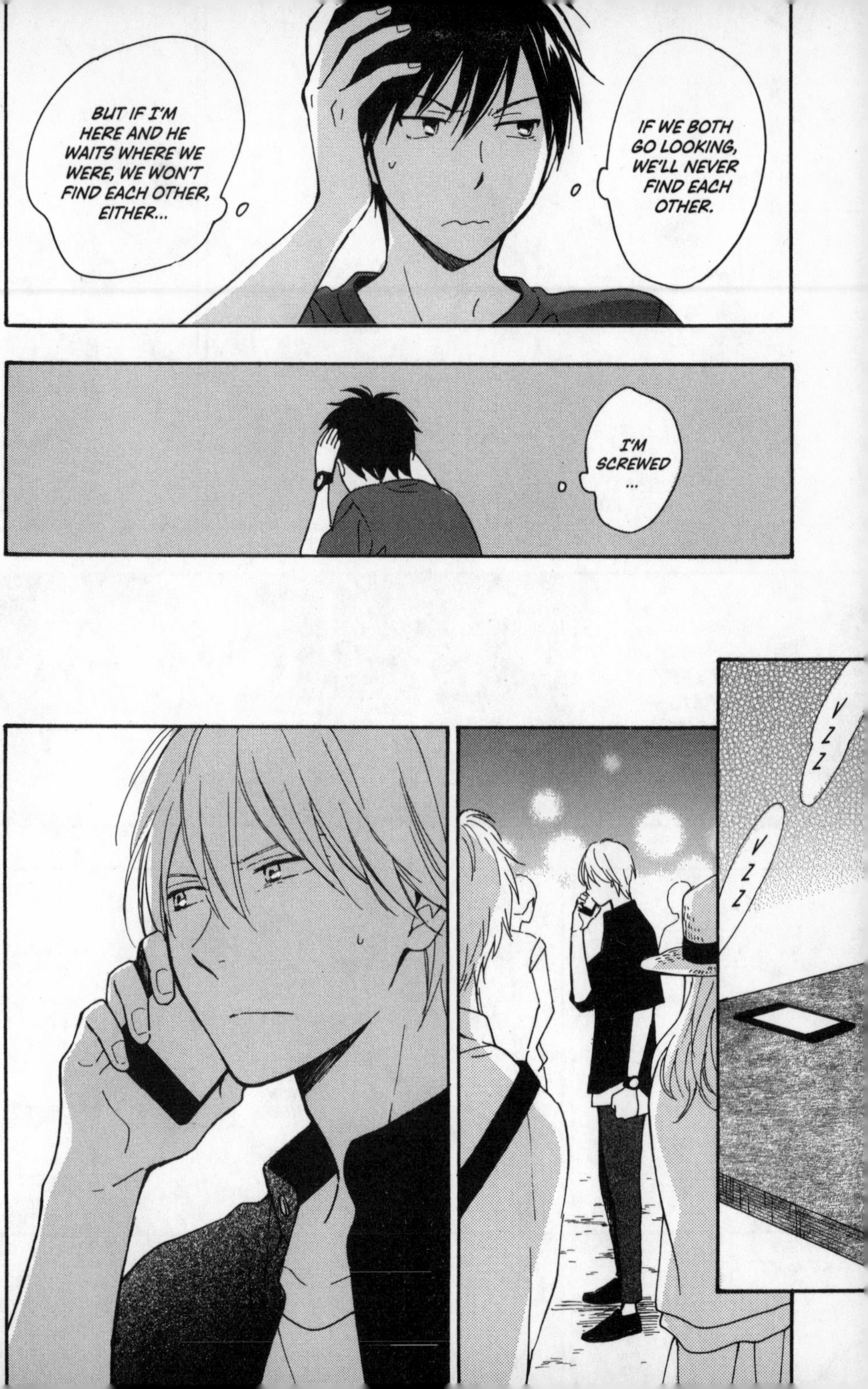
IF WE BOTH GO LOOKING, WE'LL NEVER FIND EACH OTHER.
BUT IF I'M HERE AND HE WAITS WHERE WE WERE, WE WON'T FIND EACH OTHER, EITHER...
I'M SCREWED ...
VZZ
VZZ

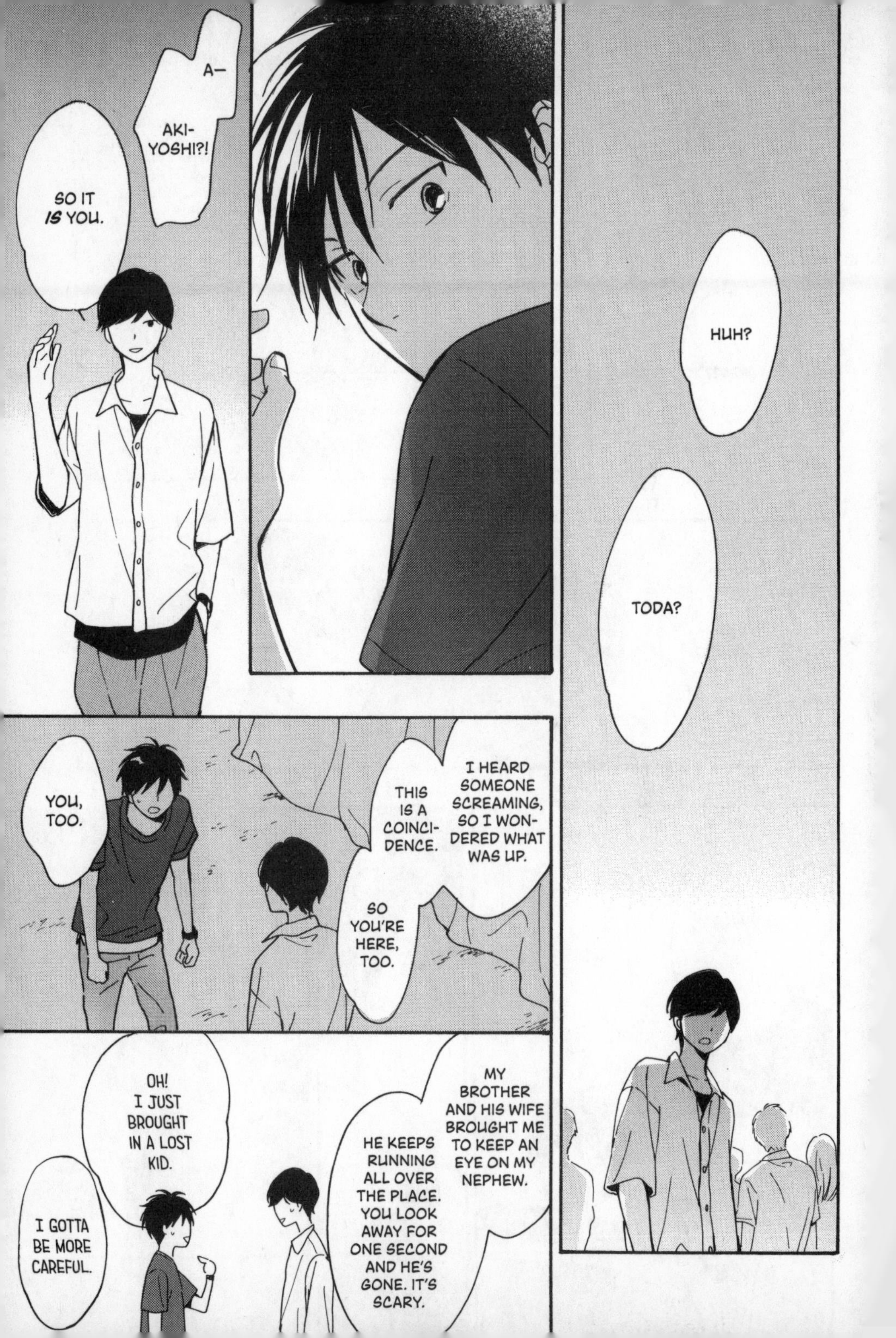
HUH?
TODA?
A— AKI-YOSHI?!
SO IT *IS* YOU.
I HEARD SOMEONE SCREAMING, SO I WONDERED WHAT WAS UP.
THIS IS A COINCIDENCE.
SO YOU'RE HERE, TOO.
YOU, TOO.
MY BROTHER AND HIS WIFE BROUGHT ME TO KEEP AN EYE ON MY NEPHEW.
HE KEEPS RUNNING ALL OVER THE PLACE. YOU LOOK AWAY FOR ONE SECOND AND HE'S GONE. IT'S SCARY.
OH! I JUST BROUGHT IN A LOST KID.
I GOTTA BE MORE CAREFUL.

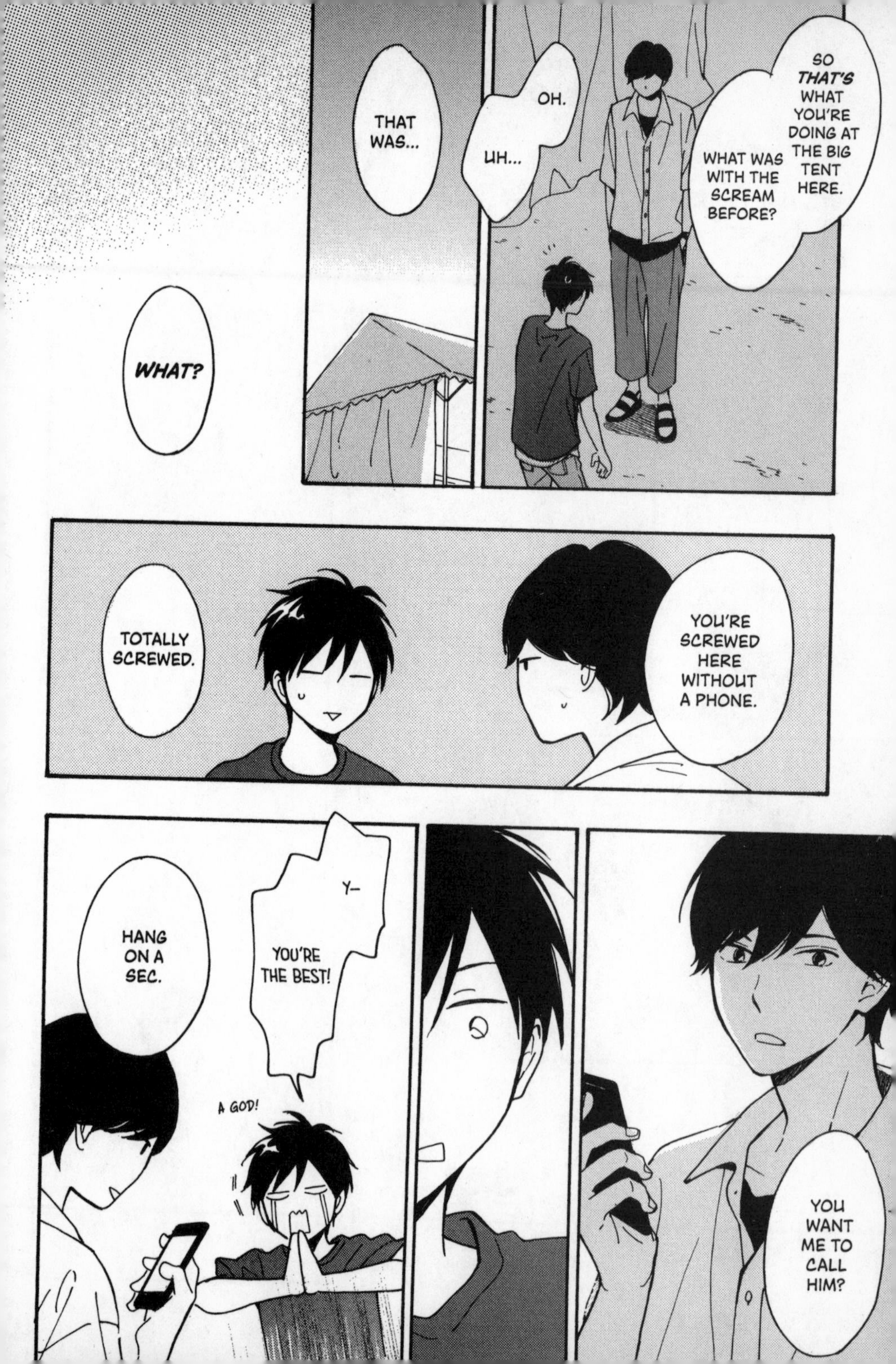

SO *THAT'S* WHAT YOU'RE DOING AT THE BIG TENT HERE.
WHAT WAS WITH THE SCREAM BEFORE?
OH.
UH...
THAT WAS...
WHAT?
YOU'RE SCREWED HERE WITHOUT A PHONE.
TOTALLY SCREWED.
YOU WANT ME TO CALL HIM?
Y—
YOU'RE THE BEST!
HANG ON A SEC.
A GOD!

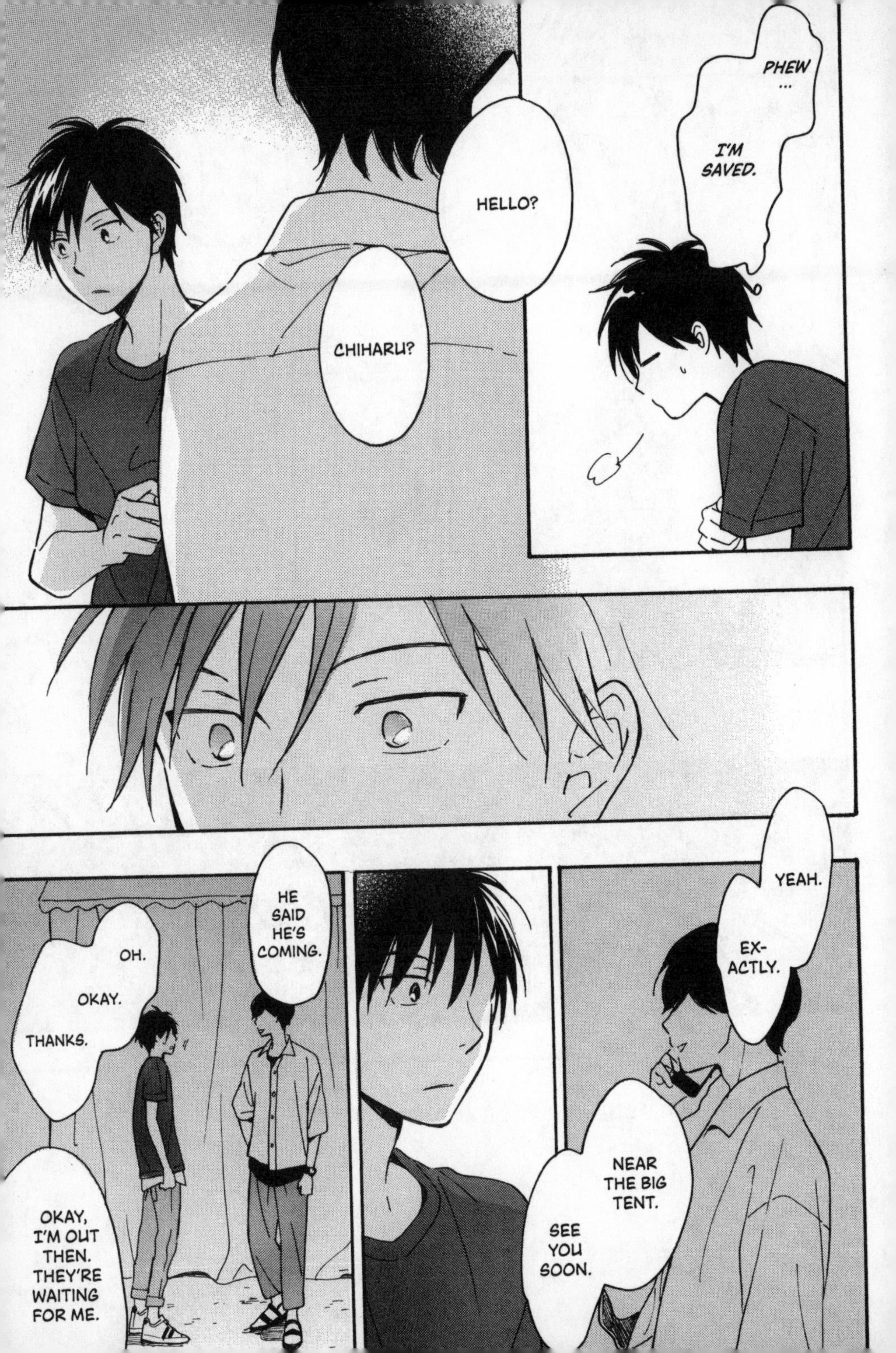
PHEW ... I'M SAVED.
HELLO?
CHIHARU?
YEAH.
EX-ACTLY.
NEAR THE BIG TENT.
SEE YOU SOON.
HE SAID HE'S COMING.
OH.
OKAY.
THANKS.
OKAY, I'M OUT THEN. THEY'RE WAITING FOR ME.

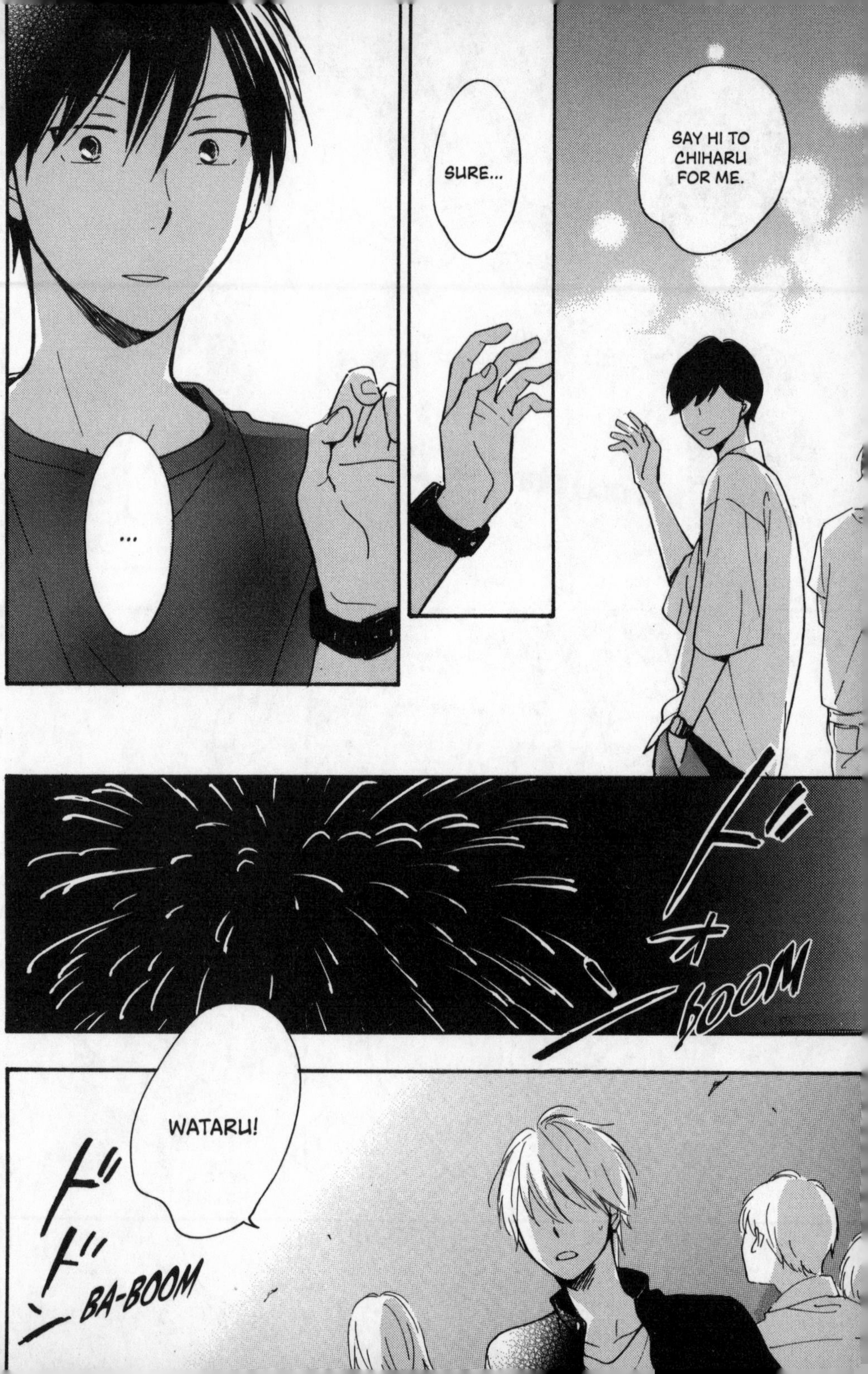
SAY HI TO CHIHARU FOR ME.
SURE...
...
ドォ
BOOM
WATARU!
ドド
BA-BOOM

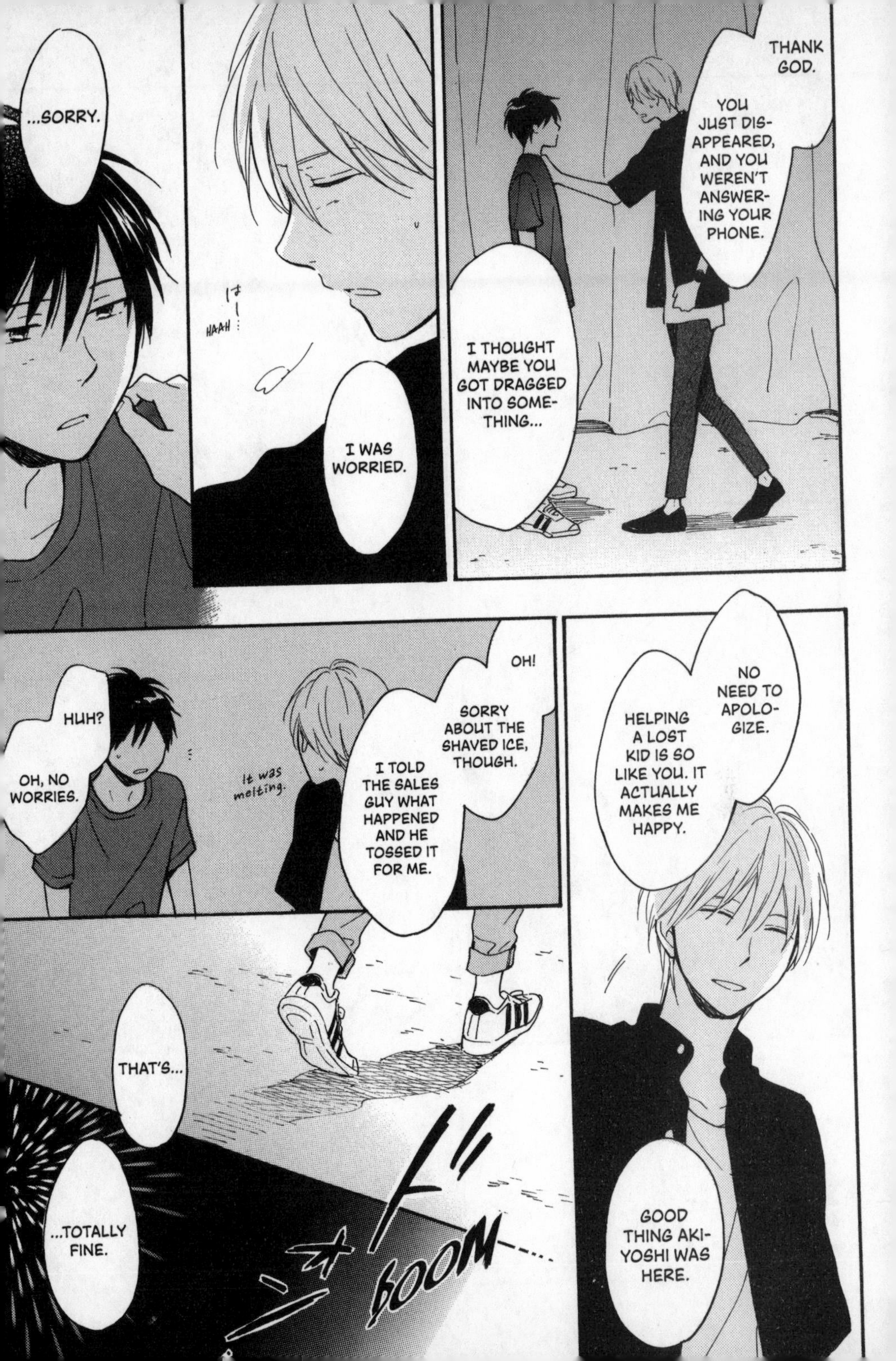
THANK GOD.
YOU JUST DISAPPEARED, AND YOU WEREN'T ANSWERING YOUR PHONE.
I THOUGHT MAYBE YOU GOT DRAGGED INTO SOMETHING...
HAAH
I WAS WORRIED.
...SORRY.
NO NEED TO APOLOGIZE.
HELPING A LOST KID IS SO LIKE YOU. IT ACTUALLY MAKES ME HAPPY.
GOOD THING AKIYOSHI WAS HERE.
OH!
SORRY ABOUT THE SHAVED ICE, THOUGH.
I TOLD THE SALES GUY WHAT HAPPENED AND HE TOSSED IT FOR ME.
It was melting.
HUH?
OH, NO WORRIES.
THAT'S...
...TOTALLY FINE.
BOOM

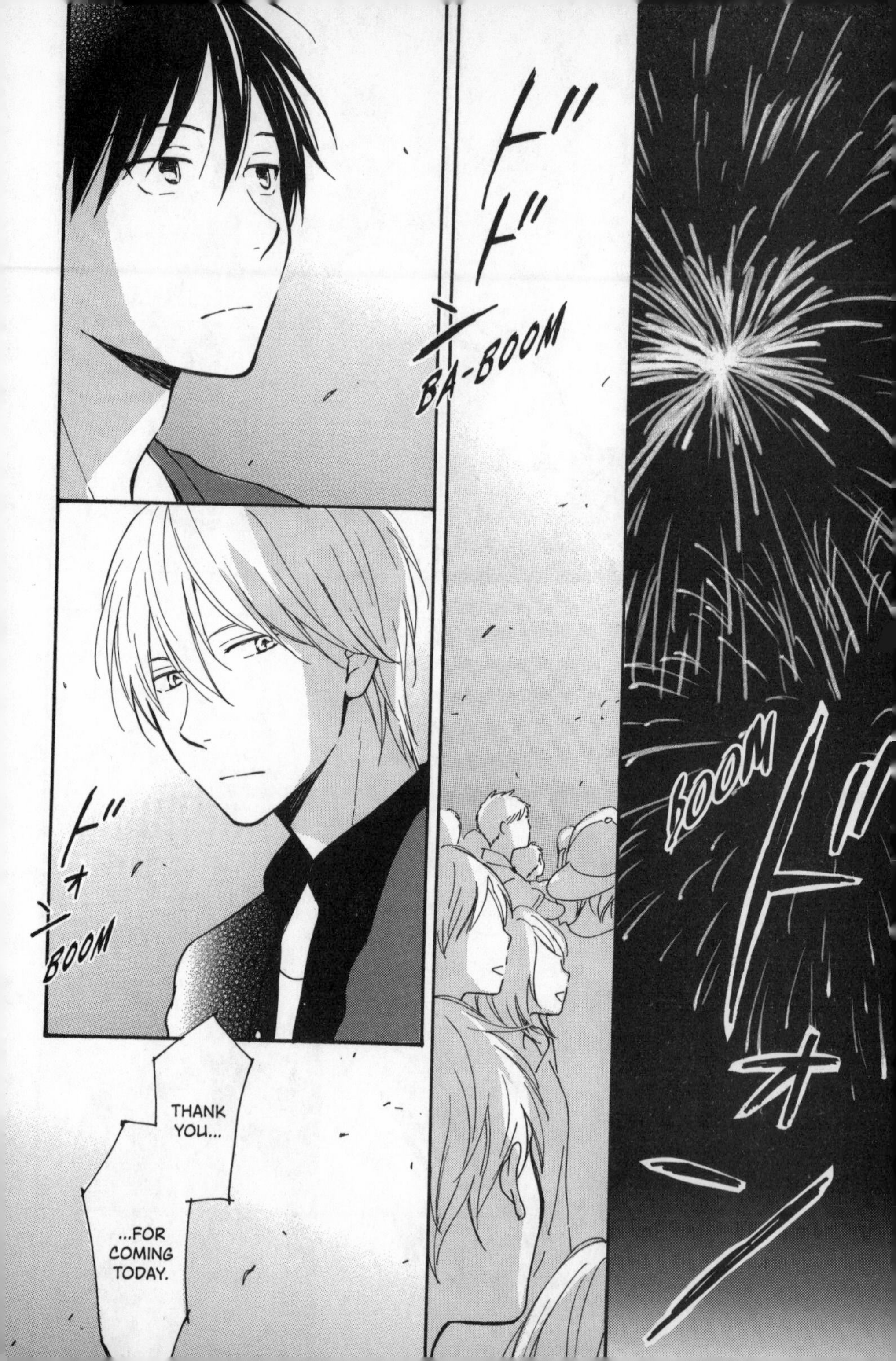
BOOM
BA-BOOM
BOOM
THANK YOU...
...FOR COMING TODAY.

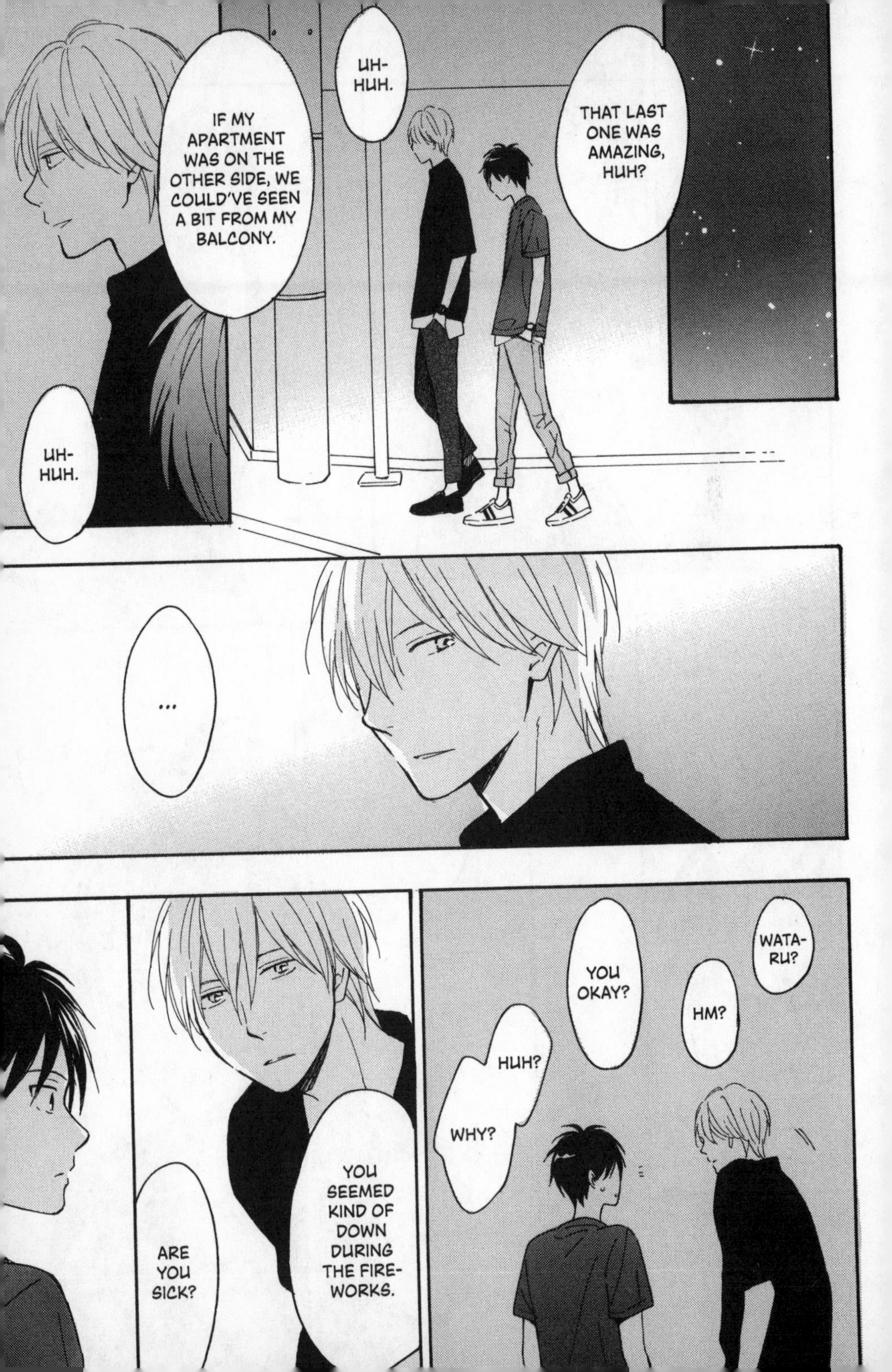
THAT LAST ONE WAS AMAZING, HUH?
UH-HUH.
IF MY APARTMENT WAS ON THE OTHER SIDE, WE COULD'VE SEEN A BIT FROM MY BALCONY.
UH-HUH.
...
WATA-RU?
HM?
YOU OKAY?
HUH?
WHY?
YOU SEEMED KIND OF DOWN DURING THE FIRE-WORKS.
ARE YOU SICK?

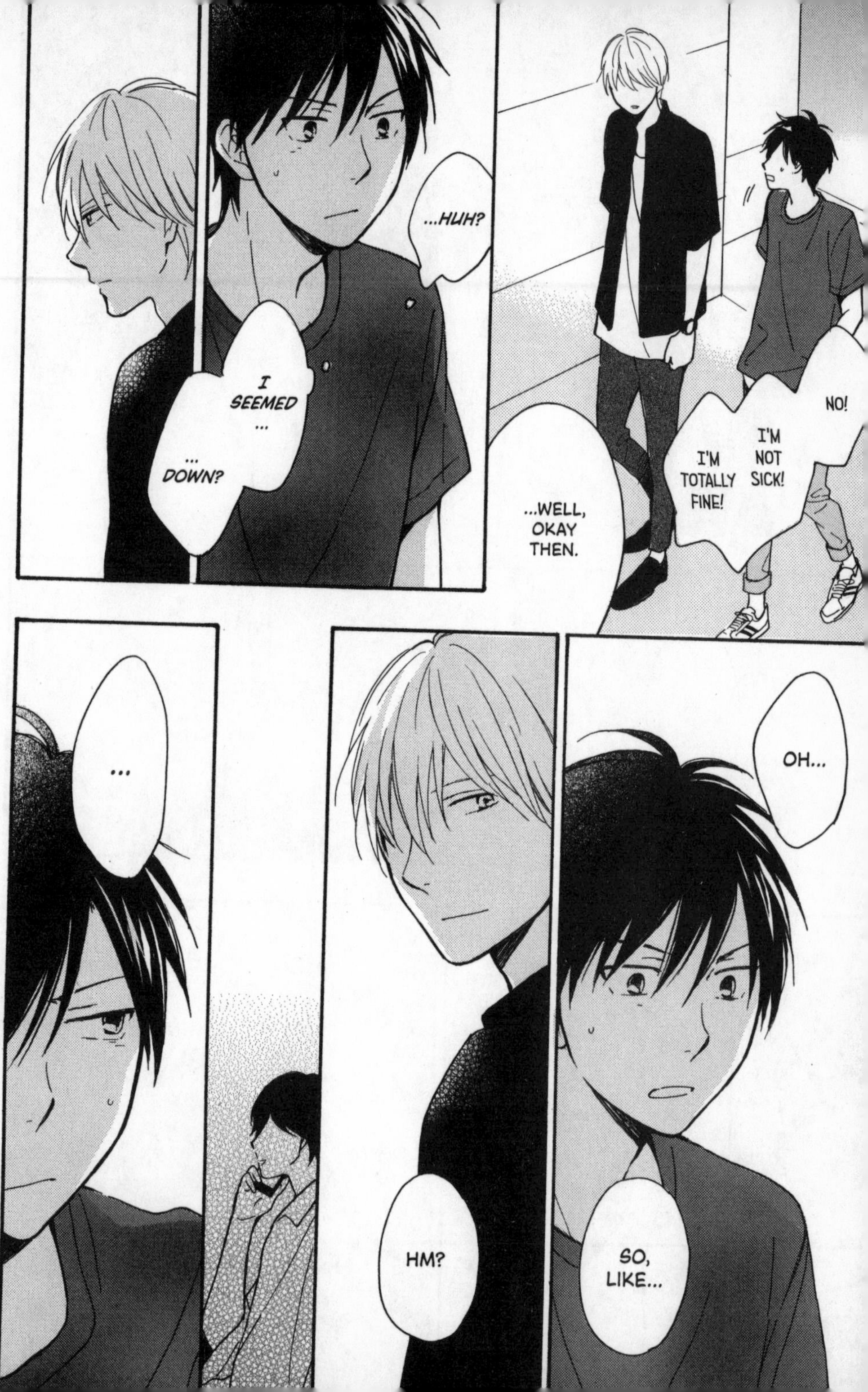
NO!
I'M NOT SICK!
I'M TOTALLY FINE!
...WELL, OKAY THEN.
...HUH?
I SEEMED ... ... DOWN?
OH...
SO, LIKE...
HM?
...

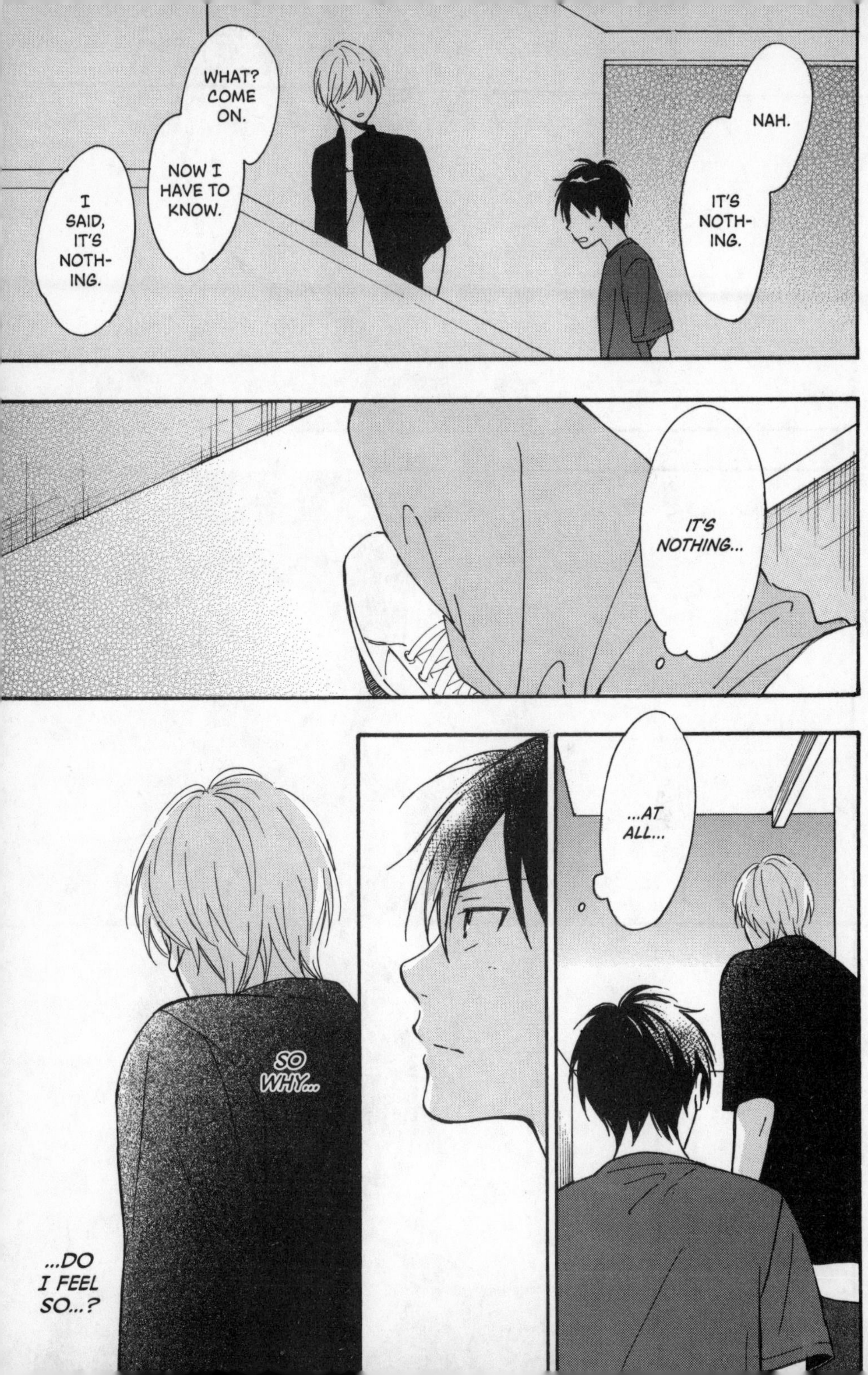
NAH.
IT'S NOTHING.
WHAT? COME ON.
NOW I HAVE TO KNOW.
I SAID, IT'S NOTHING.
IT'S NOTHING...
...AT ALL...
SO WHY...
...DO I FEEL SO...?

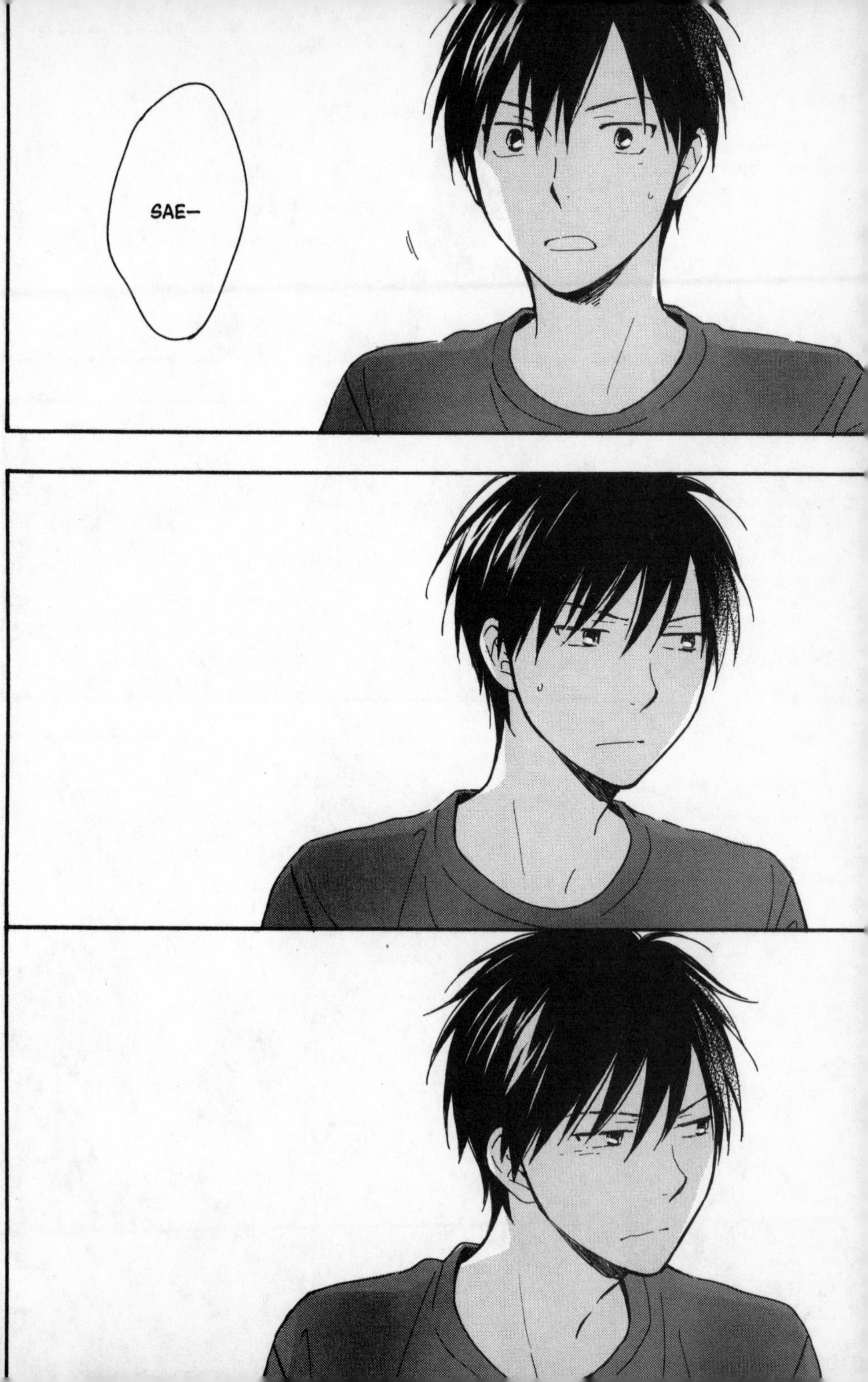
SAE—

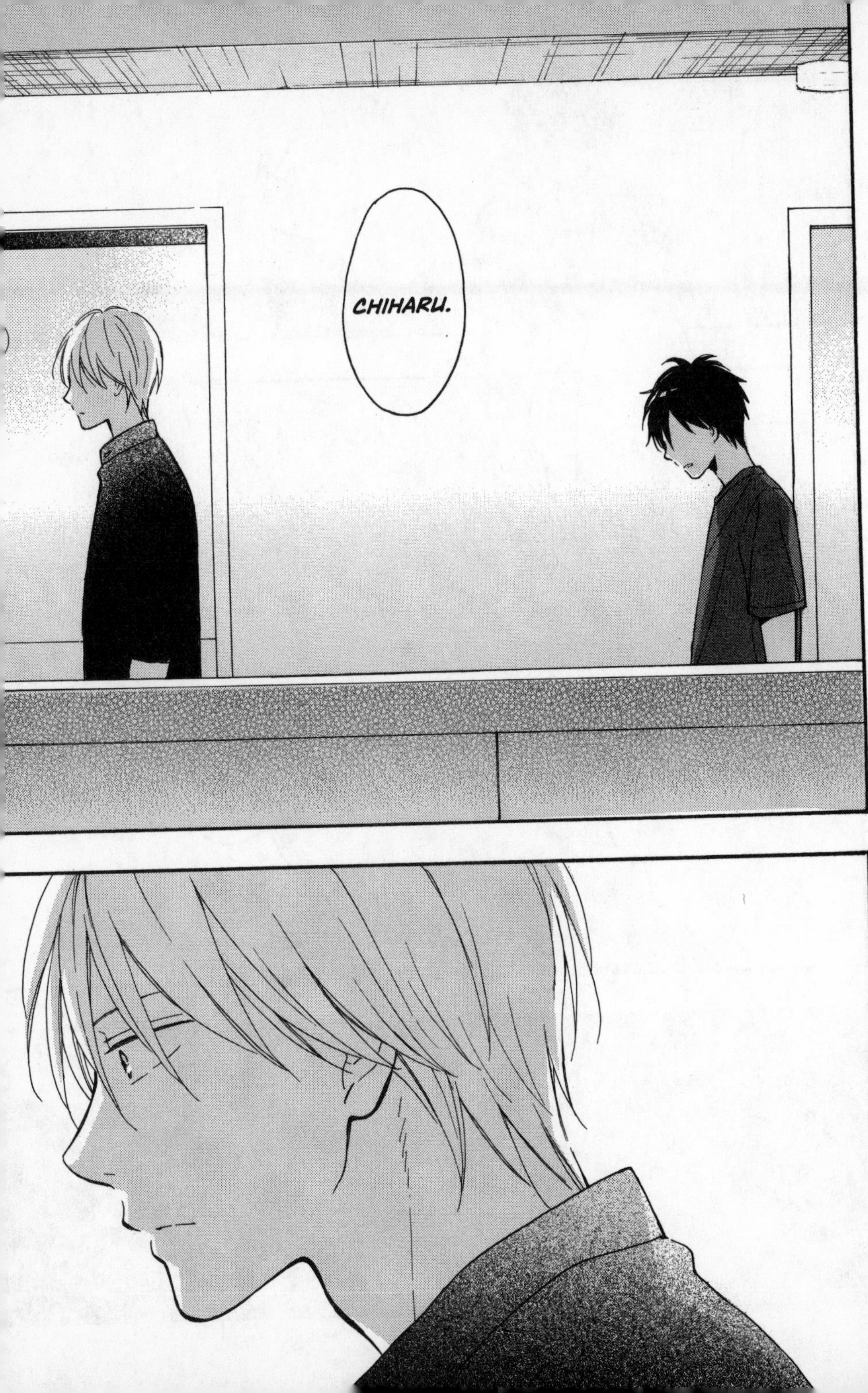
CHIHARU.

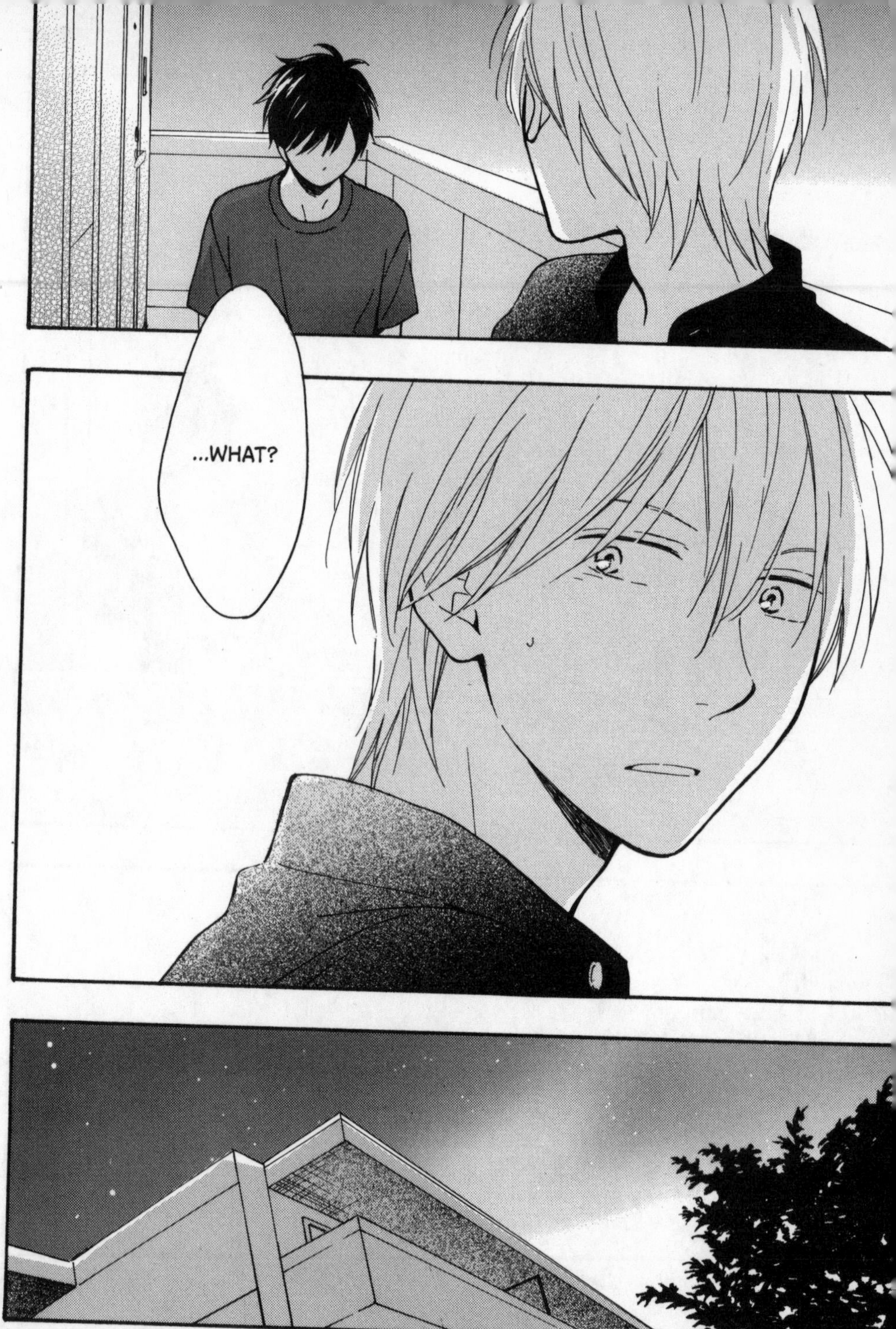
...WHAT?

MY **SUMMER** OF **YOU**

VOL.2: **THE SUMMER WITH YOU**

MY SUMMER OF YOU

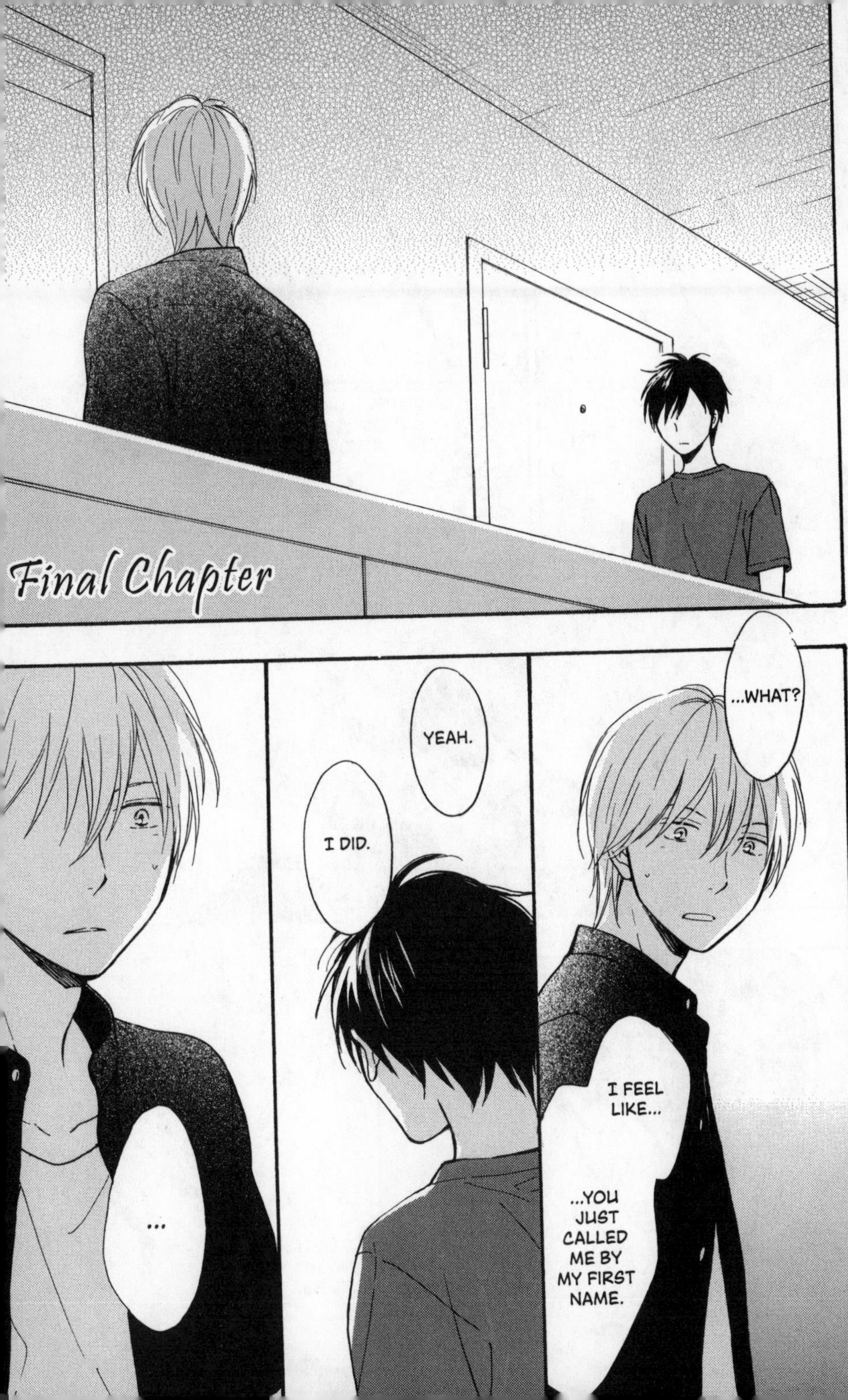
Final Chapter
...WHAT?
I FEEL LIKE...
...YOU JUST CALLED ME BY MY FIRST NAME.
YEAH.
I DID.
...

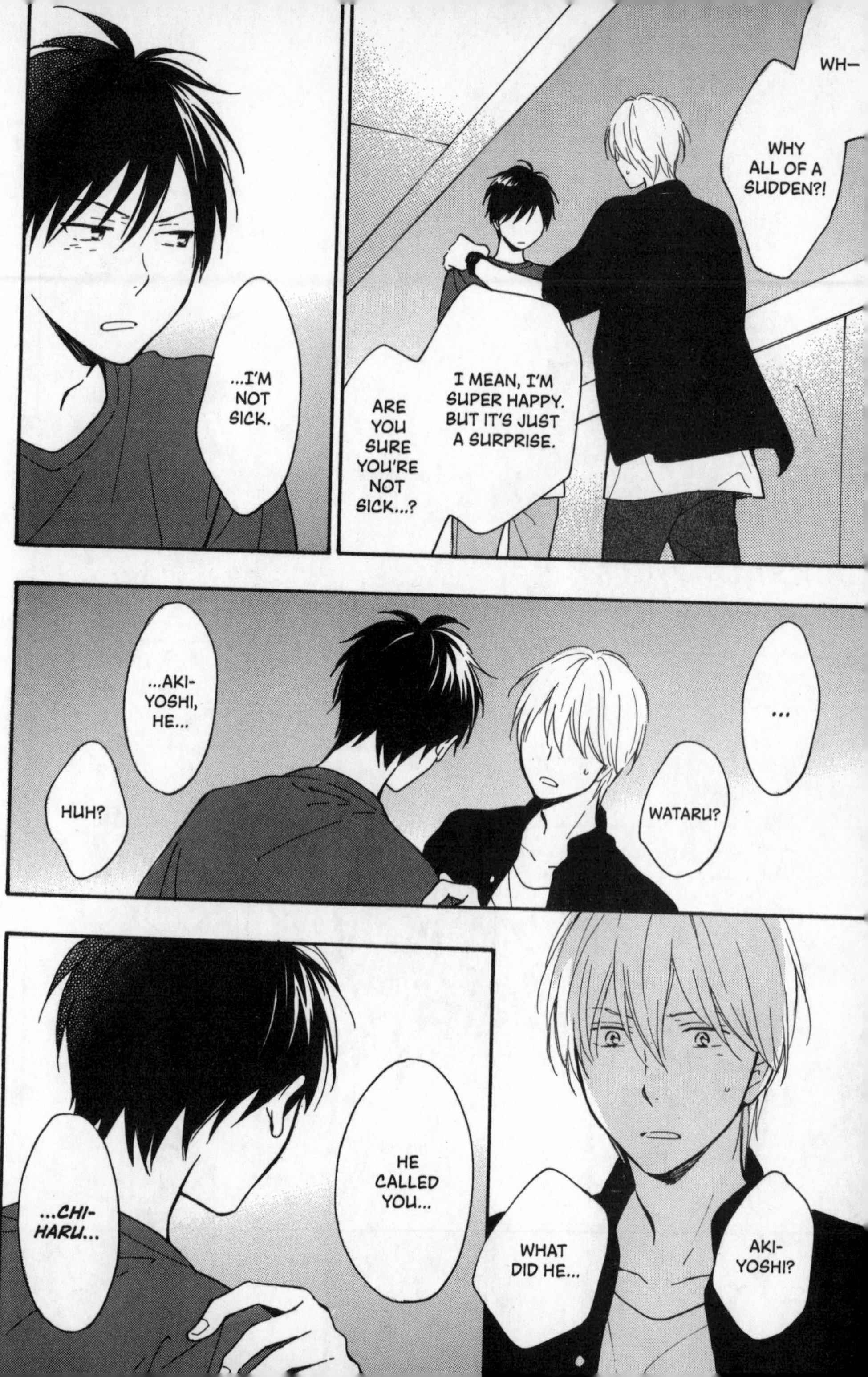
WH—
WHY ALL OF A SUDDEN?!
I MEAN, I'M SUPER HAPPY. BUT IT'S JUST A SURPRISE.
ARE YOU SURE YOU'RE NOT SICK...?
...I'M NOT SICK.
...
WATARU?
...AKI-YOSHI, HE...
HUH?
AKI-YOSHI?
WHAT DID HE...
HE CALLED YOU...
...CHI-HARU...

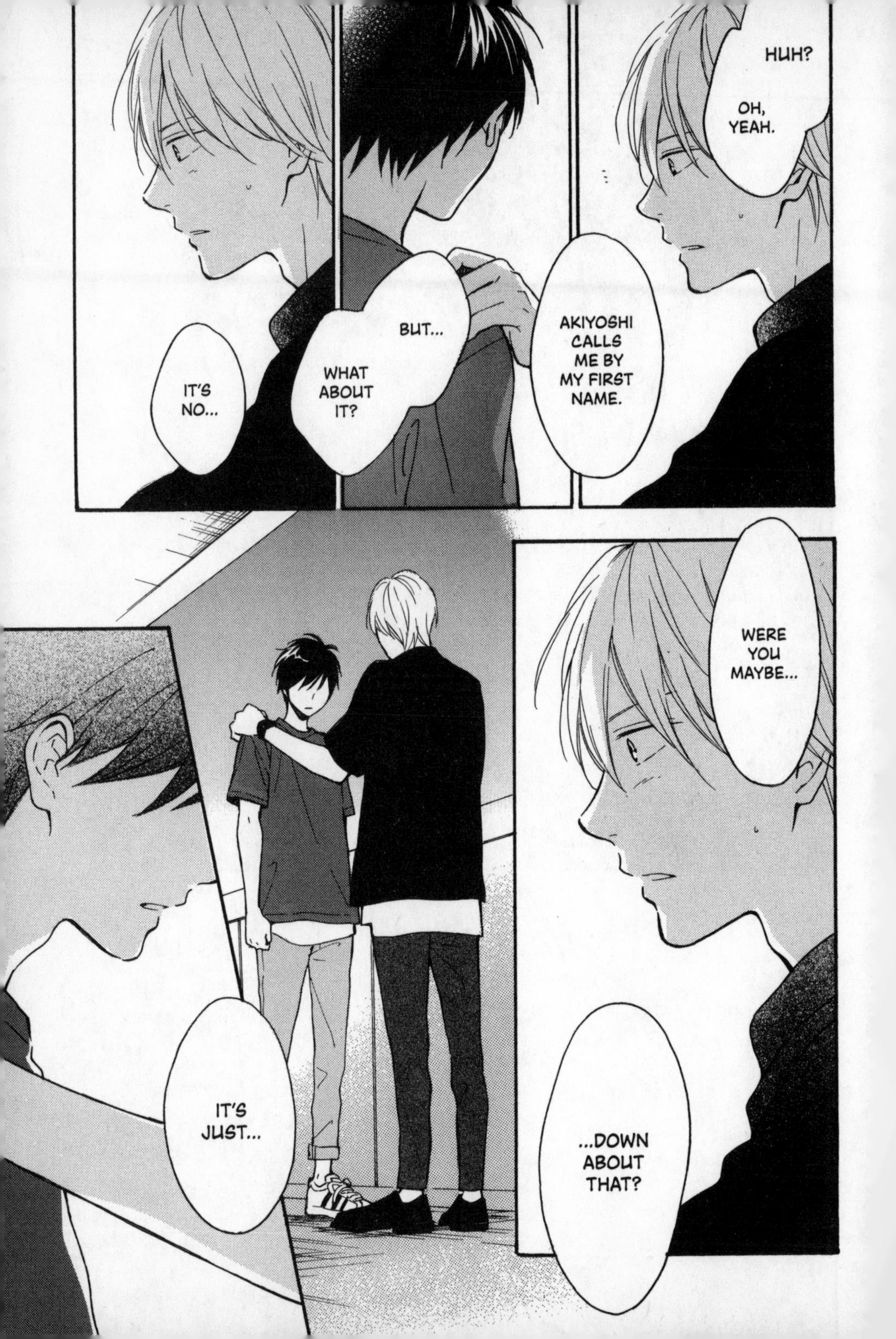
HUH?
OH, YEAH.
AKIYOSHI CALLS ME BY MY FIRST NAME.
BUT...
WHAT ABOUT IT?
IT'S NO...
WERE YOU MAYBE...
...DOWN ABOUT THAT?
IT'S JUST...

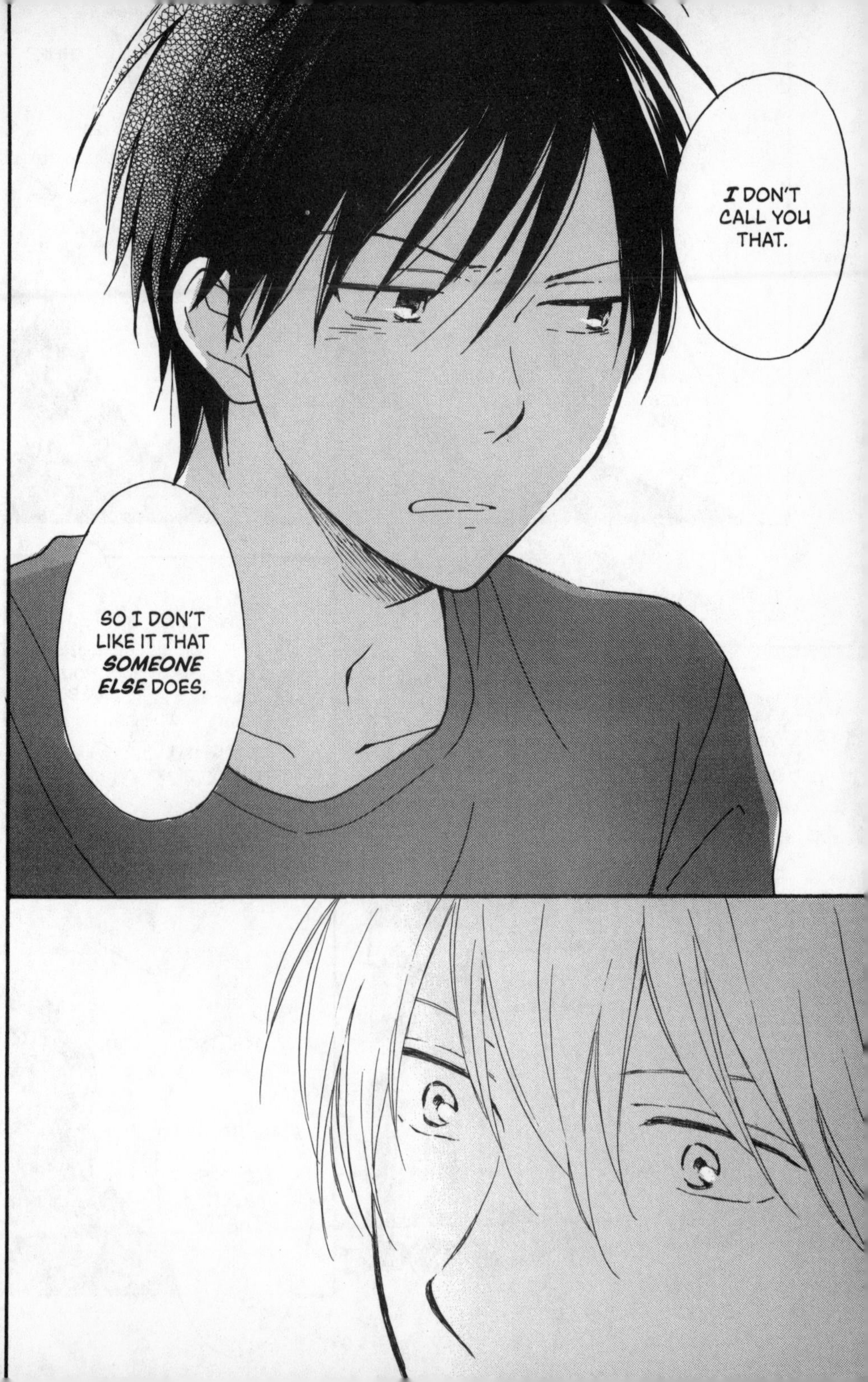
I DON'T CALL YOU THAT.
SO I DON'T LIKE IT THAT SOMEONE ELSE DOES.

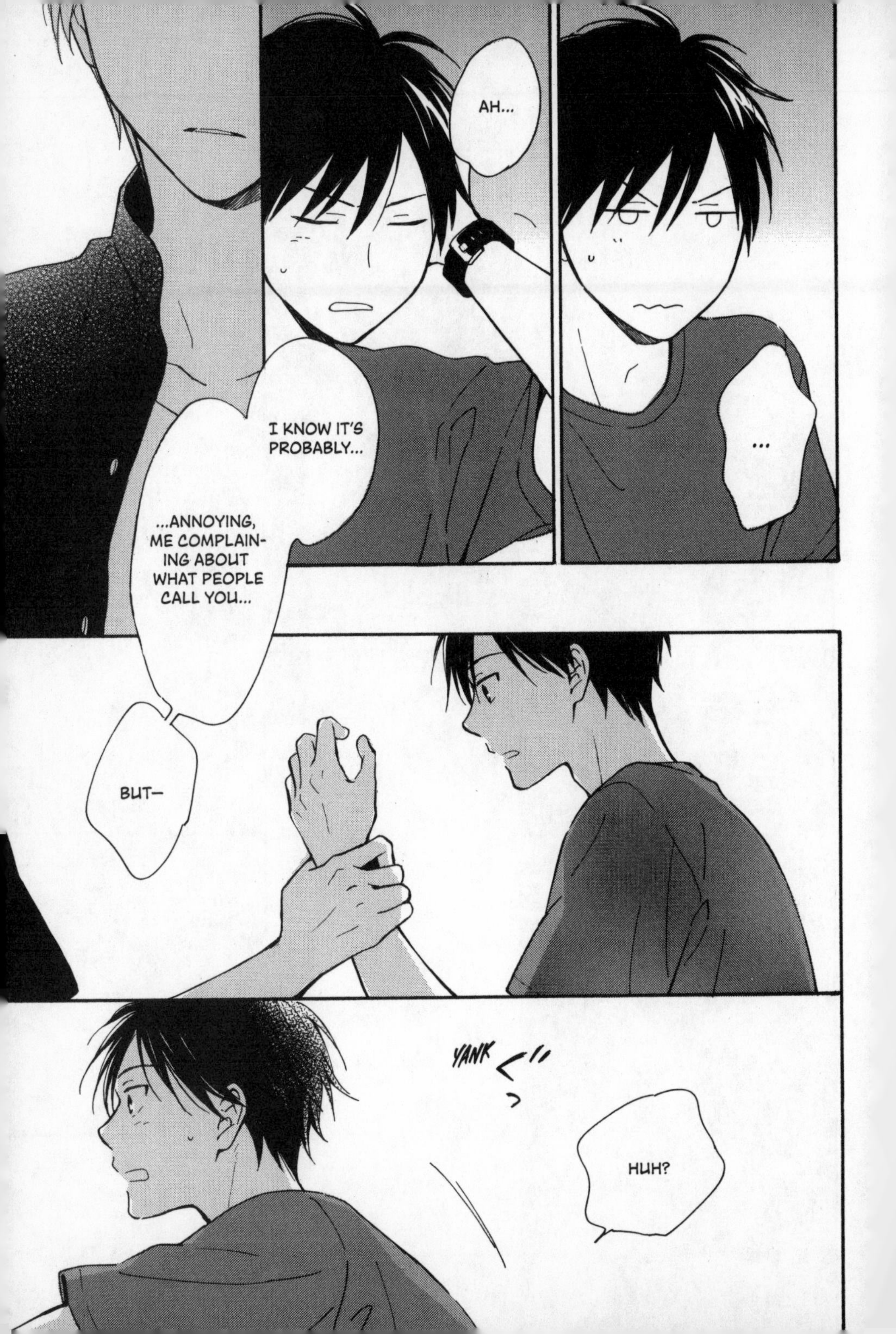
...
AH...
I KNOW IT'S PROBABLY...
...ANNOYING, ME COMPLAINING ABOUT WHAT PEOPLE CALL YOU...
BUT–
YANK
HUH?

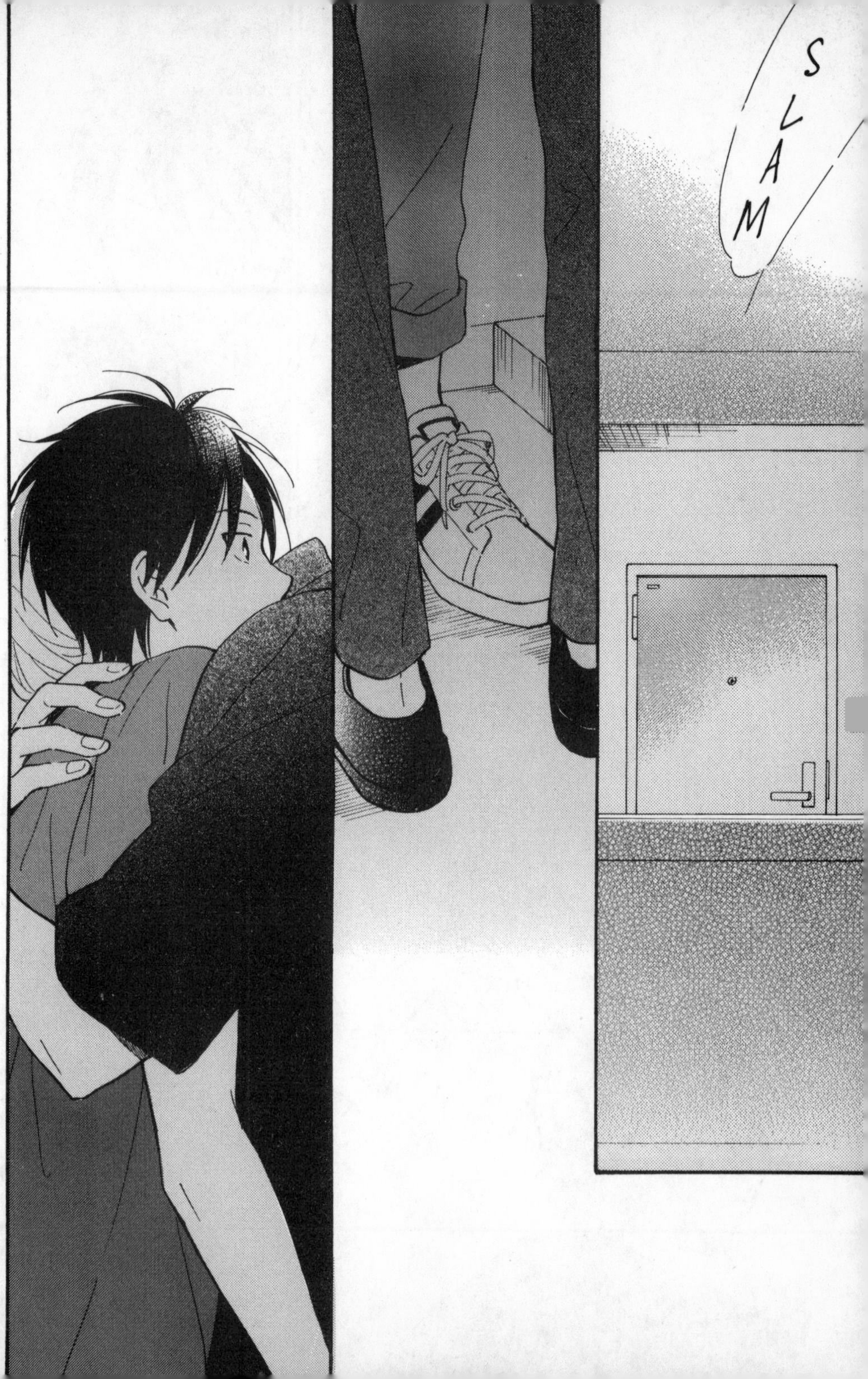
SLAM

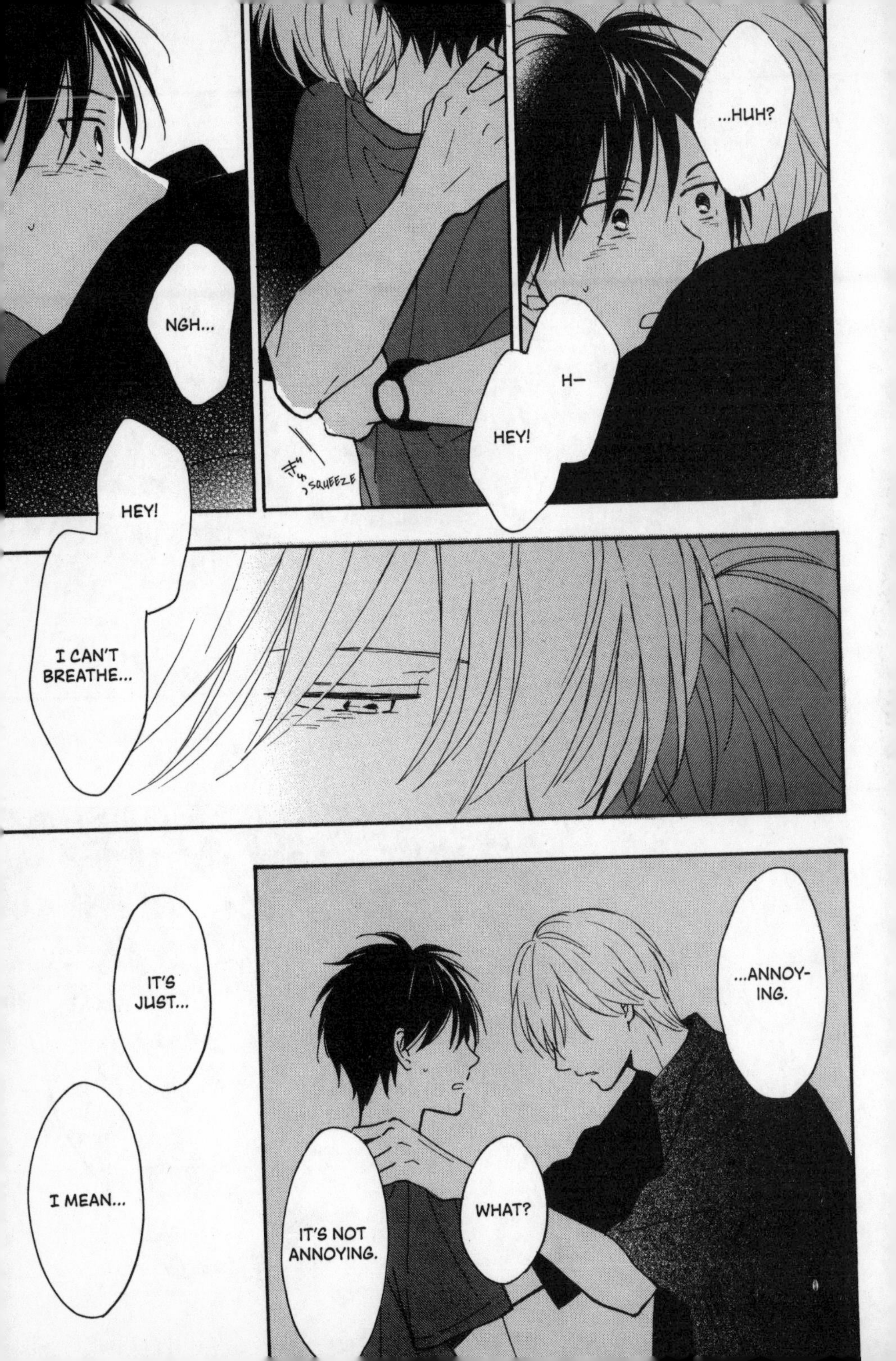
...HUH?
H— HEY!
SQUEEZE
NGH...
HEY!
I CAN'T BREATHE...
...ANNOYING.
WHAT?
IT'S NOT ANNOYING.
IT'S JUST...
I MEAN...

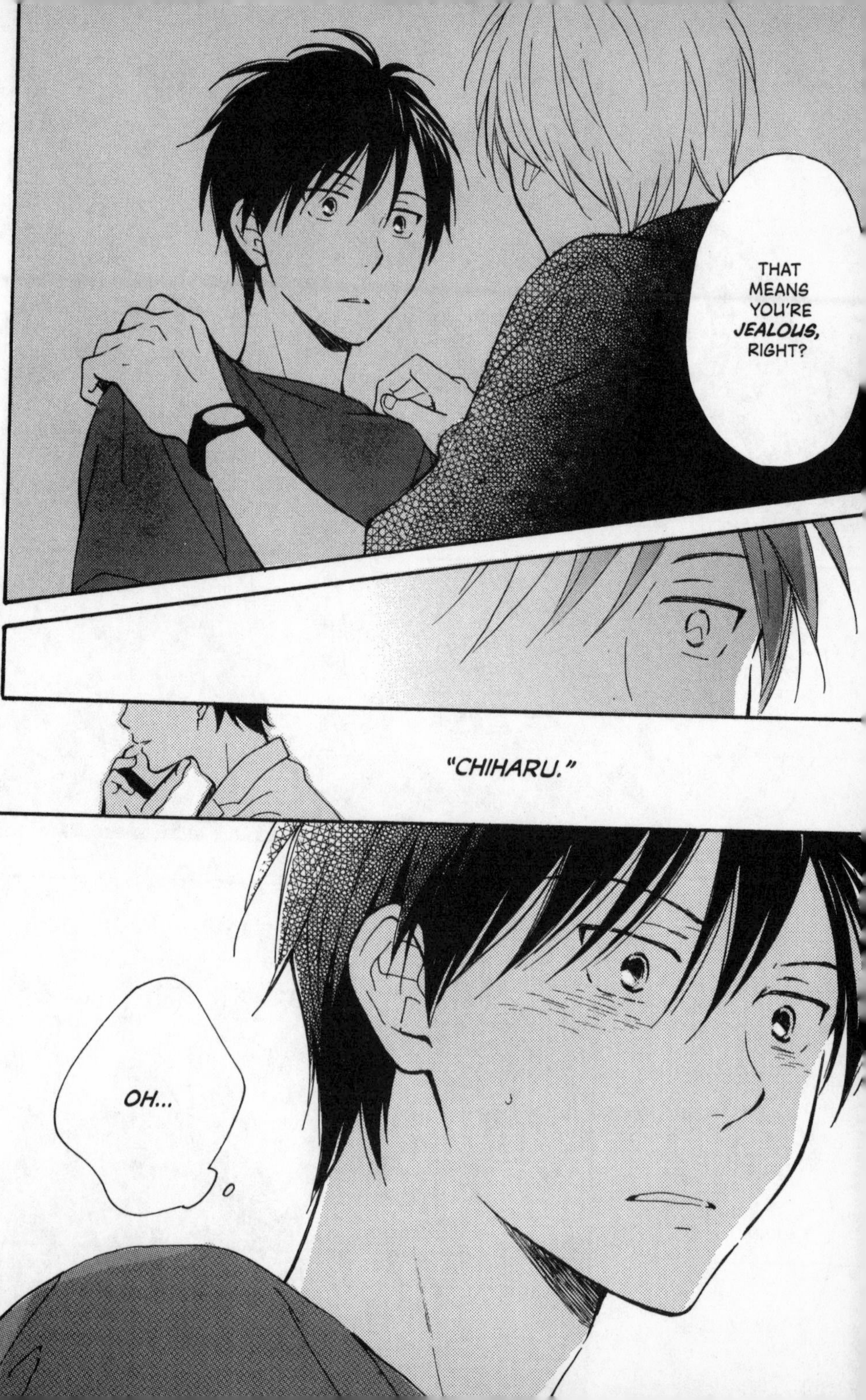
THAT MEANS YOU'RE JEALOUS, RIGHT?
"CHIHARU."
OH...

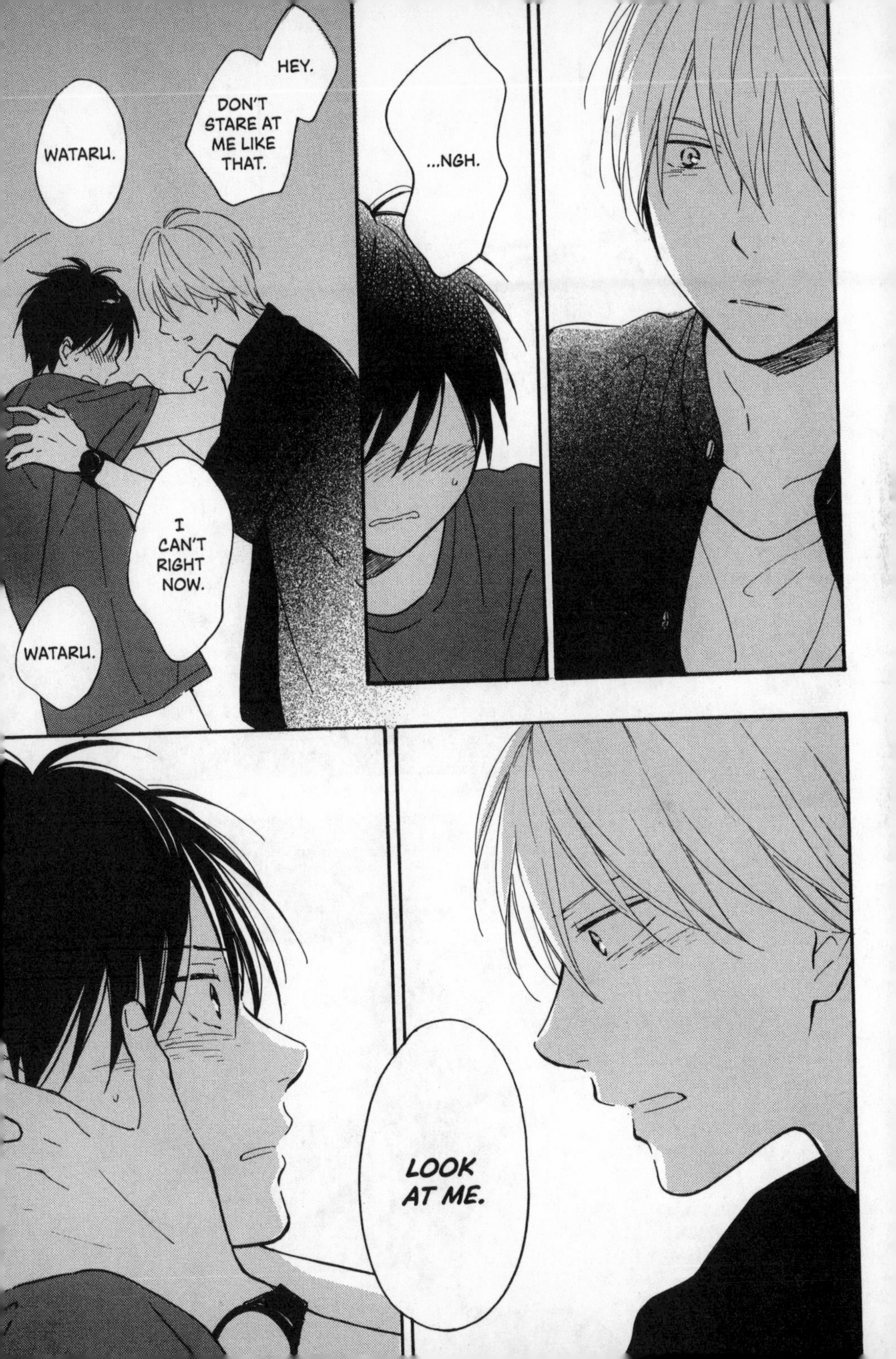
...NGH.
HEY.
DON'T STARE AT ME LIKE THAT.
WATARU.
I CAN'T RIGHT NOW.
WATARU.
LOOK AT ME.

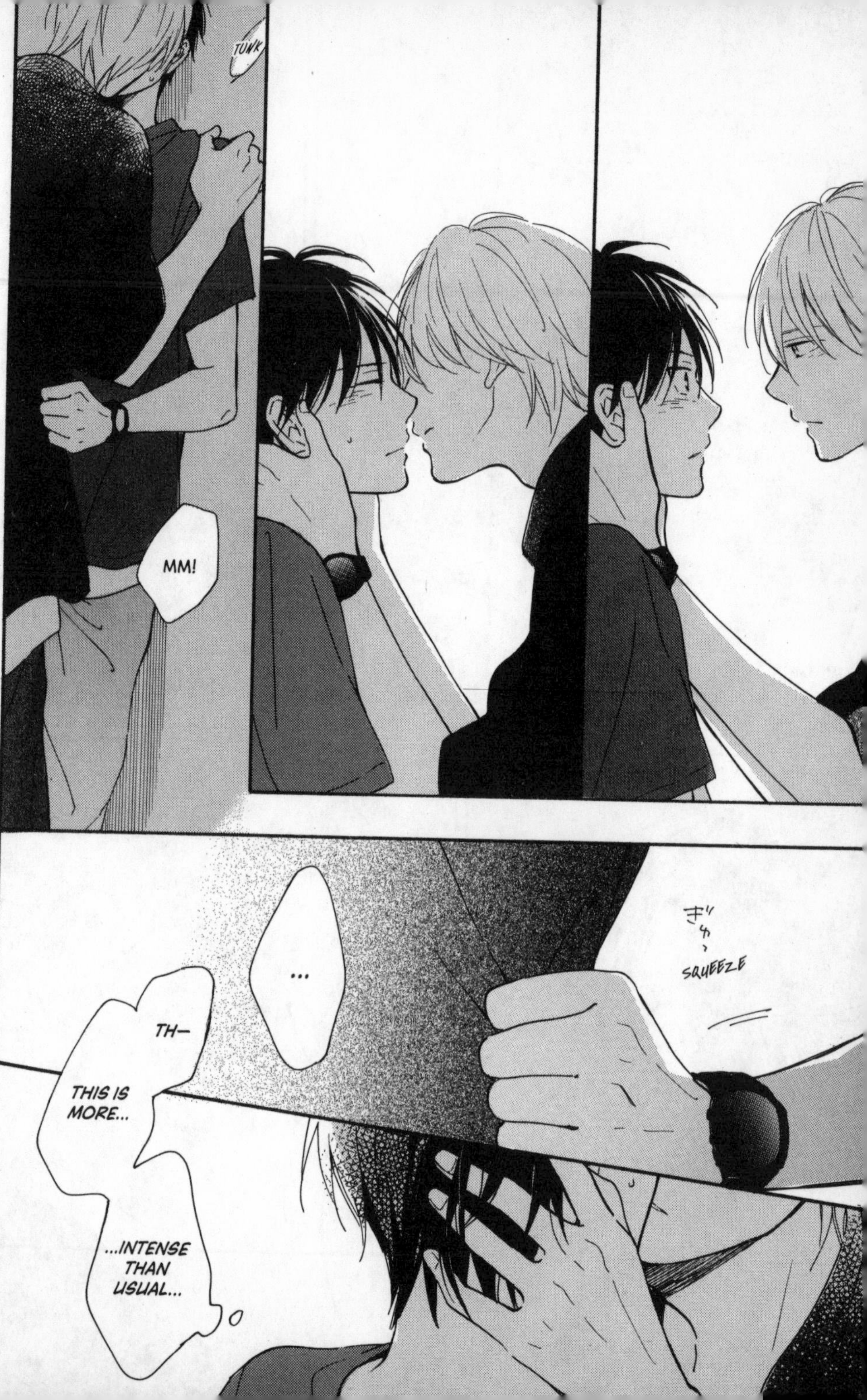
TUNK
MM!
ぎゅっ
SQUEEZE
...
TH—
THIS IS MORE...
...INTENSE THAN USUAL...

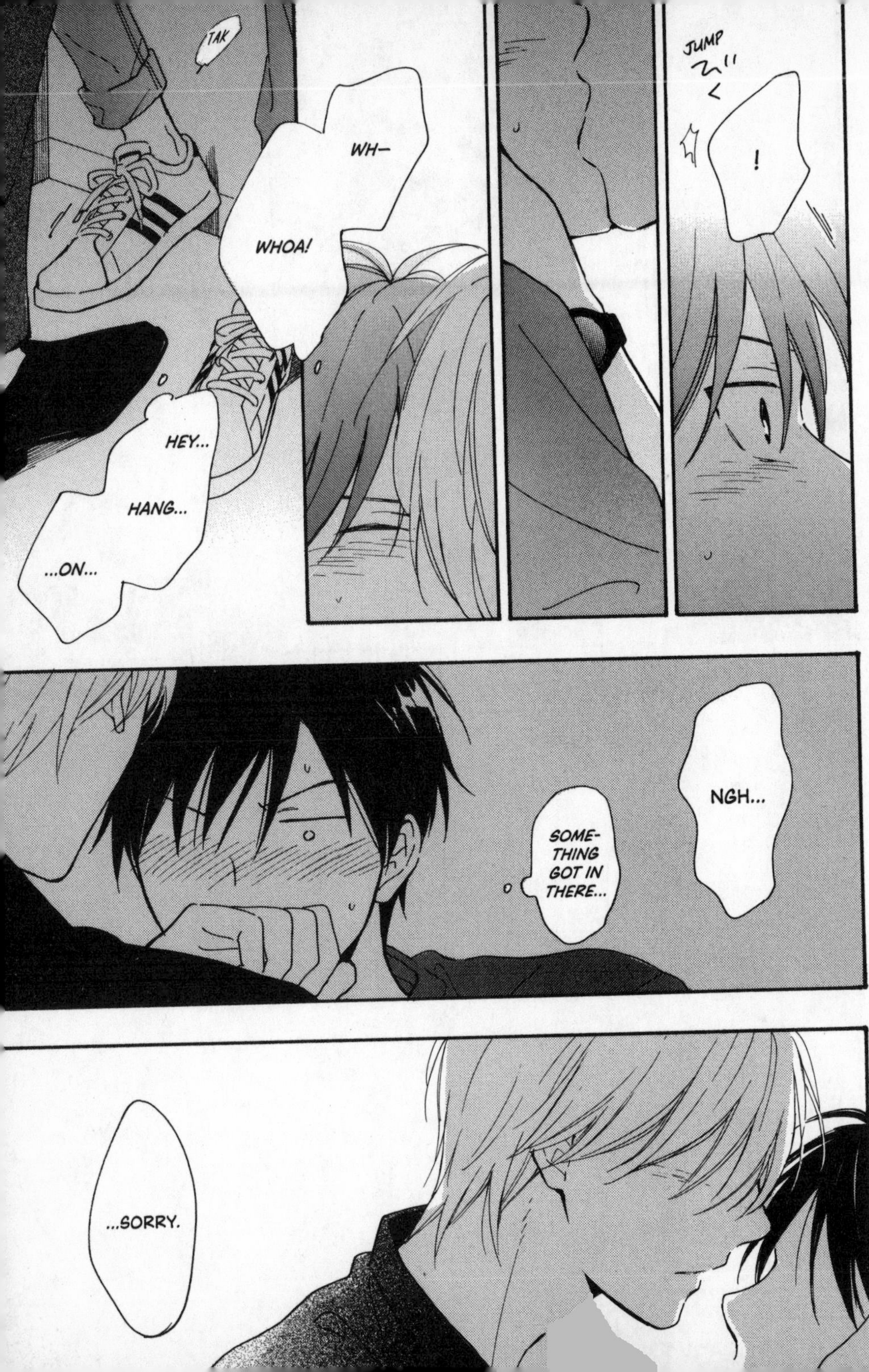
JUMP
!
TAK
WH— WHOA!
HEY... HANG... ...ON...
NGH...
SOME-THING GOT IN THERE...
...SORRY.

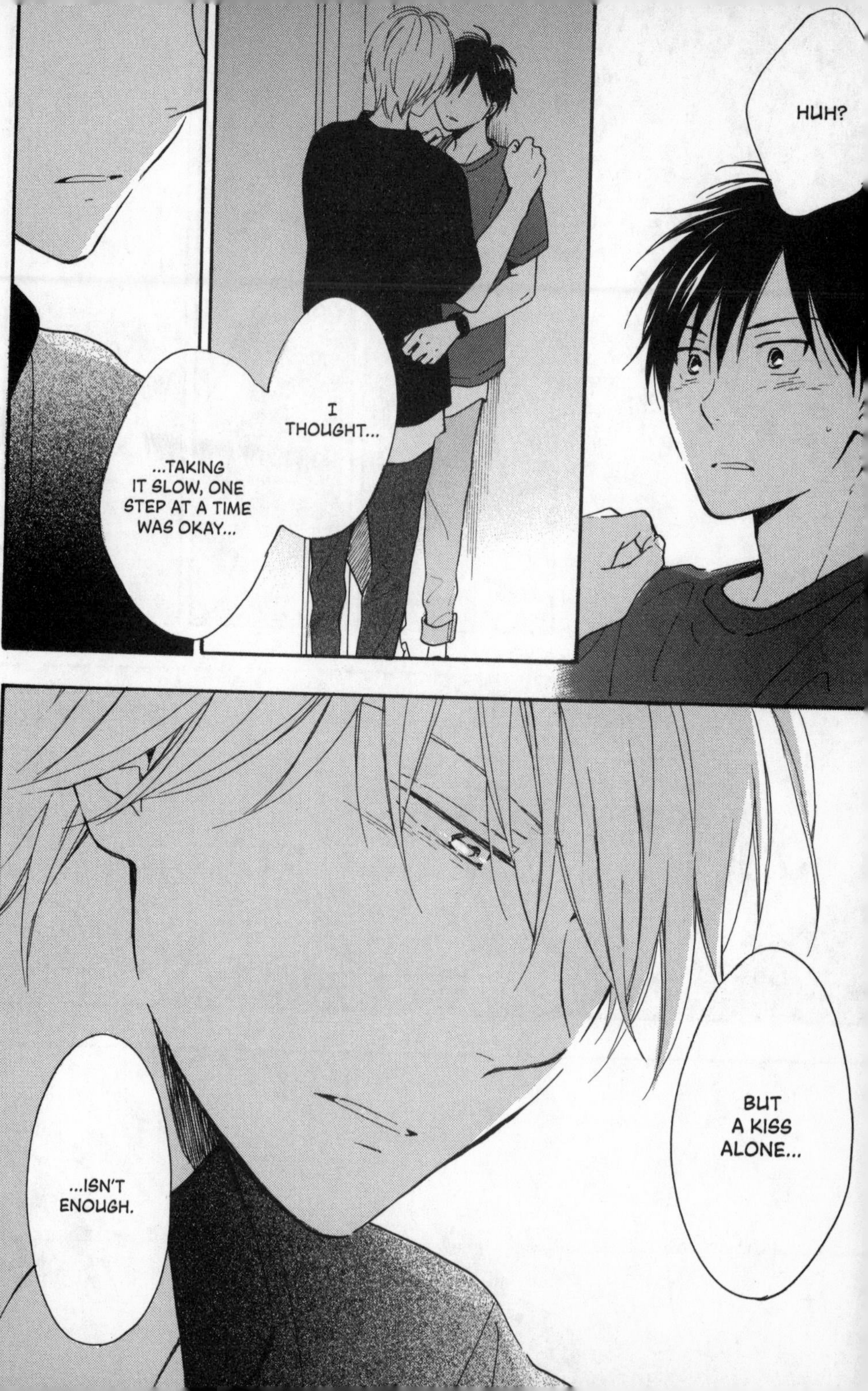
HUH?
I THOUGHT...
...TAKING IT SLOW, ONE STEP AT A TIME WAS OKAY...
BUT A KISS ALONE...
...ISN'T ENOUGH.

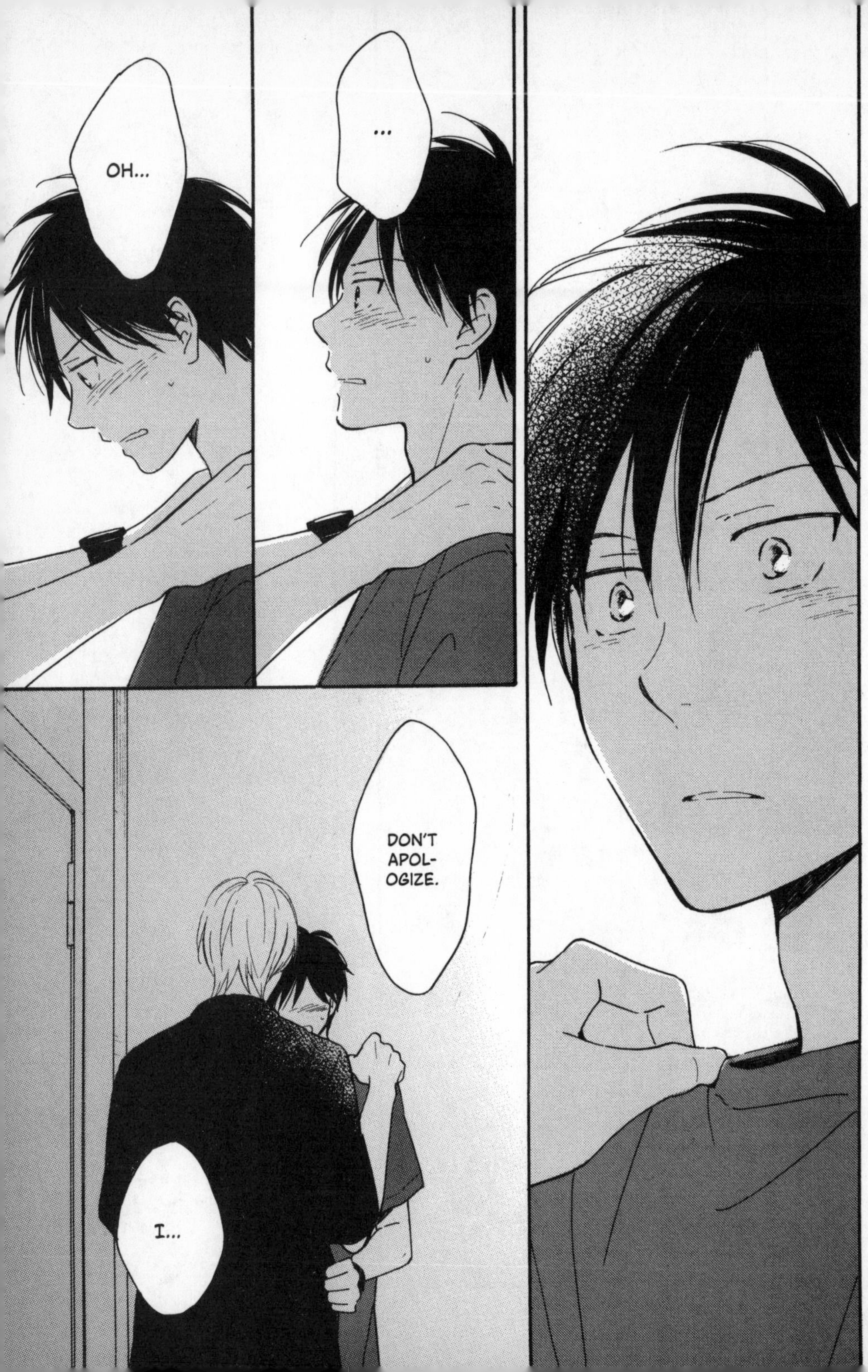
...
OH...
DON'T APOL-OGIZE.
I...

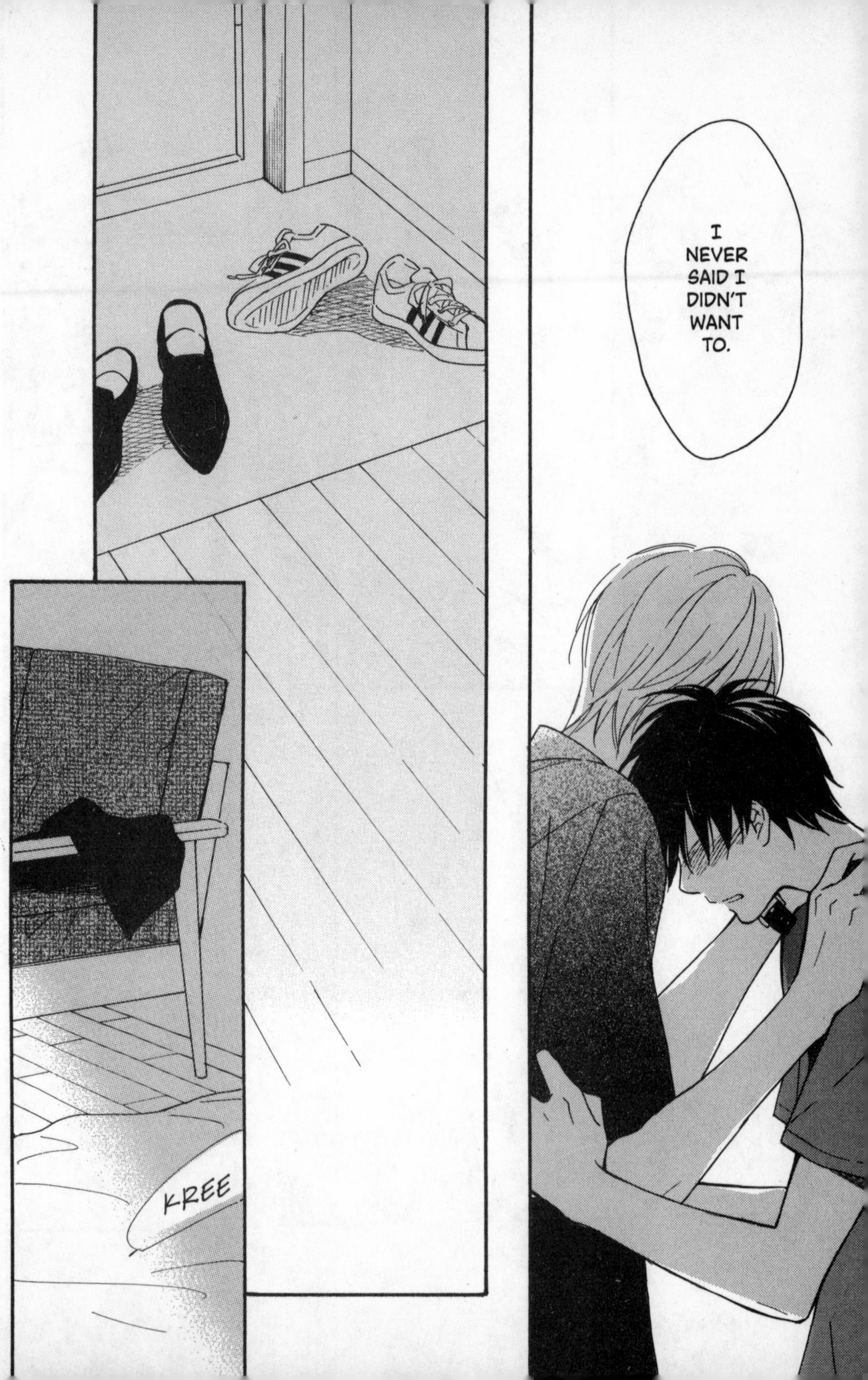
I NEVER SAID I DIDN'T WANT TO.
KREE

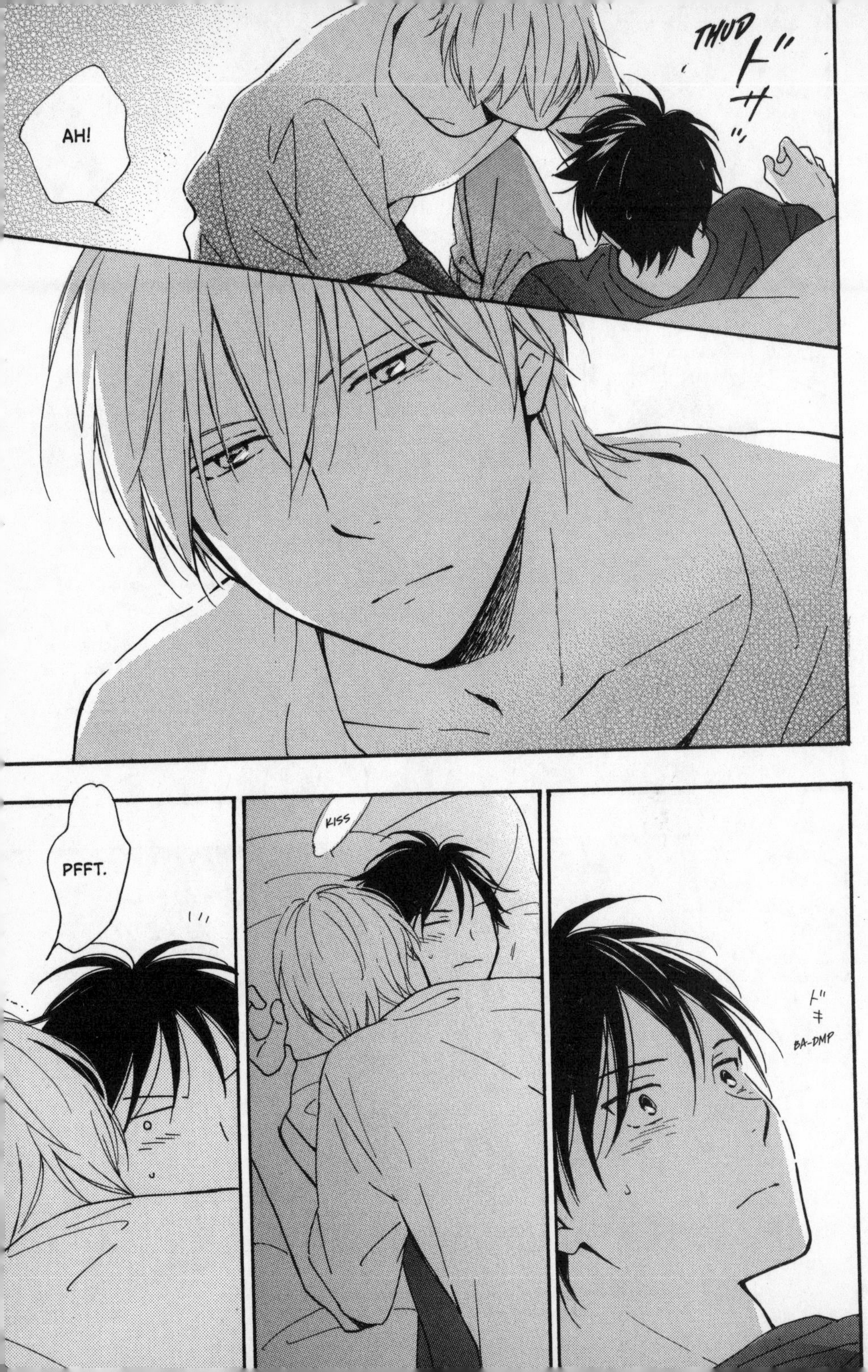
THUD
ドサ
AH!
ドキ
BA-DMP
KISS
PFFT.

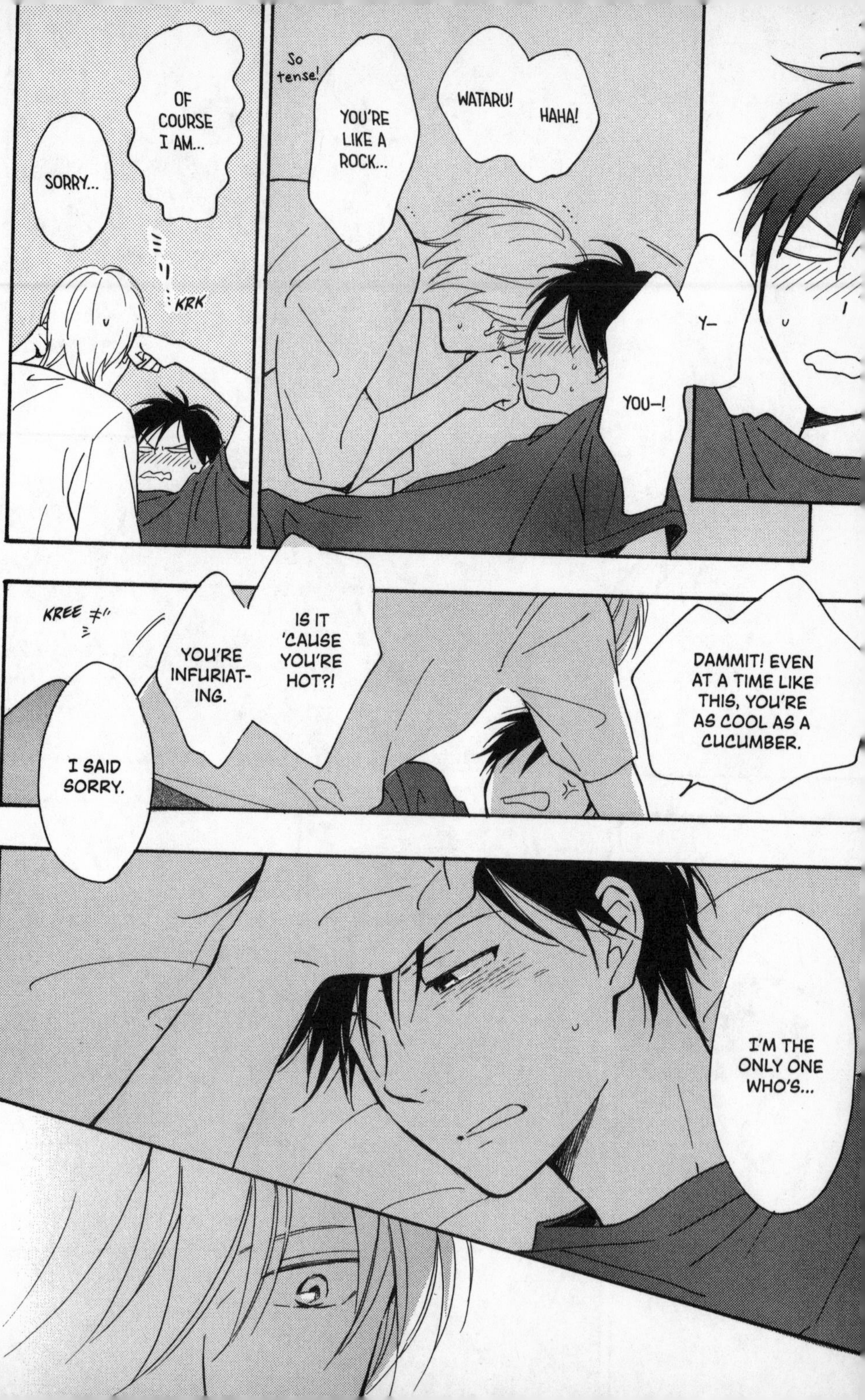
Y—
YOU—!
WATARU!
HAHA!
So tense!
YOU'RE LIKE A ROCK...
OF COURSE I AM...
SORRY...
KRK
DAMMIT! EVEN AT A TIME LIKE THIS, YOU'RE AS COOL AS A CUCUMBER.
IS IT 'CAUSE YOU'RE HOT?!
YOU'RE INFURIAT-ING.
KREE
I SAID SORRY.
I'M THE ONLY ONE WHO'S...

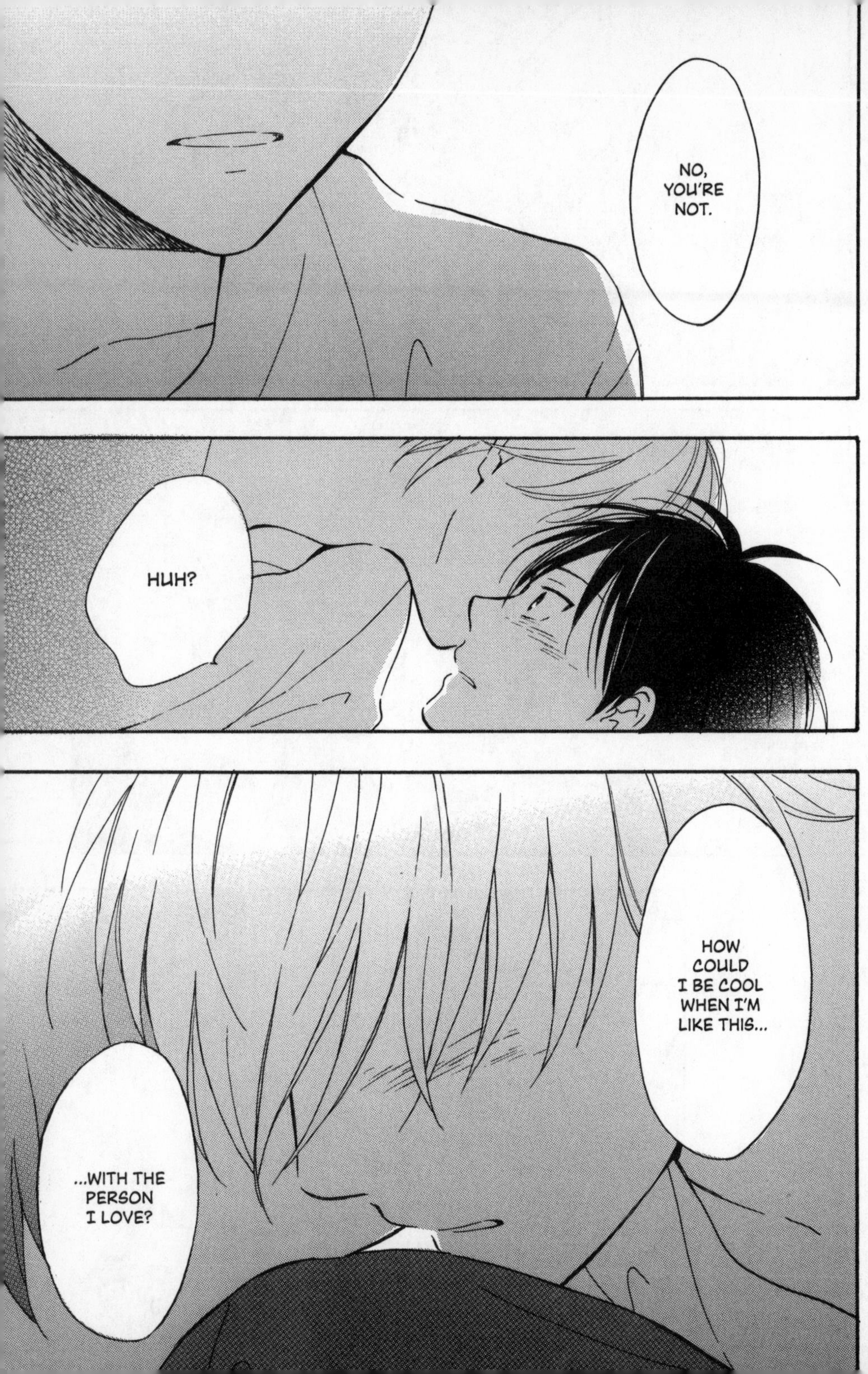
NO, YOU'RE NOT.
HUH?
HOW COULD I BE COOL WHEN I'M LIKE THIS...
...WITH THE PERSON I LOVE?

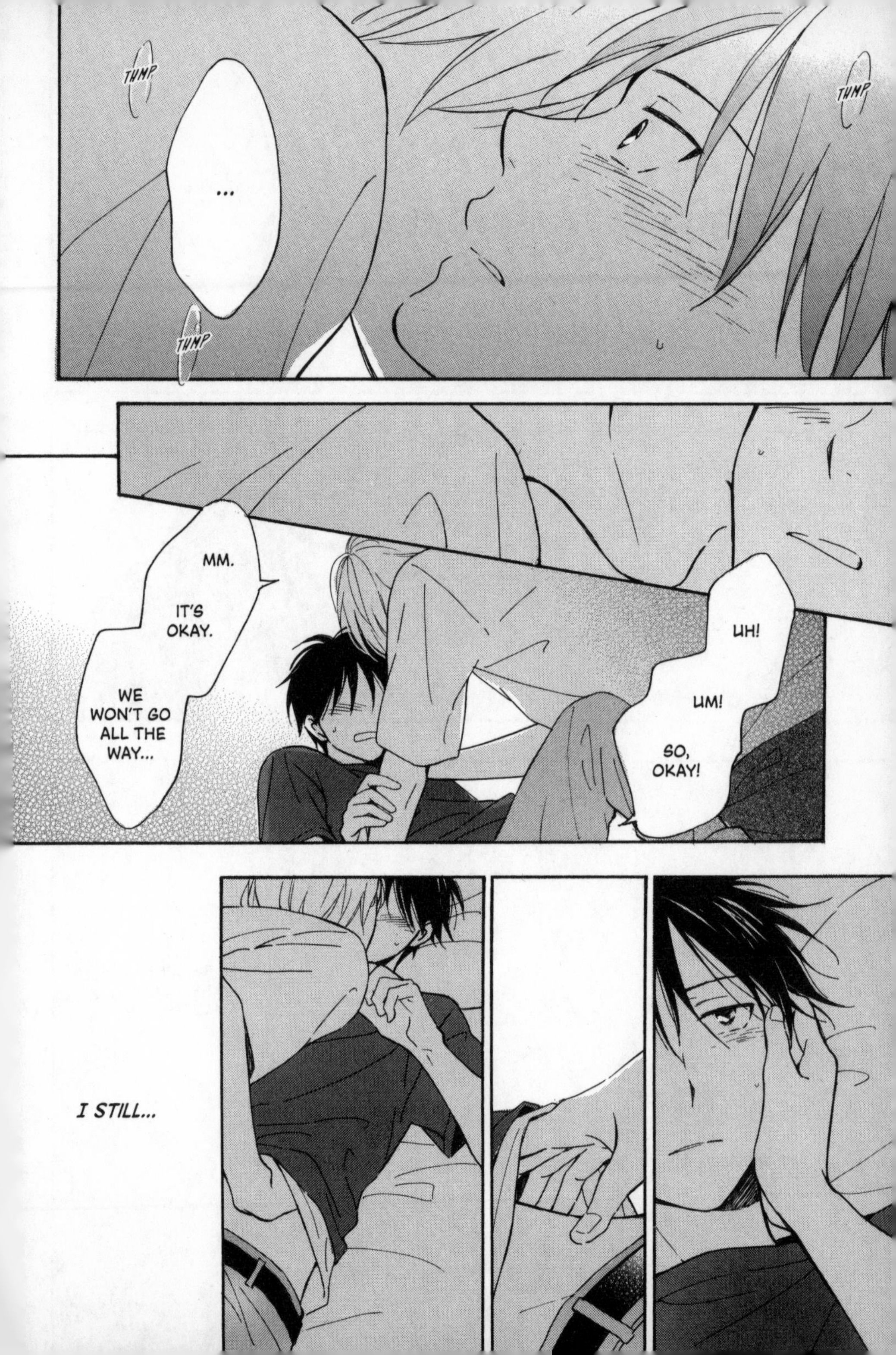
THUMP
THUMP
...
THUMP
UH! UM! SO, OKAY!
MM. IT'S OKAY. WE WON'T GO ALL THE WAY...
I STILL...

I STILL...

...HAVEN'T
CAUGHT UP...

...WITH HIM
AT ALL.

MAYBE I **CAN'T**
CATCH UP.

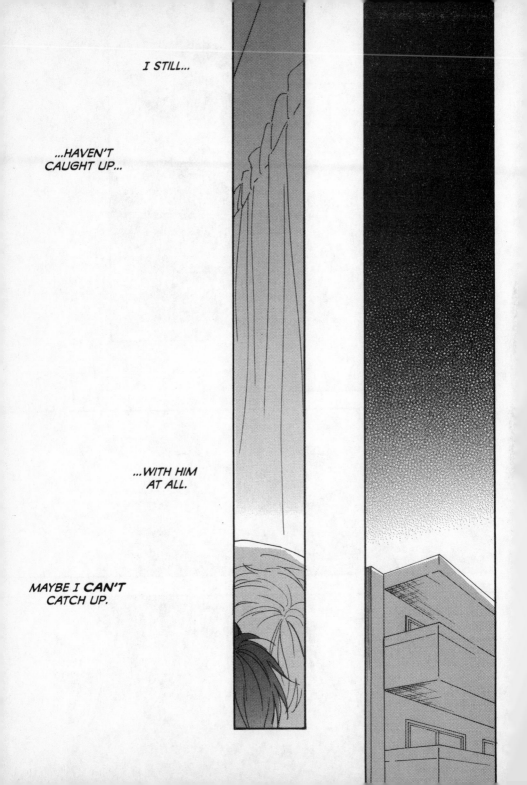

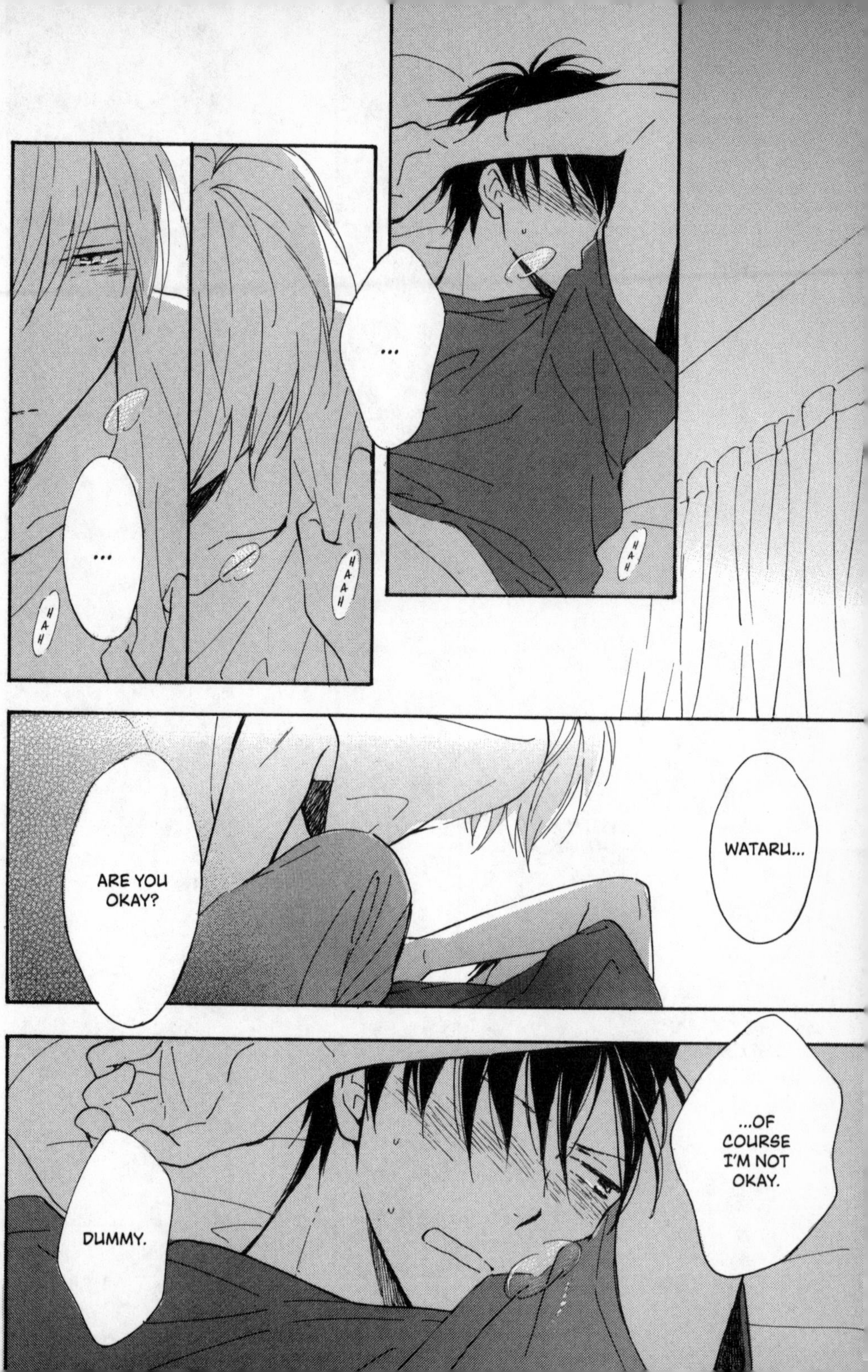
...
HAH
HAAH
...
HAH
WATARU...
ARE YOU OKAY?
...OF COURSE I'M NOT OKAY.
DUMMY.

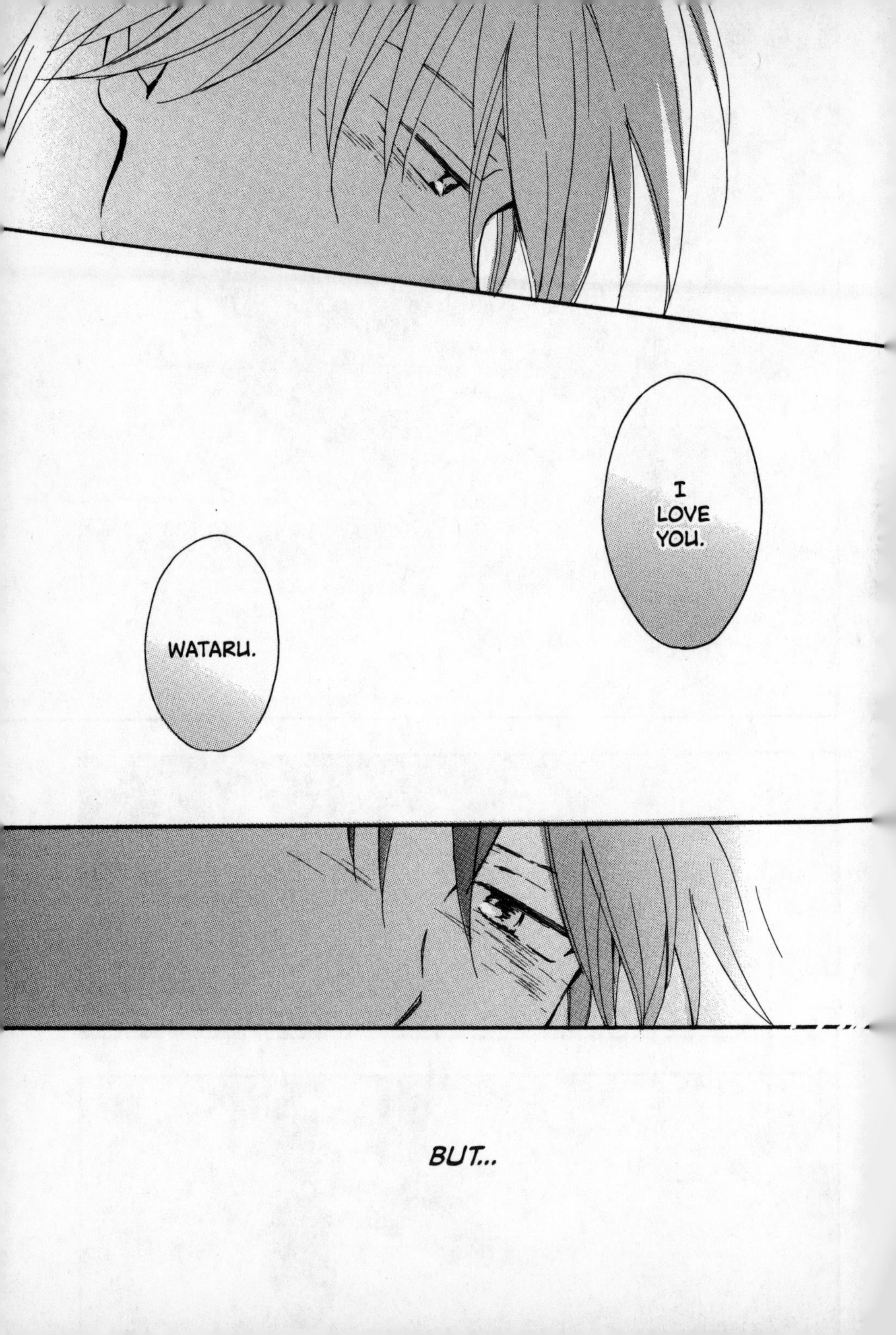
I LOVE YOU.
WATARU.
BUT...

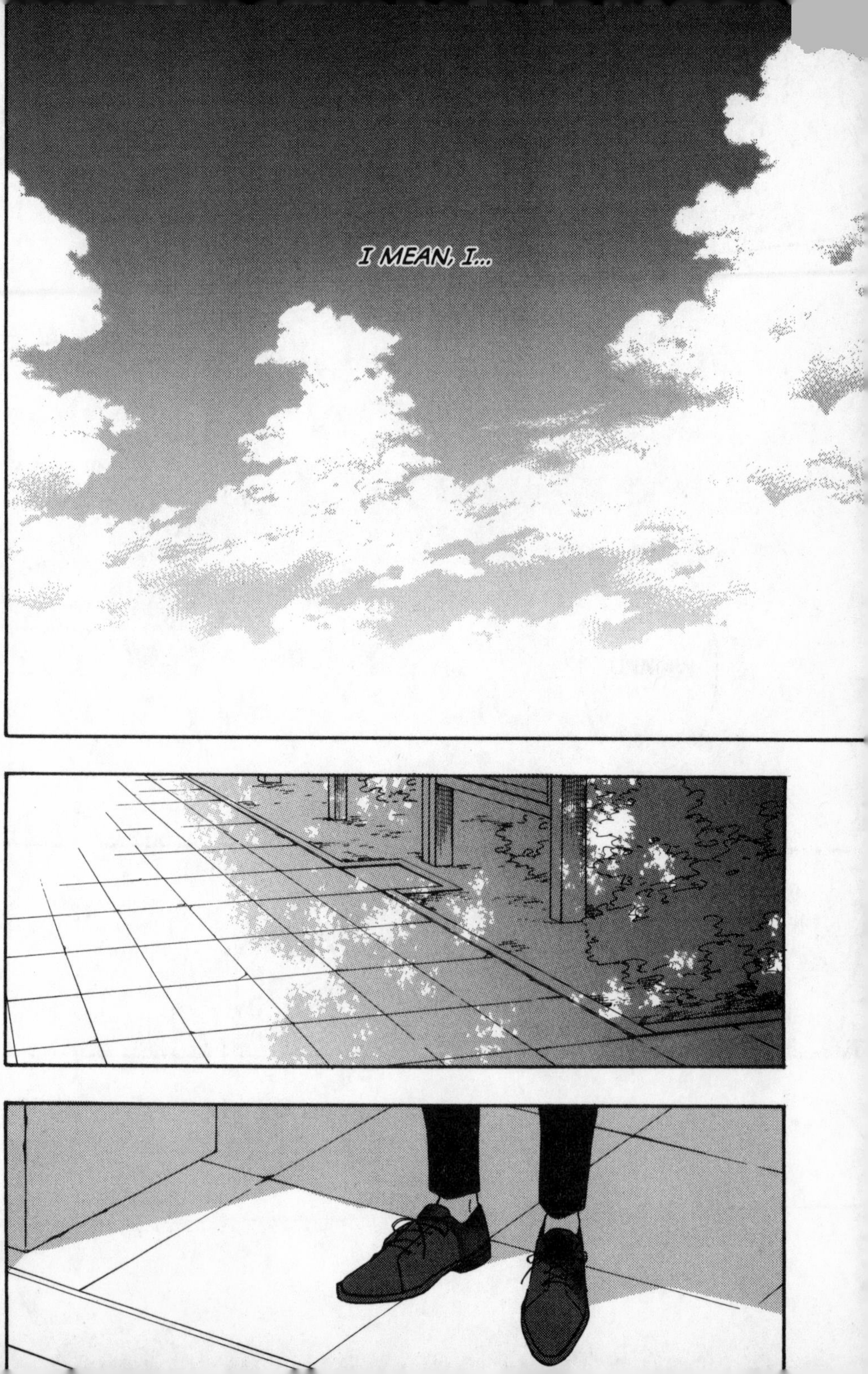
I MEAN, I...

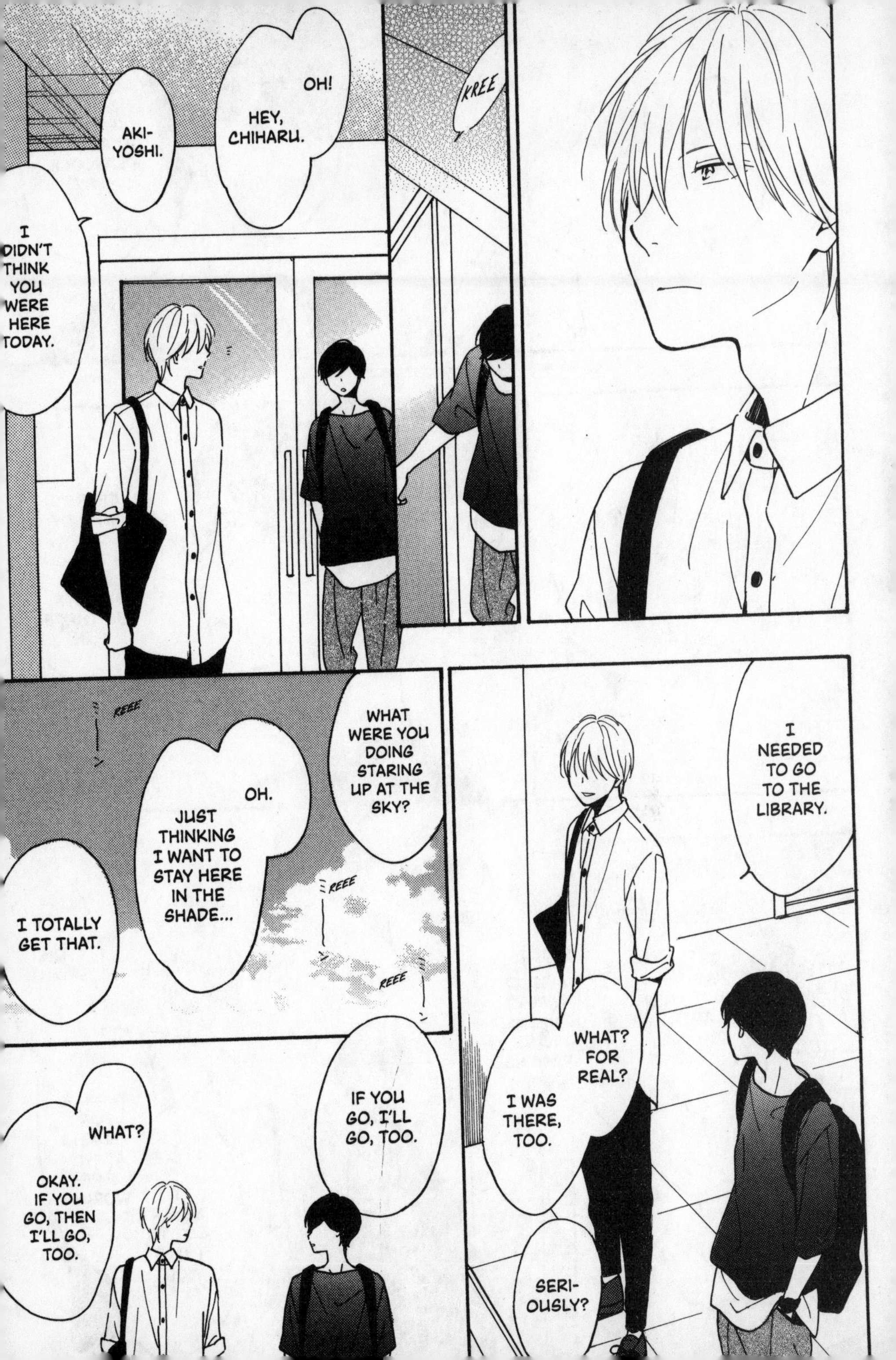
KREE
OH!
HEY, CHIHARU.
AKI-YOSHI.
I DIDN'T THINK YOU WERE HERE TODAY.
I NEEDED TO GO TO THE LIBRARY.
WHAT? FOR REAL?
I WAS THERE, TOO.
SERI-OUSLY?
WHAT WERE YOU DOING STARING UP AT THE SKY?
OH.
JUST THINKING I WANT TO STAY HERE IN THE SHADE...
I TOTALLY GET THAT.
REEE
REEE
REEE
IF YOU GO, I'LL GO, TOO.
WHAT?
OKAY. IF YOU GO, THEN I'LL GO, TOO.

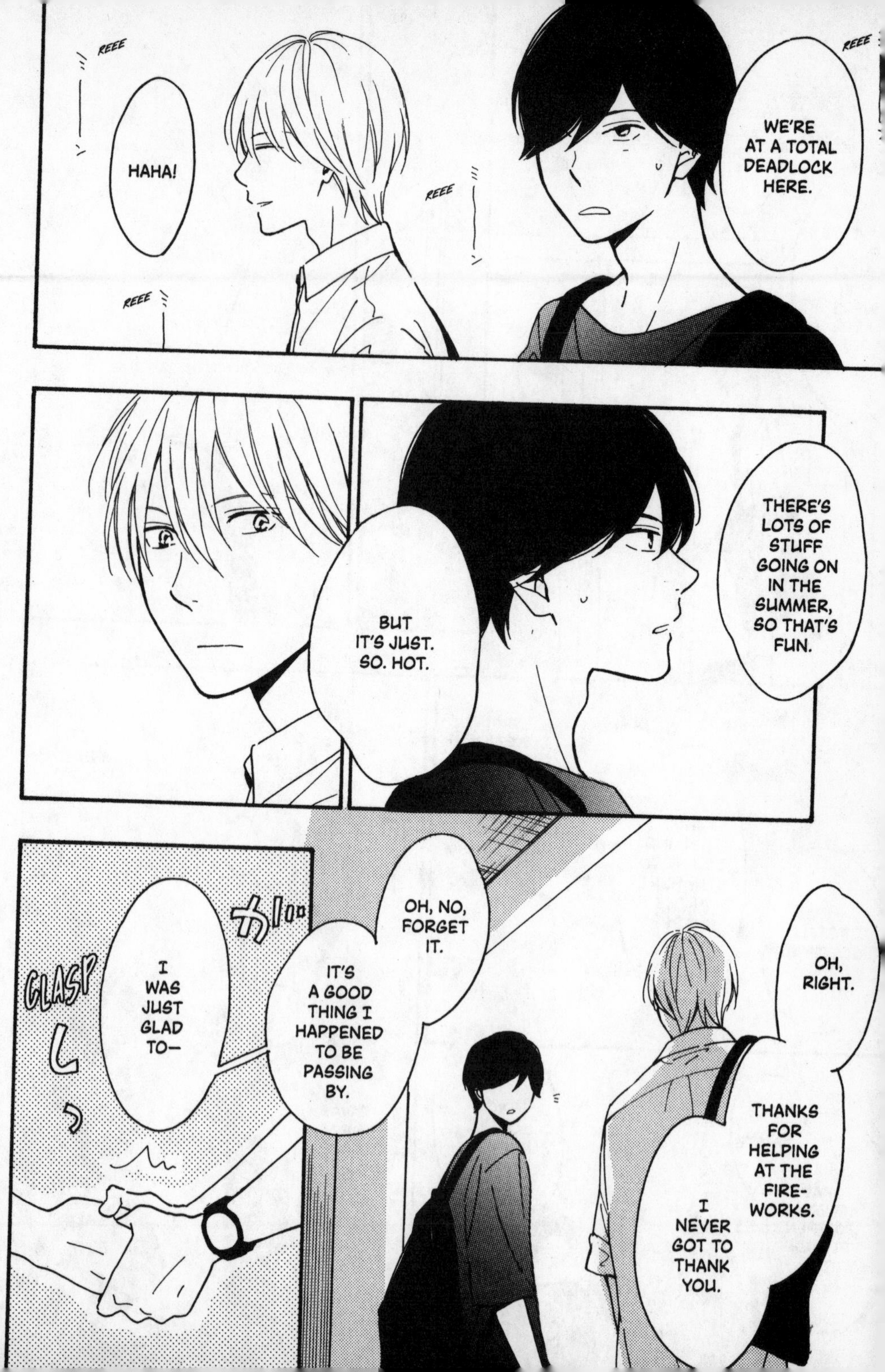
REEE
WE'RE AT A TOTAL DEADLOCK HERE.
REEE
HAHA!
REEE
THERE'S LOTS OF STUFF GOING ON IN THE SUMMER, SO THAT'S FUN.
BUT IT'S JUST. SO. HOT.
OH, RIGHT.
THANKS FOR HELPING AT THE FIRE-WORKS.
I NEVER GOT TO THANK YOU.
OH, NO, FORGET IT.
IT'S A GOOD THING I HAPPENED TO BE PASSING BY.
I WAS JUST GLAD TO—
CLASP

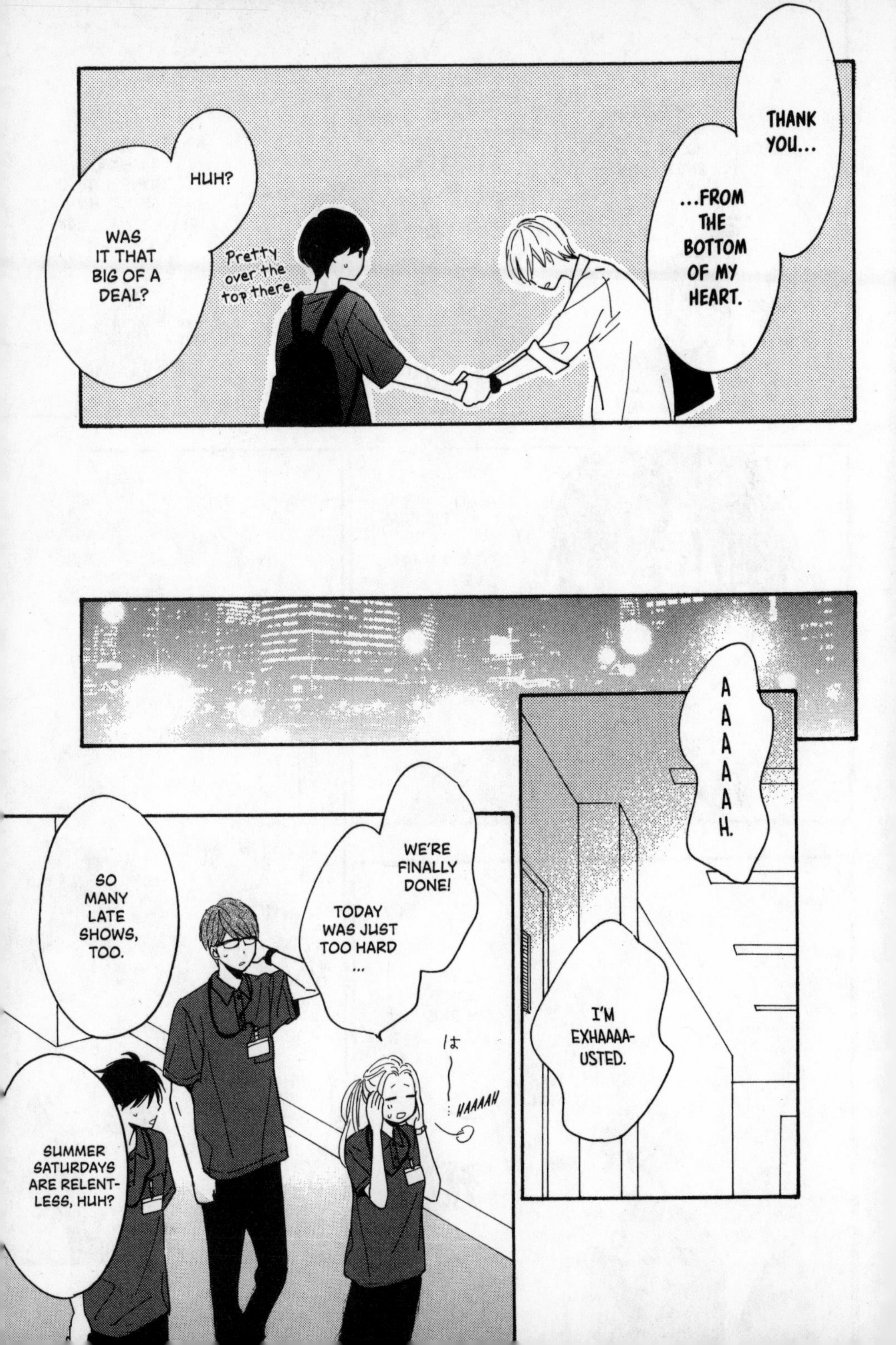
THANK YOU...
...FROM THE BOTTOM OF MY HEART.
HUH?
WAS IT THAT BIG OF A DEAL?
Pretty over the top there.
AAAAAAH.
I'M EXHAAAA-USTED.
WE'RE FINALLY DONE!
TODAY WAS JUST TOO HARD...
はー
HAAAAH
SO MANY LATE SHOWS, TOO.
SUMMER SATURDAYS ARE RELENT-LESS, HUH?

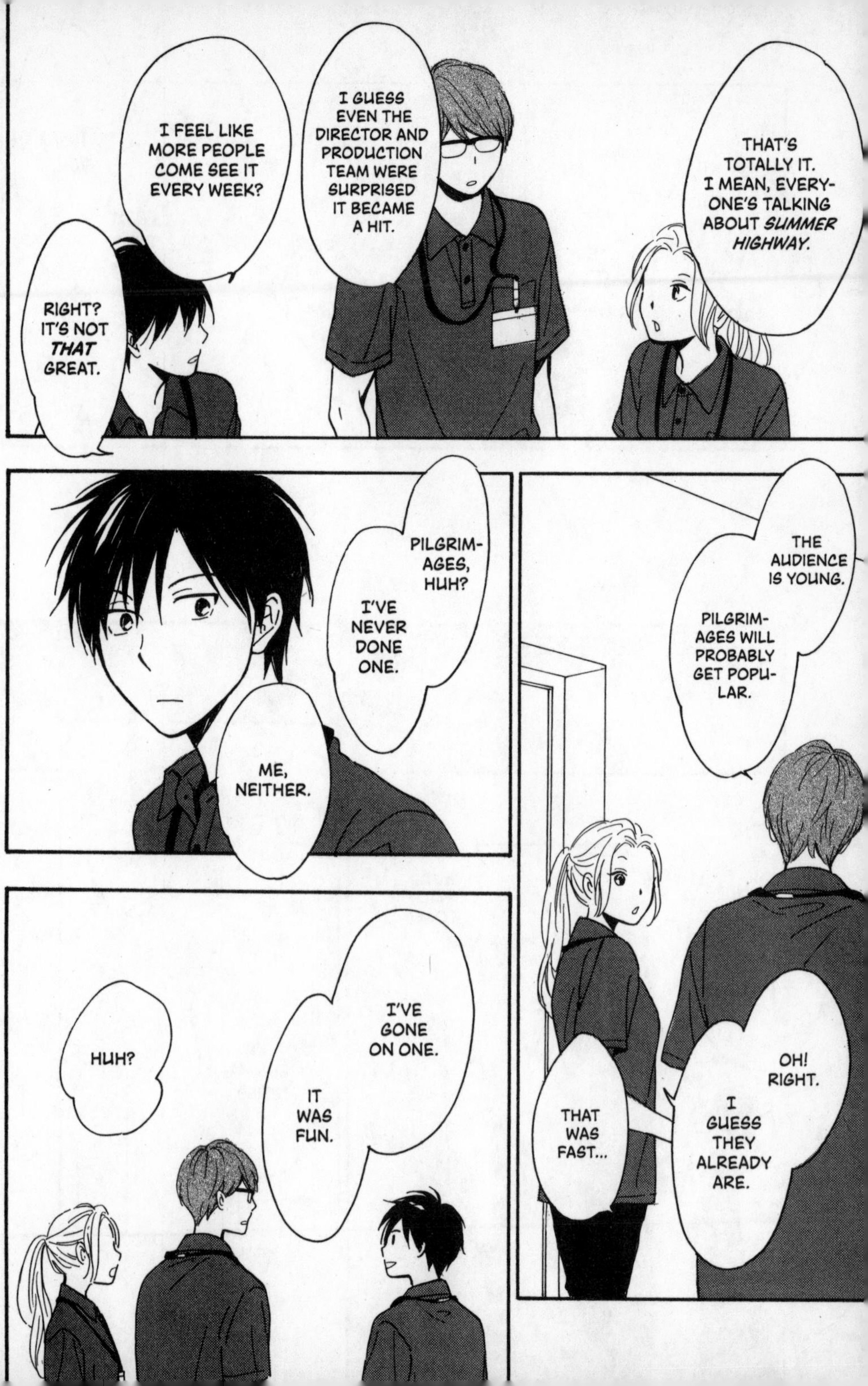
THAT'S TOTALLY IT. I MEAN, EVERYONE'S TALKING ABOUT *SUMMER HIGHWAY.*
I GUESS EVEN THE DIRECTOR AND PRODUCTION TEAM WERE SURPRISED IT BECAME A HIT.
I FEEL LIKE MORE PEOPLE COME SEE IT EVERY WEEK?
RIGHT? IT'S NOT *THAT* GREAT.
THE AUDIENCE IS YOUNG.
PILGRIMAGES WILL PROBABLY GET POPULAR.
OH! RIGHT.
I GUESS THEY ALREADY ARE.
THAT WAS FAST...
PILGRIMAGES, HUH?
I'VE NEVER DONE ONE.
ME, NEITHER.
I'VE GONE ON ONE.
IT WAS FUN.
HUH?

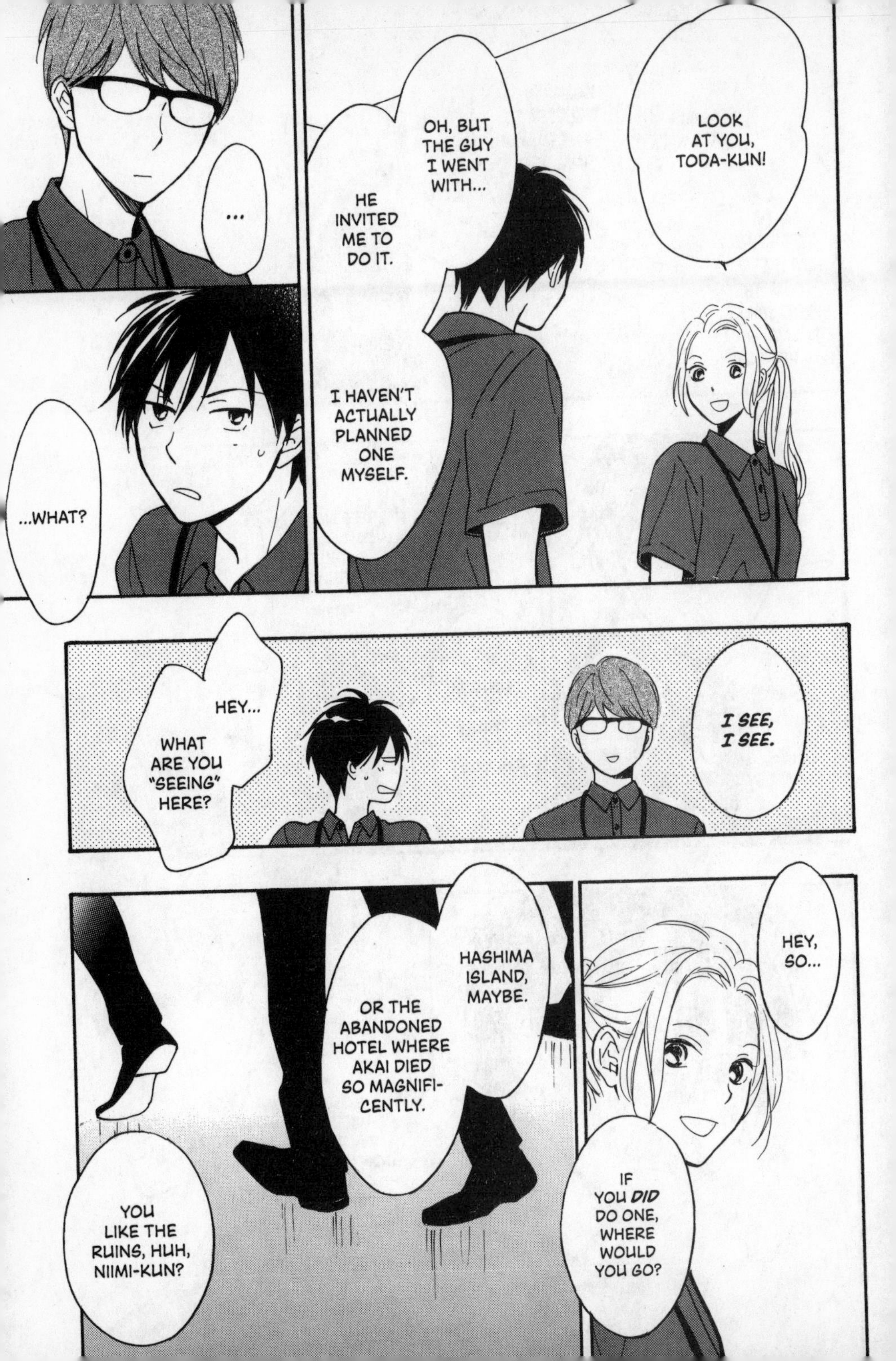
LOOK AT YOU, TODA-KUN!
OH, BUT THE GUY I WENT WITH...
HE INVITED ME TO DO IT.
I HAVEN'T ACTUALLY PLANNED ONE MYSELF.
...
...WHAT?
I SEE, I SEE.
HEY... WHAT ARE YOU "SEEING" HERE?
HEY, SO...
IF YOU *DID* DO ONE, WHERE WOULD YOU GO?
HASHIMA ISLAND, MAYBE.
OR THE ABANDONED HOTEL WHERE AKAI DIED SO MAGNIFI-CENTLY.
YOU LIKE THE RUINS, HUH, NIIMI-KUN?

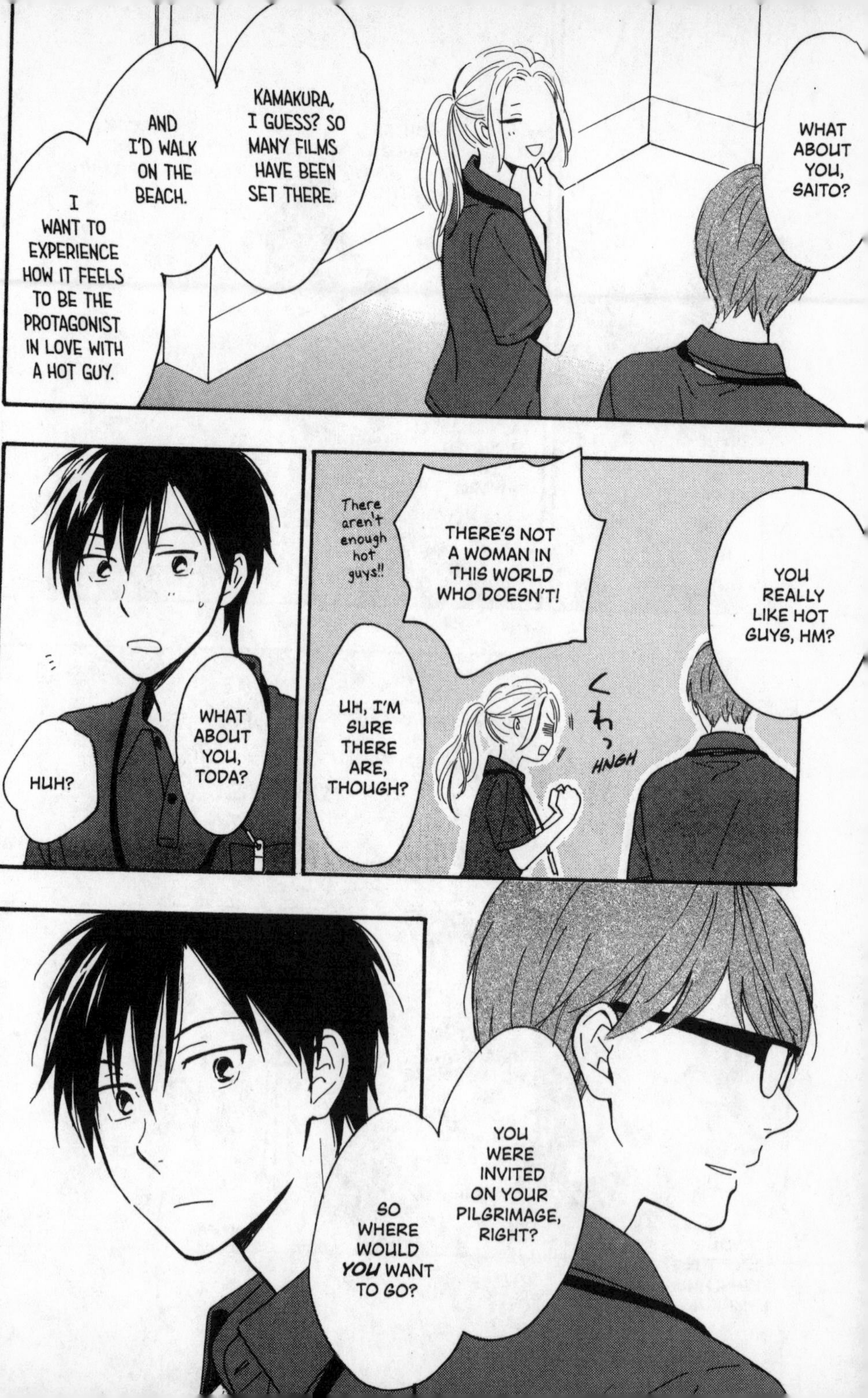

WHAT ABOUT YOU, SAITO?
KAMAKURA, I GUESS? SO MANY FILMS HAVE BEEN SET THERE.
AND I'D WALK ON THE BEACH.
I WANT TO EXPERIENCE HOW IT FEELS TO BE THE PROTAGONIST IN LOVE WITH A HOT GUY.
YOU REALLY LIKE HOT GUYS, HM?
THERE'S NOT A WOMAN IN THIS WORLD WHO DOESN'T!
There aren't enough hot guys!!
HNGH
UH, I'M SURE THERE ARE, THOUGH?
WHAT ABOUT YOU, TODA?
HUH?
YOU WERE INVITED ON YOUR PILGRIMAGE, RIGHT?
SO WHERE WOULD *YOU* WANT TO GO?

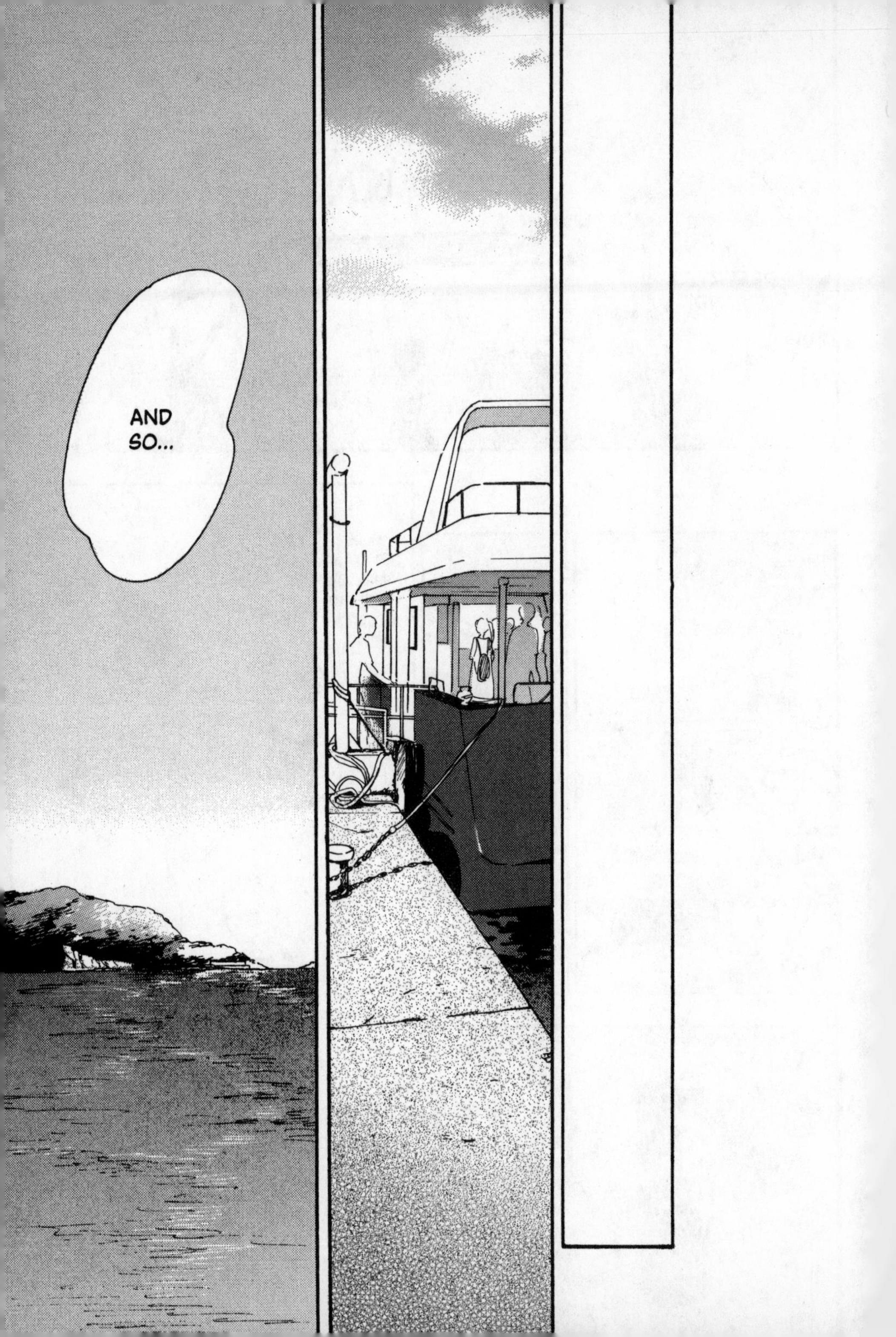
AND SO...

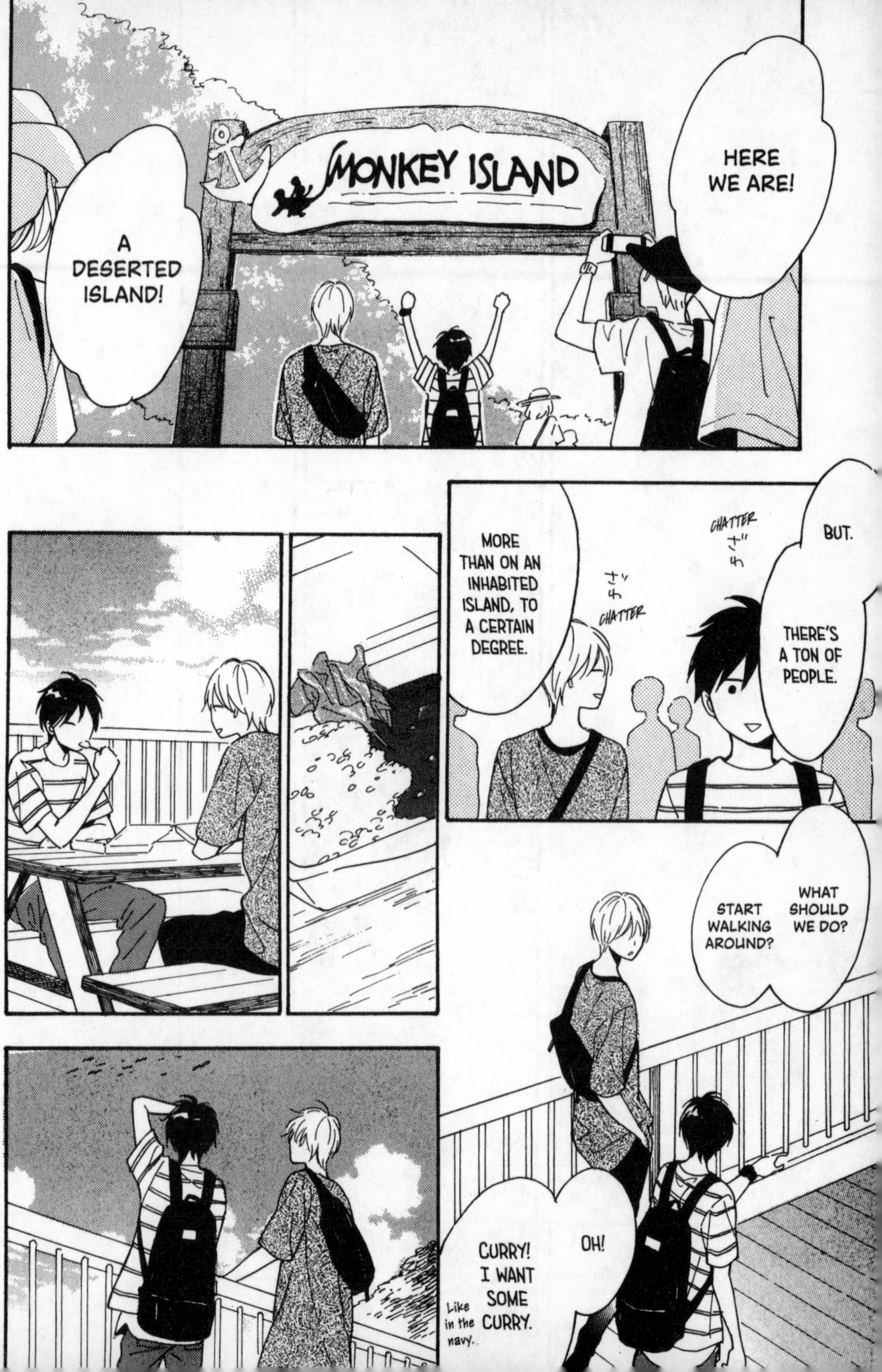
MONKEY ISLAND
HERE WE ARE!
A DESERTED ISLAND!
BUT.
THERE'S A TON OF PEOPLE.
CHATTER
CHATTER
MORE THAN ON AN INHABITED ISLAND, TO A CERTAIN DEGREE.
WHAT SHOULD WE DO?
START WALKING AROUND?
OH!
CURRY! I WANT SOME CURRY.
Like in the navy..

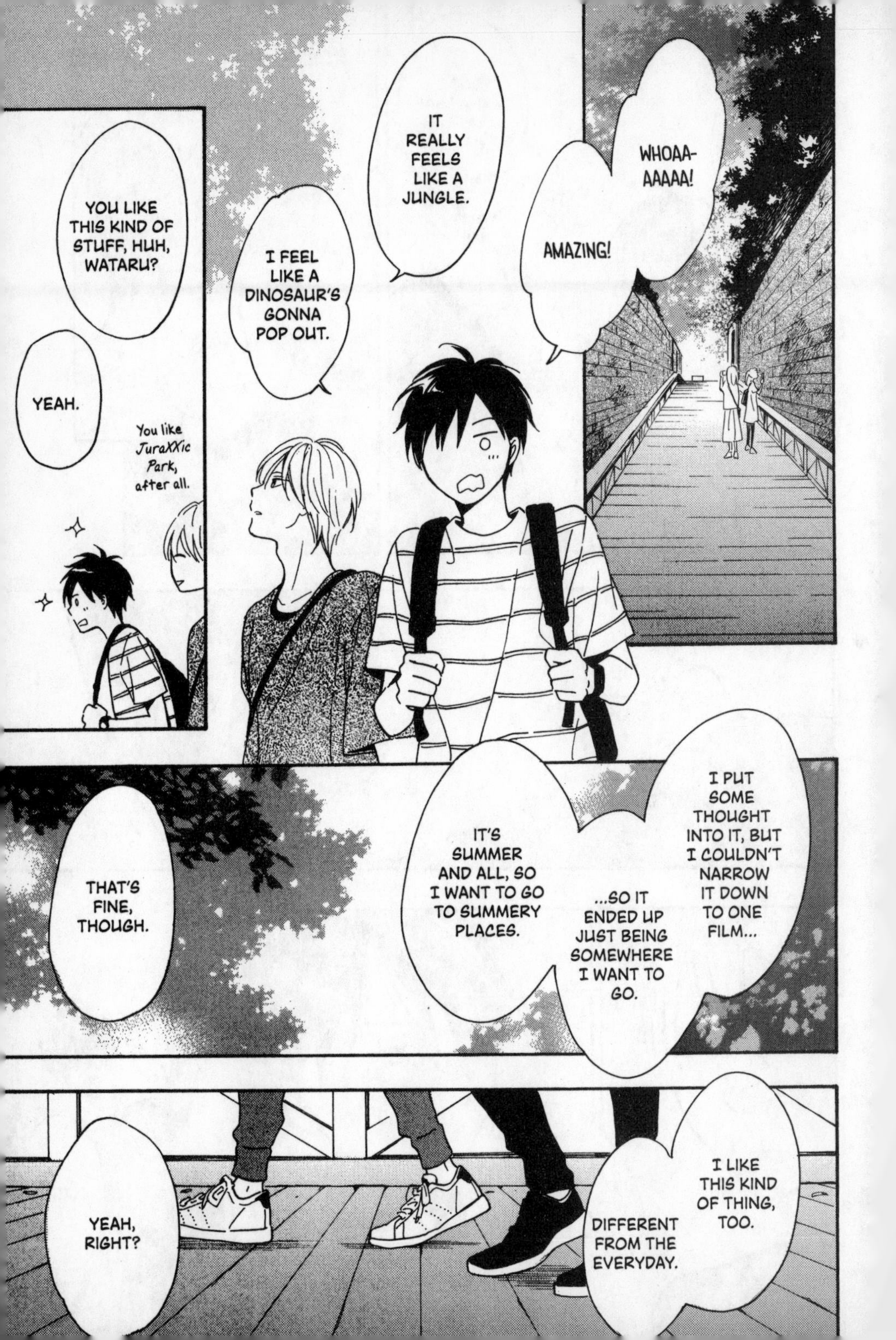
WHOAA-AAAAA!
AMAZING!
IT REALLY FEELS LIKE A JUNGLE.
I FEEL LIKE A DINOSAUR'S GONNA POP OUT.
YOU LIKE THIS KIND OF STUFF, HUH, WATARU?
YEAH.
You like JuraXXic Park, after all.
I PUT SOME THOUGHT INTO IT, BUT I COULDN'T NARROW IT DOWN TO ONE FILM...
...SO IT ENDED UP JUST BEING SOMEWHERE I WANT TO GO.
IT'S SUMMER AND ALL, SO I WANT TO GO TO SUMMERY PLACES.
THAT'S FINE, THOUGH.
I LIKE THIS KIND OF THING, TOO.
DIFFERENT FROM THE EVERYDAY.
YEAH, RIGHT?

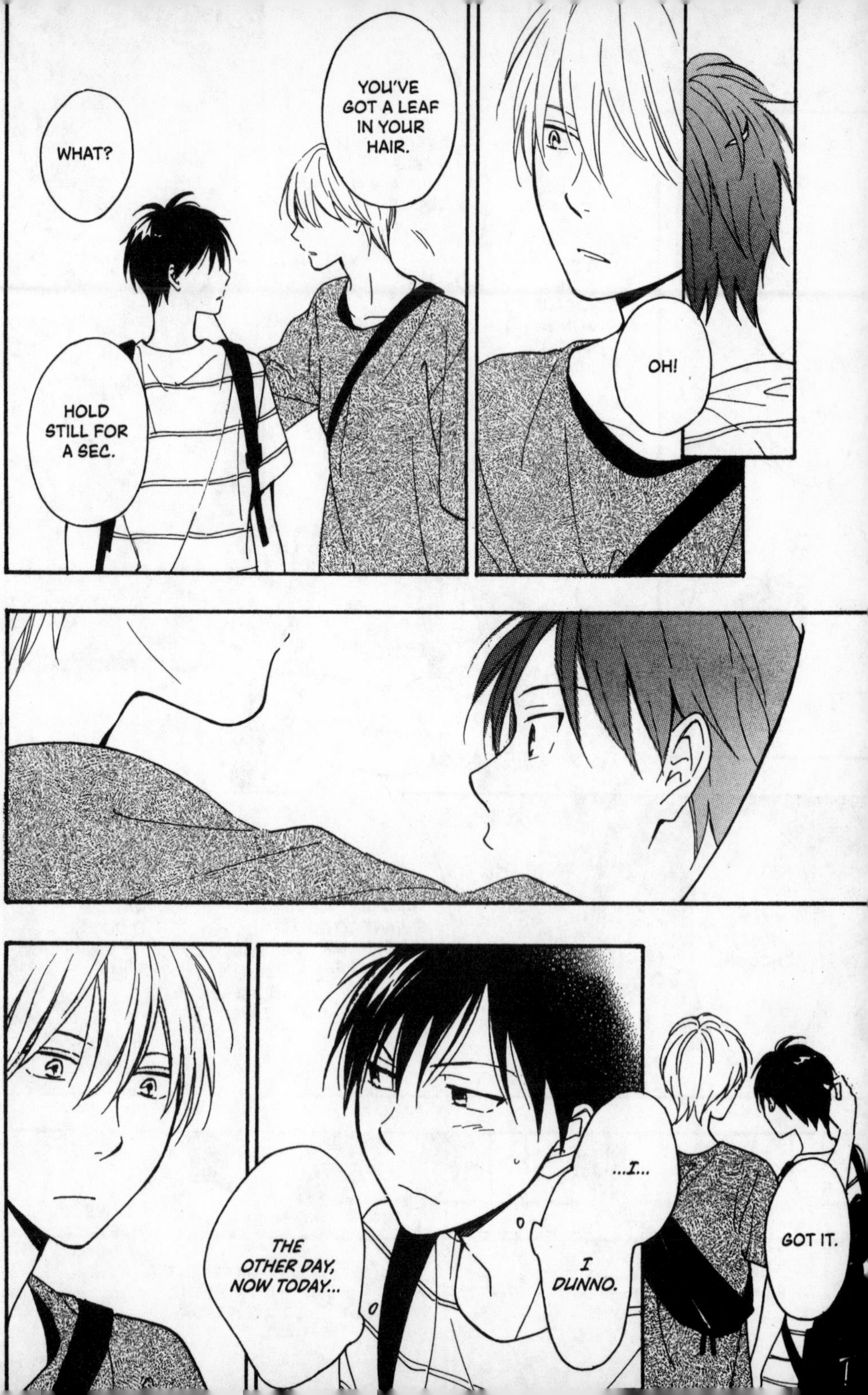
OH!
YOU'VE GOT A LEAF IN YOUR HAIR.
WHAT?
HOLD STILL FOR A SEC.
GOT IT.
...I...
I DUNNO.
THE OTHER DAY, NOW TODAY...

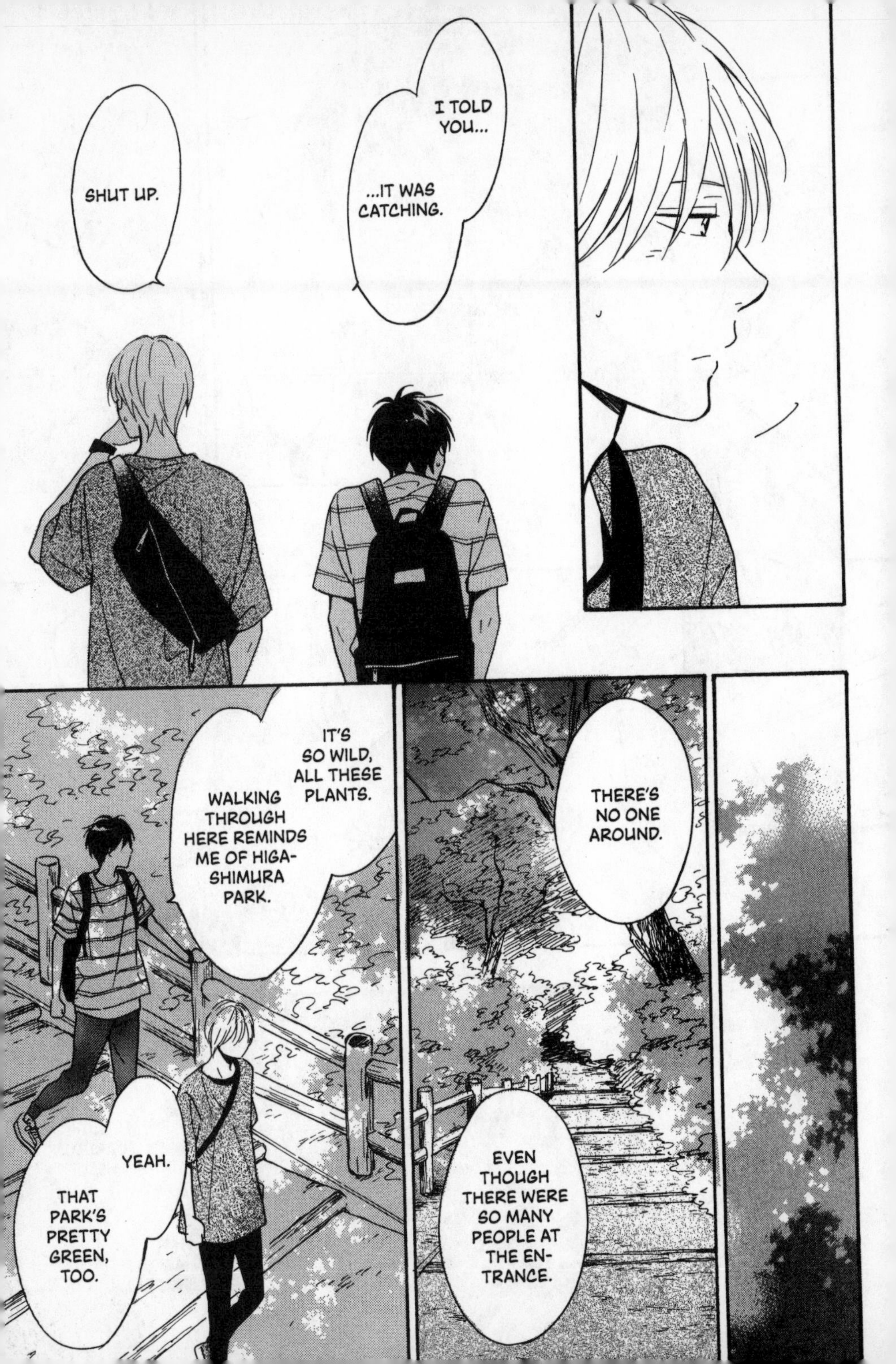
I TOLD YOU...
...IT WAS CATCHING.
SHUT UP.
THERE'S NO ONE AROUND.
EVEN THOUGH THERE WERE SO MANY PEOPLE AT THE EN-TRANCE.
IT'S SO WILD, ALL THESE PLANTS.
WALKING THROUGH HERE REMINDS ME OF HIGA-SHIMURA PARK.
YEAH.
THAT PARK'S PRETTY GREEN, TOO.

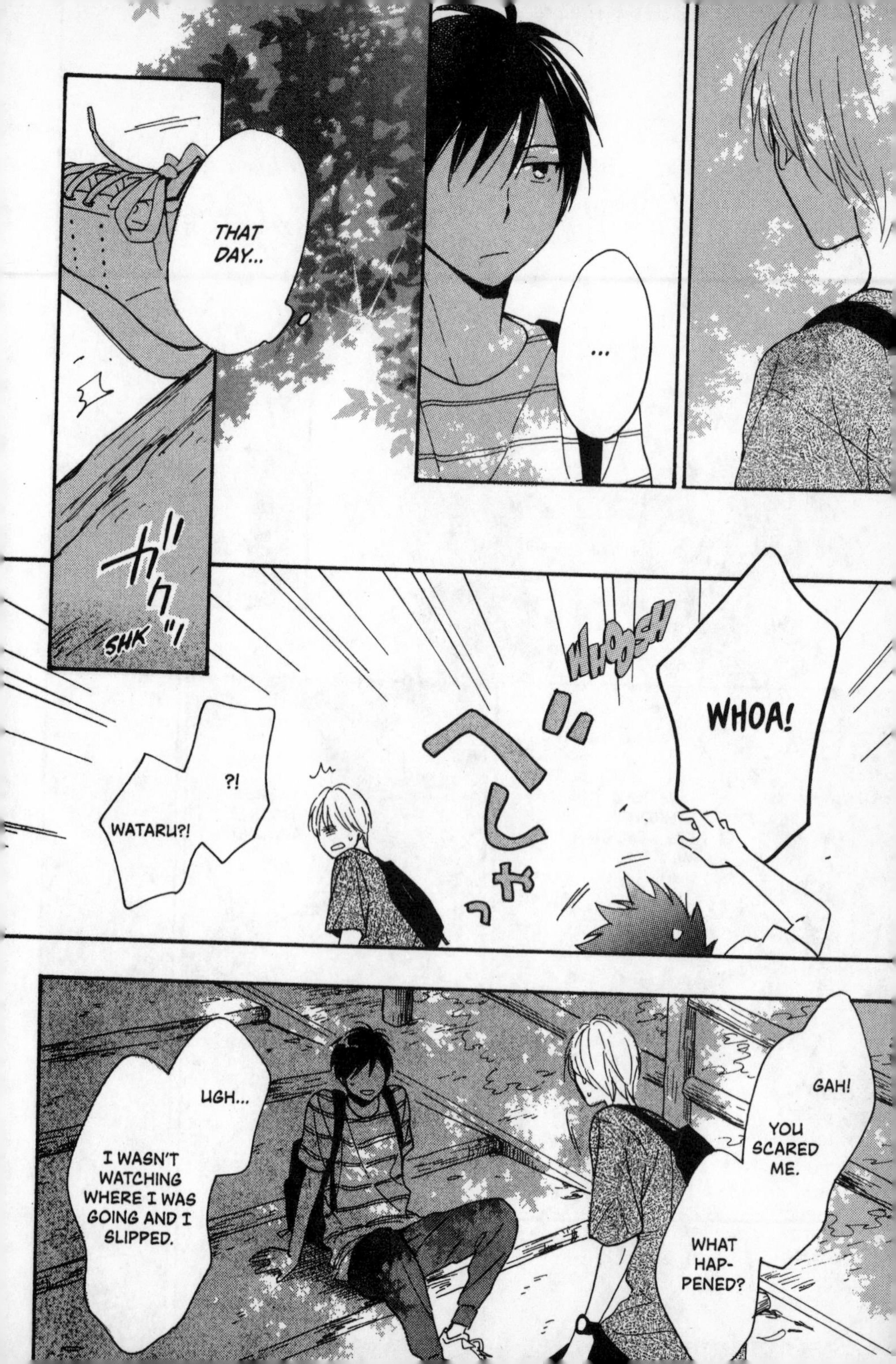
...
THAT DAY...
SHK
WHOOSH
WHOA!
?!
WATARU?!
GAH!
YOU SCARED ME.
WHAT HAP-PENED?
UGH...
I WASN'T WATCHING WHERE I WAS GOING AND I SLIPPED.

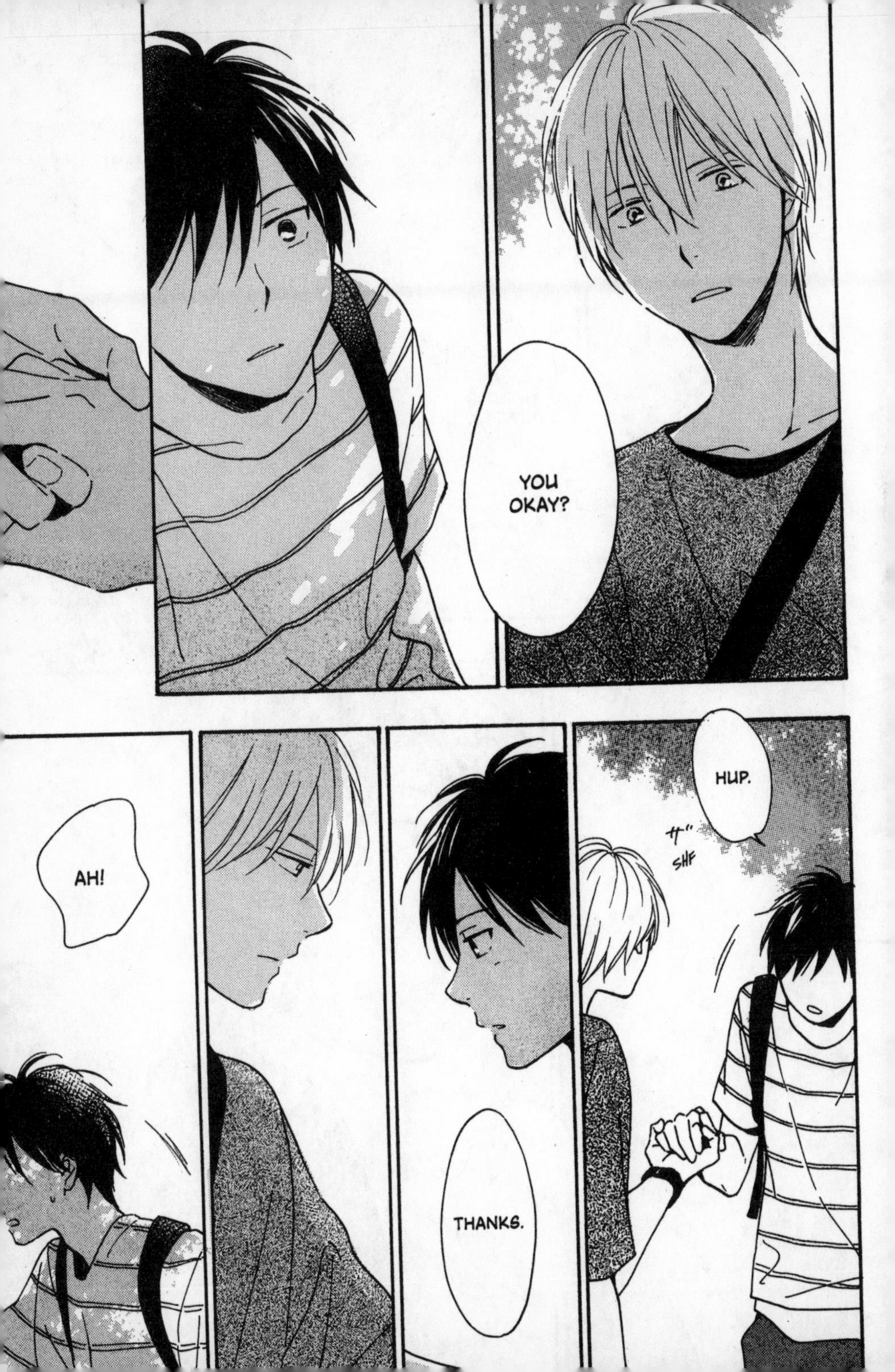
YOU OKAY?
HUP.
SHF
THANKS.
AH!

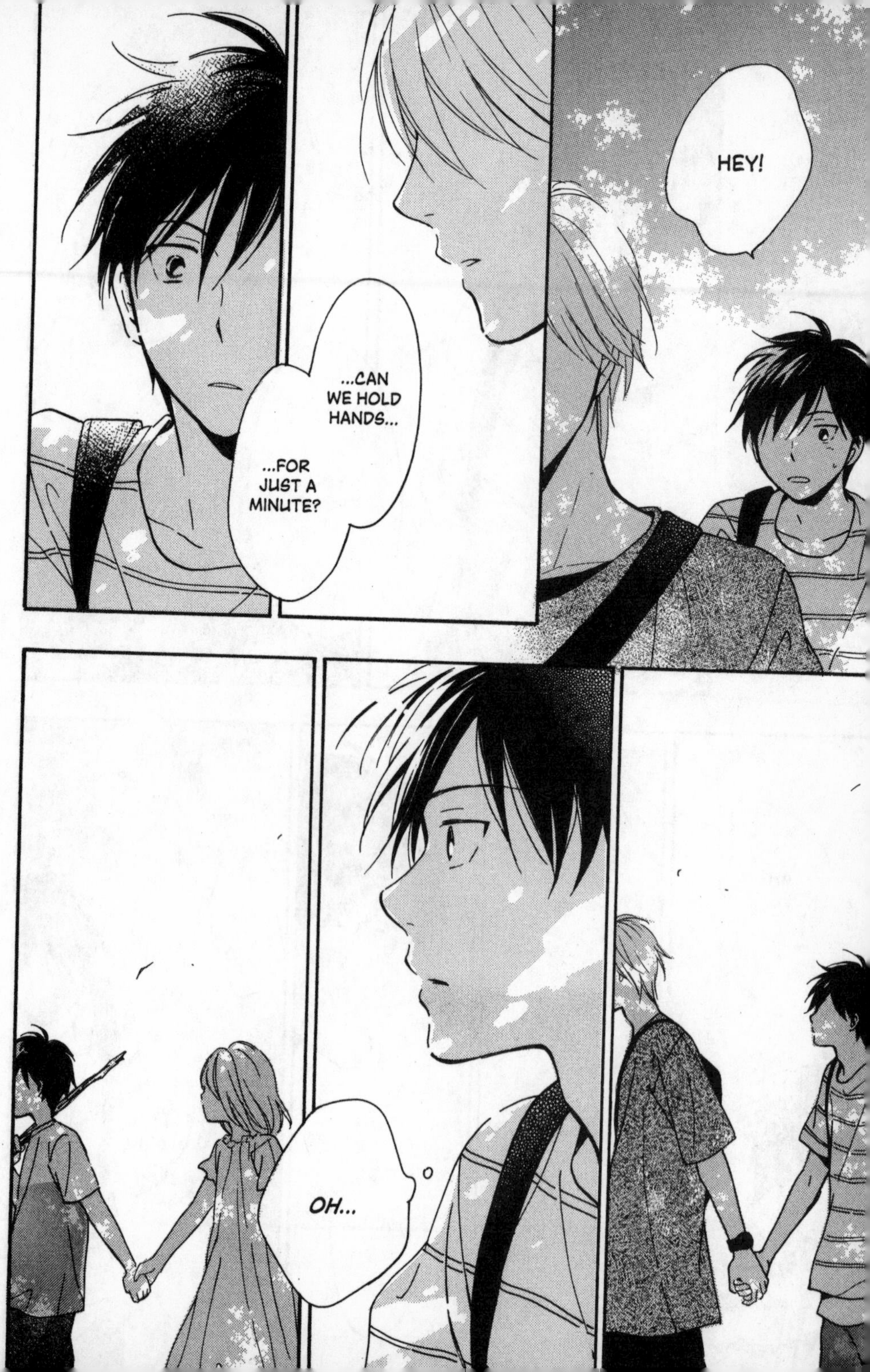
HEY!
...CAN WE HOLD HANDS...
...FOR JUST A MINUTE?
OH...

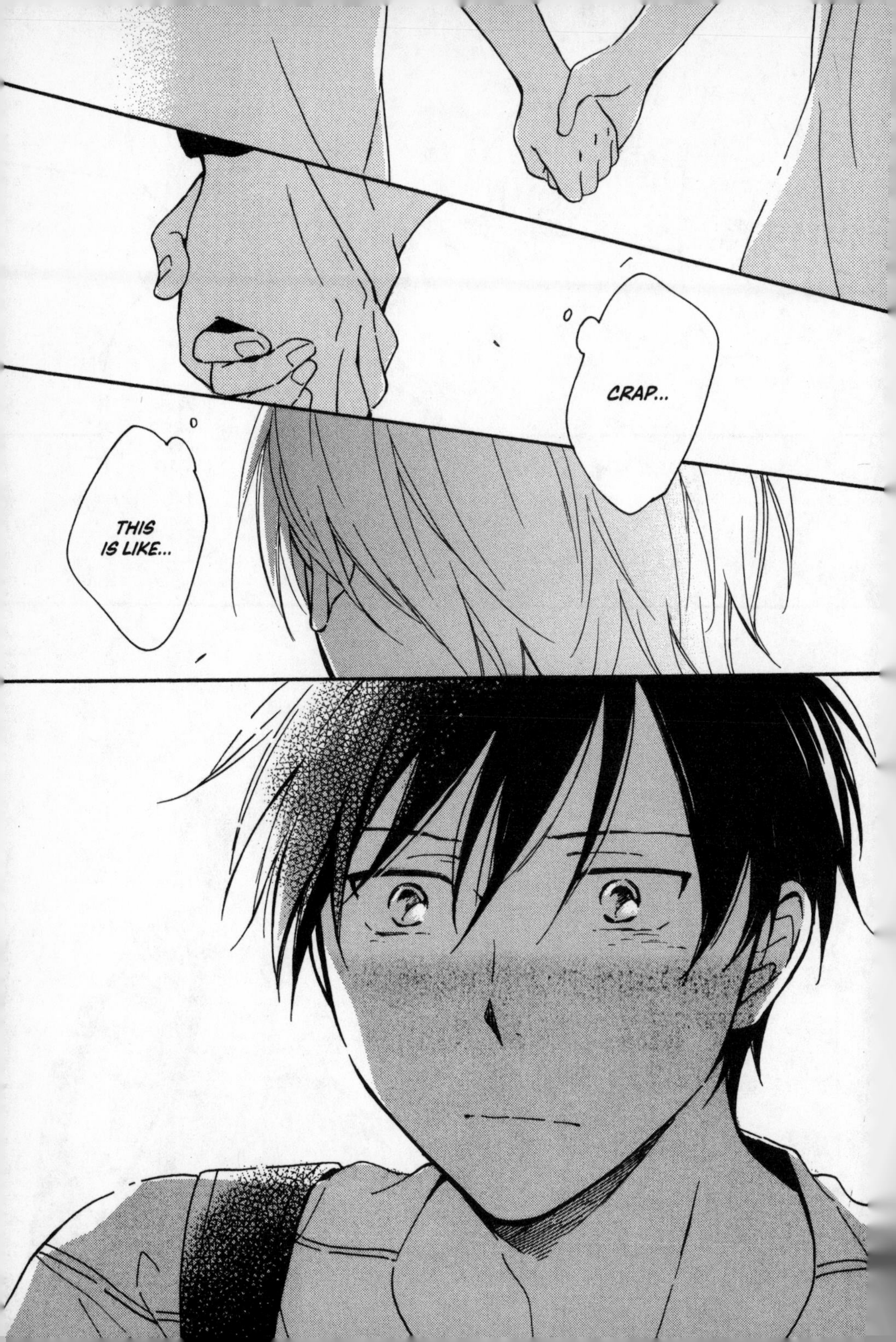
CRAP...
THIS IS LIKE...

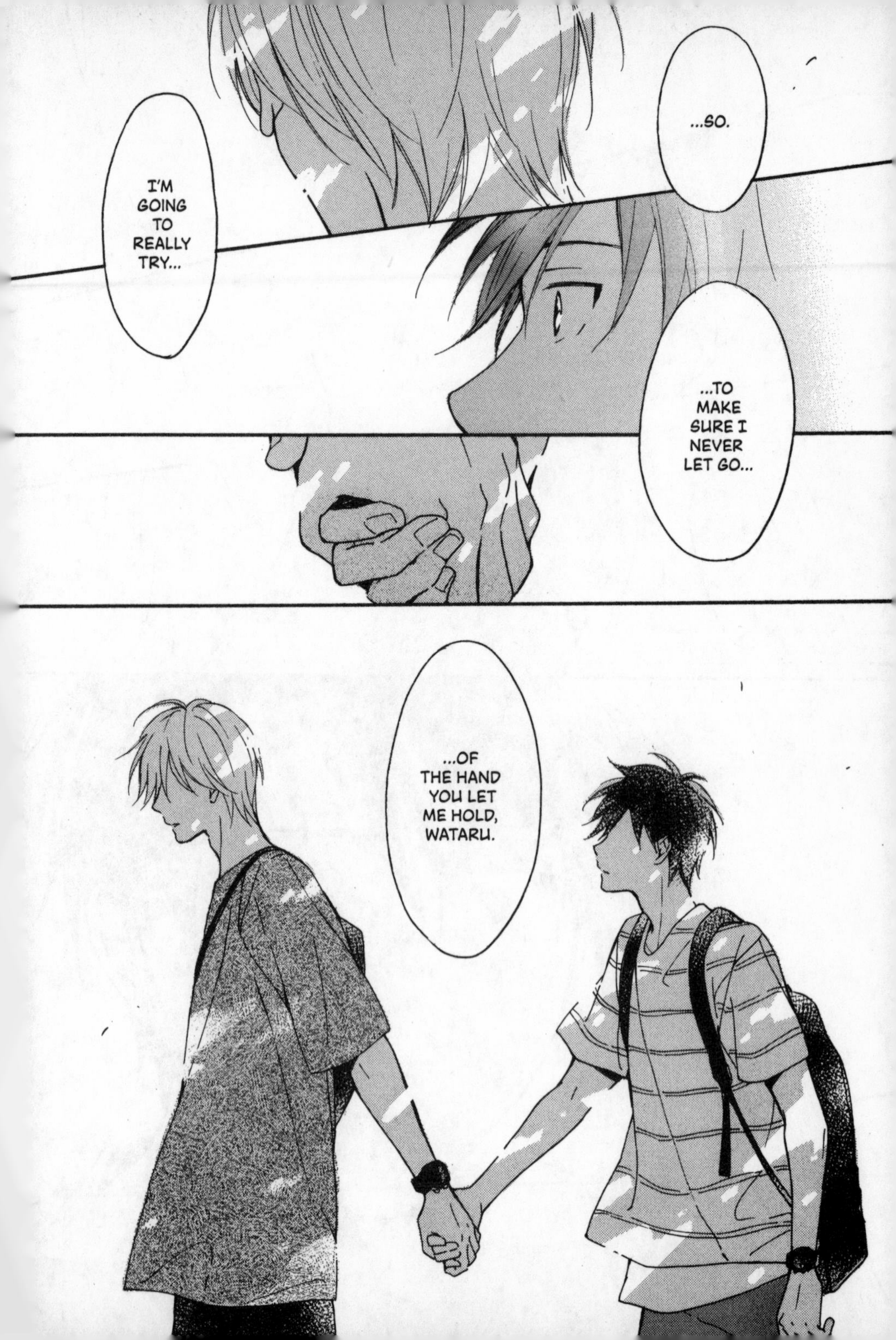
...SO.
I'M GOING TO REALLY TRY...
...TO MAKE SURE I NEVER LET GO...
...OF THE HAND YOU LET ME HOLD, WATARU.

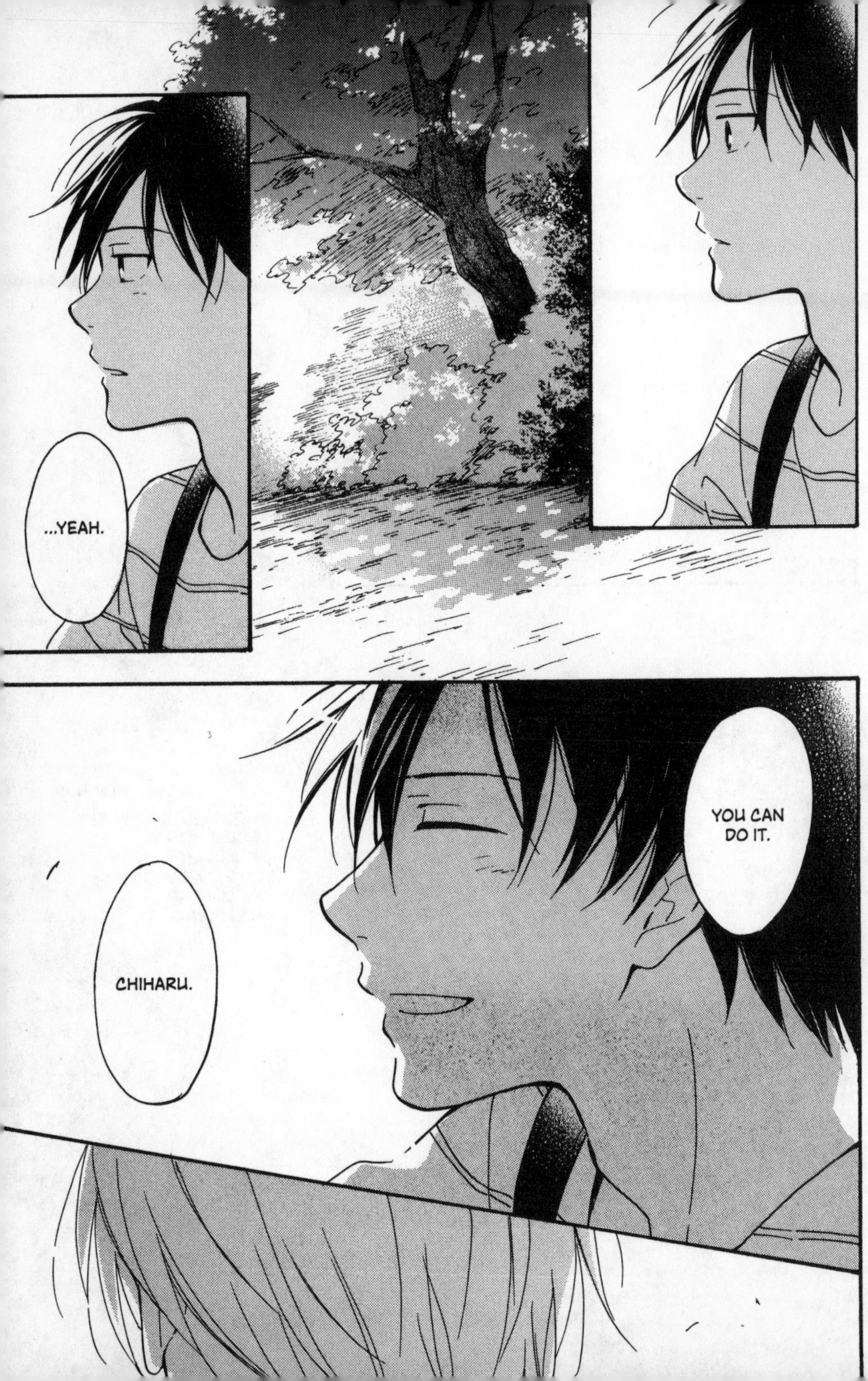
...YEAH.
YOU CAN DO IT.
CHIHARU.

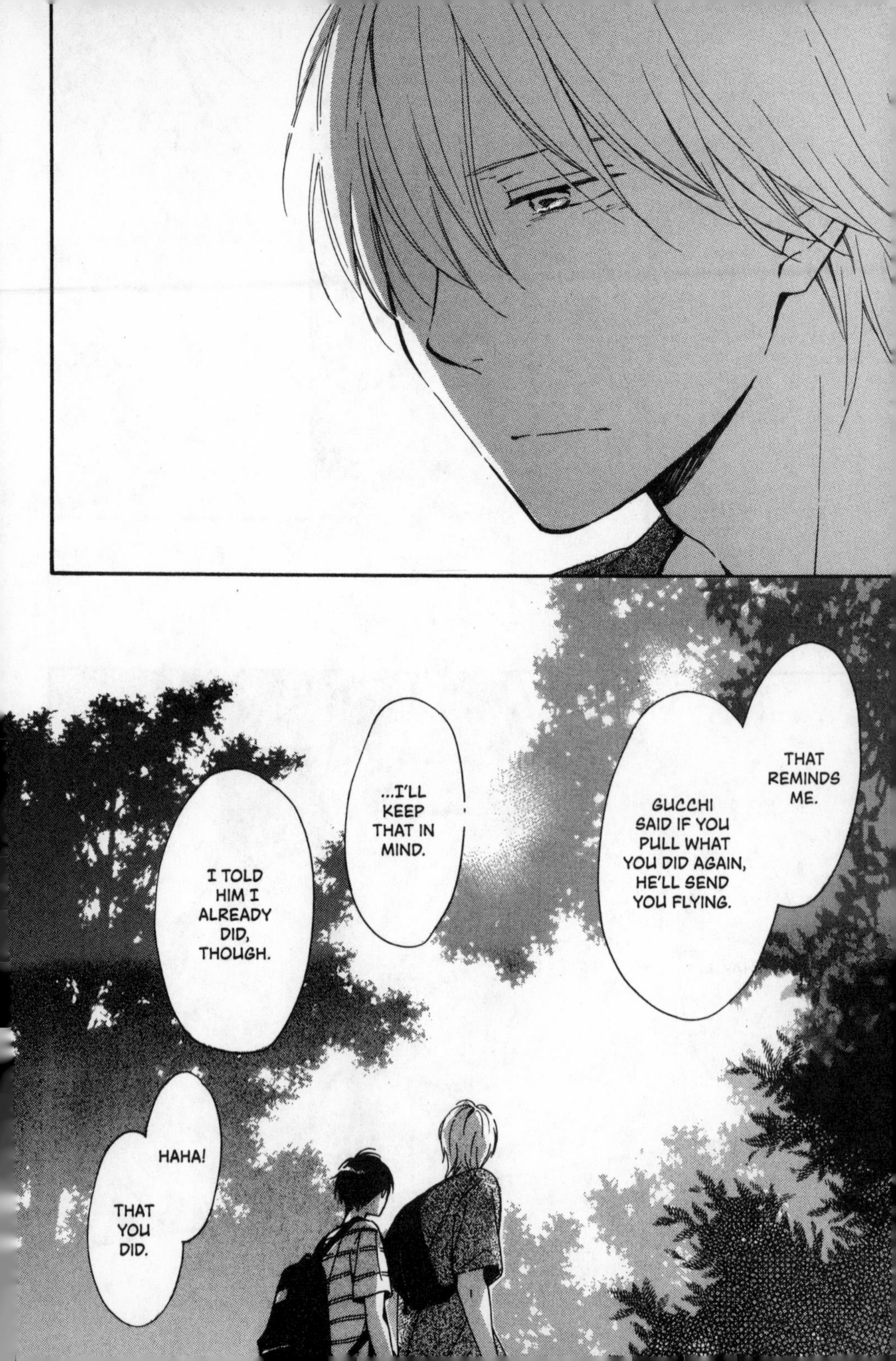
THAT REMINDS ME.
GUCCHI SAID IF YOU PULL WHAT YOU DID AGAIN, HE'LL SEND YOU FLYING.
...I'LL KEEP THAT IN MIND.
I TOLD HIM I ALREADY DID, THOUGH.
HAHA!
THAT YOU DID.

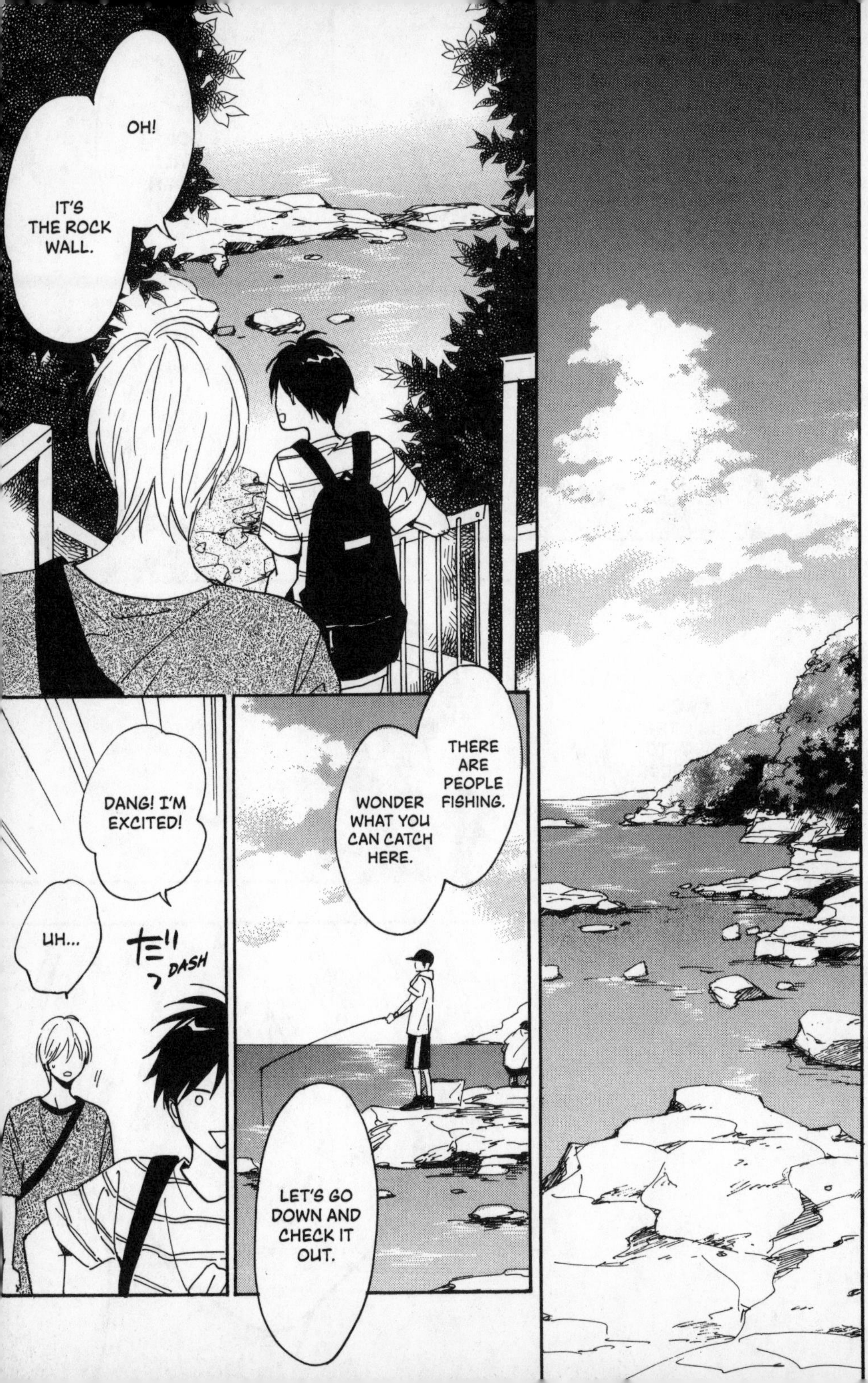
OH!
IT'S THE ROCK WALL.
THERE ARE PEOPLE FISHING. WONDER WHAT YOU CAN CATCH HERE.
LET'S GO DOWN AND CHECK IT OUT.
DANG! I'M EXCITED!
UH...
DASH

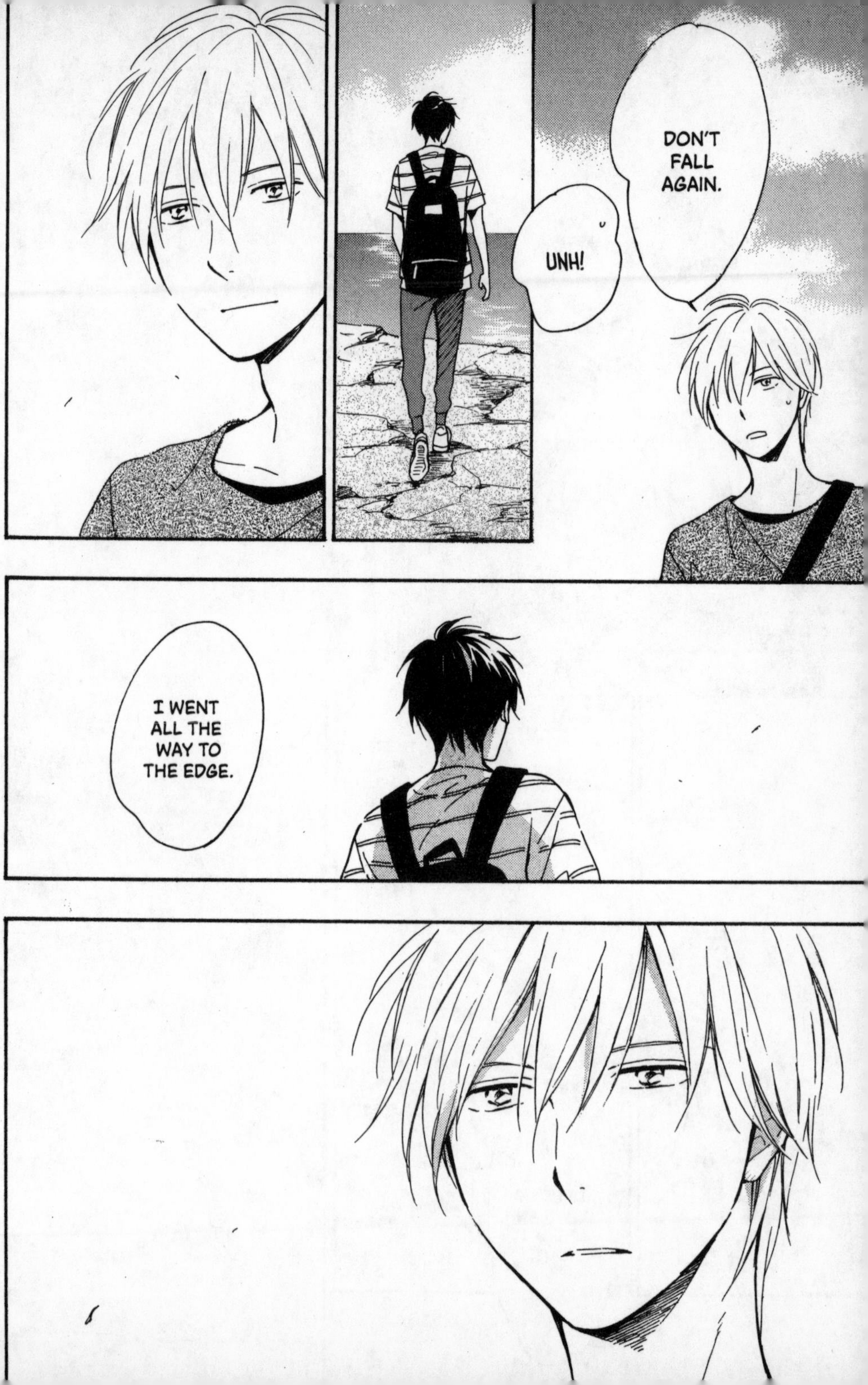
DON'T FALL AGAIN.
UNH!
I WENT ALL THE WAY TO THE EDGE.

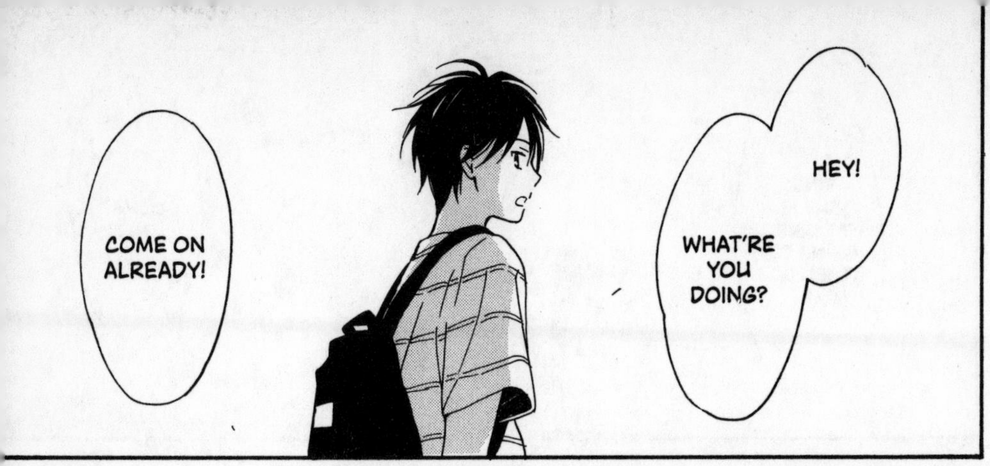
HEY!
WHAT'RE YOU DOING?
COME ON ALREADY!

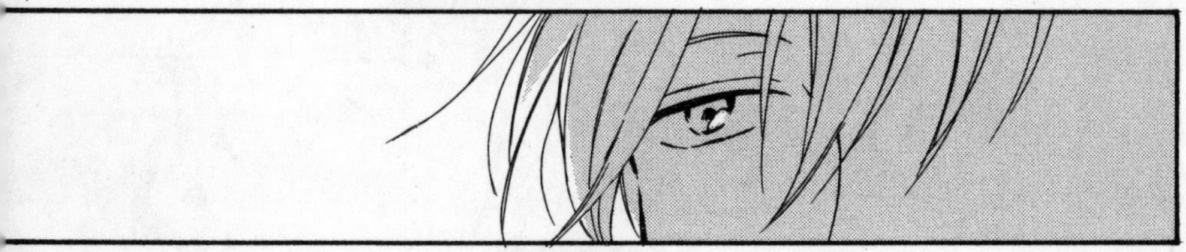

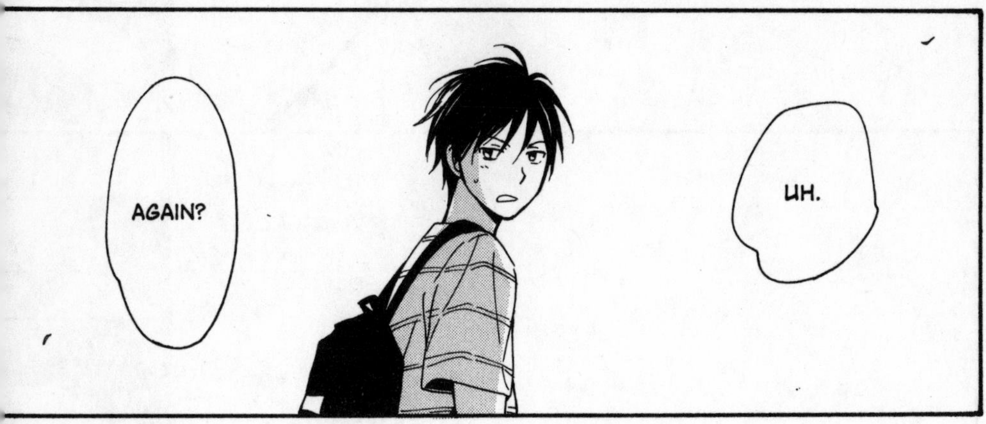
UH.
AGAIN?

WHY...?

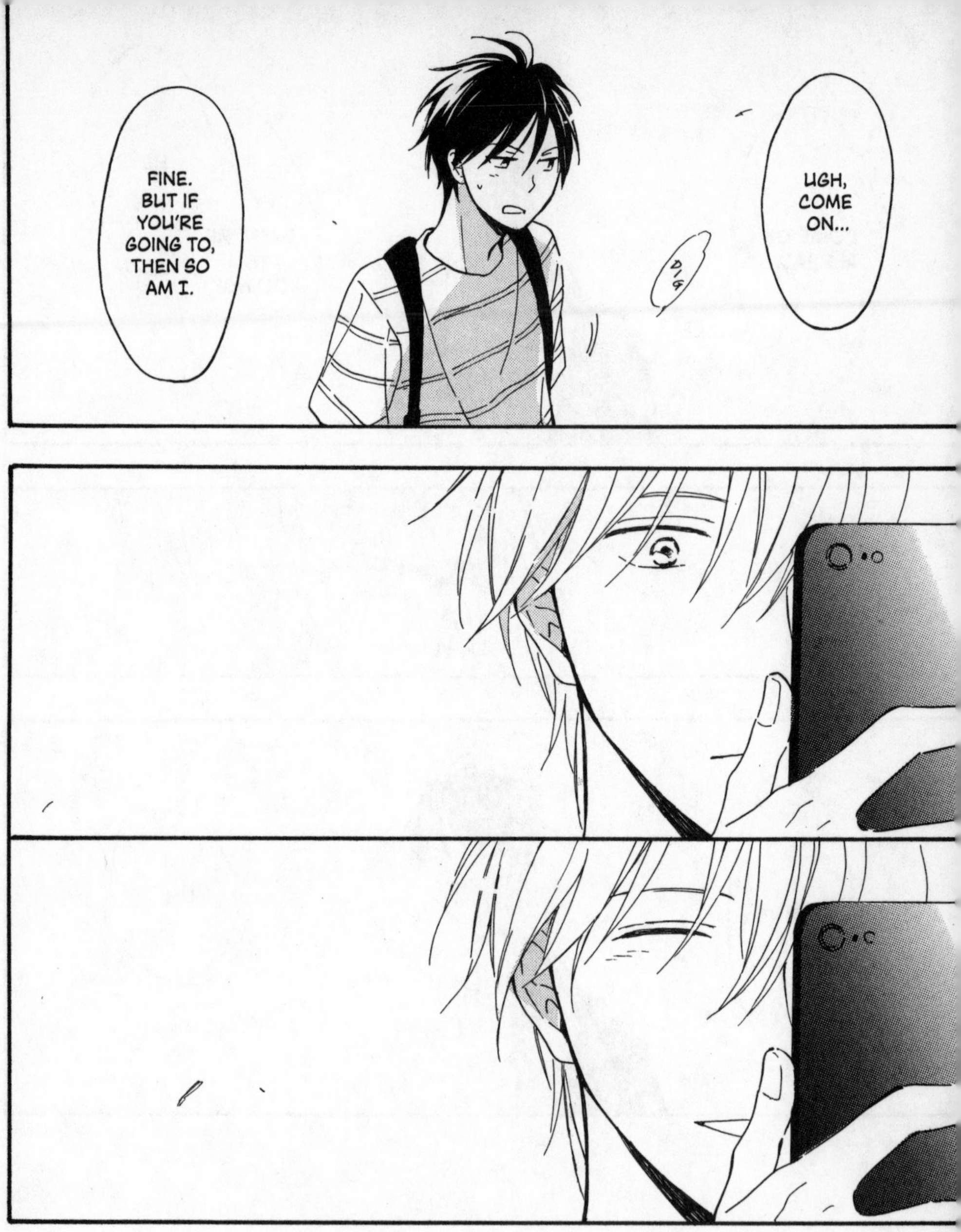
UGH, COME ON...
FINE. BUT IF YOU'RE GOING TO, THEN SO AM I.

YOU'RE HERE, RIGHT IN FRONT OF ME...

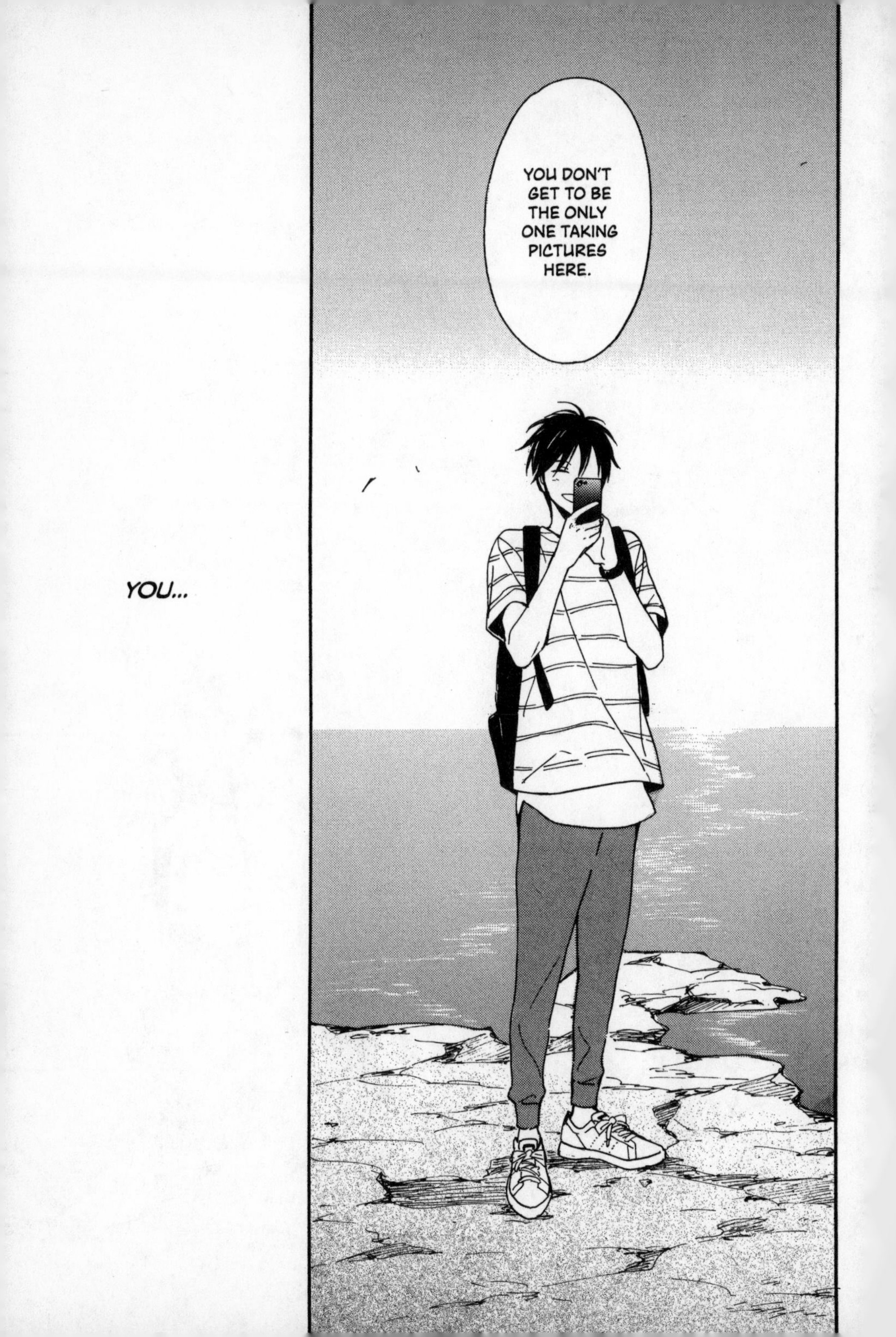
YOU DON'T GET TO BE THE ONLY ONE TAKING PICTURES HERE.
YOU...

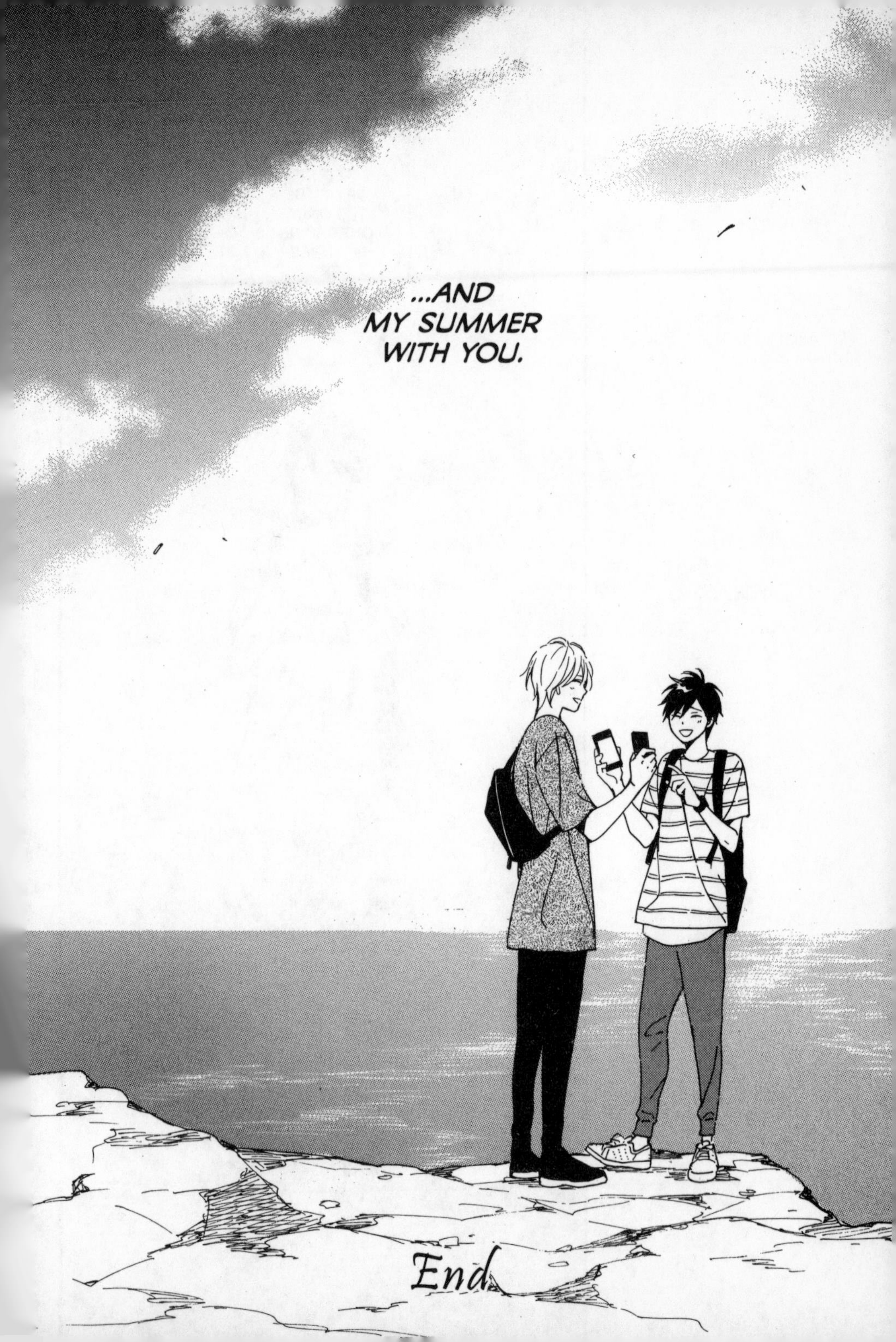
...AND MY SUMMER WITH YOU.
End

MY **SUMMER** OF **YOU**

VOL.2: **THE SUMMER WITH YOU**

MY SUMMER OF YOU

Bonus Story: A Certain Summer Night and Morning

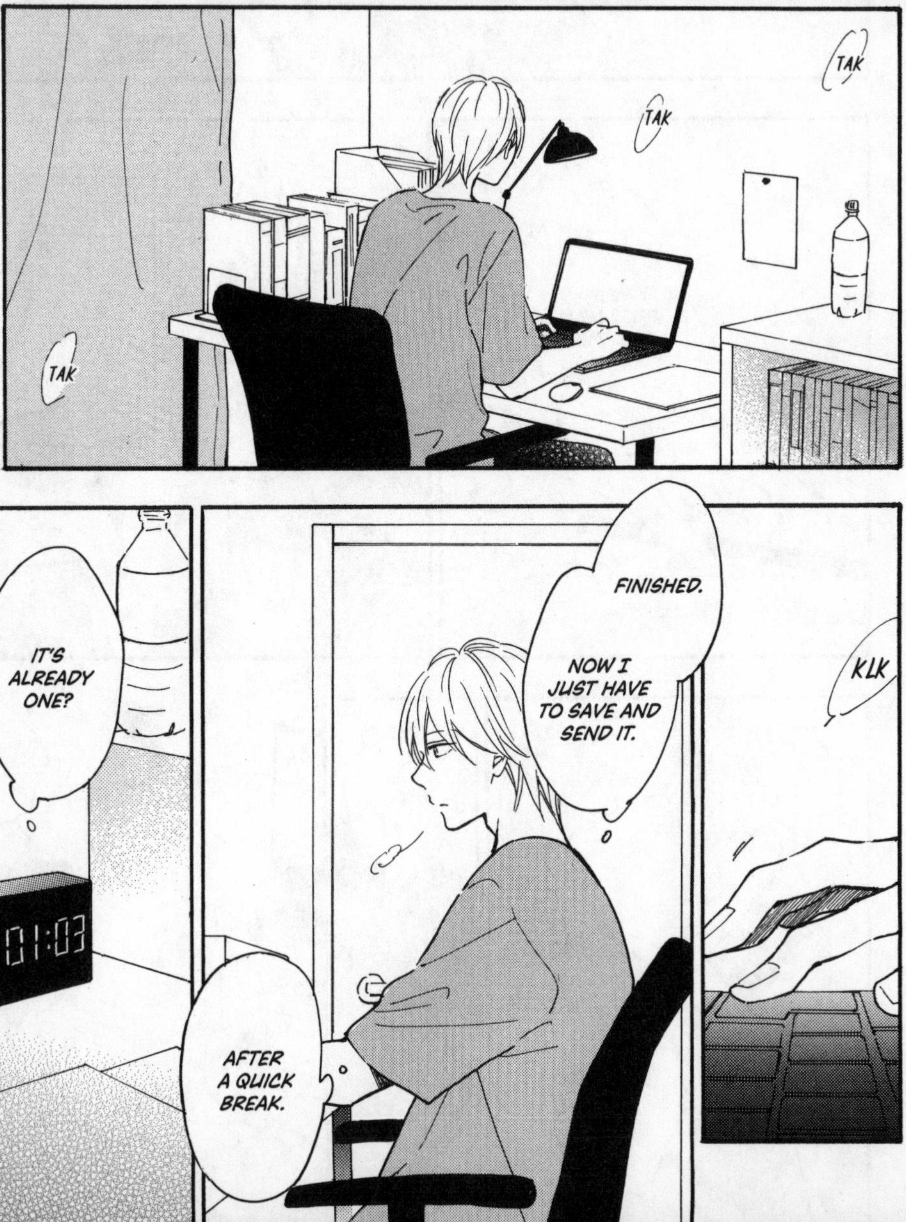
TAK
TAK
TAK
KLK
FINISHED.
NOW I JUST HAVE TO SAVE AND SEND IT.
IT'S ALREADY ONE?
AFTER A QUICK BREAK.
01:03

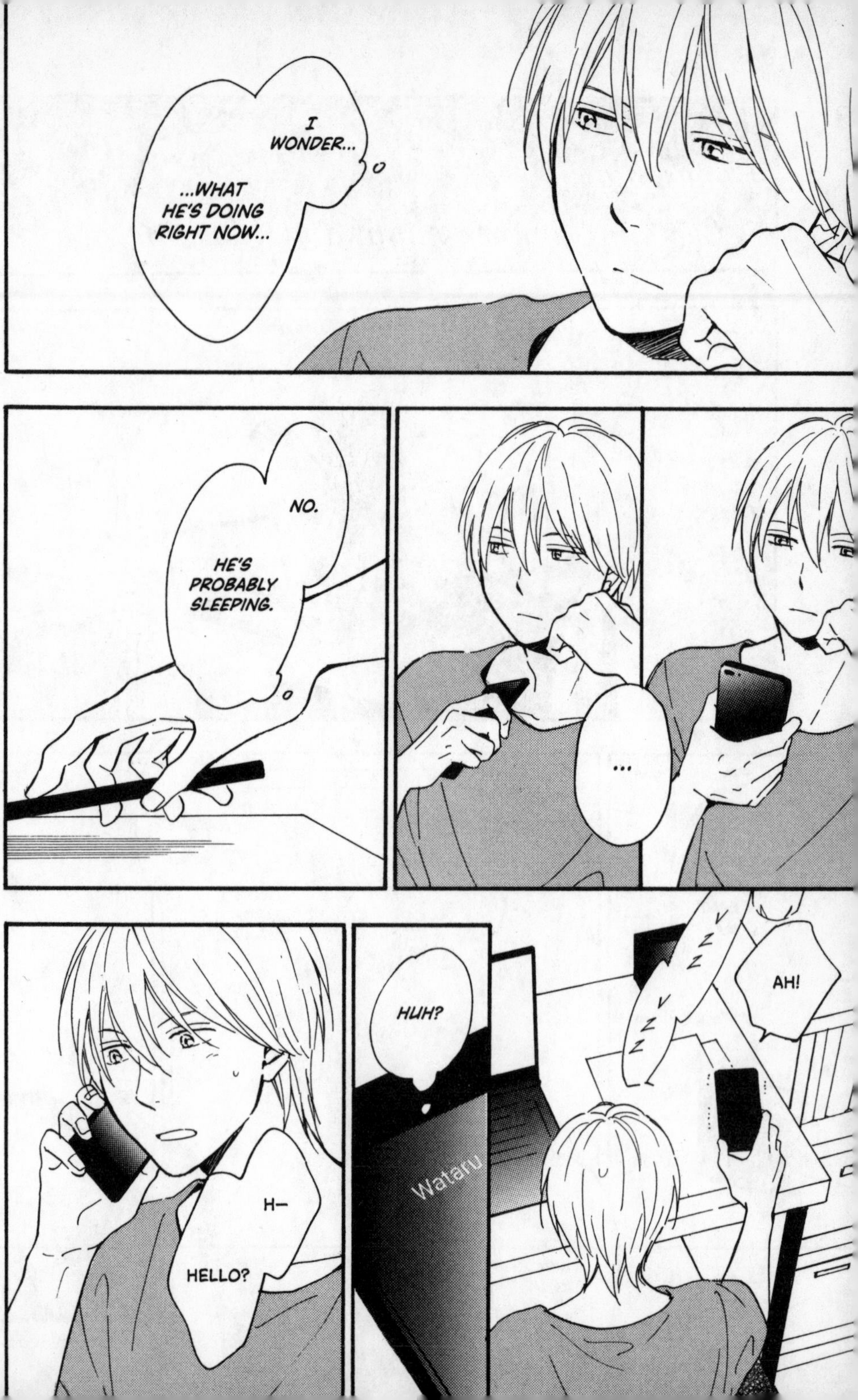
I WONDER... ...WHAT HE'S DOING RIGHT NOW...
...
NO.
HE'S PROBABLY SLEEPING.
AH!
VZZZ
VZZ
HUH?
Wataru
H—
HELLO?

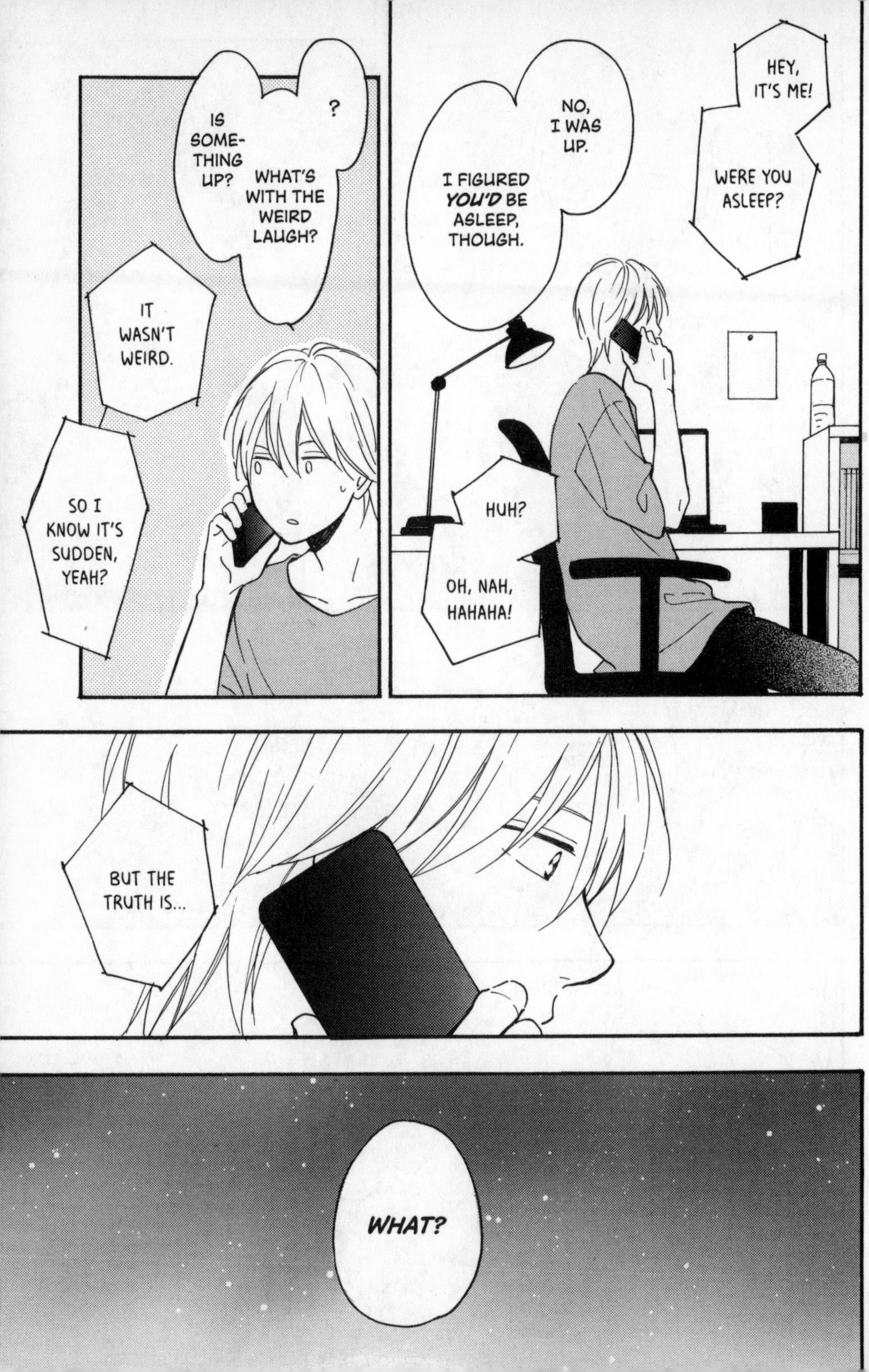
HEY, IT'S ME!
WERE YOU ASLEEP?
NO, I WAS UP.
I FIGURED *YOU'D* BE ASLEEP, THOUGH.
HUH?
OH, NAH, HAHAHA!
?
IS SOMETHING UP?
WHAT'S WITH THE WEIRD LAUGH?
IT WASN'T WEIRD.
SO I KNOW IT'S SUDDEN, YEAH?
BUT THE TRUTH IS...
WHAT?

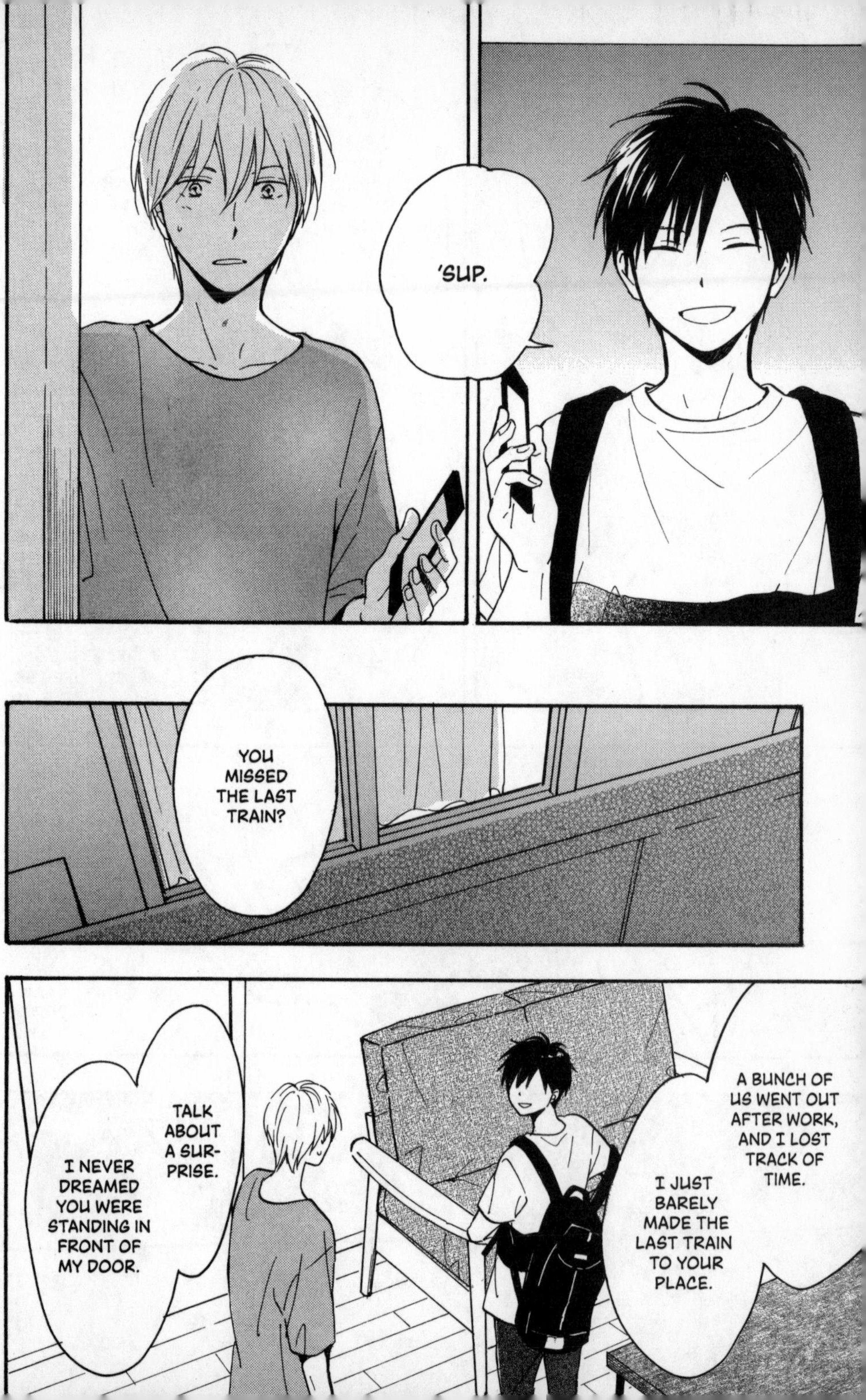
'SUP.
YOU MISSED THE LAST TRAIN?
A BUNCH OF US WENT OUT AFTER WORK, AND I LOST TRACK OF TIME.
I JUST BARELY MADE THE LAST TRAIN TO YOUR PLACE.
TALK ABOUT A SUR-PRISE.
I NEVER DREAMED YOU WERE STANDING IN FRONT OF MY DOOR.

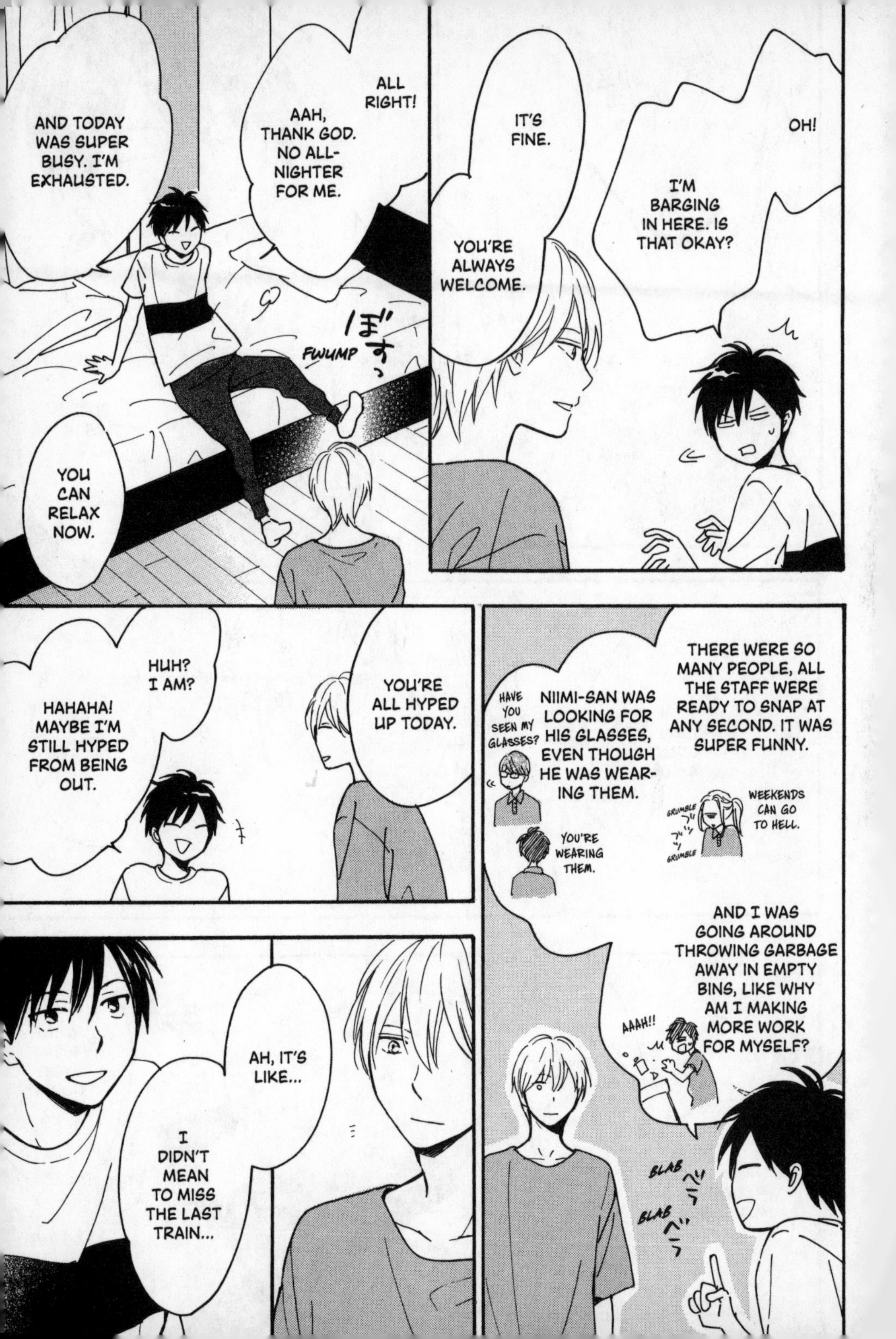
OH!
I'M BARGING IN HERE. IS THAT OKAY?
IT'S FINE.
YOU'RE ALWAYS WELCOME.
ALL RIGHT!
AAH, THANK GOD. NO ALL-NIGHTER FOR ME.
AND TODAY WAS SUPER BUSY. I'M EXHAUSTED.
FWUMP
YOU CAN RELAX NOW.
THERE WERE SO MANY PEOPLE, ALL THE STAFF WERE READY TO SNAP AT ANY SECOND. IT WAS SUPER FUNNY.
NIIMI-SAN WAS LOOKING FOR HIS GLASSES, EVEN THOUGH HE WAS WEARING THEM.
HAVE YOU SEEN MY GLASSES?
YOU'RE WEARING THEM.
WEEKENDS CAN GO TO HELL.
GRUMBLE
GRUMBLE
AND I WAS GOING AROUND THROWING GARBAGE AWAY IN EMPTY BINS, LIKE WHY AM I MAKING MORE WORK FOR MYSELF?
AAAH!!
BLAB
BLAB
YOU'RE ALL HYPED UP TODAY.
HUH? I AM?
HAHAHA! MAYBE I'M STILL HYPED FROM BEING OUT.
AH, IT'S LIKE...
I DIDN'T MEAN TO MISS THE LAST TRAIN...

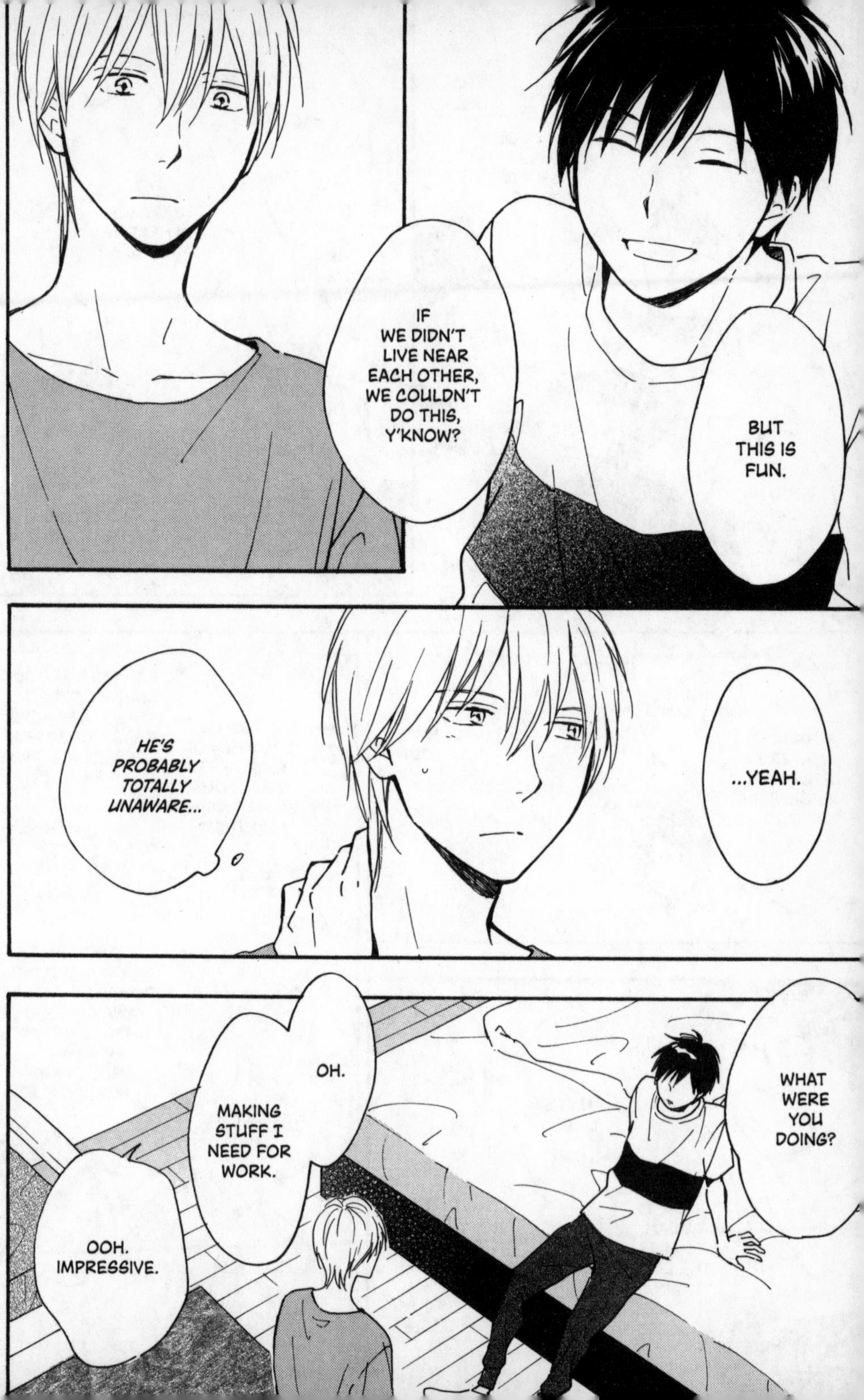
BUT THIS IS FUN.
IF WE DIDN'T LIVE NEAR EACH OTHER, WE COULDN'T DO THIS, Y'KNOW?
...YEAH.
HE'S PROBABLY TOTALLY UNAWARE...
WHAT WERE YOU DOING?
OH.
MAKING STUFF I NEED FOR WORK.
OOH. IMPRESSIVE.

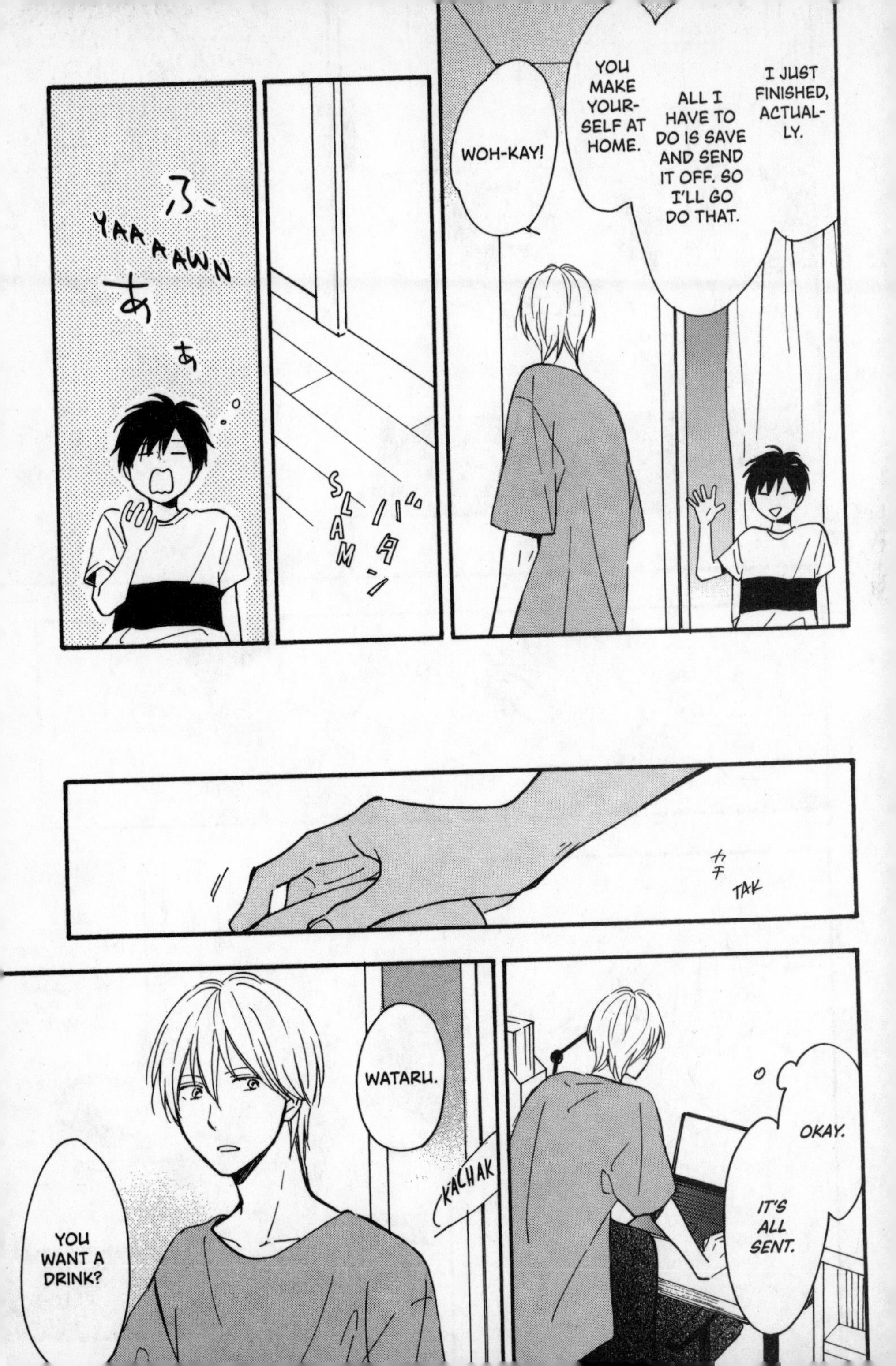
I JUST FINISHED, ACTUAL-LY.
ALL I HAVE TO DO IS SAVE AND SEND IT OFF. SO I'LL GO DO THAT.
YOU MAKE YOUR-SELF AT HOME.
WOH-KAY!
バタン
SLAM
ふぁあ
YAAAAAWN
カチ
TAK
OKAY.
IT'S ALL SENT.
KACHAK
WATARU.
YOU WANT A DRINK?

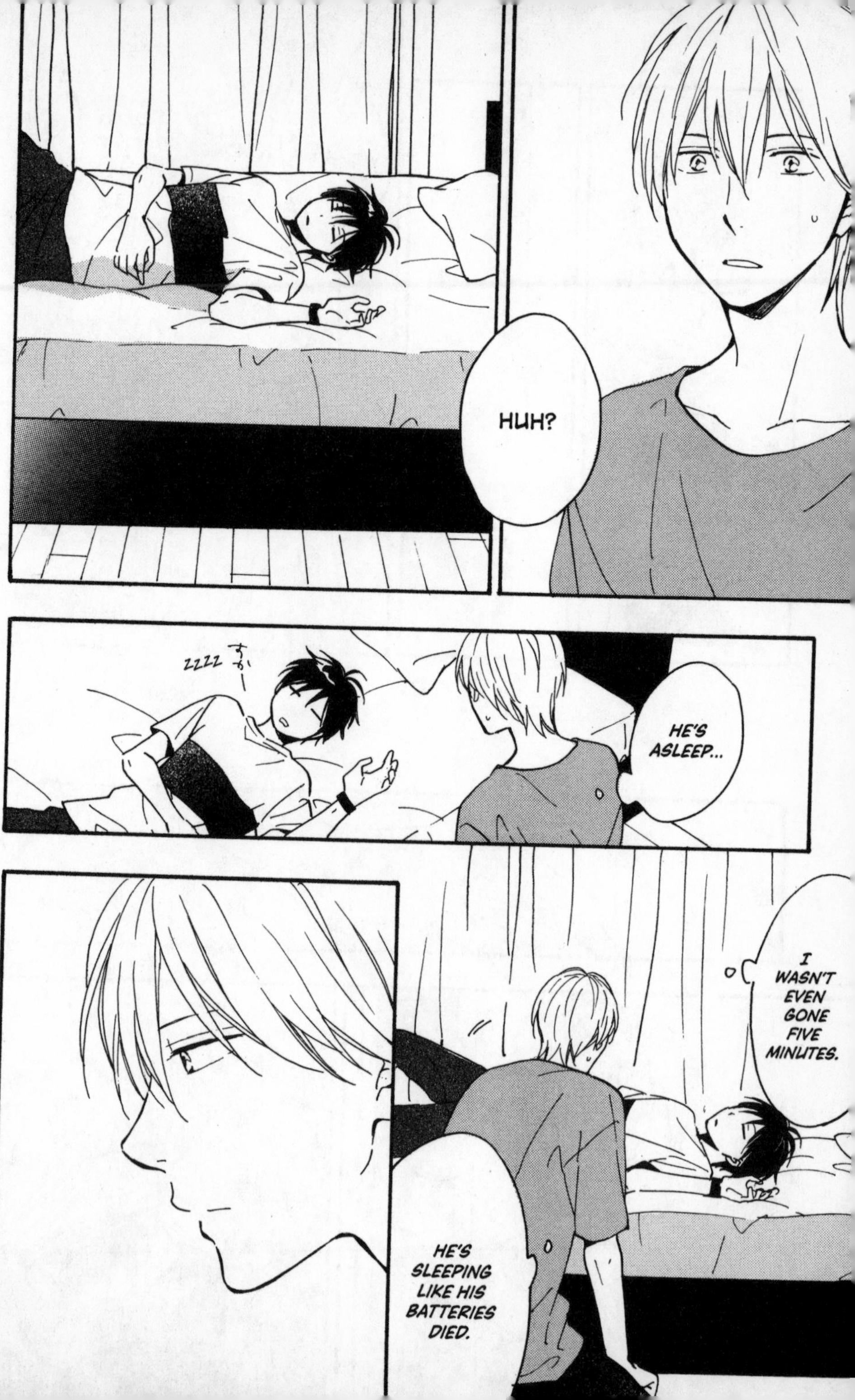
HUH?
HE'S ASLEEP...
ZZZZ
すかー
I WASN'T EVEN GONE FIVE MINUTES.
HE'S SLEEPING LIKE HIS BATTERIES DIED.

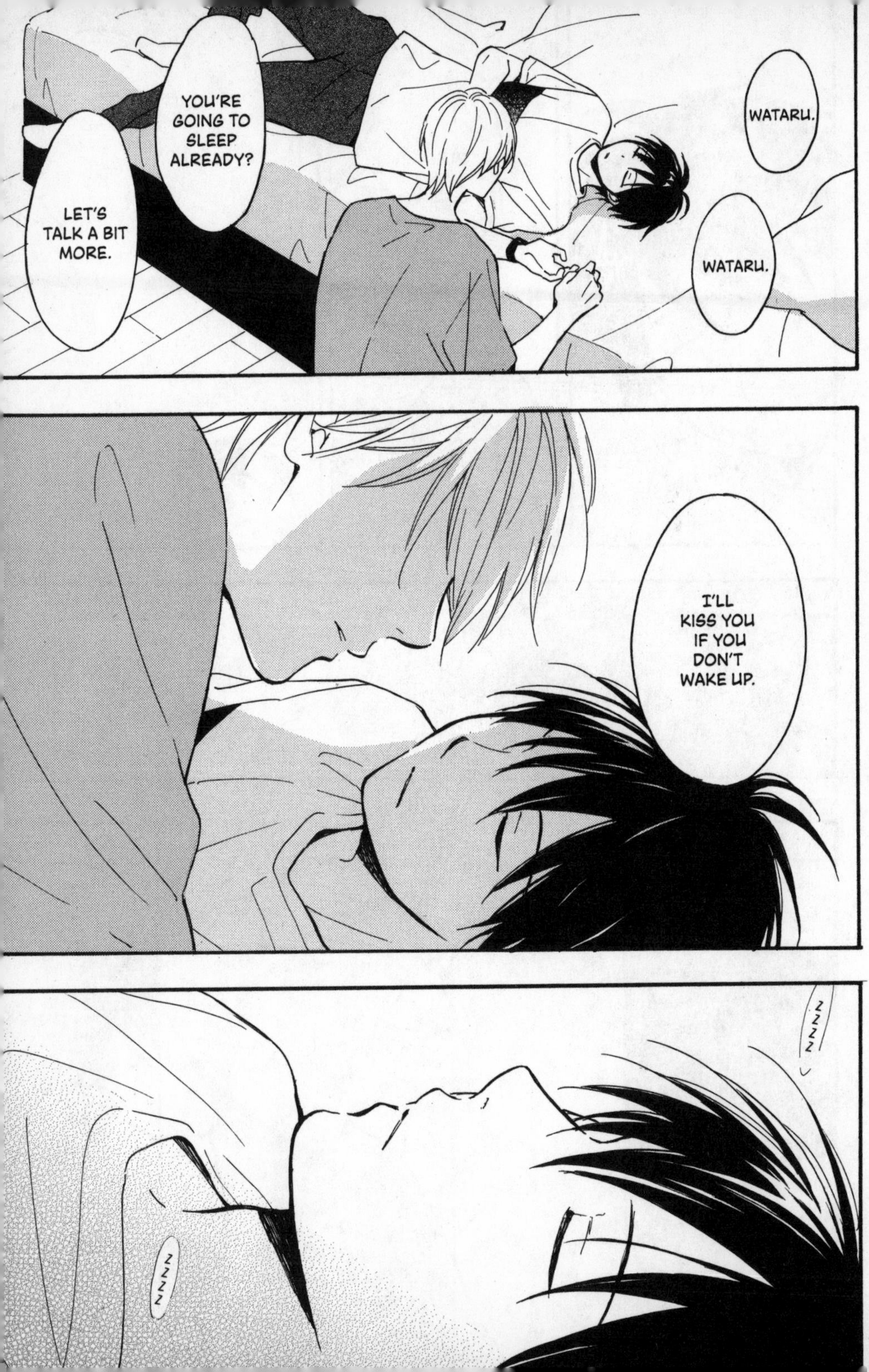
WATARU.
WATARU.
YOU'RE GOING TO SLEEP ALREADY?
LET'S TALK A BIT MORE.
I'LL KISS YOU IF YOU DON'T WAKE UP.
ZZZ
ZZZ

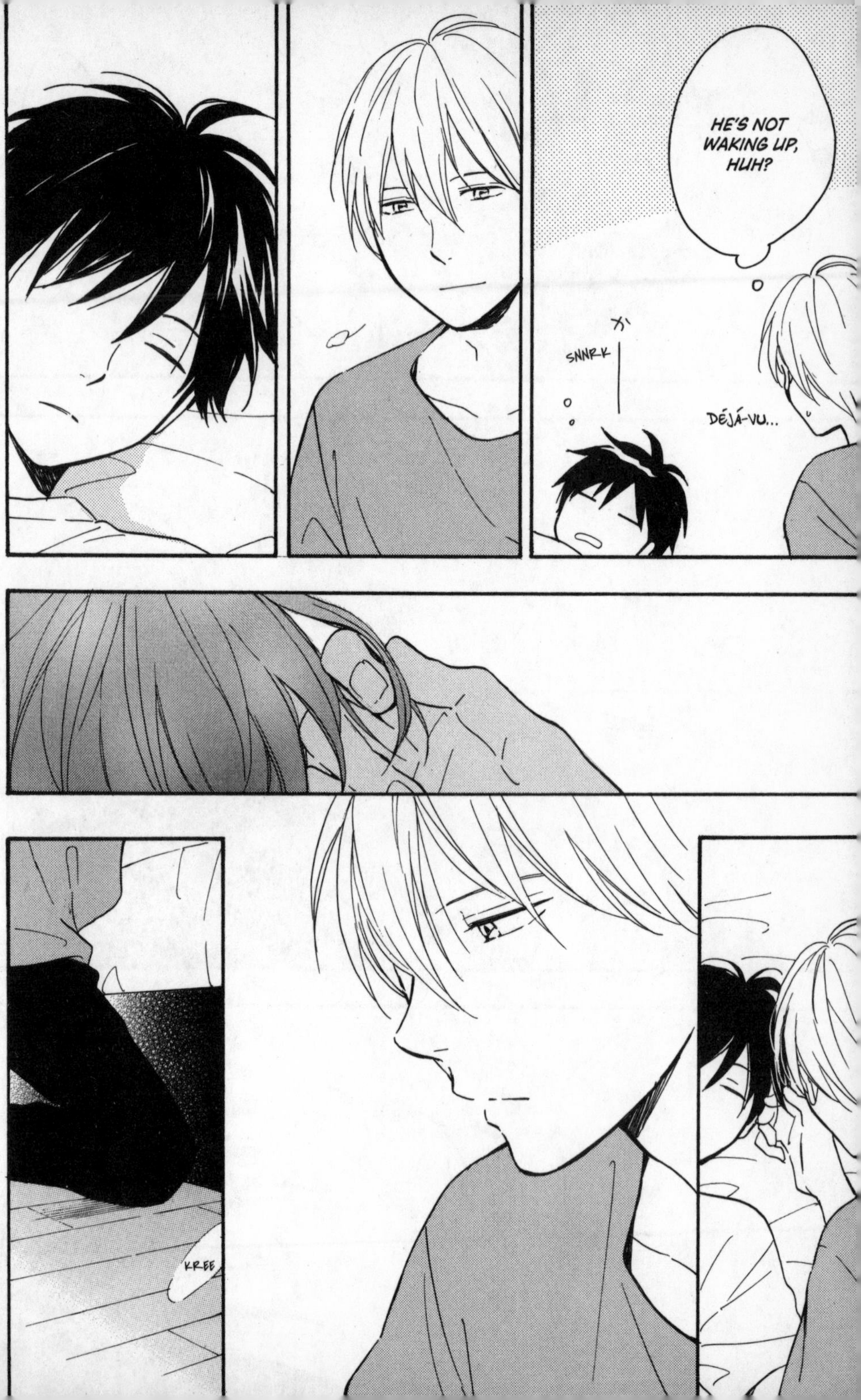
HE'S NOT WAKING UP, HUH?
DÉJÁ-VU...
ガ
SNNRK
KREE

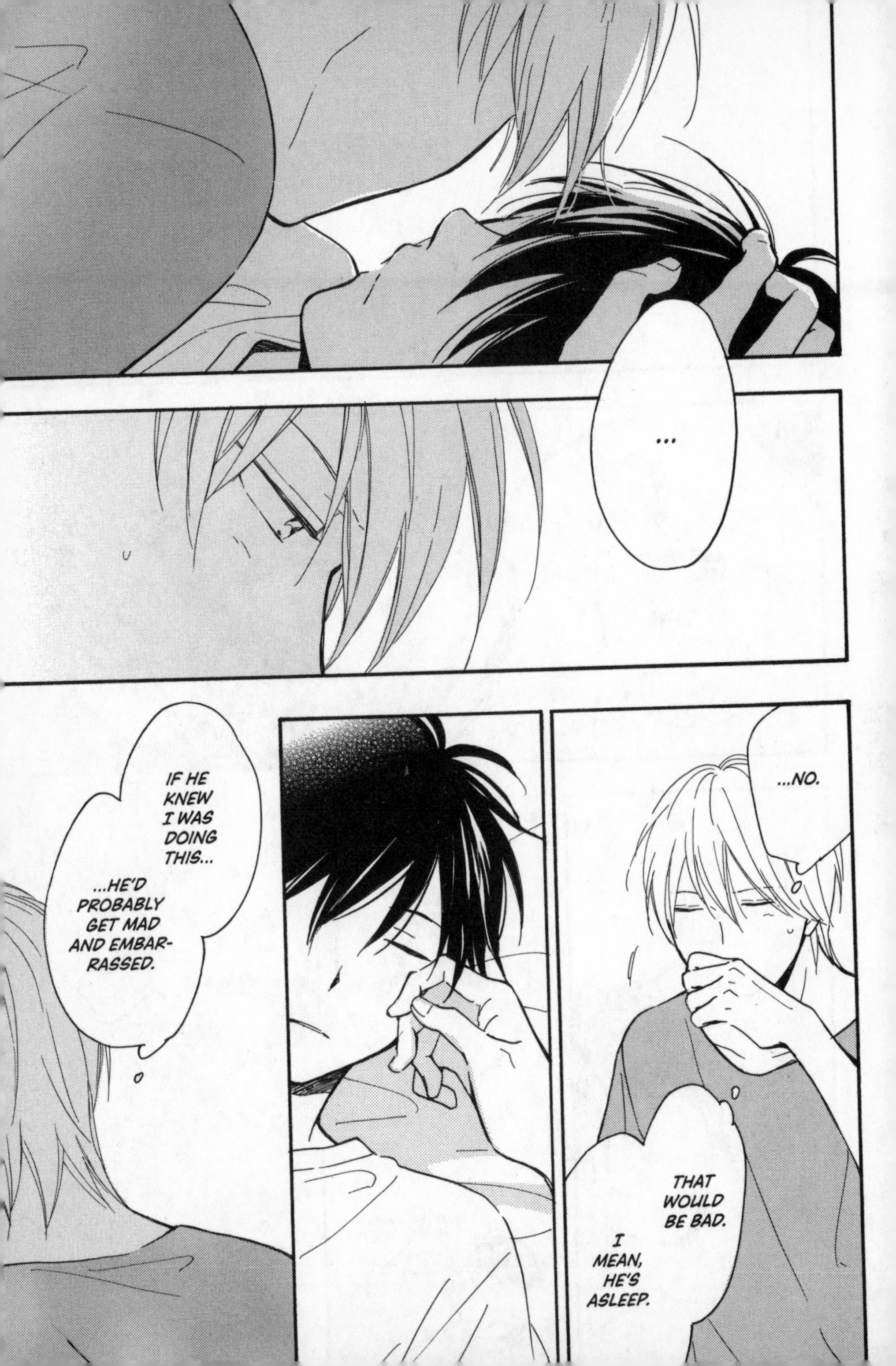
...
...NO.
THAT WOULD BE BAD.
I MEAN, HE'S ASLEEP.
IF HE KNEW I WAS DOING THIS...
...HE'D PROBABLY GET MAD AND EMBAR-RASSED.

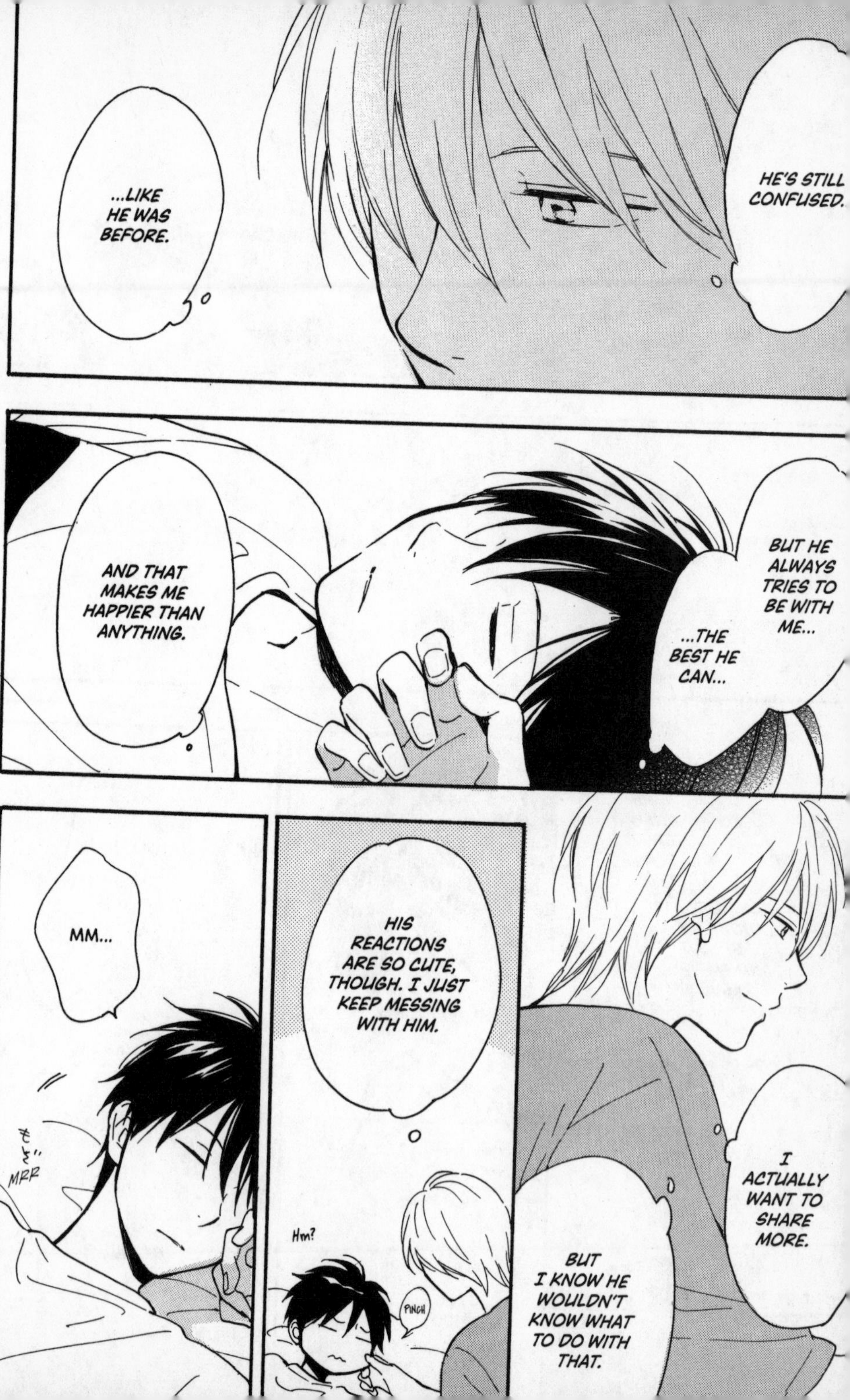

HE'S STILL CONFUSED.
...LIKE HE WAS BEFORE.
BUT HE ALWAYS TRIES TO BE WITH ME...
...THE BEST HE CAN...
AND THAT MAKES ME HAPPIER THAN ANYTHING.
I ACTUALLY WANT TO SHARE MORE.
BUT I KNOW HE WOULDN'T KNOW WHAT TO DO WITH THAT.
HIS REACTIONS ARE SO CUTE, THOUGH. I JUST KEEP MESSING WITH HIM.
Hm?
PINCH
MM...
MRR

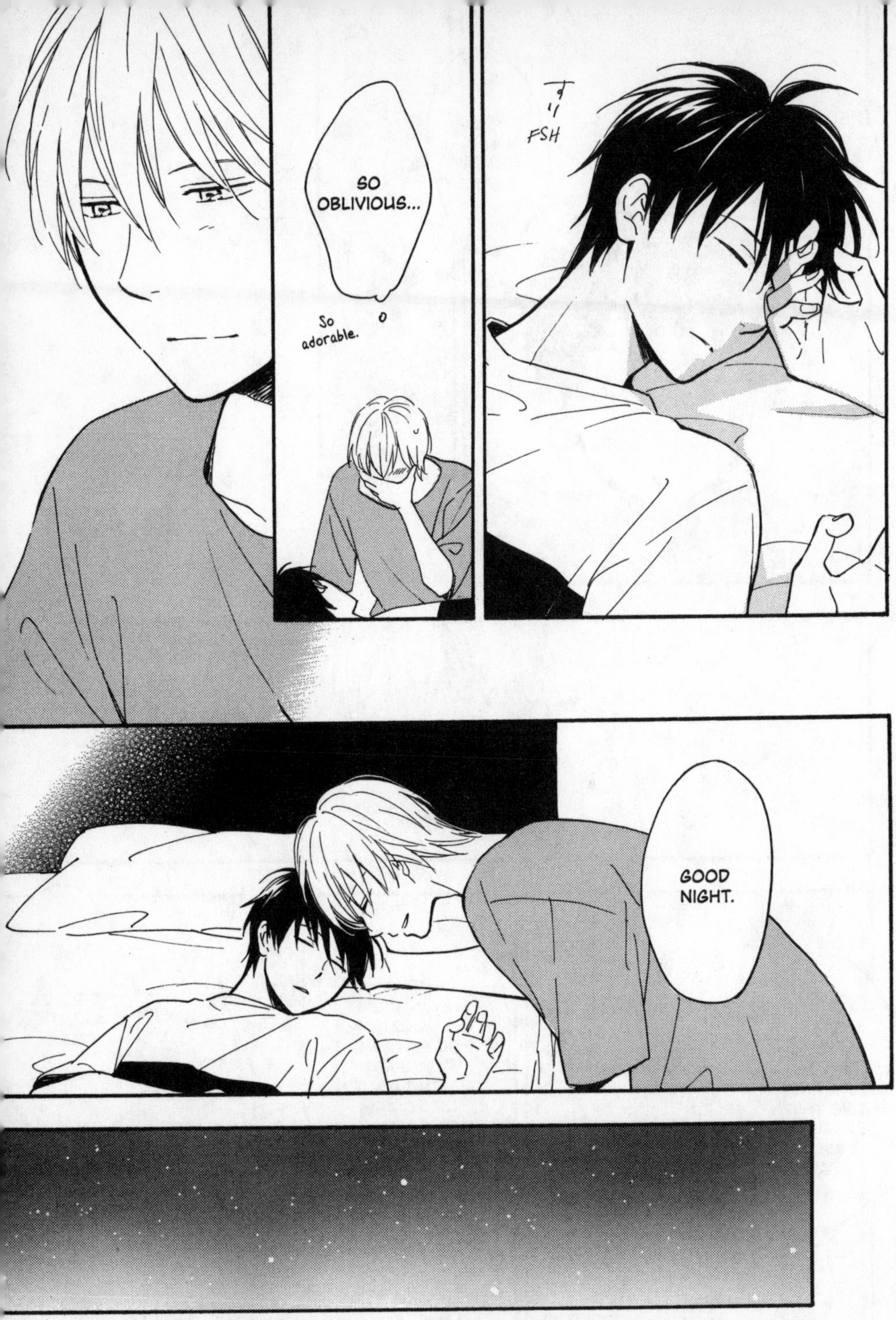
すり
FSH
SO OBLIVIOUS...
So adorable.
GOOD NIGHT.

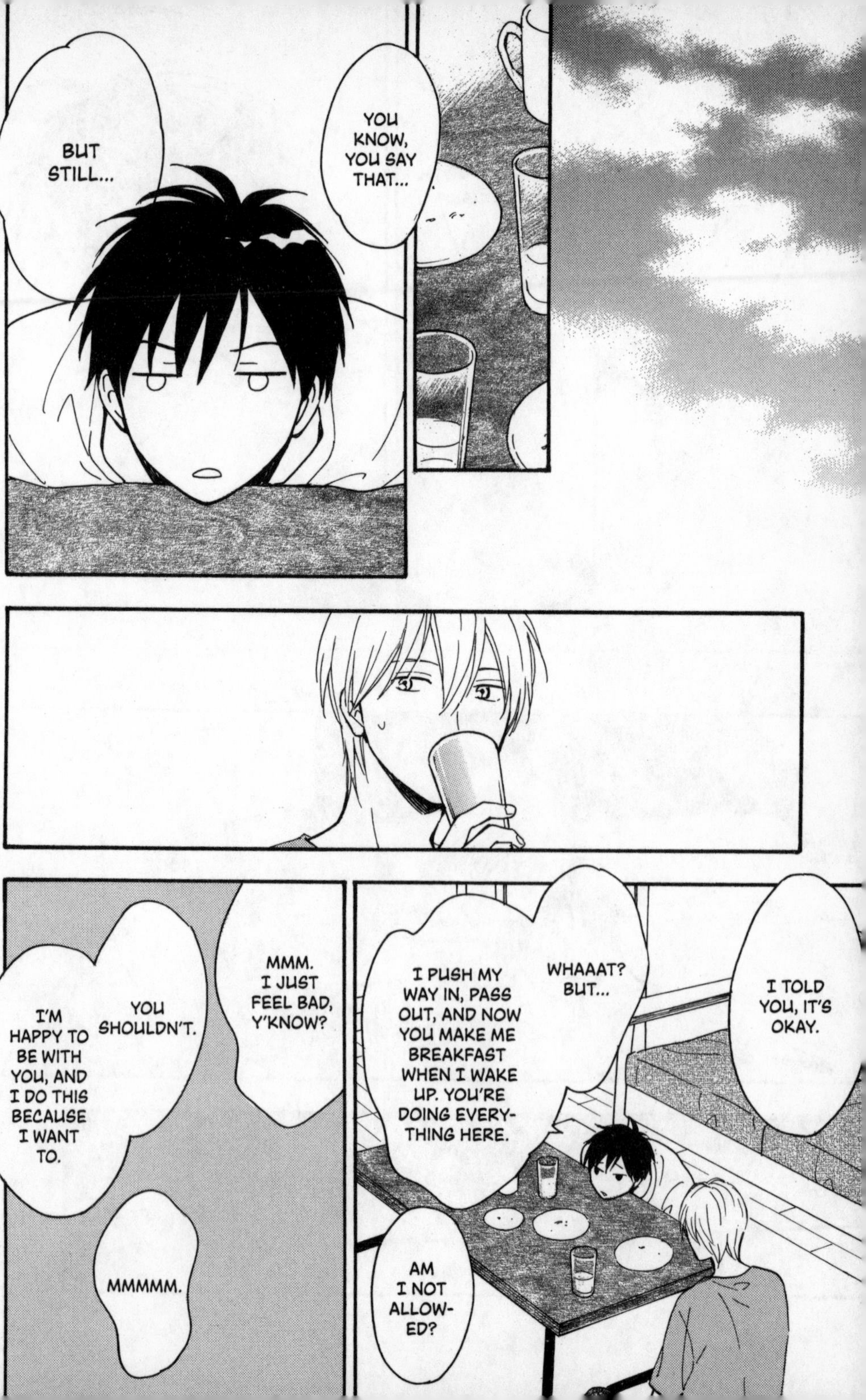
YOU KNOW, YOU SAY THAT...
BUT STILL...
I TOLD YOU, IT'S OKAY.
WHAAAT? BUT...
I PUSH MY WAY IN, PASS OUT, AND NOW YOU MAKE ME BREAKFAST WHEN I WAKE UP. YOU'RE DOING EVERY-THING HERE.
AM I NOT ALLOW-ED?
MMM. I JUST FEEL BAD, Y'KNOW?
YOU SHOULDN'T.
I'M HAPPY TO BE WITH YOU, AND I DO THIS BECAUSE I WANT TO.
MMMMM.

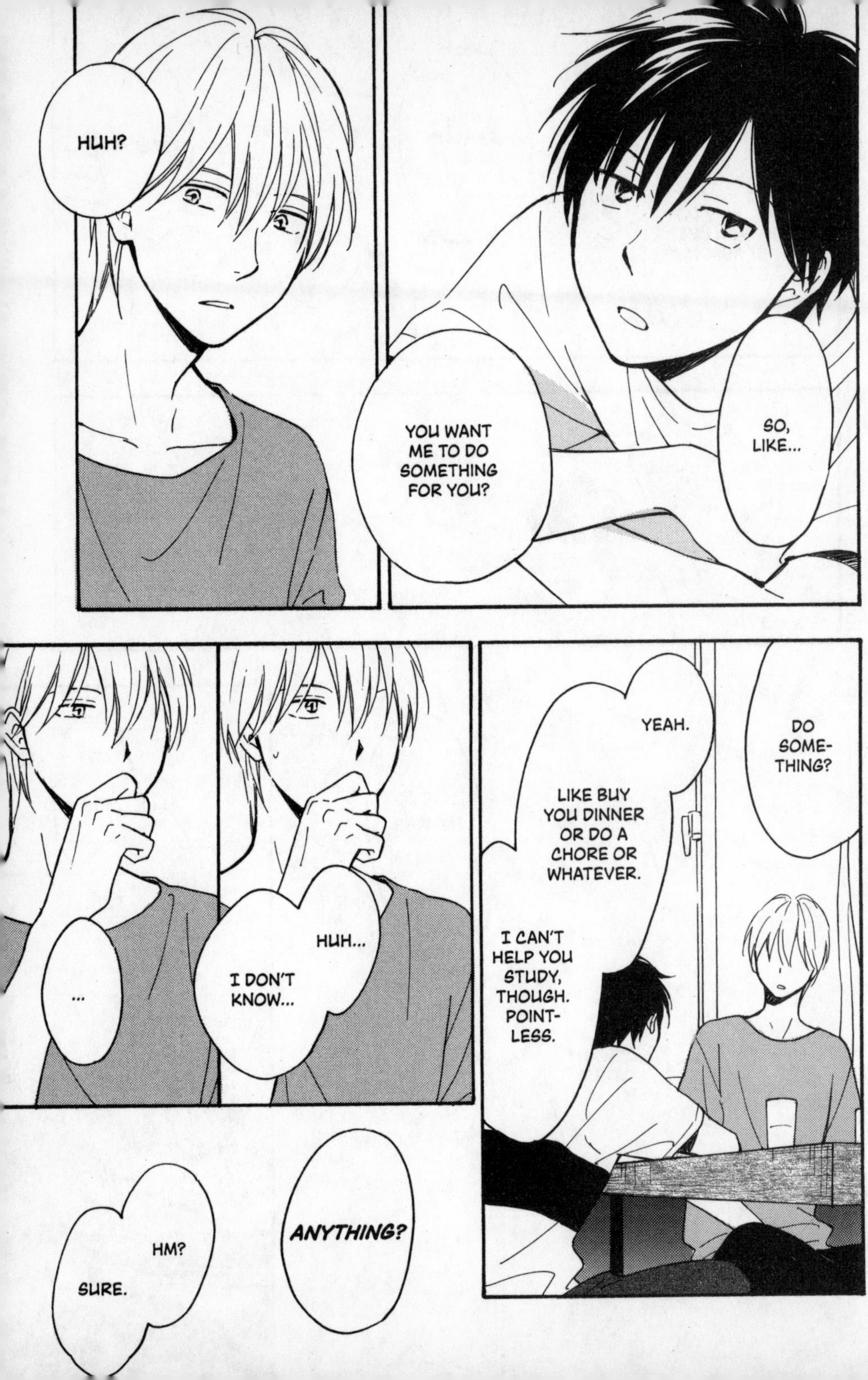

SO, LIKE...
YOU WANT ME TO DO SOMETHING FOR YOU?
HUH?
DO SOME-THING?
YEAH.
LIKE BUY YOU DINNER OR DO A CHORE OR WHATEVER.
I CAN'T HELP YOU STUDY, THOUGH. POINT-LESS.
HUH...
I DON'T KNOW...
...
ANYTHING?
HM?
SURE.

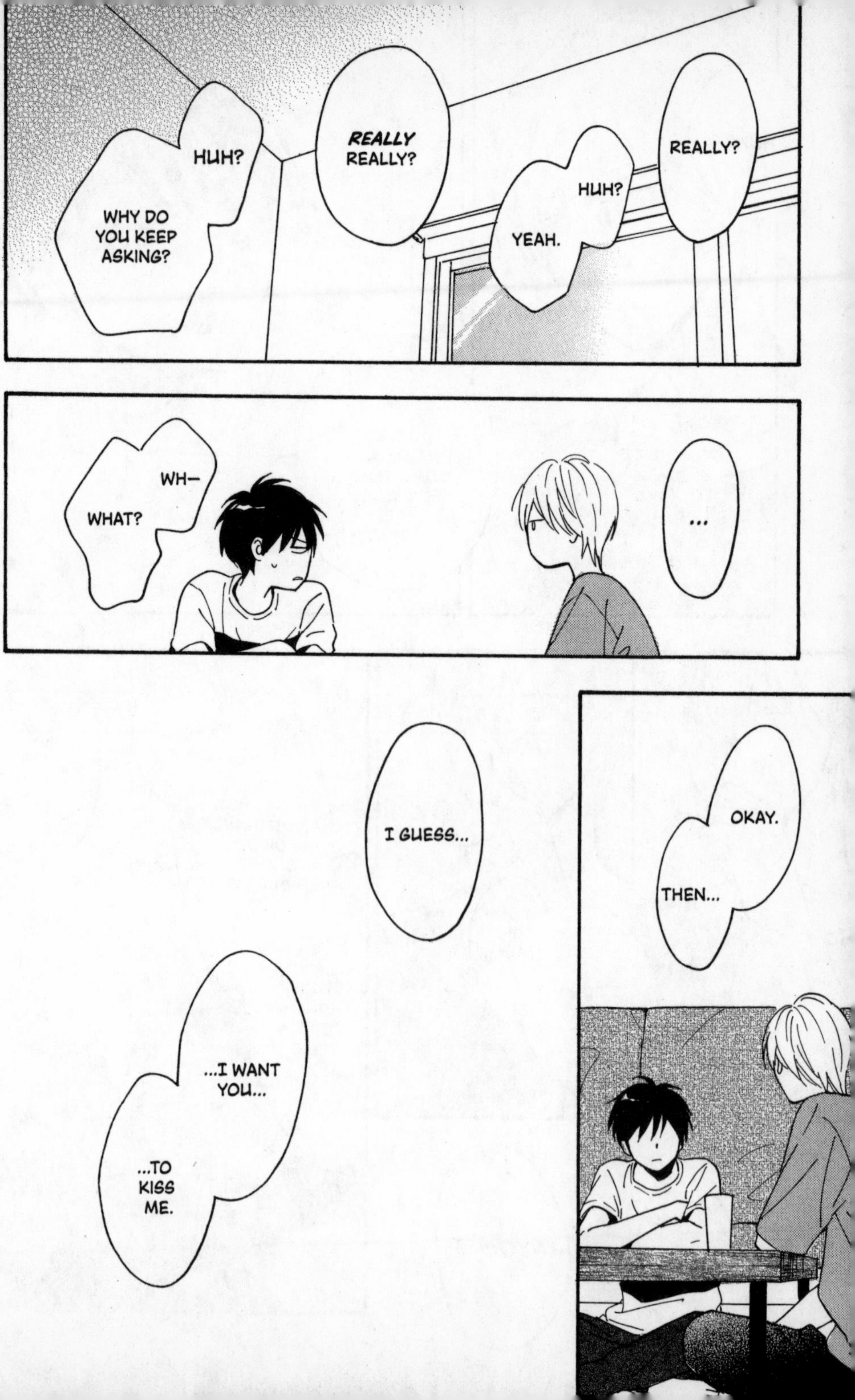
REALLY?
HUH?
YEAH.
REALLY REALLY?
HUH?
WHY DO YOU KEEP ASKING?
...
WH—
WHAT?
OKAY.
THEN...
I GUESS...
...I WANT YOU...
...TO KISS ME.

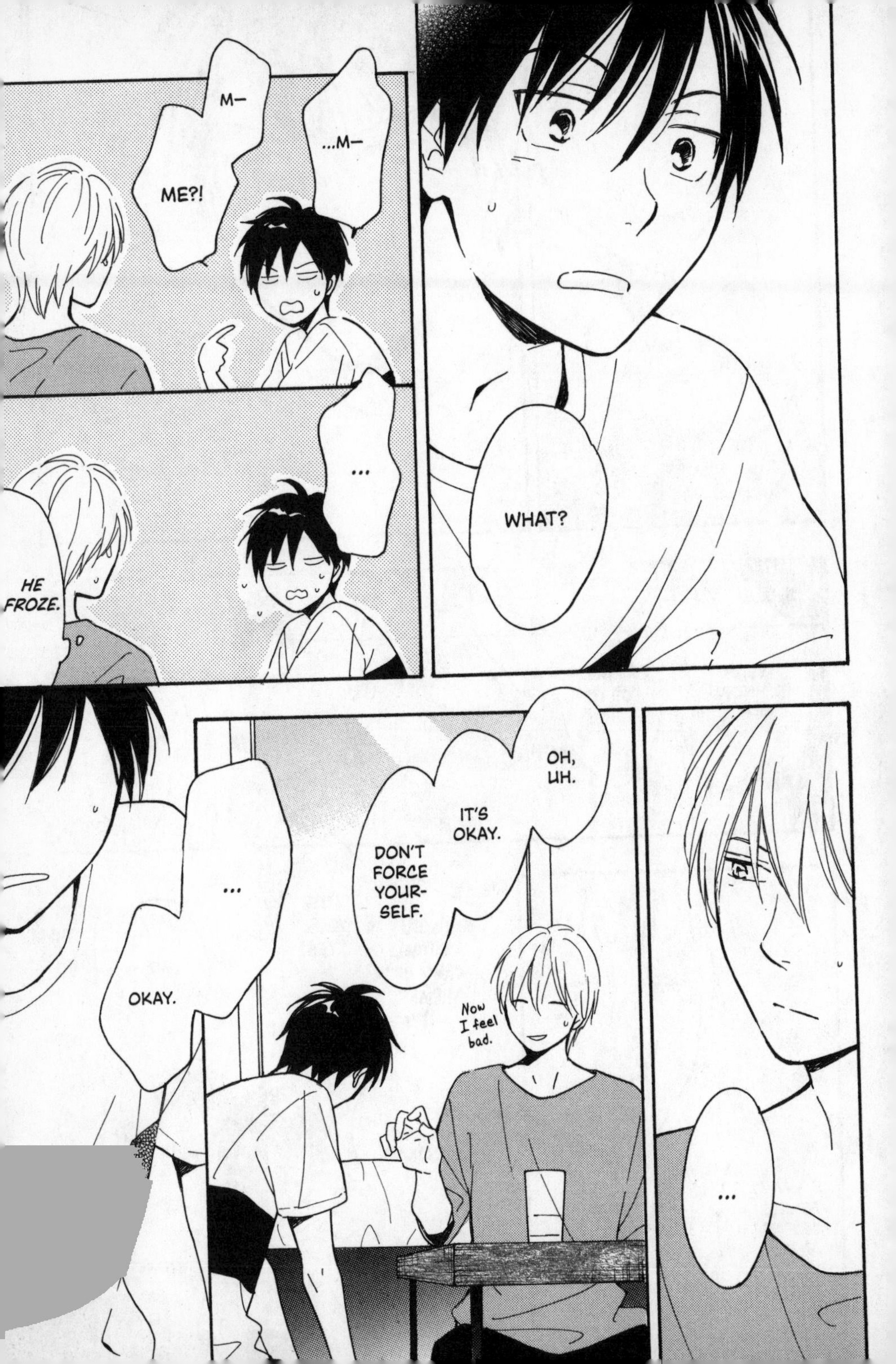
WHAT?
M—
...M—
ME?!
...
HE FROZE.
...
OH, UH.
IT'S OKAY.
DON'T FORCE YOUR-SELF.
Now I feel bad.
...
OKAY.

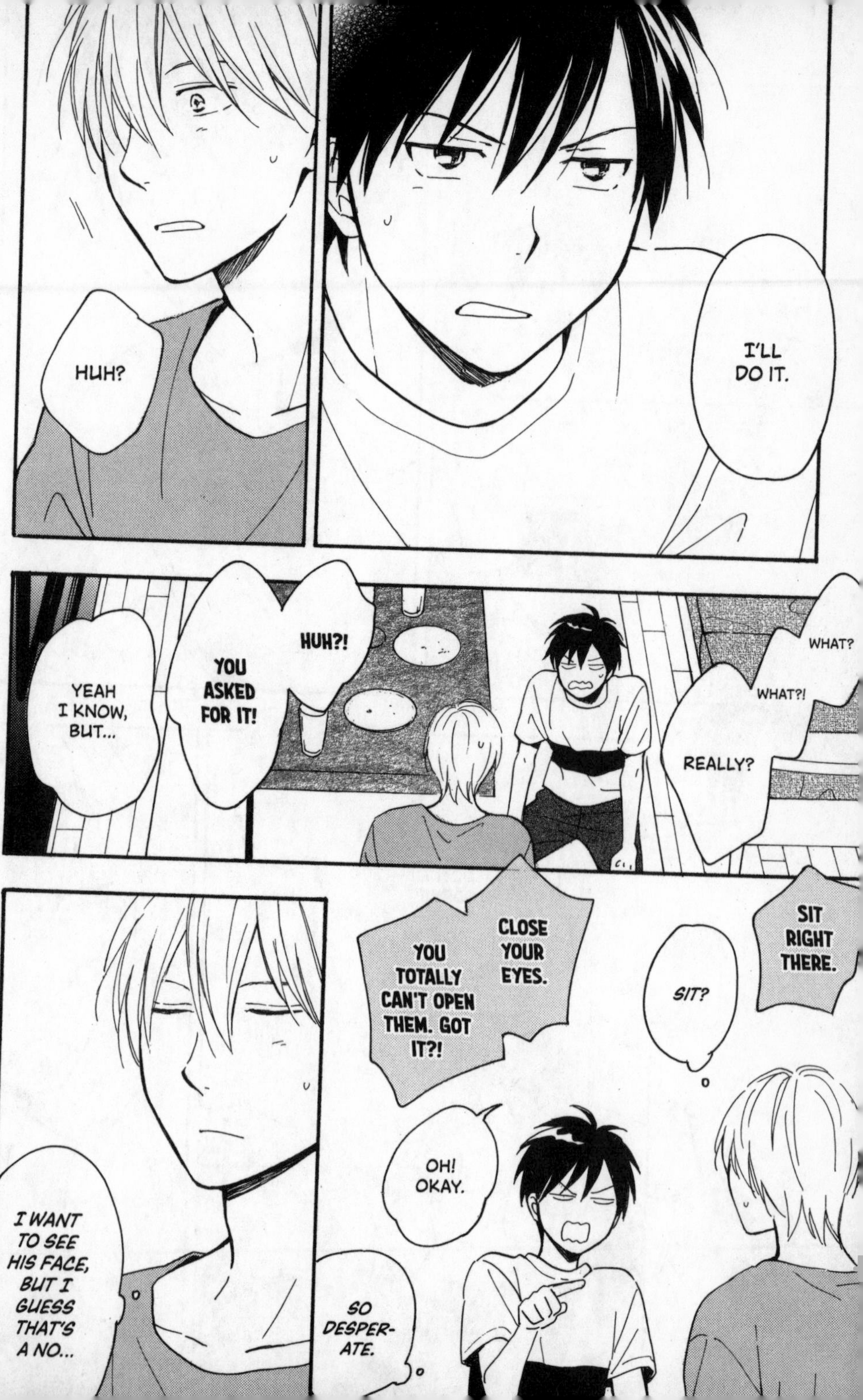
I'LL DO IT.
HUH?
WHAT?
WHAT?!
REALLY?
HUH?!
YOU ASKED FOR IT!
YEAH I KNOW, BUT...
SIT RIGHT THERE.
SIT?
CLOSE YOUR EYES.
YOU TOTALLY CAN'T OPEN THEM. GOT IT?!
OH! OKAY.
SO DESPERATE.
I WANT TO SEE HIS FACE, BUT I GUESS THAT'S A NO...

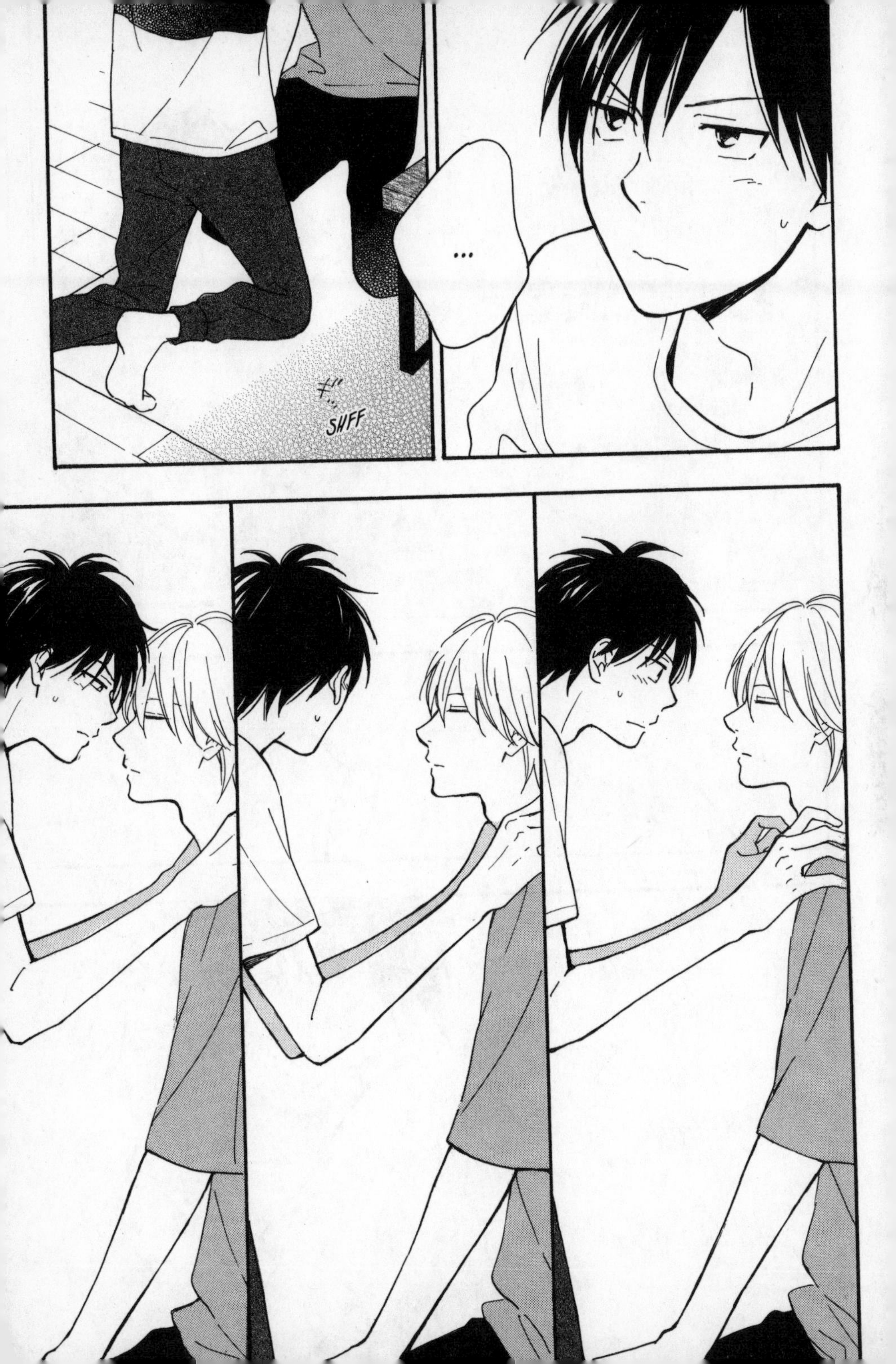
...
SHFF

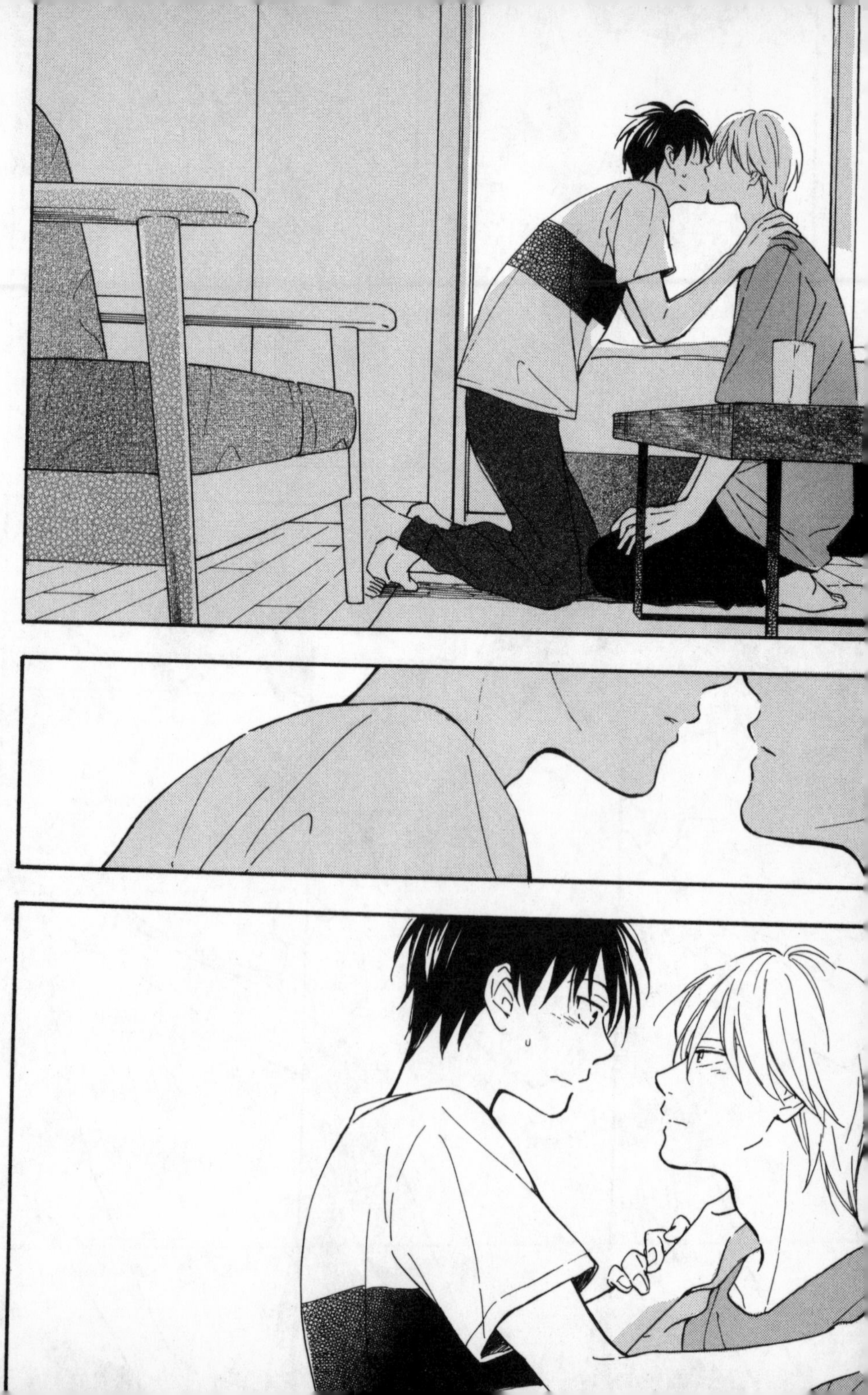

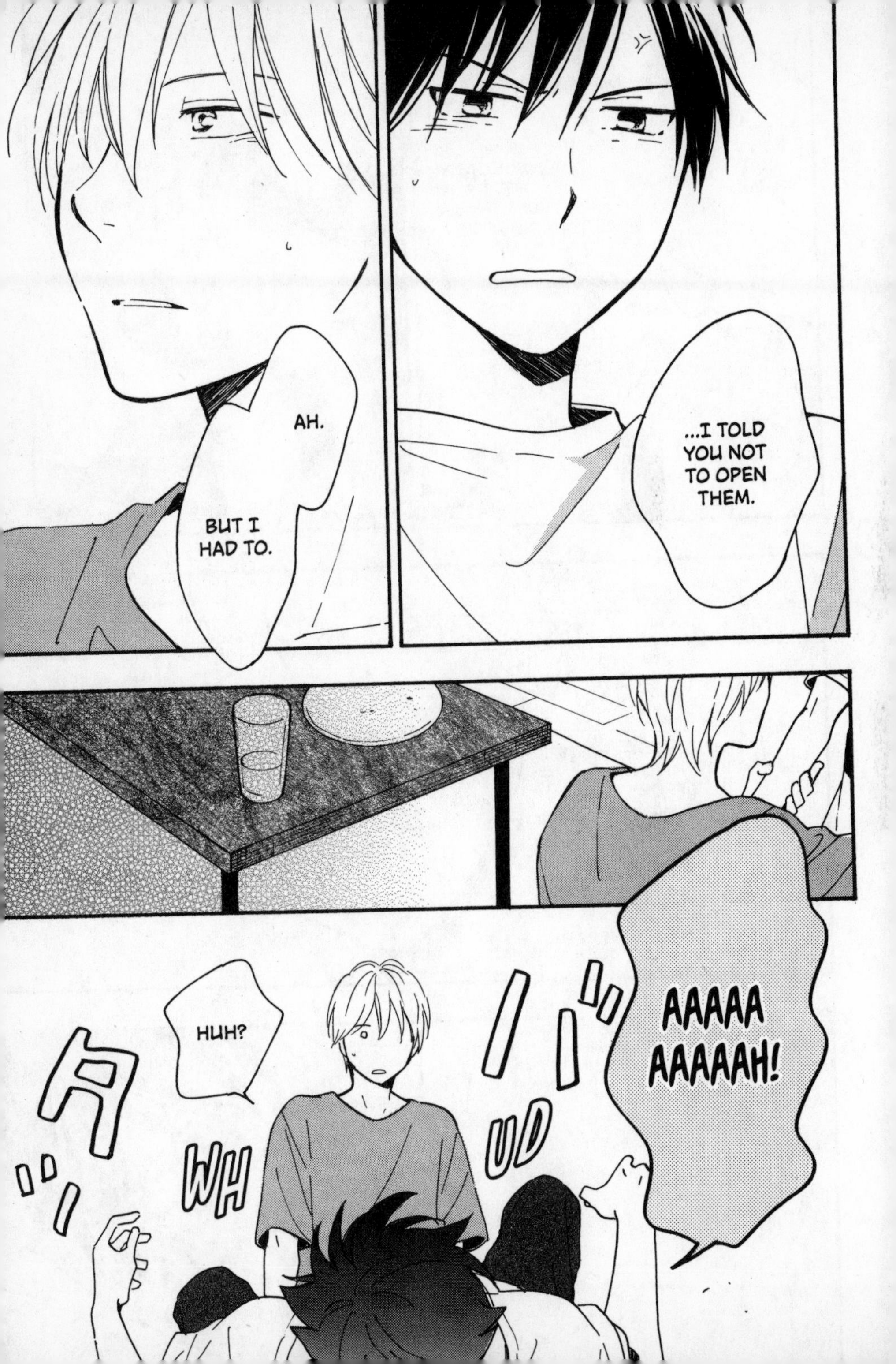
...I TOLD YOU NOT TO OPEN THEM.
AH.
BUT I HAD TO.
AAAAA AAAAAH!
WHUD
HUH?

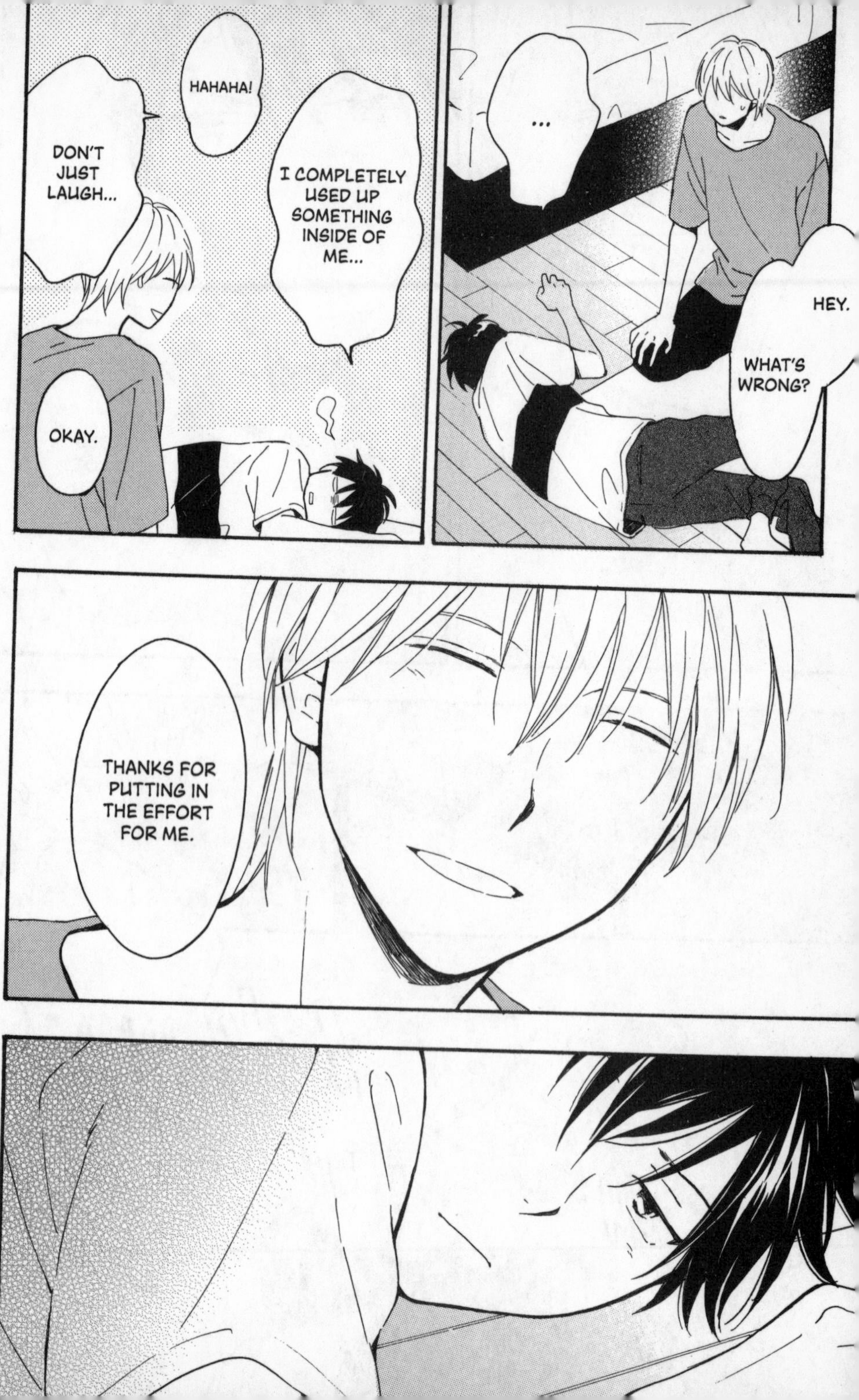
...
HEY.
WHAT'S WRONG?
I COMPLETELY USED UP SOMETHING INSIDE OF ME...
HAHAHA!
DON'T JUST LAUGH...
OKAY.
THANKS FOR PUTTING IN THE EFFORT FOR ME.

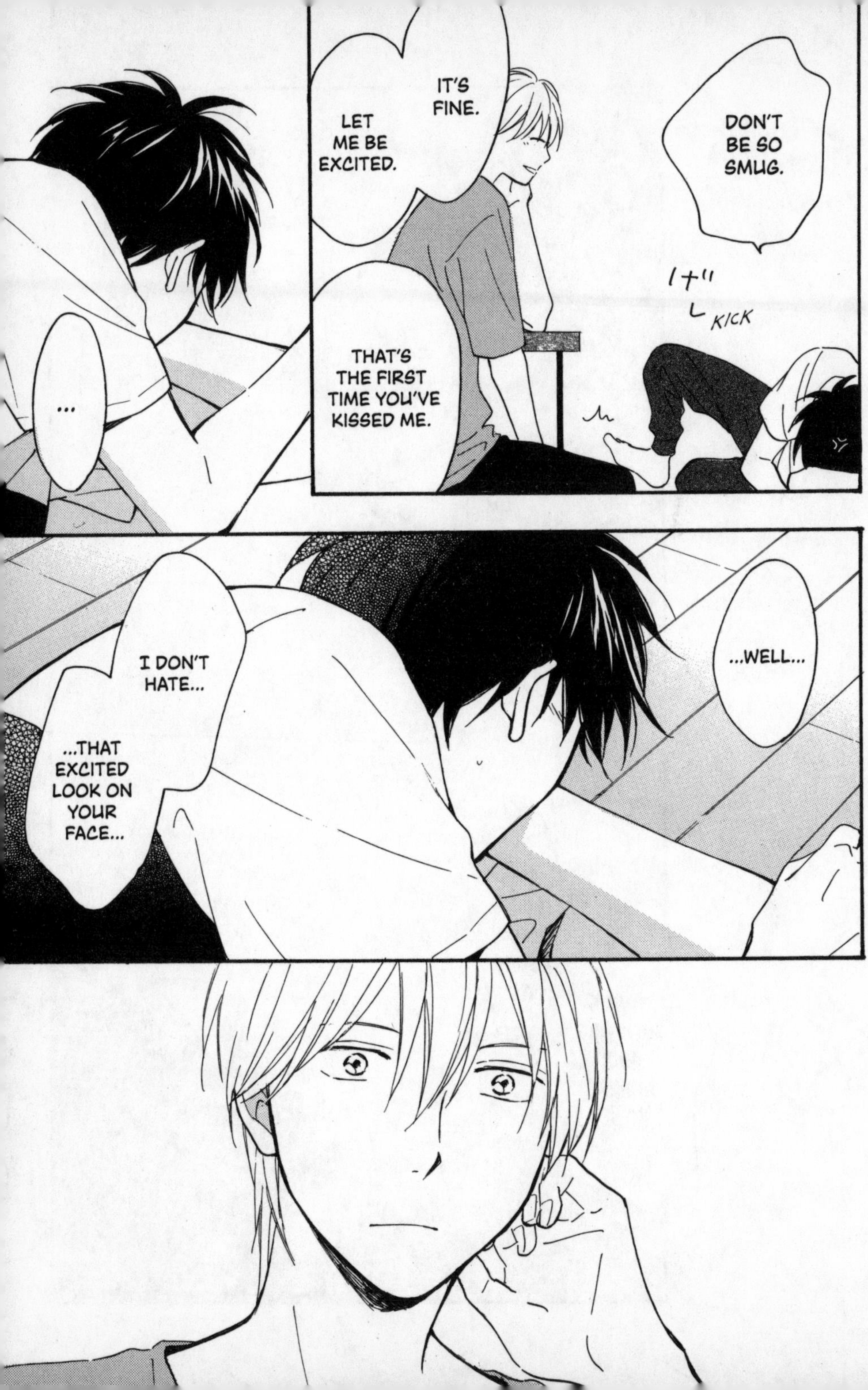
DON'T BE SO SMUG.
KICK
IT'S FINE. LET ME BE EXCITED.
THAT'S THE FIRST TIME YOU'VE KISSED ME.
...
...WELL...
I DON'T HATE...
...THAT EXCITED LOOK ON YOUR FACE...

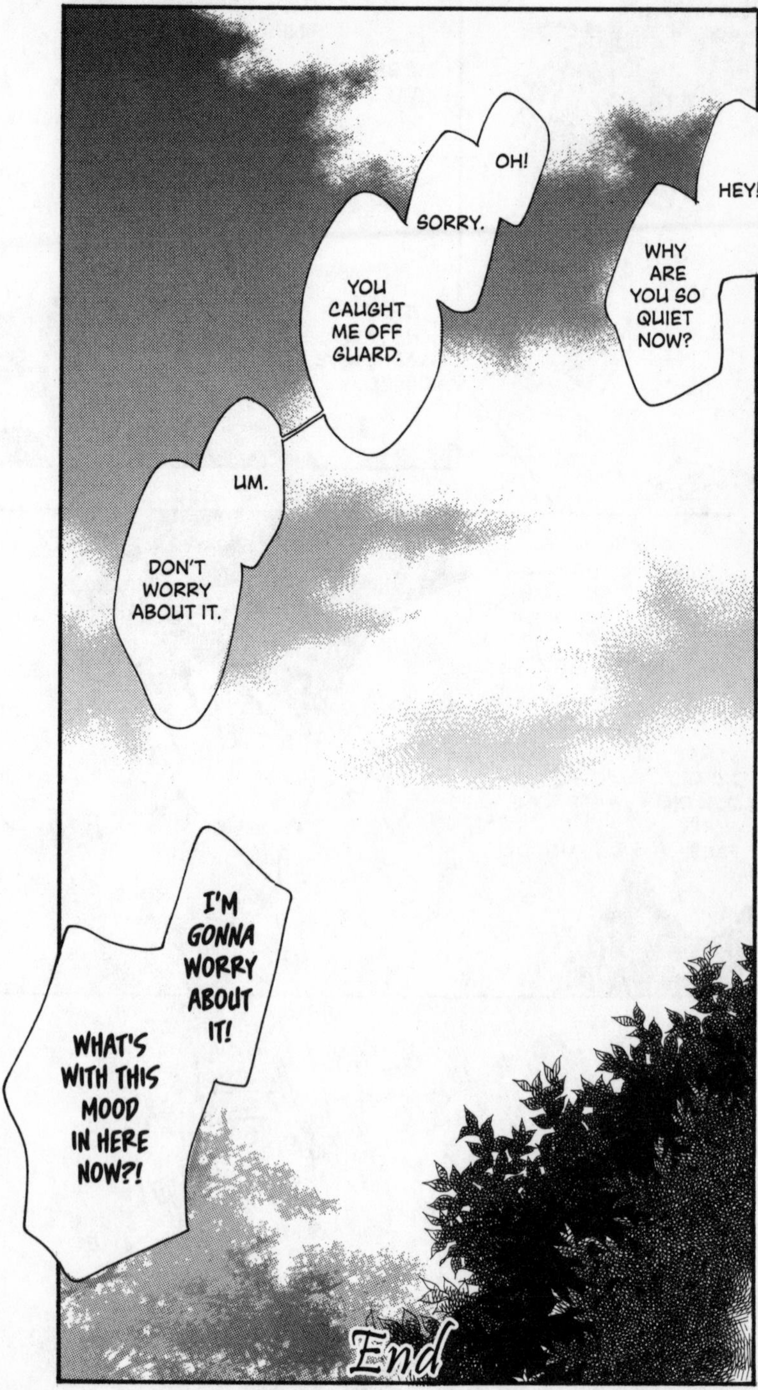
HEY!
WHY ARE YOU SO QUIET NOW?
OH!
SORRY.
YOU CAUGHT ME OFF GUARD.
UM.
DON'T WORRY ABOUT IT.
I'M GONNA WORRY ABOUT IT!
WHAT'S WITH THIS MOOD IN HERE NOW?!
End

MY SUMMER OF YOU

AFTERWORD

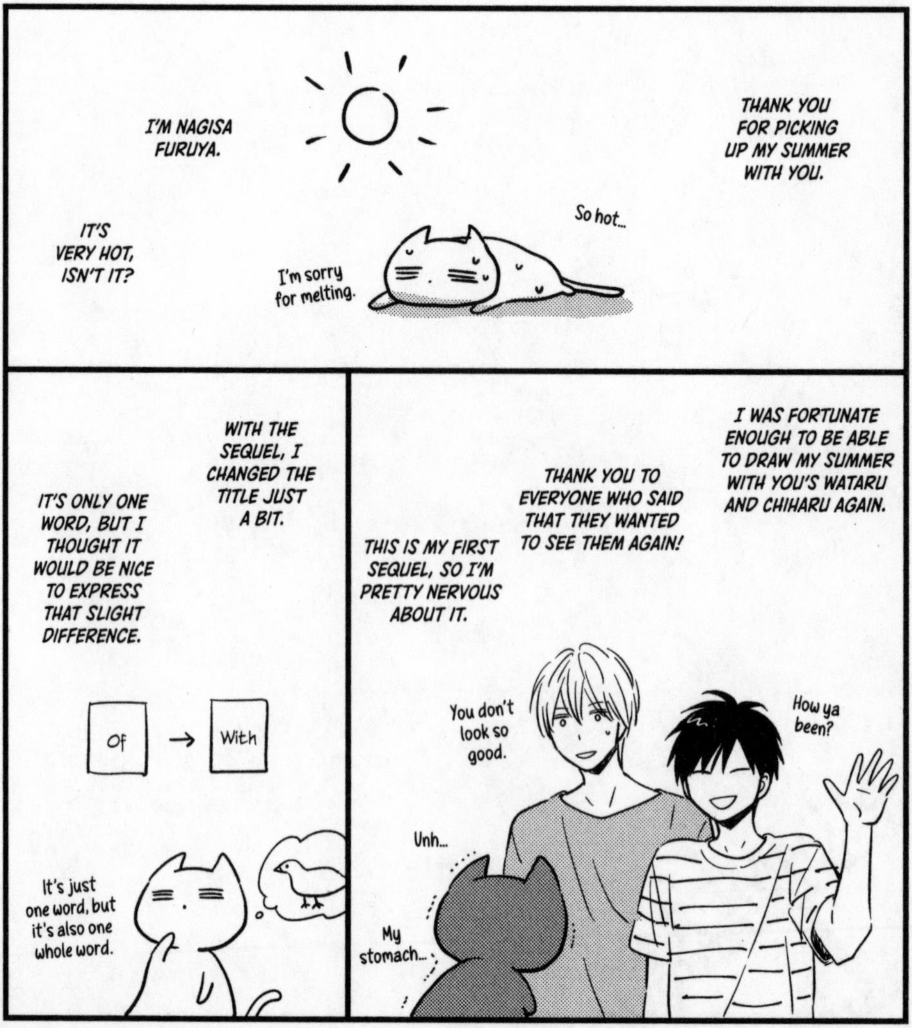
THANK YOU FOR PICKING UP MY SUMMER WITH YOU.
I'M NAGISA FURUYA.
So hot...
I'm sorry for melting.
IT'S VERY HOT, ISN'T IT?
I WAS FORTUNATE ENOUGH TO BE ABLE TO DRAW MY SUMMER WITH YOU'S WATARU AND CHIHARU AGAIN.
THANK YOU TO EVERYONE WHO SAID THAT THEY WANTED TO SEE THEM AGAIN!
THIS IS MY FIRST SEQUEL, SO I'M PRETTY NERVOUS ABOUT IT.
How ya been?
You don't look so good.
Unh...
My stomach...
WITH THE SEQUEL, I CHANGED THE TITLE JUST A BIT.
IT'S ONLY ONE WORD, BUT I THOUGHT IT WOULD BE NICE TO EXPRESS THAT SLIGHT DIFFERENCE.
Of
With
It's just one word, but it's also one whole word.

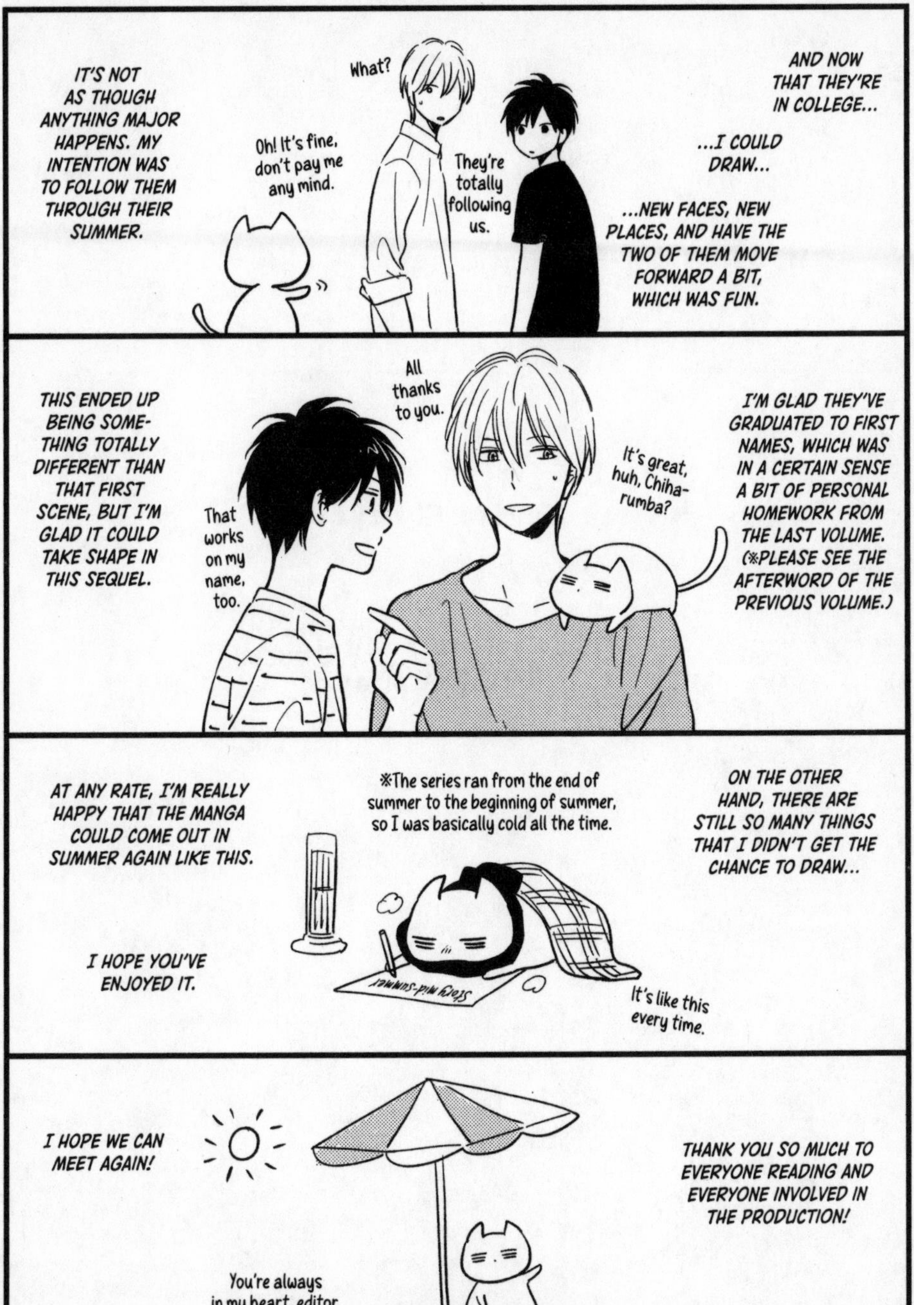
AND NOW THAT THEY'RE IN COLLEGE...
...I COULD DRAW...
...NEW FACES, NEW PLACES, AND HAVE THE TWO OF THEM MOVE FORWARD A BIT, WHICH WAS FUN.
What?
They're totally following us.
Oh! It's fine, don't pay me any mind.
IT'S NOT AS THOUGH ANYTHING MAJOR HAPPENS. MY INTENTION WAS TO FOLLOW THEM THROUGH THEIR SUMMER.
I'M GLAD THEY'VE GRADUATED TO FIRST NAMES, WHICH WAS IN A CERTAIN SENSE A BIT OF PERSONAL HOMEWORK FROM THE LAST VOLUME. (※PLEASE SEE THE AFTERWORD OF THE PREVIOUS VOLUME.)
It's great, huh, Chiha-rumba?
All thanks to you.
That works on my name, too.
THIS ENDED UP BEING SOME-THING TOTALLY DIFFERENT THAN THAT FIRST SCENE, BUT I'M GLAD IT COULD TAKE SHAPE IN THIS SEQUEL.
ON THE OTHER HAND, THERE ARE STILL SO MANY THINGS THAT I DIDN'T GET THE CHANCE TO DRAW...
※The series ran from the end of summer to the beginning of summer, so I was basically cold all the time.
It's like this every time.
Story mid-summer
AT ANY RATE, I'M REALLY HAPPY THAT THE MANGA COULD COME OUT IN SUMMER AGAIN LIKE THIS.
I HOPE YOU'VE ENJOYED IT.
THANK YOU SO MUCH TO EVERYONE READING AND EVERYONE INVOLVED IN THE PRODUCTION!
You're always in my heart, editor, designer, K-shi!
I HOPE WE CAN MEET AGAIN!

Nagisa Furuya

This is the sequel,
a second summer.

TRANSLATION NOTES

Gacha, page 43
A gacha game is a genre of video games that often feature a gacha, or lottery, mechanic to them. Gacha games encourage players to spend in-game currency to draw a random virtual item, or, depending on the kind of game, an in-game character.

-sama, page 44
In Japanese, the honorific -sama signifies formality. It is often used when someone is addressing someone who is of a higher ranking than them, such as a celebrity, a god or divine entity (kamisama), a guest or a customer (okyakusama), or can also be used when one addresses someone they greatly admire. In this instance, Wataru's classmate is holding him in high regard for his good luck with gacha-pulling.

Onigiri and umeboshi, page 46
On this page, we see Chiharu and Wararu making onigiri, or rice balls. Onigiri are traditionally formed into triangular or cylindrical shapes, are often wrapped in nori, or dried seaweed, and can be made plain or, as we see Chiharu and Wataru doing here, include fillings. Umeboshi, or pickled plum, is one such popular filling.

Friday night movie, page 54
Here, Wataru says he set his alarm for the kin-ro, short for kinyoubi roodshoo —"Friday night road show", or Friday night movie. This is in reference to the movie of the week that Nippon TV (NTV) broadcasts each Friday evening, ranging from popular domestic offerings to Hollywood blockbusters. The term "road show" went out of use long ago in the US, but remains standard in Japan to refer chiefly to a movie's theatrical release (though in this case, means it's being shown on television).

Yukata, page 115
A yukata is an unlined cotton kimono, often worn during the summer and in casual settings, such as at summer festivals, traditional style inns, and bathhouses.

"I feel like you just called me by my first name.", page 145
In Japan, people generally don't address one another by their first names—and, unless given explicit person from someone, doing so can even be considered rude. Rather, it's more common for people to address one another by their last name, coupled with the approriate honorific (Such as -san for Mr./Ms./Mx., -senpai for an elder or upperclassman, -sensei for a teacher, etc.) However, addressing someone by their first name signifies that you have a close relationship with them, and can sometimes be used in casual settings, such as between friends (as Akiyoshi does to Chiharu), or lovers, as Wataru addresses Chiharu here.

TRANSLATION NOTES

"I want some curry. Like in the navy.", page 174
Although curry originates from Indian cuisine, the dish was popularized in Japan during the Meiji Era (1868-1912), when it was brought to Japan from India by the British. Due to it being rich in vitamin b, the dish was soon adopted by the Japanese Navy in order to prevent beriberi, where it quickly became a favorite aboard Japanese naval ships. Today, curry is a popular dish in Japan, and is often served with rice, over noodles, or in bread. Japanese curry often includes onions, carrots, and potatoes, with beef, pork, and chicken as popular meat additions.

"It's just one word, but it's also one whole word.", page 218
The Japanese titles of *The Summer of You* and *The Summer With You* are *Kimi wa natsu no naka* and *Kimi to natsu no naka*, respectively. Here, the author is referring to how when combined, the particles *ha* (an alternative romanization of *wa*) and *to* form the word *hato*, or pigeon, hence the pigeon imagery next to the author.

MY SUMMER OF YOU

MY **SUMMER** OF YOU

MY SUMMER OF YOU

A Kodansha Comics Trade Paperback Original
My Summer of You Vol. 2: The Summer With You copyright © 2019 Nagisa Furuya
English translation copyright © 2021 Nagisa Furuya

Published in the United States by Kodansha Comics, an imprint of
Kodansha USA Publishing, LLC, New York.

Publication rights for this English edition arranged through
Kodansha Ltd., Tokyo.

First published in Japan in 2019 by Ichijinsha Inc., Tokyo
as *Kimi to natsu no naka.*

ISBN 978-1-64651-244-7

Printed in the United States of America.

www.kodanshacomics.com

1st Printing
Translation: Jocelyne Allen
Lettering: Nicole Roderick
Editing: Tiff Joshua TJ Ferentini
Kodansha Comics edition cover design by Adam Del Re

Publisher: Kiichiro Sugawara

Director of publishing services: Ben Applegate
Associate director of operations: Stephen Pakula
Publishing services managing editors: Alanna Ruse, Madison Salters
Assistant production managers: Emi Lotto, Angela Zurlo
Logo and character art ©Kodansha USA Publishing, LLC

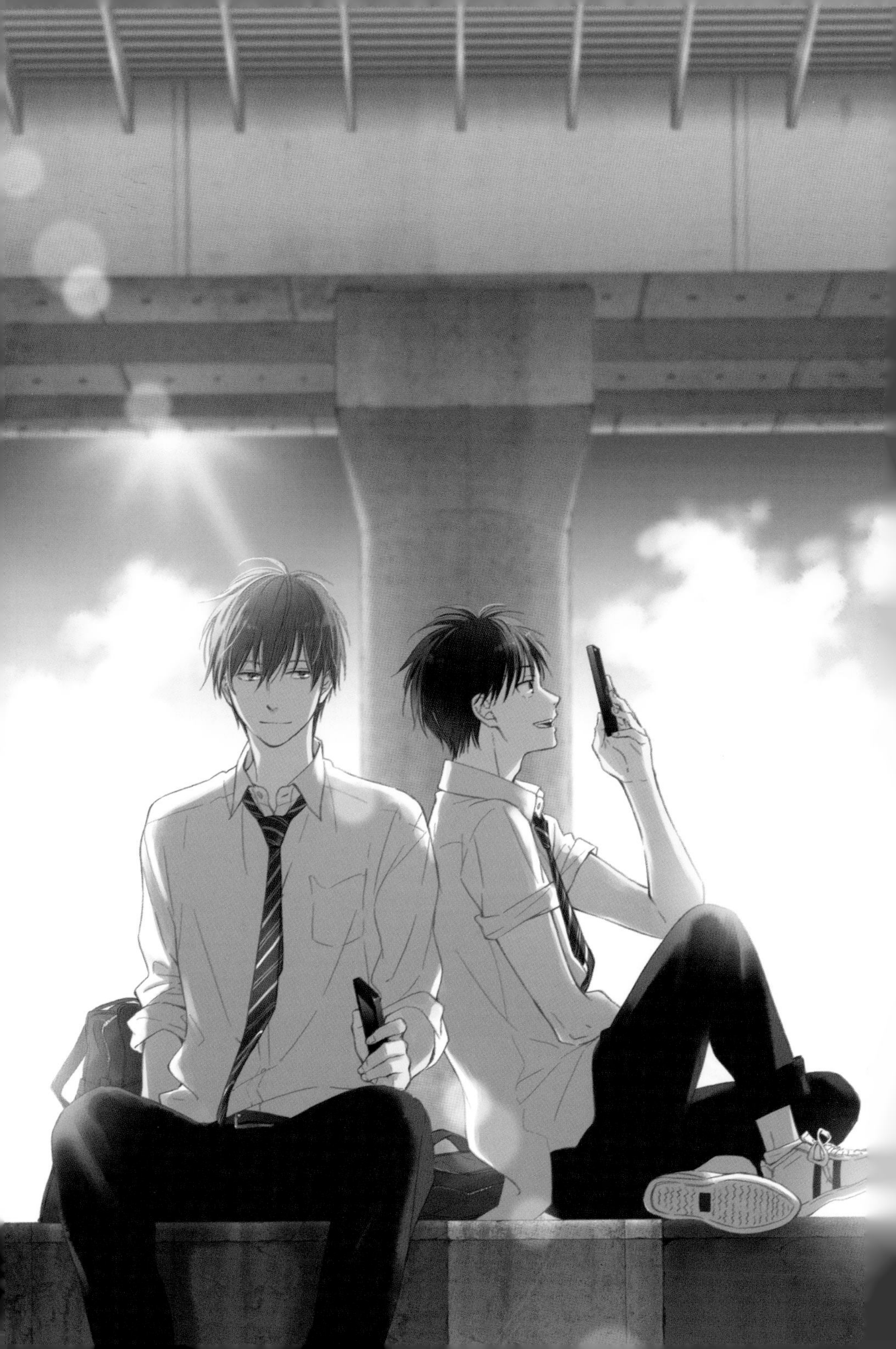

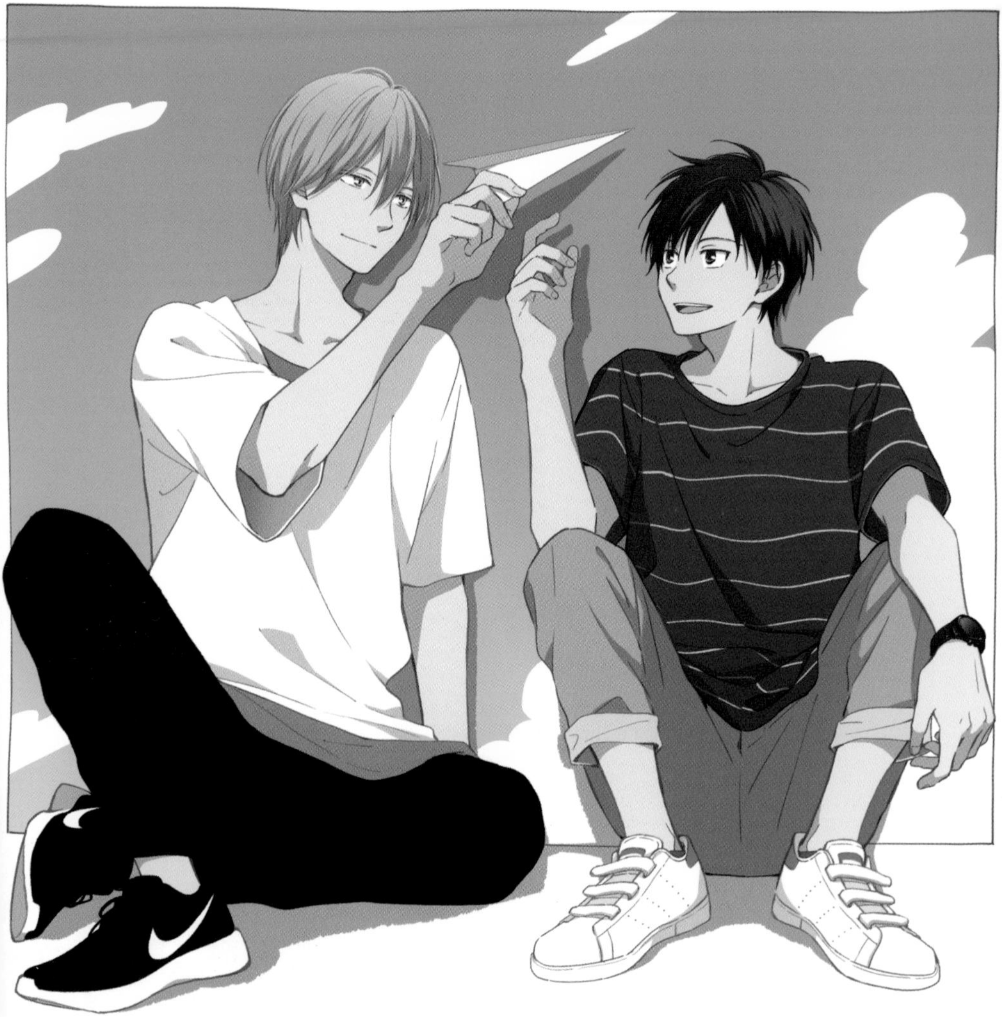

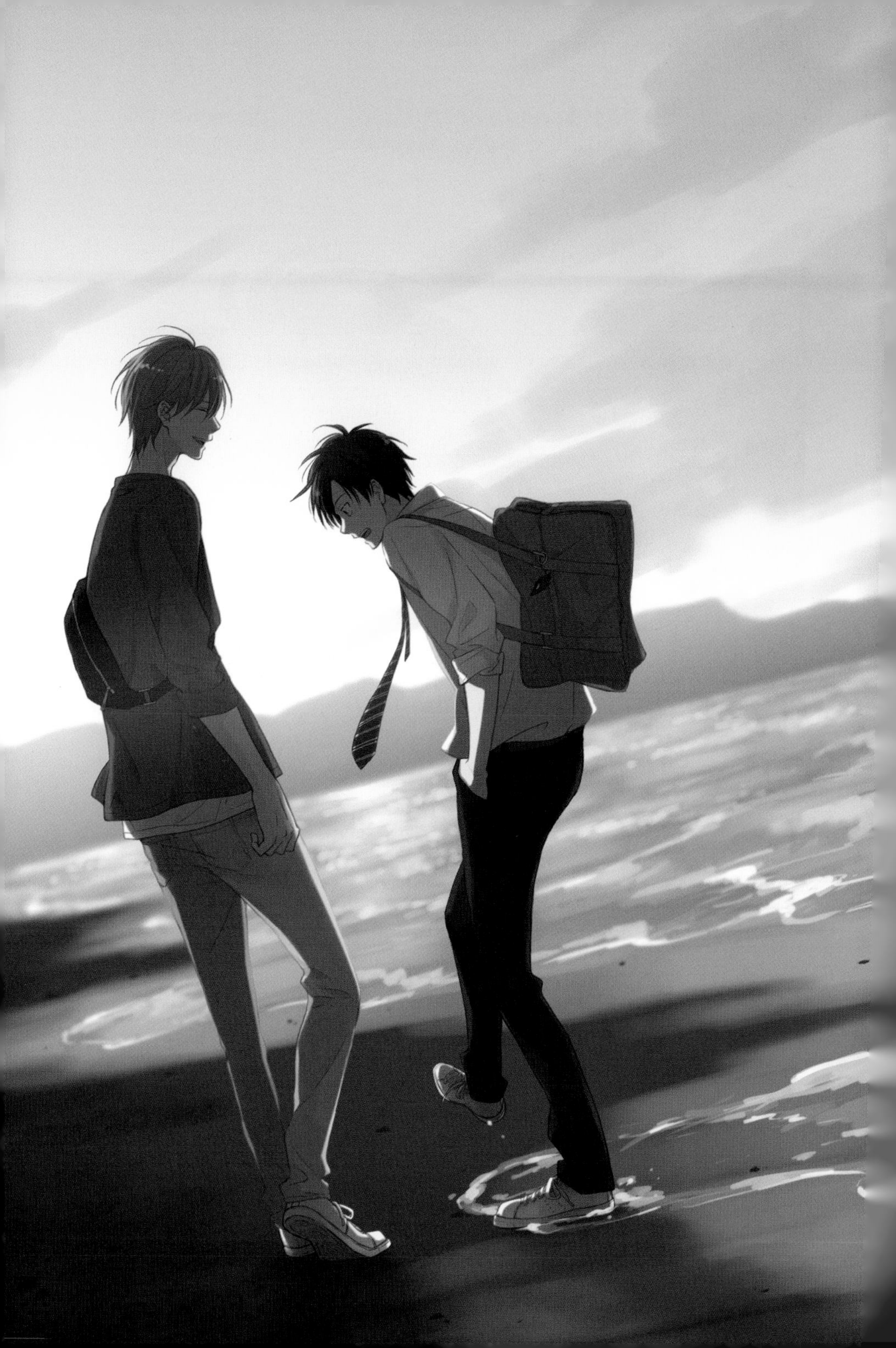

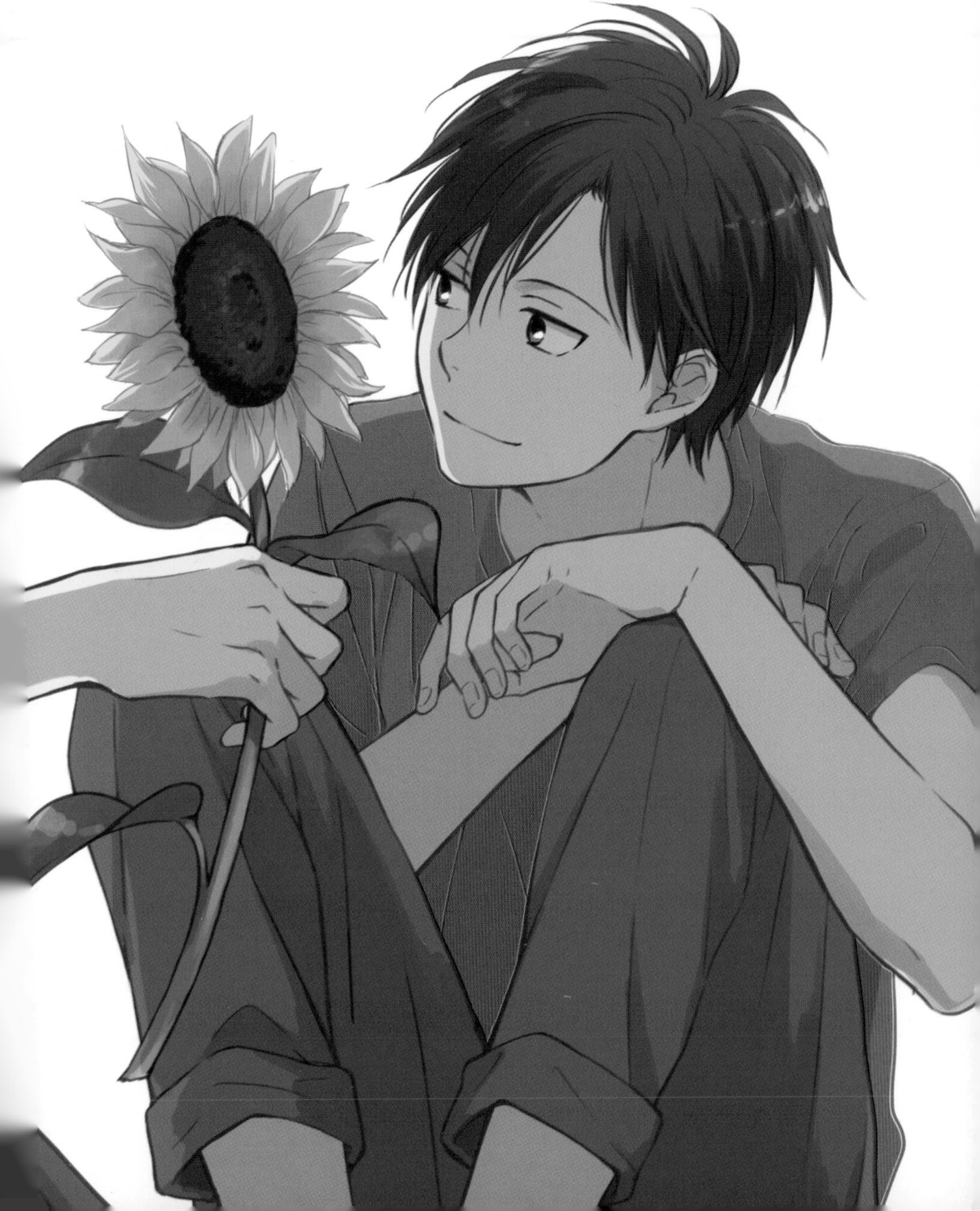

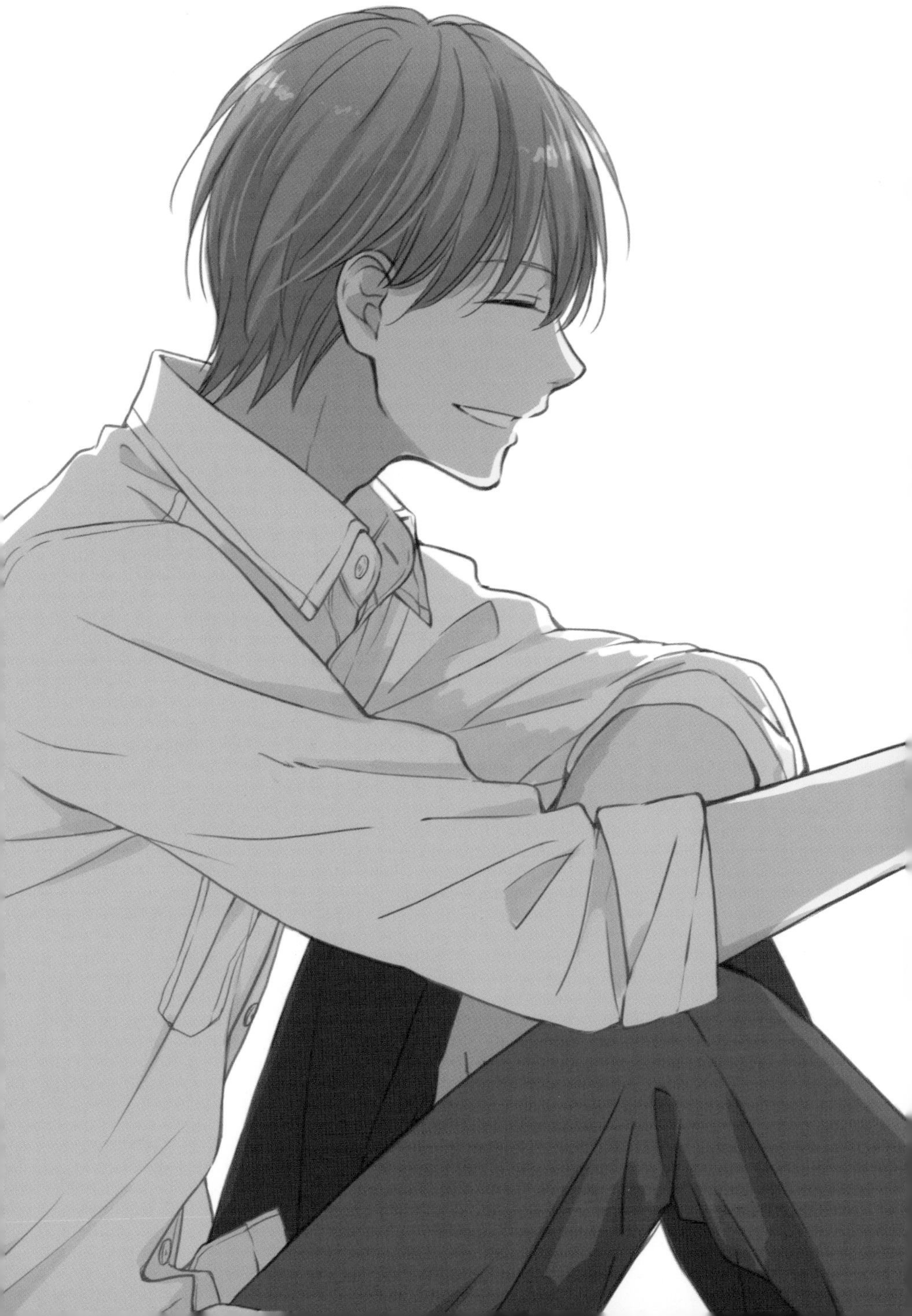

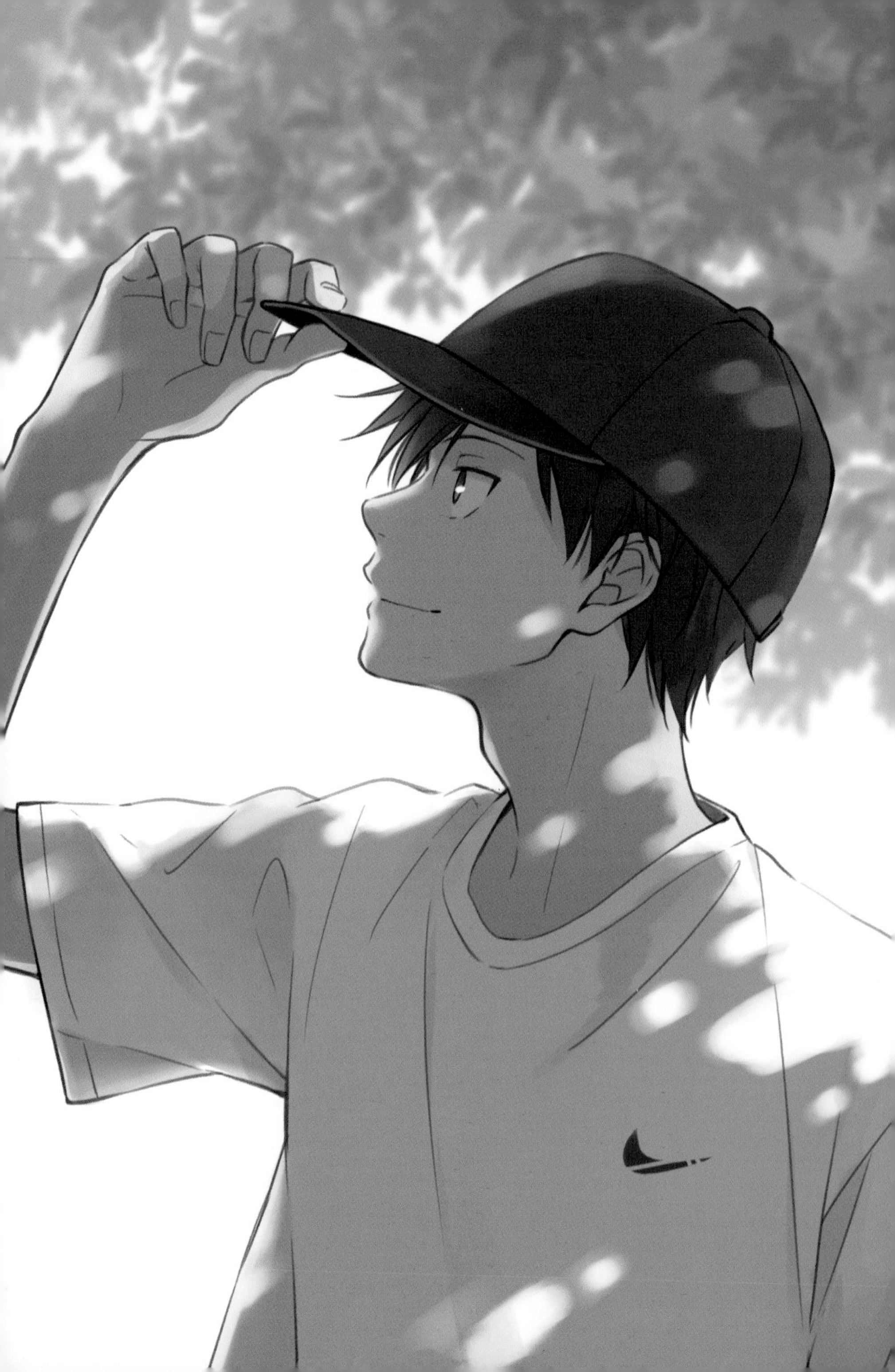

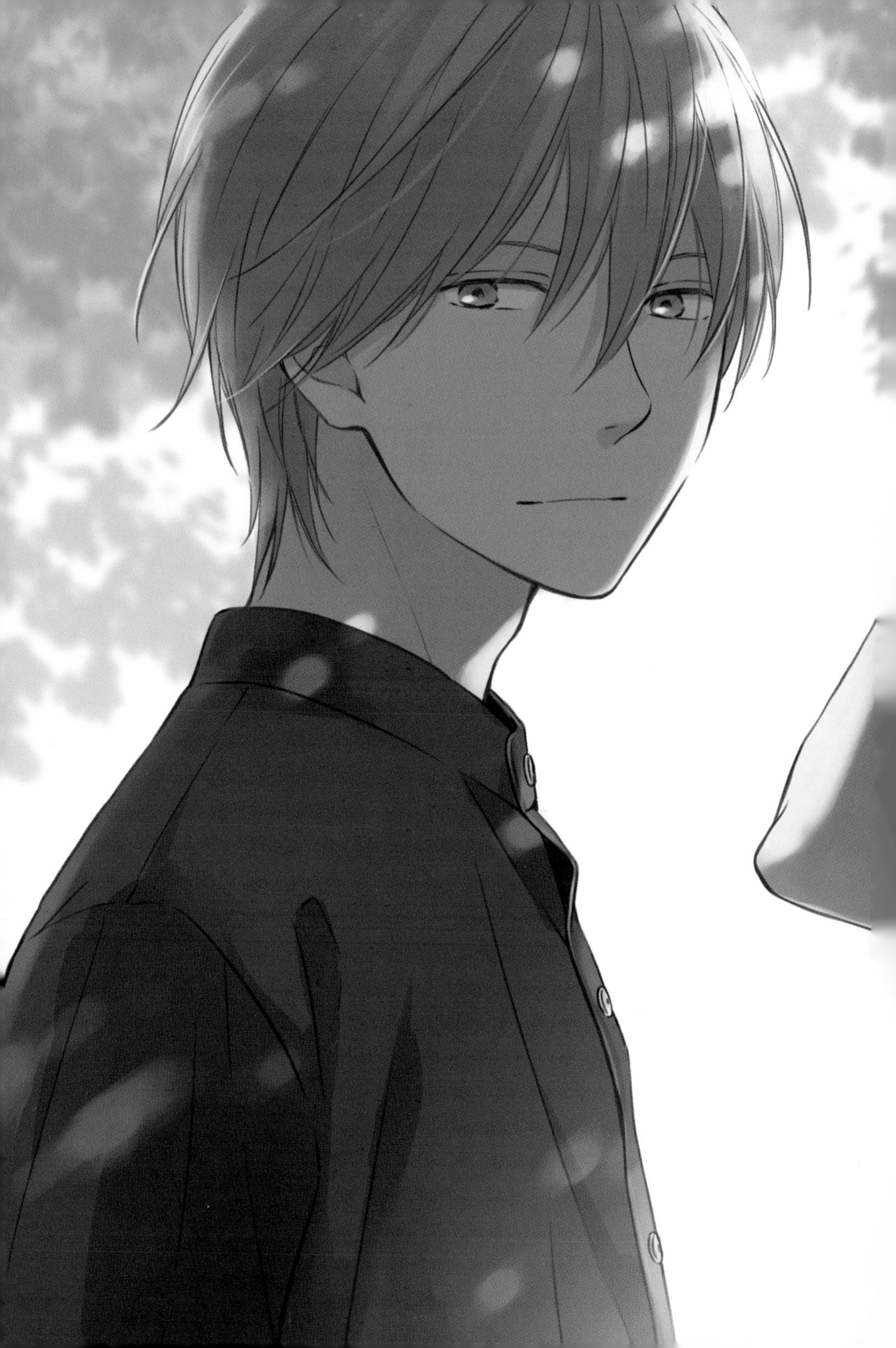

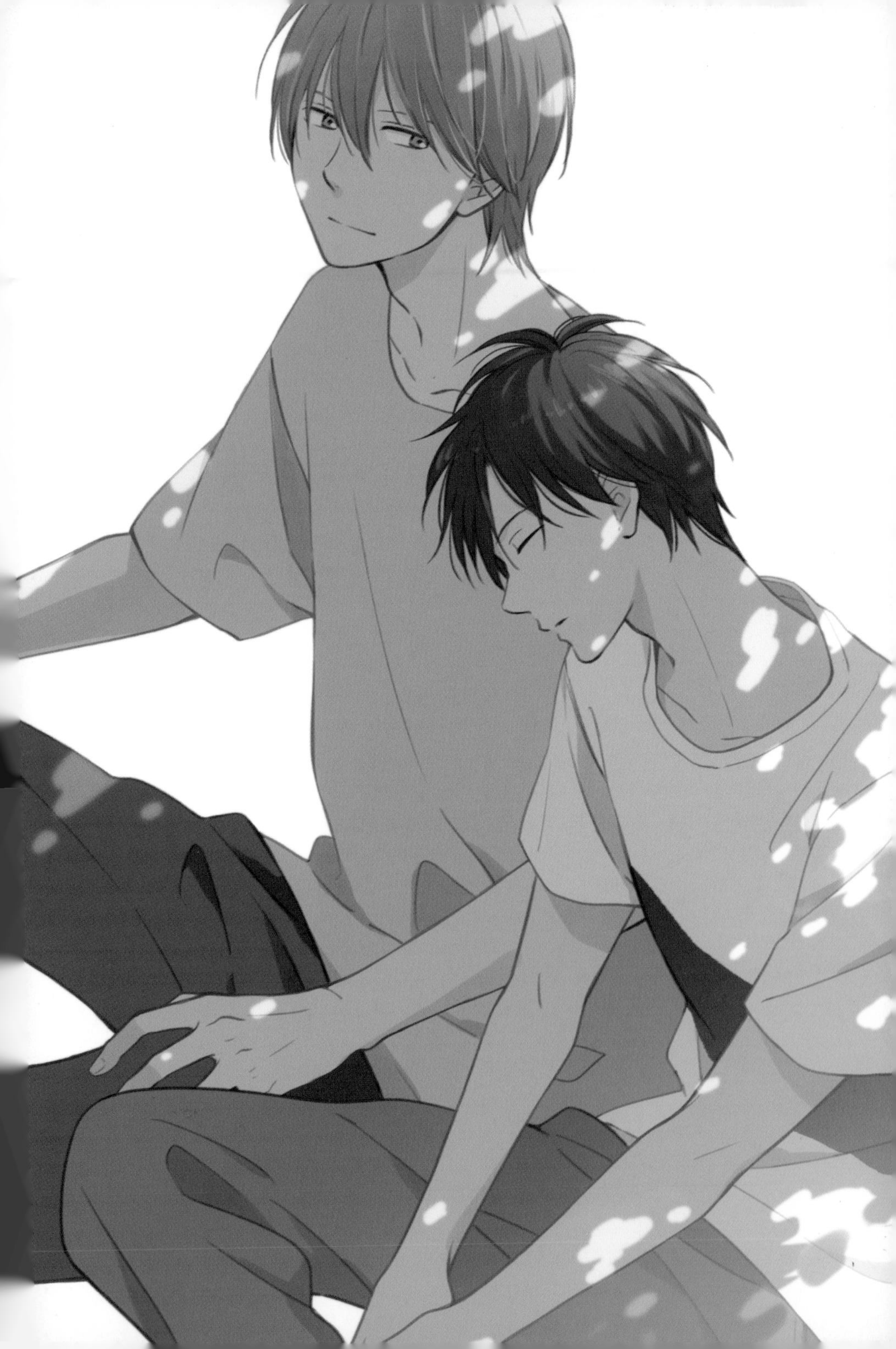

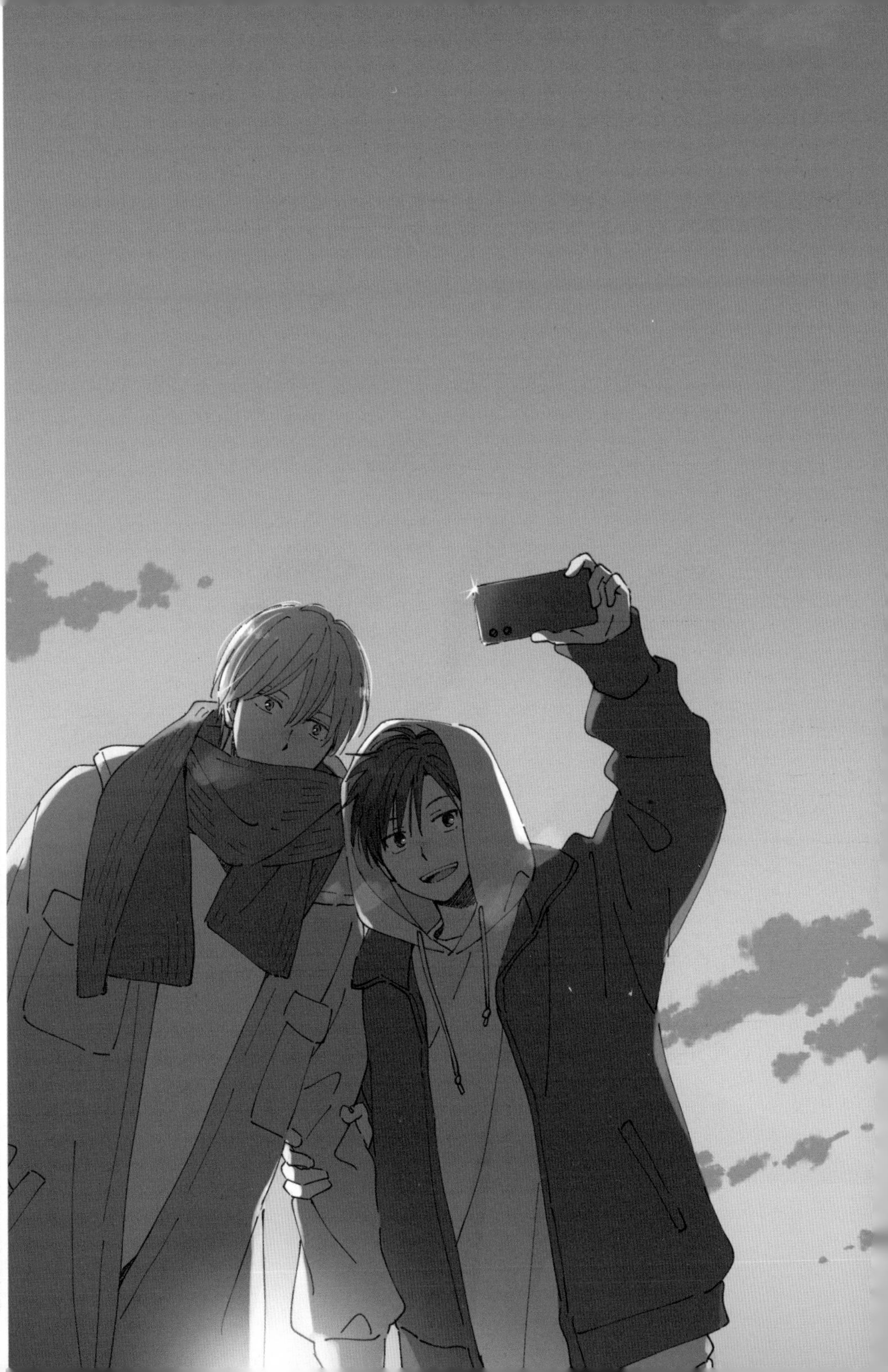

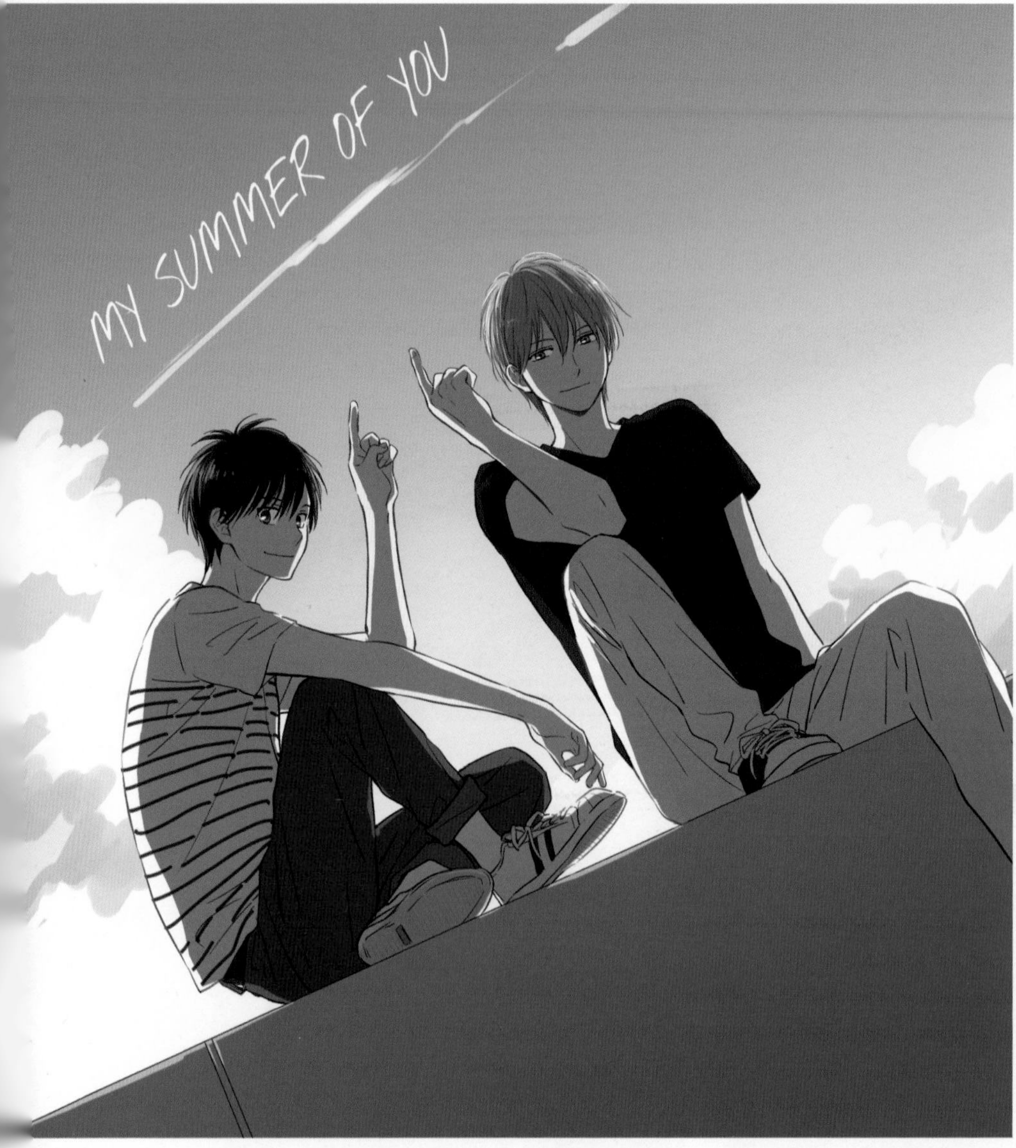
MY SUMMER OF YOU